"The Seth books present an alternate map of reality with a new diagram of the psyche . . . useful to all explorers of consciousness."

— Deepak Chopra, author of *The Seven Spiritual Laws of Success*

"Seth was one of my first metaphysical teachers. He remains a constant source of knowledge and inspiration in my life."

— Marianne Williamson, author of *A Return to Love*

"I would like to see the Seth books as required reading for anyone on their spiritual pathway. The amazing in-depth information in the Seth books is as relevant today as it was in the early '70s when Jane Roberts first channeled this material."

— Louise Hay, author of *You Can Heal Your Life*

"Seth's teachings had an important influence on my life and work, and provided one of the initial inspirations for writing *Creative Visualization*."

— Shakti Gawain, author of *Creative Visualization*

"The Seth books were of great benefit to me on my spiritual journey and helped me to see another way of looking at the world."

— Gerald G. Jampolsky, author of *Love is Letting Go of Fear*

"As you read Seth's words, you will gain more than just new ideas. Seth's energy comes through every page — energy that expands your consciousness and changes your thoughts about the nature of reality."

— Sanaya Roman, author of *Living with Joy*

"Quite simply one of the best books I've ever read."

— Richard Bach, author of *Jonathan Livingston Seagull*

"To my great surprise — and slight annoyance — I found that Seth eloquently and lucidly articulated a view of reality that I had arrived at only after great effort and an extensive study of both paranormal phenomena and quantum physics. . . . "

— Michael Talbot, author of *The Holographic Universe*

BOOKS BY JANE ROBERTS

The Rebellers (1963)

The Coming of Seth (How to Develop Your ESP Power) (1966)

The Seth Material (1970)

Seth Speaks: The Eternal Validity of the Soul, A Seth Book (1972)

The Education of Oversoul Seven (1973)

The Nature of Personal Reality, A Seth Book (1974)

Adventures in Consciousness (1975)

Dialogues of The Soul and Mortal Self in Time (1975)

Psychic Politics: An Aspect Psychology Book (1976)

The World View of Paul Cézanne: A Psychic Interpretation (1977)

The Afterdeath Journal of an American Philosopher: The World View of William James (1978)

The "Unknown" Reality: Vol. 1, A Seth Book (1977)

The "Unknown" Reality: Vol. 2, A Seth Book (1979)

The Further Education of Oversoul Seven (1979)

Emir's Education in the Proper Use of Magical Powers (1979)

The Nature of the Psyche: Its Human Expression, A Seth Book (1979)

The Individual and the Nature of Mass Events, A Seth Book (1981)

The God of Jane: A Psychic Manifesto (1981)

If We Live Again: Or, Public Magic and Private Love (1982)

Oversoul Seven and the Museum of Time (1984)

Dreams, "Evolution," & Value Fulfillment: Vol. 1, A Seth Book (1986)

Dreams, "Evolution," & Value Fulfillment: Vol. 2, A Seth Book (1986)

Seth, Dreams, and Projection of Consciousness (1986)

The Magical Approach, A Seth Book (1995)

The Way Toward Health, A Seth Book (1997)

A
Seth
BOOK

The Way
TOWARD
HEALTH

Jane Roberts

FOREWORD AND EPILOGUE BY ROBERT F. BUTTS

AMBER-ALLEN PUBLISHING
SAN RAFAEL, CALIFORNIA

Published by Amber-Allen Publishing, Inc.
P.O. Box 6657
San Rafael, CA 94903

Cover Art: Robert F. Butts
Cover Design: Beth Hansen
Editorial: Janet Mills

Library of Congress Cataloging-in-Publication Data

Seth (Spirit)
The way toward health / [channeled by] Jane Roberts;
foreword and notes by Robert F. Butts.
    p.   cm. — (A Seth book)
    Includes index.
1. Health.   2. Spirit writings.   I. Roberts, Jane, 1929–1984.
II. Title.   III. Series: Seth (Spirit). Seth book.
613 — DC21   97-18255   CIP

ISBN 978-1-878424-30-3
Printed in U.S.A. on acid-free paper

22   21   20   19   18   17   16   15   14   13   12   11

CONTENTS

FOREWORD

The Way Toward Health is more than an account of the stay — and death — of my wife, Jane Roberts, in a hospital in Elmira, New York, just 13 years ago. I've long wanted to see it published while feeling, knowing, that it has much else to offer, too. Not only about Jane's fine ability to speak in a trance or dissociated state for Seth, that "energy personality essence," as he calls himself, but about all of the vastly complicated challenges that can, and do, arise in the course of a human life.

Our lives, I've learned, don't simply proceed nicely and directly from "birth" to "death." Instead, I see each one of us as traveling a most curious and branching-out or circuitous route, one that is creative in ways that are both known and, I'm sure now, unknown.

Ah, there's the challenge, then — to understand our inherent creativity. We can try to mold it, to make it conform or behave, but each life has a life of its own. How fortunate! My wife's life and work show that we can even create challenges and goals before birth, then in physical life plunge into fulfilling those qualities as we don flesh and clothing and beliefs. Yet what great, unexpected convolutions we can encounter in those challenges we've created! Even so, I think, ultimately we come to understand, whether on conscious or unconscious levels — or both — that we were utterly ourselves while learning along the way.

Jane died in the hospital at 2:08 A.M. on Wednesday, September 5, 1984, after being there, quite helpless in certain ways, for a year and nine months. It was the third time she'd been hospitalized since February 1982. Since her death many have written to both sympathize and to ask "Why?" She had Seth, didn't she — for whom she spoke for some 21 years; she also produced six books with him along the way (plus a number of books on her "own"). Why hadn't Seth gotten her out of her dilemma, turned the magic key in the proper psychic lock? She was only 55 years old when she died. She could have lived for another 20 years, say, and contributed even more to our knowledge, both with Seth and by herself. She could have become world famous had she chosen to go that route.

The answers to such questions that Jane, Seth, and I arrived at are in this book. Jane was a human being first, and a very gifted psychic second. Seth *did* help her, many many times over the years. Beyond that, Jane and I learned that there exist great realms of knowledge and feeling as yet largely unrevealed. It would have been even finer to tap into those wondrous mazes much more, but we did the best we could. Seth still helps my wife, I'm sure. They're united now, and in larger terms also meeting with many others they know from the "past," "present," and "future." Because of certain dreams I believe that even portions of my own entity (Seth calls me Joseph) are joining in. Well, why not, since as Seth describes reality, everything exists at the same "time?" Tricky concepts and questions to wrestle with, I know, and sometimes contradictory. Enough to last for a lifetime in just this mundane reality.

I think this book shows, then, that the ways toward health can and do vary tremendously. In some stubborn and psychically grounded way we each are going to make our own choices, as human beings always have. Surely Jane's life shows this, and in ways that neither of us were even remotely aware of consciously when we married 42 years ago.

During those 21 months in the hospital, Jane, Seth, and I said much about her physical/psychic condition, and I recorded it all in my homemade shorthand as best I could under often very stressful conditions. In all that time I missed spending up to six or more hours a day with my wife only once, because of a heavy snowstorm. For weeks after her admittance in April, I didn't know if Jane would ever do any "psychic" work again, but three months later she surprised me by beginning a series of dialogues similar to the "worldview" material she'd produced for her books on the psychologist and philosopher William James, and the artist Paul Cézanne. Once again, she was inspired by my questions on art and related matters. "At least I feel I'm doing something I'm made for," she said when starting the new project. She concluded it in September 1983, then over the next four months delivered a series of 71 mostly short, mostly personal Seth sessions. She finished that series on January 2, 1984 — and began *The Way Toward Health* the next day.

During all of this time, we told no one in the hospital what we were specifically doing — staff accepted our conventional explanation that we were writers and "just working." It all worked very well, even when we were often interrupted, as the sessions show.

Inevitably, however, much had to be omitted from *The Way Toward Health* as it's presented here — not Seth's material, but from Jane's and my work and notes. I owe a great deal to the very considerate help of Janet Mills, the proprietor of Amber-Allen Publishing. We saw that if all of the peripheral material for each session was included, the book would be very long. (I had a number of personal experiences and insights that I thought enhanced concepts of the Seth material, for example.) But what to cut, when to stop? This presented a dilemma for me.

When Jane began delivering the Seth material in 1963, I became very conscious of the record we'd leave, not with Seth but concerning our private lives. The one can't help but add to the other, increasing the marvelous complexity of both. Long ago I came to believe that nothing exists in isolation; to omit some of the record leaves gaps, obviously. Hardly an original idea, yet one that I often see ignored in the surface activities of our daily lives. Other facets of our physical and nonphysical lives could help us tremendously if more conscious attention was given to them, regardless of "when" they happened.

But how can we — how can anyone — bring more of our inherent knowledge to consciousness, to use? How can we become more keenly aware of the facts and implications of our dreams, for example, and the very great influences they exert in our lives? Often our dreams are doorways to other realities. Yet I know that we're delving ever more deeply into our psyches; Jane's work with Seth, as well as her poetry and other writings, show that. The great gifts of our psyches are all there, waiting . . .

Robert F. Butts
Elmira, New York
September 1997

PART ONE

DILEMMAS

CHAPTER 1

The Purpose of This Book, and Some Important Comments About Exuberance and Health

JANUARY 3, 1984
4:50 P.M. TUESDAY

(T*his morning at 10:00, I took a special delivery package from the postman — a translation in French of* The Individual and the Nature of Mass Events. *Others of our books are being translated also.*

(I left the house for the post office and to take Jane's typewriter in for cleaning. So I was twenty minutes late getting to Jane's hospital room 330 this afternoon. The day was warmer — 32 degrees.

(My wife was late getting back from hydro* — the staff was very busy. The tray was late also, but Jane ate a good lunch.

(3:15. Jane began reading yesterday's session — and she did very well, even better than yesterday. She finished at 3:35. "If your eyes keep improving," I said, "maybe eventually you'll end up with weaker glasses." She was obviously surprised at the thought, but then, why not? Mine had improved a few years ago.

(3:40. I cut Jane's fingernails and toenails. The job went easier than it used to — and indeed, the doubled-up fingers on her right hand loosened up considerably as I worked on them. Another improvement, I told her.

---

*Hydro, as staff members call it, is short for the hospital's hydrotherapy department. Each morning, Jane is placed upon a litter that is lowered into a large tub of gently-swirling warm water that massages her whole body. The treatment is very relaxing, very beneficial, especially for bedsores.

(4:01. A new nurse named Betty took all of Jane's vitals. I worked on mail as Jane had a piece of candy and a cigarette. I thought she was going to pass up having a session, it was getting so late, but finally she decided to have a short one as the time to turn her on her side arrived.)

Now: I bid you another fond good afternoon.

("Good afternoon, Seth.")

I will speak briefly.

I wanted you to know *(pause)* that new developments concerning the [medical] insurance situation are occurring, to your benefit.

("Oh. Okay.")

An added note: <u>When you can</u>, a gentle massaging of the <u>tops</u> of Ruburt's* toes, by the nails, and perhaps down a bit toward the first joints, will help increase the body's entire circulation. Earlier, he would not have been able to respond. This only need take a few moments.

As always, the session format sets up its own accelerated healing framework.

I may or may not return, according to those rhythms of which I speak, but know that I am present and approachable.

("Well, we have time if you want to say something more."

(Pause.) I will merely make a few comments. As you know, or have suspected, I am indeed adding book dictation — at our own pace, considering the circumstances. It should be relatively easy to identify those portions —

("Yes.")

— and Ruburt will be able to do so easily, if ever you have difficulty, knowing when one portion begins and another ends.

("It's not a problem. Any idea of a title, or do you want to wait on that?")

I will give you that material later, with other introductory passages.

("Okay."

("Oh, it's me," Jane said.

---

*When he began dictating *Seth Speaks* way back in January 1970, Seth told us: "I write this book through the auspices of a woman of whom I have become quite fond. To others it seems strange that I address her as 'Ruburt,' and 'him,' but the fact is that I have known her in other times and places, by other names. She has been both a man and a woman, and the entire identity who has lived these separate lives can be designated by the name of Ruburt."

(4:56 P.M. Jane said that as soon as she gave the last sentence from Seth she thought the title of the book would be The Way Toward Health. *She didn't actually pick that up from Seth, it just came to her. And I told her that her statement reminded me that the same thought had come to me a couple of times previously after I'd been pretty sure that Seth was giving book work.*

(Upon checking, I verified my original guess, that she'd first done an outline for The Way Toward Health *in* Volume One *of* The "Unknown" Reality. *That book was published in 1977. See Appendix 7.*

("That first line of the session is an entertaining one," I said, and read her Seth's statement about the insurance matter. I'd been surprised, since I hadn't expected him to comment today.

("The minute before I said I was going to have a session, that idea came into my mind," Jane said. "I knew it was from Seth." She hadn't had time to mention it to me before the session began.

(A note: I'll have the details on tap in my collection of Time *magazines — but today there took place the freeing of the American airman through the visit of the Reverend Jesse Jackson to President Assad of Syria. This is a great moral and political accomplishment on Jackson's part, especially after President Reagan hadn't wanted him to go to Syria.*

(Of more importance, it seems on the surface at least, is a reaching-out on Assad's part toward a dialogue with the Western world — quite an unexpected development, I thought. As I discussed the events of today with Jane, and watched them on TV, it came to me that they might signal at least a beginning of those very beneficial world events Seth had referred to for the coming year in the session for December 28, 1983. Jane didn't know, and I'm not leaping to any conclusions. Seth had referred to "many countries changing their alliances," however. Syria is now allied with Russia. Fascinating to follow, I told Jane.)

JANUARY 4, 1984
3:54 P.M. WEDNESDAY

(In yesterday's session, Seth said that "new developments concerning the insurance situation are occurring, to your benefit." It appears that he's right so far, considering what our lawyer told me this morning about talking with the hospital, doctors, and Blue Cross.

(Jane ate a good lunch as we talked. While I answered mail she began reading yesterday's session, and once again did very well, holding the pages in her left hand as usual. She said that last night she'd had a brief blue period, in which she'd wondered if she'd ever walk out on the street again, but got herself out of it by saying "cancel" to herself, and remembering Seth's material.

(She also thought of a chapter in Seth's new book, one that was titled "Food and You" — then found herself stewing about saying something wrong in the book and leading people astray — more signs of old habits. "But then," she said, "I told myself to trust myself and Seth, and I said to hell with it."

("You've got to," I said. "We can't afford to do anything else anymore. Keep that word 'trust' in mind."

(When the nurse took Jane's temperature it was 98.8. "My God," I joked, "that's almost perfect."

(Jane got tired waiting for people to take all of her vital signs, like blood pressure and temperature, so she launched into the session.)

Now: I bid you another fond good afternoon.

("The same to you, Seth.")

The will to live can be compromised by doubts, fears, and rationalizations.

Some people, for example, definitely want to live, while they try to <u>hide</u> from life at the same time. Obviously, this leads them into conflicts. Such people will impede their own motions and progress. They become overly concerned about their own safety. If any of my readers feel this way, they may even hide these feelings from themselves. They will concentrate upon all of the dangers present in society in their own country, or in other portions of the world, until their own frightened overall concern for safety seems to be a quite natural, rational response to conditions over which they have no control.

(Pause.) What is actually involved is a kind of paranoia, which can become such a powerful response that it can take over a person's life, and color all projects. If this has happened to any of my readers, you might recognize yourself in any number of different scenarios. You might be a "survivalist," setting up stores and provisions to be used in case of a nuclear disaster. It may seem to you that you are quite justified in protecting yourself and your family from disaster. In many

such cases, however, the people so worried about the occurrence of danger from the outside world are instead concerned about the nature of their <u>own energy</u>, and afraid that it might destroy them.

(4:03.) In other words, they do not trust the energy of their own lives. They do not trust the natural functioning of their bodies, or accept this functioning as a gift of life. Instead they question it at every point — even holding their breath at times, waiting for something to go wrong.

Other people may actually impede those portions of the body given to mobility, so that they limp, or tighten their muscles, or otherwise tamper with their bodies so that the end result is one that requires a cautious, hesitating approach to motion. Some may even cause themselves to have severe accidents, in which they sacrifice portions of their bodies to retain a sense of —

(4:07. The nurse came in to take Jane's blood pressure. Jane asked for some iced ginger ale. She said that she was doing well — obviously — then added that when she spoke a sentence for Seth she also sensed the other sentences to come, or those around the spoken one. "Like even if I give one that's at the bottom, like a brick at the bottom of a building, I know the ones up at the top of the building."

(I read this note to her and she agreed that it was an accurate version of what she'd just said. "It's almost like instantly sensing a new tall structure, only it's made of words."

(After getting the ginger ale, I read the session to her that she'd given so far, then made sure the door to 330 was closed as much as possible. Resume at 4:17.)

— false safety.

These rather self-deceptive feelings are not hidden deeply in the subconscious mind, as you might suppose. Instead, in the majority of cases they consist of quite conscious decisions, made at one time or another on quite surface levels.

(Long pause at 4:19.)

They are not forgotten, but the people involved simply <u>close their own eyes</u>, so to speak, to those decisions, and <u>pretend</u> (underlined) that they do not exist, simply to make their lives appear smooth and to save face with themselves, when they know very well that the decisions really rest on very shaky ground indeed.

I do not wish to simplify matters, but such decisions can be uncovered very easily <u>in children</u>. A child might fall and badly scrape a knee — so badly that limping is the result, at least temporarily. Such a child will often be quite conscious of the reason for the affair: he or she may openly admit the fact that the injured part was purposefully chosen so that a dreaded test at school could be missed, and the child might well think that the injury was little enough to pay for the desired effect that it produced.

An adult under the same circumstances might become injured to avoid a dreaded event at the office — but the adult may well feel ashamed of such a reaction, and so hide it from himself or herself in order to save feelings of self-esteem. In such cases, however, the adults will feel that they are victims of events over which they have little or no control.

(4:27.) If the same kind of event occurs with any frequency, their fear of the world and of daily events may grow until it becomes quite unreasonable. Still, in most such instances those inner decisions can be easily reached — but while people are determined to "save face," they will simply refuse to accept those decisions as their own. People <u>will</u> (underlined) to live, to act or not to act. To a large extent they <u>will</u> (underlined) the events of their lives — whether or not they are willing to admit this to themselves, and they <u>will</u> (underlined) to die.

(4:32.) Comments.

All of this, of course, applies to Ruburt's situation — for once, indeed, he <u>willed</u> himself into immobility, willing to sacrifice certain kinds of motion in order to safely use <u>other</u> kinds of psychological motion, because he was afraid of his spontaneous nature, or his spontaneous self.

He was afraid that it acted according to <u>its own reasons</u> which might not be his own — or so he thought. Now he is beginning to understand that his energy is the gift of his life — <u>to be expressed</u>, not repressed — and to understand, again, that <u>spontaneity knows its own order</u>.

He just told you that when he begins to speak for me he senses an entire tall structure of words, and unhesitatingly he lets that structure form *(intently)*. The same is true with his ability to move and walk; the more he trusts his energy, the more his spontaneity forms its own beautiful order that results in the spontaneous physical <u>art</u> of walking — and he is indeed well along the way. The changes have already begun in his mind, and they <u>will</u> (underlined) be physically expressed.

It is no coincidence, in your language, that the word "will" refers to the future, as in a line like "it will happen," and also refers to the decision-making quality of the mind.

I may or may not return, again according to those rhythms of which I speak — but I am present and approachable.

("Thank you, Seth."

(4:39 P.M. "Well, that's your longest session yet," I said. Jane agreed. She sipped ginger ale and had a smoke while I read her the rest of the session. It's very good.

("I didn't want to interrupt while you were reading," Jane said, "but I began to get what he's going to say about a whole lot of things . . . He's going to get into epilepsy, and say that it's a result of your fear of your own power, and short-circuits it. The same thing with secondary personalities, so you can blame your actions on something else."

("I also got that he's going to say that in ordinary terms we don't have access to all the information we've got at one time because consciously it would be so hard to sort through it — but that we really are conscious of it, and for working purposes we just pretend that we aren't. He's said that before — that the so-called unconscious portions of ourselves are in themselves quite conscious."

(7:10. I left Jane after saying the prayer we always use with her, and went shopping at ACME supermarket on Elmira's south side. Finished eating supper at 9:45 P.M.

(I meant to note: Some of today's Seth material reminds me of Jane's "sinful-self" material. Probably inevitable in this book, at least at times . . .)

JANUARY 5, 1984
4:25 P.M. THURSDAY

(I typed yesterday's session this morning, and didn't get to work on Dreams, "Evolution," and Value Fulfillment *until after 10:30. I also made arrangements to get our taxes for 1983 done. It worked out well, but I lost time — and when I got to Room 330 this afternoon, my legs were itching again. I told Jane.*

(The day was warm — over 36 degrees. The ice in the driveway is melting. I'd put rock salt on it last night and this morning.

(Jane said she had a long wait for hydro this morning. She's been having a lot of spasms, and fears the catheter was loosened enough yesterday that she'll have to have it changed tonight. She saw her doctor briefly in hydro.

(One of the nurse's aides stopped by for a visit. She had been injured and suffered a relapse when she fell and twisted or pulled on some of the staples in her leg. Now a prolonged recovery period is predicted. Jane and I soon noticed the negative suggestions her doctor had given her, as she talked with us. She also told us that another nurse will be out for at least a week with a strained back, which she evidently got from trying to lift a patient. It made us wonder about working in hospitals — it seemed everyone was sick at one time or another.

(Jane ate a good lunch, then at 3:05 began reading the session from yesterday. She did fairly well, though not as good as yesterday, and finally got through the six pages at 3:34. She held the pages okay in her left hand, though. She said her ability to perceive had varied considerably, and that she'd had to strain to read. I'd seen that her eyes were very red when I gave her drops.

(3:45. I read a batch of recent sessions to Jane. She told me of a dream she'd had last night, vivid, involving her walking, putting on new clothes while in the middle of a street, of leaving the hospital and going across a street into a Five and Ten, of putting pretty decorations in her hair. I said the dream was a very good one, and once more set the stage for the act of walking. She agreed. I worked on some mail.

(4:00–4:11. A nurse took Jane's vitals — temperature, 98.5. When all was clear and quiet — except for the patient, Karina, hollering next door — Jane said she'd like to have a short session.)

Now: I bid you another fond good afternoon.

("Good afternoon, Seth.")

People who have epilepsy are also afraid of their own energy.

They do not trust it, nor do they trust the spontaneous portions of the self. They are afraid that left alone their energy might strike out against others, and so they short-circuit its use, having attacks that momentarily render themselves helpless.

People with so-called secondary personalities also fear their own energy. They divide it up so that it seems to belong *(long pause)* to different personalities, and is therefore effectively divided. In basic terms, true amnesia does not exist in such cases, though it appears to. The people involved are quite aware of their activity at all times, but they behave in a fashion that is not continual — that is, the main personality does not seem to behave in a continual manner, but is broken up, or again, seemingly divided. This psychological ploy neatly prevents the so-called main personality from using all of its energy at any one time.

(Long pause.) The individuals concerned pretend to themselves that they have no memory of the other personalities' existences or activities. These personalities, however, <u>store up</u> their energy so that one personality often exhibits explosive behavior, or makes certain decisions that <u>seem</u> (underlined) to go against the wishes of the main entity. In this way *(pause),* different kinds of behavior may be exhibited, and while it would seem that many decisions are made by one portion of the self, without another portion of the self knowing anything about it, such usually is not the case. In fact, the main personality is able to express many different kinds of probable action, but the entire personality is prevented from acting with its full energy or power. Instead the energy is diverted into other channels.

All portions of the self are indeed conscious, and they are also basically <u>conscious of each other</u>, though for working purposes they may seem to be separate or isolated.

(Pause at 4:37.) Comments.

For a few days — at least when possible — read Ruburt those portions of yesterday's session that were devoted to his condition.

I may or may not return, again according to those rhythms of which I speak, but know that I am present and approachable.

("Okay. Thank you."

(4:40 P.M. I told Jane that I'd thought she would speak longer, but she said she often feels that if she did I'd never get the sessions typed. "I notice that around seven o'clock you start getting nervous," she said. It's true that by then I'm restless and getting tired, but I can always make exceptions. "You wouldn't get anything done on Dreams if you had to type longer sessions," she added. Probably true.

(I've also thought of re-reading yesterday's excellent session to her often, as a sort of reminder.)

JANUARY 6, 1984
4:22 P.M. FRIDAY

(The day was again warm — about 38 degrees when I left for Room 330.

(Jane was okay, although she said she'd had another long wait before and after hydro. Things aren't too well organized, or are too busy. Jane got blue over the hydro situation, the waiting, new people lifting her and not knowing how, etc. I met a couple of new nurses or aides myself. One looked in for a moment after her own therapy — didn't look good, Jane said. My own theory is that the people who work there get sick of it after a while, and then get sick in order to get a rest or a vacation with pay.

(Jane ate a good lunch, though, in spite of having some spasms. I told her my scratching had subsided considerably since yesterday. "There's only one answer," I said in answer to her news about the hospital. "I know," she said, "and that's what I'm trying to do." Truly, I added, it was the only way to get rid of all the basic negativity in the place. I sometimes wondered why Jane's body didn't recognize that to an even more profound degree, and see to it that her physical body healed itself even more rapidly so that we could get out.

(3:16. Jane began reading yesterday's session, and did quite well — better than yesterday. She was done at 3:25, while I worked on mail. At 3:36 a new nurse came in to take her temperature — 98.2. At 3:50 another nurse took her blood pressure.

(After holding a session on November 10, 1982, Jane went eleven months before her next one on October 9, 1983. In the meantime, she'd gone into the hospital on April 20, 1983. Now, starting at 4:00, I read her portions of some of the sessions she'd held since resuming them in October. There are many good points therein, and I don't want to lose track of them. Jane did say that she wanted to have a session. We'd wondered about her lack of physical motion to any great degree recently.)

Now: I bid you another fond good afternoon.

("Good afternoon, Seth.")

The idea of the sinful self will not be predominant in our own book, but we certainly will delve into the many unfavorable concepts that are held by the various religions — concepts that certainly make many people feel that the self is indeed sinful rather than blessed.

The self is indeed blessed, and just the reminder of that fact can often short-circuit negative beliefs, particularly if they are not too deep-seated.

As far as Ruburt's motions are concerned, the body is following its own rhythms, which will sometimes involve overt, noticeable exercise and activity on the one hand, while on the other it exercises internally, so to speak, making all preparations for the other later exercises and motion. It seemed, for example, sudden when Ruburt fed himself, even if briefly, but that exterior improvement followed many inner manipulations, which until then had not <u>connected</u> in that particular manner.

(*Pause at 4:27.*) Reading some of the earlier sessions of this sequence also serves to remind you both of the progress that has taken place since those sessions began (*on October 9, 1983*), and therefore invite even newer improvements.

I may or may not return, again according to those rhythms, but know that I am <u>indeed, once more</u>, present and approachable.

(*"Okay."*

(*4:29 P.M. I read the session to Jane. We thought his comment about the sinful self might have come about through my reading to her earlier today my question to him of last October about what part the sinful self might be playing in her challenges.*

(*4:45. I wanted to exercise Jane's right leg while she was still on her back, as Seth suggested I do each day, but she decided to wait until I'd turned her. I also massaged with Oil of Olay the toes of her feet, as Seth had mentioned doing. The right leg moved well. Jane said the toe touching sent sensations up her legs — as Seth had said it would.*

(*As I drifted off into my nap at 5:15, after finishing my dehypnotizing massage of Jane, I remembered the dream I'd had last night. After the nap I described it to her, and said I'd wanted to do so earlier, so Seth could comment if he wanted to. I'd dreamed, in color, that Jane rebroke her right leg several times in the same place. Insurance hassles were involved also. I woke up stewing, and finally had to get up from my chair to take some baking soda to relieve my stomach. I slept well after that.*

(*After a few minutes, Jane said the dream could have been related to the injuries the nurse's aide had suffered to her own impaired leg — the one that had been stapled inside that I described in a recent session. The doctor's negative suggestions to her could have been involved.*

(*Then Jane told me that she, too, had had a negative dream last night. A woman she met had cancer of the face, and was taking the drug interferon as treatment. The woman told Jane that Jane had the same kind of facial skin that she had — with all of its negative suggestions.*

(It sounds almost as though Jane and I had our worrisome dreams in tandem. We agreed that they represented fears on our parts — that they weren't literal or precognitive in any sense.)

JANUARY 7, 1984
4:11 P.M. SATURDAY

(The day was colder — 28 degrees — when I left for 330. I'd worked on taxes for an hour this morning, and Dreams. *No calls from anybody. I'd envisioned Jane getting back to her room around 11:00, after hydro, but when I got there she said she didn't get back until almost noon. She'd just had her fresh bandages put on and been turned, before I arrived. She ate a good lunch, though, and seemed to be doing okay.*

(2:45. I began working with mail, and Jane started reading yesterday's session. She zipped right through it — doing the best she has in some little while — and finished at 2:55. Very good indeed.

(3:00. Dana came in to empty Jane's catheter bag, or Foley, as everyone calls it. Shawn took her temperature at 3:20 — 98.5; and at 3:45 Lynn gave Jane eyedrops.

(In between all of this activity, when we were alone for quiet moments, I mentioned a question to Jane that I'd thought of last night; I hoped Seth might go into it, I said. The question had been triggered by a sentence of mine in the notes for yesterday's session, to the effect that I sometimes wondered why Jane's body, particularly her body consciousness, didn't simply take over to "even a more profound degree, and see to it that her physical body healed itself even more rapidly so that we <u>could</u> get out" of the hospital. Jane had had an emotional reaction, I'd noticed, when she read that line aloud yesterday, and it set me thinking.

(The question contains many implications. "Maybe such a thing even happens at places like this," I said. "If it never happened, it would mean the body consciousness was always subservient to other more dominant portions of the personality, and I don't think that's true either. After all, if that was the case and things went wrong, the body consciousness could see its own death approaching, even, and not be able to do anything about it . . . "

(I also reminded Jane that we'd like a word from Seth on our negative-type dreams of the night before last, and which I'd described in yesterday's session.)

Now: I bid you another most fond good afternoon.

("Same to you, Seth.")

The body consciousness, on its own, is filled with exuberance, vitality, and creativity.

Each most microscopic portion of the body is conscious, strives toward its own goals of development, and is in communication with all other parts of the body.

The body consciousness is indeed independent. To a large degree its own defense mechanisms protect it from the mind's negative beliefs — at least to a large extent. As I have mentioned before, almost <u>all</u> persons pass from a so-called disease state back into healthy states without ever being aware of the alterations. In those cases the body consciousness operates unimpeded by negative expectations or concepts.

When those negative considerations are multiplied, however, when they <u>harden</u>, so to speak, then they do indeed begin to diminish the body's own natural capacity to heal itself, and to maintain that overall, priceless organization that should maintain it in a condition of excellent strength and vitality.

There are also occasions when the body consciousness itself rises up in spite of a person's fears and doubts, and throws aside a condition of illness in a kind of sudden victory. Even then, however, the person involved has already begun to question such negative beliefs. The individual may not know <u>how</u> to cast them off, even though he or she desires to do so. It is in those instances that the body consciousness arises and throws off its shackles.

With free will, however, it is not possible for the body consciousness to be given full and clear dominion, for that would deny large areas of choices, and cut off facets of learning. The main direction and <u>portent</u>, however, of the body consciousness on its own is always toward health, expression, and fulfillment.

The molecules, and even the smaller aspects of the body act and react, communicate, cooperate with each other, and share each other's knowledge, so that one particle of the body knows what is happening in all other parts. Thus, the amazing organization usually works in a smooth, natural fashion. Many body events that you think of in your society as negative — certain viruses, for example — are instead meant as self-corrective devices, even as <u>fever</u> actually promotes health rather than impedes it.

(4:26.) The main characteristic of bodily consciousness is its spontaneity. *(Long pause.)* This allows it to work at an incredibly swift rate that could not be handled by the topmost conscious portions of the mind. Its operation is due to an almost instantaneous kind of consciousness, in which what is known is known, with no distance between, say, the knower and the known.

The act of seeing, and all of the body's senses, are dependent upon this inner spontaneity.

(4:29.) Comments.

Both of your "negative" dreams express left-over doubts and fears, and the old concept that the poorest rather than the best outcome of any event will happen. The working of Ruburt's eyes, and the continuous changes in his vision, give indications of the <u>other</u> kind of improvements, happening in the circulatory systems and other portions of the body. The eyes, knowing his intent now to read, read. Reason does not have to tell him how to do this.

In the same way, simply and gently, let him address his legs, telling them his intent to walk again. The actions involved in normal walking will begin to return. <u>They are, now</u>, beginning to return *(as I was just going to ask Seth).* On some days his eyes do not read as easily as on others, and on those days they simply reflect an unevenness as they prepare themselves for still other improvements. The same occurs in other portions of the body.

(Pause at 4:35.) At this particular time, it is indeed a good idea for him to imagine himself walking, almost in a detached manner. Certainly without too much seriousness — but lightly.

Now I may or may not return, again according to those rhythms of which I speak — but I am present and approachable.

("Yes. Okay."

(4:36 P.M. "It's me," Jane said. She had a cigarette before I turned her on her side. I massaged her toes as Seth had recently suggested, which got good results, then after I'd turned her, I gently worked her right leg back and forth as Seth had suggested. The knee of the broken leg actually works quite

freely, I remarked — much more so than the left knee. Jane agreed. In fact, when she's lying down, her left foot impedes the motion of her right foot and leg. But this will pass.

(Jane ate a good supper, and I left at 7:10 after reading the prayer with her. Sleep well, sweetheart.)

JANUARY 9, 1984
4:17 P.M. MONDAY

(No session was held yesterday, Sunday, January 8. However, there are several events from yesterday that I want to summarize here.

(First is my dream of the night before, which I described to Jane in case she had a session and Seth wanted to comment. I dreamed in color that Jane and I had moved back to Sayre, Pennsylvania — my home town — to Mrs. Potter's old apartment at 317 S. Elmer Avenue. However, the place was more spacious, and bore elements of 458 W. Water Street, in Elmira, New York, also. I walked around the large rooms, saying to Jane, "See, this place isn't bad at all. It's a nice setting, we can make a go of it here." We were in town, protected, and looking out the windows I saw more spacious yards than actually exist there. I liked the near-downtown setting, and so did Jane. Elmira is only 18 miles from Sayre.

(Second: At 5:30 I went to the restroom off Room 330. While in there, the sum of $20,000 popped into my head as I idly thought very briefly about our friend, Maude Cardwell. In fact, I'd almost forgotten I'd written a letter to her last week. I didn't try to pick up anything more. "I don't know whether the $20,000 represents all we'll get from donations — the fund — whether it's from one person, is a start of something larger, or what," I told Jane. But I wanted her to know my impression just in case.* She was about to have supper.

(Third: At 6:10, as I began feeding Jane, the thought of Steve and Tracy Blumenthal crossed my mind quite definitely, without being terribly intrusive. Here too, I hadn't been thinking of them — had forgotten, in fact, that the day was Sunday, when they usually visit. I suddenly knew

---

*Maude Cardwell publishes a Seth-oriented newsletter, *Reality Change*, from her home in Austin, Texas. We've met only by telephone. Maude wants to ask the readers of *RC* to help Jane and me pay for certain very large medical bills not covered by insurance. A most humbling suggestion for my wife and me — we've always prided ourselves on making our own way.

they were going to call the hospital. A few seconds later I heard high-heeled footsteps in the hall, coming around the corner, approaching 330. A woman we didn't know knocked, then came in to tell us that Steve was on the line, and wanted to visit Jane this evening. Jane said okay — after 8:00 P.M. I told Jane I hadn't even had time to tell her of my impression before the woman — who perhaps was a volunteer answering the phone — came to us. In other words, I'd picked up the fact of the call while the woman walked toward us and I heard her. It's possible, I speculated, that the very sound and rhythm of her footsteps helped trigger my conscious realization of the call from Steve.

(I asked Jane if the Cardwell experience could be said to validate the Blumenthal affair, or vice versa, and she said yes, since they'd happened so close together. Note that the money affair by-passed entirely the question of insurance money. I hadn't been thinking of the insurance money at all.

(Jane had a good day, although a bit of a problem trying to read the session from the day before. She also wore a small patch on her left elbow, which she'd knocked somehow — perhaps in hydro — so that it was quite sore.)

∼

(No interruptions this morning, Monday, January 9. I worked on taxes for an hour, Dreams *the rest of the time. I took the Christmas bell, made in Switzerland and sent to us by a reader in upstate New York, in to 330; when wound up it plays* Silent Night *most evocatively. The woman who sent it wanted Jane to write the founder of a Seth group in Syracuse; the lady is dying of cancer. I wrote both women last night.*

(Jane ate a good lunch. I told her that I got mad this morning because I felt that the Seth material wasn't — and wouldn't — get the hearing it deserved in our society. I asked why the material, if it was inherent within human beings, was so much ignored. "I don't mean just lately," I said, "but for thousands of years." I felt that mankind seemed to have deliberately or perversely chosen to ignore it, for probably innumerable reasons historically. Yet, why not use it, if it could help solve some of our species' great challenges? Jane didn't show much of a reaction, beyond saying "They'll use it."

(If I wasn't at my best today, neither was Jane. She admitted it, that she'd been blue. She tried reading previous sessions, and after taking a break in-between, did manage to get through them, but it wasn't easy. As usual, though, she finished up better than she'd been when she started.

(4:05. After her vitals had been taken — temperature 97.4 — Jane talked about having a session. Robert, the male nurse, had taken her blood pressure, and had to stop and readjust her position to a more comfortable one before he could proceed.

(Jane's Seth voice was a bit stronger today.)

Now: I bid you another fond good —

("Good afternoon, Seth.")

Exuberance *(pause)* and a sense of vitality are always present to some degree or another.

Some people —

(4:18. Diana, an RN, came in to see Jane's hair, which she'd thought had been cut. Jane had forgotten to tell me, but someone from downstairs had wanted to cut Jane's hair this morning, but then couldn't because of a clash of schedules with Jane going to hydro. Jane had canceled the deal. I read her the material she'd just given.)

— are always aware of their own joy regardless of circumstances. They feel safe and protected even when the events of their lives do not seem favorable. Regardless of their own doubts and worries, such people feel themselves supported, and feel that in the end everything will work to their advantage. Many other people, however, lose this sense of safety —

(4:24. Penny, an RN whom we like a lot, stopped in to say good-bye for the day. "I'm going crazy," she said twice, referring to the hectic day she'd had on Surgical 3 today. She's a friend of Luke and Lois Hutter, of Sayre, whom Jane and I knew many years ago. Through a call Penny had arranged, I talked to Luke around the holidays, and Lois subsequently wrote us a letter giving us all the latest news about their family, Mrs. Potter, etc. I'd idly speculated with Jane about whether the reacquaintance with the Potters — Lois is Mrs. Potter's adopted daughter — had any connection with my dream about our moving back to the apartment we'd had in the Potter house in Sayre.)

— and abundance, and it may seem as if joy in living was an attribute only of the young.

Exuberance and joy, however, basically have nothing to do with time or age. They may be expressed as vividly and beautifully at the age of 80 as at the age of 8. For whole segments of the population, however, it seems as if joy and health are fleeting attributes expressed briefly in childhood, and then lost forever.

(There was much noise in the hall. Penny had left the door to 330 half open.)

There are innumerable ways of reclaiming joy in living, however, and in so doing *(long pause)* physical health may be reclaimed by those who have found it lacking in their experience.

(Long pause at 4:29.) The quality of life is intensely important, and is to a large extent dependent upon a sense of well-being and self-confidence. While these attributes are expressed in the body, they also exist in the mind, and there are some cumbersome mental beliefs that may severely impede mental and physical well-being.

We will not concentrate upon these, but we will indeed discuss them, so that each person can understand the relationship between poor beliefs and poor health, for through understanding these connections the individual can re-experience the great <u>mental</u> variety that is possible. No individual is helpless, for example, in the face of negative beliefs. He or she can learn to make choices once again, and thus to <u>choose</u> positive concepts, so that they become as natural as negative beliefs once did.

One of the greatest detriments to mental and physical well-being is the unfortunate belief that any unfavorable situation is bound to get worse instead of better. *(Pause.)* That concept holds that any illness will worsen, any war will lead to destruction, that any and all known dangers will be encountered, and basically that the end result of mankind's existence is extinction. All of those beliefs impede mental and physical health, erode the individual's sense of joy and natural safety, and force the individual to feel like an unfortunate victim of exterior events that seem to happen despite his own will or intent.

(4:39.) Comments.

The ideas I have just mentioned are all prominent in your society, and now and then they return to darken your senses of joy and expectation.

Today Ruburt experienced a small-enough, but still potent enough, recurrence of those ideas. It is very important that they be recognized when they appear. For now, often that recognition alone can clear your thoughts and mind.

(Long pause.) You had your own experiences last evening: your foreknowledge of your friend's phone call, and the unorthodox

(long pause) knowledge about the money — and those two events happened because you did indeed want another small assurance of the mind's capabilities despite the official concepts of the mind, by which you are so often surrounded.

Such experiences let you taste, again, the feeling of your own greater abilities and freedom. Tell Ruburt to remind himself again that he is <u>free</u> to move and to walk normally.

("Can I ask a question?")

You may.

("You're saying that to some extent at least, he still feels that he isn't free to move and walk. I've thought of this several times myself lately.")

I am saying that to varying degrees those concepts sometimes return, that it should be obvious that this happens less and less. Remind him also to remember that he does not have any particular disease. Society would be much better off if man labeled multitudinous levels of physical health rather than dignifying negative concepts by giving them names and designations.

Now, I may or may not return, again according to those rhythms of which I speak — but know that I am present and approachable.

We will shortly be finished with Chapter One. It should be a simple matter to separate personal material from book dictation.

("Yes, Okay."

(4:48 P.M. "Well," Jane said with a sigh, "I'm glad I had a session."

("Well," I joked, "at least you did something useful today." She had a cigarette. The supper tray came. As we talked before I turned her on her left side, I said that I felt she still did not feel entirely free to walk, that something — some beliefs, or set of them — still held her back. I've been conscious of this feeling of my own for some time, and have thought of mentioning it at times. I didn't want to overdo it, either.

("Well, whatever it is," Jane said with some desperation, "I've got to get over it . . . "

(While she ate I told Jane of another question I'd had in mind for some time, and asked that Seth comment: Our situation, for which we're both responsible, is one of extremes. That is, it seems that we could achieve the same results with less exaggerated, less damaging extremes of behavior. Why did we have to go so far? I've always wondered about this. I granted that one could always say that the same end couldn't be achieved by <u>not</u> going as

far, but then, I told Jane, if one followed that line of reasoning to its logical conclusion, physical death would result — that state would be the final extreme of any form of behavior.

(It wasn't until I was ready to leave 330 that I realized I hadn't asked Seth to comment on my dream of the night before — involving our returning to the Potter apartment-house in Sayre. It looks like we'll have plenty of questions lined up for you-know-who.

(It was snowing as I went out to the car. Not as badly as last night, though, when I'd had to be quite careful driving home.

(Jane called, with nurse Carla's help, as I finished this session after 10:00 P.M.)

JANUARY 10, 1984
4:30 P.M. TUESDAY

(I'm typing this session on May 23, 1985. My friend, Debbie Harris, found the original in notebook #39 when she was copying it for Yale University Library. I'd evidently laid the notes aside to type the next day because I was so busy, then forgot to type them. I seem to have a vague memory about this. I think it's the first time I ever skipped typing a session that way.

(How strange — here I am, typing another session from my notes, when I thought that part of my life was over — that I'd never have another session to type. I wish there were more of them to do. Jane has been dead for 259 days.

(This material came through after Jane and I had watched a program yesterday and today called In Search Of *— old reruns featuring Leonard Nimoy. I don't recall the shows. In my original notes I had noted that today's "session material was quite unexpected."*

(Jane obviously gave this material from her hospital bed in Room 330.)

Now: I bid you another fond good afternoon.

("Good afternoon, Seth.")

A few comments.

There are many, many species that man has not discovered, in all the categories of life — insects onward.

There are multitudinous species of <u>viruses</u> and so forth that man has not encountered and recognized, and there are connections between viruses and other species of living matter that remain unknown. There are indeed two different kinds of upward-walking mammals, much like your own species, but much larger, and with infinitely keener senses. They are indeed amazingly swift creatures, and through scent alone they are aware of the presence of man when any member of your species is at all in the immediate area — standing, say, at least several miles away. Vegetable matter is a main diet, though often supplemented by insects, which are considered a delicacy.

They have, for that matter, devised many ingenious insect traps, so that hundreds or more can be caught, for many are needed since insects are so small. These traps are often constructed on trees, in the bark, in such a fashion that the tree gum itself is used to trap the insects. The traps appear to be part of the tree itself, so as to protect them.

These creatures do indeed remember, but their remembering operates extremely rapidly — a kind of almost instantaneous deduction that comes as sense data is interpreted. That is, received and interpreted almost at once, or simultaneously.

(Pause at 4:40.) Offspring do not occur until the individuals are well past the age that you would consider normal for breeding. Otherwise the procedure is the same. With some territorial variation, such creatures reside in many of the world areas on your planet, though their overall population is very small — altogether, perhaps, several thousand. They rarely congregate in large groups, but do have a family and tribal-like organization, with at the very most twelve adults in any given area. As offspring are added, the groups break up again, for they know well that in larger numbers they would be much more easy to discover.

They all use tools of one kind or another, and live indeed in close concord with the animals. There is no competition between them and animals, for example, and they are not basically aggressive, though they could be extremely dangerous if they were cornered, or if their young were attacked.

They grow quite sluggish in wintertime, in very cold climates, and their temperature drops, as is characteristic of hibernating animals, except that their temperature is more sensitive to daily variations, so that on some winter days they can forage for food very well, while on the other hand they may hibernate for even weeks on end.

(4:46.) They have a keen understanding of nature, and of natural phenomena. Language is not developed to any great degree, for their sensual ordinary equipment is so pure and swift that it almost

becomes a language of its own, and does not need any <u>elaboration</u>. Those senses possess their own variances, so that without any word such as "now" or "then," the creatures are able to know quite accurately how many living creatures are in the vicinity, how long they have been there *(pause)* — and their experience with time is one that follows the seasons in such a way that they have formed a <u>wordless</u>, fairly accurate picture of the world, including navigational direction.

I am mentioning this material because of the program you saw today, and also because I knew of your interest.

The new relationship with Prentice-Hall should work very well. Now you are considered quite respectable *(pause)*, that you have survived so many changes within that publishing organization.

Your dream about the return to Sayre, and the more spacious surroundings, means also that as you now change the past and the future, so you have changed the past: you view it in a more extended light, so that it becomes less narrow and constricting. Then from that new past, in certain terms, the new present and future emerge — a fascinating phenomenon.

Now, I may or may not return, according to those reasons with which you are beginning to grow acquainted, but know that I am present and approachable.

("Thank you very much, Seth."

(4:55 P.M. "I should tell you," Jane said as I lit a smoke for her, "but as soon as that program was over, I knew he was going to mention the Abominable Snowman. But I thought it would be maybe a few lines — I didn't expect that much." I hadn't expected any. The TV show had ended at 3:00 P.M. Jane also said she "saw," or remembered, what the insect trap looked like, but she couldn't make a drawing of it. She said she didn't want to mislead me, but that the traps reminded her of spider webs, the way the insects became trapped in them.

(5:00 P.M. "Don't be worried — I'm not going to go on with the session, but as he said, you always go back and change the past from the present — your focus point, you know — I know what he's going to say next . . . " I said she was welcome to resume the session.

(I had to ask Jane to repeat what she said because the Russian patient in the room next door, Karina, was yelling out in the hall, as she has been all afternoon. Quite distracting. She's still at it. The girl who brought the

supper tray at the end of the session left our room door open, and Karina sounded all the louder.

(Added on Wednesday, January 11, 1984: We'd like more on changing the past from the present. Today Jane and I sort of disagreed [I think] on what Seth was saying. She seems to think the actual episode of Father Darren chasing her around the bed when she was in that hotel room with him as a teen-ager is changed, whereas I thought Seth meant that the original event remained, but that her psychological understanding of what had transpired changed a good deal. There is a difference here. Jane doesn't create a reality in which the event is absent from her memory, or never happened, that I know of.

(Seth didn't mention this in his short session of Wednesday, January 11, and I neglected to ask him about it.)

JANUARY 11, 1984
4:23 P.M. WEDNESDAY

(I haven't typed yesterday's session, on Sasquatch. I had to shovel the driveway — about four inches of snow — since snow had fallen most of the day, and I didn't want a mess out there today. Jane called me last night, courtesy of Carla, and she said Debbie Harris also visited. Debbie is a true friend indeed.

(Yesterday's session was mainly on the Sasquatch phenomenon, triggered I imagine by the program In Search Of, *and I'll probably take time off from* Dreams *one morning to get it done. That's complicated at the moment because I'm already taking time off from* Dreams *each morning now, to work on 1983 tax figures. But we'll make it.*

(This morning [and last night when I got home] the furnace was making so much noise that I called our plumber to come check it out. I left the garage door open for him, as promised, so he could get in the house in the afternoon when I wasn't there. Miracle of miracles — when the heat came on tonight the furnace was so quiet I couldn't believe it. It's always been noisy to some extent, but lately has been much worse.

(Last night in the mail I found Carol Steiner's Ph.D. thesis on the Seth material, which she'd promised in November. We knew a year ago she was writing this for her doctorate in philosophy. Quite interesting, but as I told Jane, it reminded me of just what a task it is to start at the beginning and

present an explanation of the Seth material. From our viewpoint I suppose it seems like more is left unsaid than said — but this may always be true in such cases. Carol wants to publish the work, and asks about a Butts-Roberts biography — something I think we'll probably pass upon. I'll write our publisher, Prentice-Hall.

(Jane ate a good lunch. She tried re-reading the session for January 9, but had trouble. Her eyes kept changing; at times she could see well. Seth has mentioned this acclimatization of the eye muscles. Most of the time Jane had trouble, trying to read around being given her vitals, and finally she gave up. We forgot to ask Carla what my wife's temperature was. I made an attempt to answer the mail, but didn't do well. The time seemed to be gone before we could get anything done.

(I did remind Jane that in yesterday's session Seth hadn't addressed the question I'd mentioned to her at lunch time — why were we such extremists in our behavior, considering the severity of the symptoms, and so forth? Jane did want to have a session this afternoon.)

Now: I bid you another fond good afternoon.

("Good afternoon, Seth.")

I have the following comments.

Your situations can be called extreme — but true extremes are far less fortunate. You have, for example, the extremes of poverty suffered by people in many other parts of the world — a poverty that stunts all kinds of growth, mental and physical, and brings about an early death. Or the extremes of disease, in which children are born without all the faculties needed for life, and — therefore also die an early death. Or those extremes when entire families suffer patterns of tragedy so whole numbers are wiped out at one time.

There are reasons for such cases, of course. I simply wanted you to know that many very severe extremes exist, that would make your lives seem most favorable in contrast. Since you both have such mental agility and a history in this life of health and vitality, that history can be used by Ruburt, if he recalls himself running up and down the steps of the art gallery, for example. His mind and body both must recognize the validity of those motions, so that there should be no contradictory material to block it.

The mental exercise of seeing himself vigorously cleaning the apartments at 458 *(where we used to live on W. Water Street)*, or the rooms at the hill house *(where we live now)*, can also be used most advantageously.

I may or may not return, again according to those rhythms of which I speak — but know that I am present and approachable.

("Okay."

(4:30 P.M. Jane felt better. I told her that Seth didn't go into our questions about his material in yesterday's session, concerning changing the past from the present, nor did he comment on Carol Steiner's Ph.D. thesis on the Seth material. I'd showed it to Jane, of course, but she hadn't been able to read it.

(In the session notes for January 9, I'd noted that I still felt that something was holding Jane back from feeling free to walk, in spite of all the advances we've made. Seth hadn't mentioned this is yesterday's session [for the 10th], and now I asked Jane if she had any insight into that question. I wasn't even sure I was right.

(I was getting my stuff together preparatory to leaving for the evening when Jane said she'd been thinking it over, and had something to tell me. It turned out that she was — is — impaired in feeling free to walk because of her broken right leg, she said.

(Then she revealed that more and more she's worrying about why the right leg looks so much shorter than the left one. It doesn't seem possible to her that she'll be able to walk on it even if she does straighten it out. We talked for a little while. I'm afraid the talk didn't make her feel any better. I've known for some time that a problem exists there as to why the leg is shorter-looking. "But then," I said, "we're not supposed to think that way. We're supposed to have the confidence that the body knows what it's doing, and will fix that leg in whatever manner is necessary." Jane agreed, of course, but I could see she was quite upset.

(I said she may have to get a medical opinion, but that I felt that if they wanted to X-ray the leg tomorrow, she'd say no. I would dearly love to see the leg begin to relax, to straighten out to at least a degree. I'm terribly concerned at the stress involved in her holding the right leg so doubled up against her groin. As I said, I still don't really know why the body has to do this. That even if the bones had been weakened by prolonged stress, with her improved appetite and attitude, that danger period should be at least somewhat alleviated by now. No more bones have broken.

(In short, Jane, the right leg is evidently to play a central role in your

recovery — not only a physical one, but a vital one concerning changes in belief about the whole thing. Ironic indeed, I thought as I drove home, if the broken leg would serve as the last, final impetus toward clearing our psyches of the last of the old, damaging beliefs, so that the new synthesis can finally take place: the body can heal itself . . .

(Jane called at 10:10 tonight, with Carla's help, just as I was finishing typing the session. She said she still didn't feel a whole helluva lot better. I tried to cheer her up — and myself as well.)

JANUARY 12, 1984
4:02 P.M. THURSDAY

(The day was very cold — only 12 degrees at noon. I stopped at the bank to buy a check and a money order for Blue Cross and the monthly hospital payment on our old bill. When I got to 330 Jane told me about her dream, which she had not long after I left last night.

(In the dream she was in a bathtub, without water, talking to her mother whom she could not see. This was followed by "a very sensual" episode she cannot recall at all. Then she stood in a room letting her hair down. She thinks this means that symbolically she's "letting her hair down" as she continues to learn.

(Jane was "blue and nervous" this morning, but talked herself out of it. She ate a good lunch. I had yesterday's session typed, and she tried several times to read it without success — even after I'd given her eyedrops, she just couldn't do it today. I finally read the session to her, finishing at 3:33.

(Afterward, as we talked, Jane agreed to look in the mirror, which I have had available in 330 for some months. At first she was afraid to, but it went well — with only a little catch in her throat she faced herself, and did very well at it. The main point we agreed on was that using a mirror meant one less important hassle to deal with; she'd be hiding that much less from herself.

(We put on lipstick and she looked very good, with her fine skin and lack of wrinkles that most people her age have. She's 54. I told her she looked remarkably well. Her hair also looks good — curling and alive. I said if it was dyed, as she used to do, that she'd look fine, just like her old self. I also suggested she look in the mirror, at least briefly each day, and that soon there would be nothing to it. She might even get to look forward to seeing herself continue to improve.

(Jane tried to read the session again, but soon gave up. I remarked that if she had a session today I'd like it to be on what we'd talked about before I left last night — her right leg, and related challenges. I also wanted Seth to comment on the last paragraph I'd written for yesterday's session. I thought I had a good idea there, and Jane agreed. She also wants me to bring in an eyebrow pencil, so she can use that with her lipstick.

(Finally, Jane got tired of waiting for people to do her vitals, and decided to start the session.

(Karina was hollering out in the hall, around the corner, and had been doing so steadily ever since I got there.)

Now: I bid you another fond good afternoon.

("Good afternoon, Seth."

(Long pause.) It may be far more <u>pleasant</u> to be good-humored all of the time — but in Ruburt's situation the <u>fairly</u> infrequent periods of blueness do indeed operate therapeutically, so that he is able to express those feelings through tears, and therefore relieve the body of expressing the same feelings through additional symptoms.

(Someone asked from the doorway: "Is Sharon in there?"

("Nope," I said. Jane stayed in trance.)

There is a certain residue, in other words *(pause)* of fairly desolate feelings — and these are working themselves out through such expression, thus freeing the body for additional improvements. He *(as Seth sometimes addresses Jane, because of her male entity name, Ruburt)* progresses at a certain rate, for example, and encounters some blockages, due to doubts and fears. These are then released and expressed through tears or through a recognized period of blueness. Then the system is cleared again, and the way clear for more improvements.

In the past, the <u>body itself was depressed</u> *(a very important point)*, running at low gear, and this is certainly not the case now. Each time, of course, the period of blueness is briefer, the system cleared more quickly, and the new improvements also show themselves at a quicker rate.

(Long pause at 4:10.) This is now, at least, a natural casting-off of old doubts and fears, but in such a way that they are recognized and then let go.

(Long pause.) The changing condition of the eyes shows the kind of cycles that occur: the upper edges, so to speak, of improvements continue, so that each new improvement is, obviously, superior to

the last. But in the meantime there is much variation, unevenness, and times when the vision is quite unclear. Those changes do indeed seem mysterious. Ruburt is not looking at his own eyes all of the time — so that mysteriousness is somehow taken for granted. He understands so little about the eyes' operation to begin with, that he does not bother to figure out, or try to figure out, the order that such improvements should take, or how they should happen.

The right leg is immediately before his vision, however — it is highly visible, so that he often compares its position unfavorably with that of the other leg. This is bound to lead him to consider those impediments that seem to be in the way. The body can heal the leg as easily as it can heal the eyes, and as easily as it can heal the bedsores.

It is a good idea for now not to concentrate upon that leg, or what it must do eventually in order for walking to take place. It might help if now and then he imagines his walking taking place as easily and naturally as his thoughts come and go, and in ways as mysterious as the way his vision operates, when it is suddenly clearer, and he reads so much more quickly — for the quick reading will soon be the norm.

It is indeed a step forward that he looked in the mirror today — a very important issue — and so is your suggestion that he do so briefly every day — and smiles (amused).

It shows he is ready to encounter himself, and at least willing to look kindly upon himself. Of course, the lipstick is an excellent idea, and the eyebrow pencil, so that he begins to care for his face as he used to. The face's expression accurately reflects the inner self-image, as odd as it may seem. A smile, even when he does not feel like smiling, builds up the self-image, and affects the entire bodily condition.

Ruburt has already been healed of conditions quite as complicated as the leg that was broken.

I may or may not return — but know indeed that I am present and approachable, and that I hold both of you in my attention.

("Can I ask a question?")

You may.

("Do you want to say something about our discussion yesterday, about changing the past from the present?" I felt that Seth was bound to agree with Jane's version of what he'd said, rather than mine.

(4:25.) It is very difficult to explain, because what actually happens is sometimes so directly contrary to what <u>seems</u> to have happened. You do not simply change, or enlarge, your ideas or beliefs about the past — but you <u>change the events of the past themselves</u> for yourself, and sometimes for others also.

It might help if you remember that despite appearances all events are basically subjective. Their "objectivity" happens at a certain point of focus, and as —

(4:27. A new nurse came in to take Jane's temperature — 98.3. Karina had been yelling throughout the session — so much so that at times I'd almost missed what Seth had been saying.

(A moment later Shawn Peterson came in to say hello. I made the mistake of asking how her husband was, since I'd thought about asking yesterday, but hadn't. Shawn launched into a long account of her husband's latest troubles. Yesterday the two of them had spent a day at the hospital in Sayre. With the best intentions, her account reflected all the negative beliefs about illness that Jane and I had come to expect in the hospital setting. After Shawn left, I read to Jane her material from 4:25.)

— that focus changes, so do the events.

(4:44 P.M. That was it, although Jane said she had more material available. It was time to turn her. The situation was somewhat frustrating, since I'd looked forward to some good material in changing the past from the present; I hadn't wanted the question to be forgotten.

(Maybe more on it tomorrow, Jane said at last. Karina had definitely been a bother this afternoon, and she was still calling out, her voice hoarse and much weaker. I told Jane I thought she sounded like she was reliving a reversion to her childhood. The staff people had tried to calm her down at various times, to no avail. Jane said their actions made her feel bad, because it reminded her of when she'd had her own panic feelings, and people had tried to calm her down in her early days in the hospital. Now, Jane said "cancel" to herself after she'd told me her feelings.)

JANUARY 13, 1984
3:37 P.M. FRIDAY

(Jane looked at herself in the mirror today after lunch — the second day in a row that she's done so. These events are the first like them in well over a year, she estimated. They also had their humorous side, since today she

barely looked at her image, then afterward told me that her hair was white.
It isn't, of course. "Well, I got that over with," she said with obvious relief
after I'd handed her the mirror not long after getting to 330. I gave her her
lipstick also, which she applied without trouble.

(The day was warmer at about 22 degrees. This morning I'd prepared
payments for insurance and the hospital. Karina is much quieter today —
so far. I said I wouldn't mind Seth commenting on her.

(Jane ate a good lunch. A nurse's aide brought us a copy of the regular
menu, compared to the one for soft foods that Jane has always used, and we
discovered that there isn't all that much difference between the two.

(2:35. Jane began reading yesterday's session, and obviously did better
than she had yesterday. I helped her in some spots. At 2:50 she quit for a
cigarette while on page three. Then she told me of her dream. In the first
part, she saw in a mirror that she had pink beads which she tried on to see
how they'd go with the blouse she was wearing — blouse color unknown. In
the second part, she was on her back in bed when her right hip did some-
thing and then her legs were equal in length in her vision. She doesn't know
what she did. I said it sounded as though the dream state was giving her
information on healing and motion. The leg data were especially important.

(3:20 Jane finished reading the session aloud, and did very well at it,
especially toward the end. I answered mail while she had another cigarette
before the session. She'd decided not to wait for people to do her vitals. When
she asked me if I could sort out Seth's book material from his personal stuff,
I said it was easy — that I wasn't concerned at all.

("You know why?" I asked her. "Because you're going to do all the work
on the book. When you get home, so start getting ready. I've always known you
were going to do the book. I'll do an intro if you want, and you can too, or
you-know-who can also — but you're going to be the one who does that book."

(My little speech got her talking about it and related matters, and she
soon felt Seth around. She put out her cigarette early, in fact.)

Now I bid you another most fond good afternoon.

("Good afternoon, Seth.")

Apropos of our discussion concerning time.

The nature of universal creativity is so remarkable that its <u>true</u>
<u>reaches</u> are literally beyond most understanding. The implications
are staggering — so that the affair is almost impossible to explain.

The past, and every moment of the past, are being constantly changed from the operation point of the present. <u>In your terms</u>, the present becomes the past, which is again changed at every considerable point from the latest-present — you may put a hyphen between the last two words, so that the meaning is clear. Yet through all of this immense, continuous creation, there is always a personal sense of continuity: You never really lose your way in the distance between one moment and the next —

(3:43. One of the nurses popped in on her way home to tell us that Georgia Cecce had just been admitted to the hospital — "Down the hall, in room 307." We've known Georgia, Jane's favorite nurse, ever since my wife entered the hospital in April, 1983.

("Every time we get on this subject something happens," I said. I read to Jane what she'd just given so far. "Is that clear?"

("Yes," she said. Resume at 3:46.)

In somewhat of the same fashion the objects about you are constantly in motion, as you know. The atoms and molecules are forever moving, and <u>in a way</u> the electrons are the <u>directors</u> of that motion.

Your own focus is so precisely and finely tuned that despite all of that activity, objects appear solid. Period. Now objects are also events, and perhaps that is the easiest way to understand them. They are highly dependent upon your own subjective focus. Let that focus falter for a briefest amount of time, and the whole house of cards would come tumbling down, so to speak.

Remember that you are also objects, and also events, and as physical bodies your organs are also composed of atoms and molecules whose motion, again, is directed by the electrons.

(Long pause at 3:52.) The electrons themselves have their own subjective lives. They are also subjective events, therefore, so there is always a correlation between those electrons in your bodies and those in the objects you see about you. Nevertheless again, subjective continuity itself never falters, in that it is always a part of the world that it perceives, so that you and the world <u>create each other</u>, in these terms.

When you change the past from each point of the latest-present, you are also changing events at the most microscopic levels. Your <u>intent</u> has also an electronic reality, therefore. It is <u>almost as if</u> your thoughts punched the keys of some massive computer, for your thoughts do indeed have a force. New sentence: Even as sentences are composed of words, there is no end to the number of sentences that can be spoken — so "time" is composed of an endless variety of electronic languages that can "speak" a million <u>worlds</u> instead of words.

Now I may or may not return, according to those rhythms of which I speak, but know that I am "present" and approachable.

("May I ask a question?")

You may.

("How about saying something about Karina?" I'd heard the Russian lady sounding off a few times this afternoon during the session.)

Take your break.

(4:00. Jane had a cigarette. "He means he'll be back," she said. "I thought that stuff on time was fantastic. There's something you have when you're doing it that you don't have when you read it afterward, when you're outside of it. When you're doing it you're <u>inside</u> of it."

("You mean you feel it," I said, and she agreed. I've often thought of how weak our current theories are to explain what we see around us, or in the night sky.

(4:05–4:10. Lynn came in to do all of Jane's vitals. Temperature 98. We talked about Karina, in the room on the other side of the bathroom between rooms. Lynn thinks Karina is disoriented, although some of the doctors don't. We speculated as to why Karina has never learned any language other than Russian. Lynn said the hospital even has a list of Russian words, but that Karina doesn't respond adequately to them — perhaps they're poorly pronounced, say.

(I told Jane after Lynn left that she could continue with the material on time if she preferred. Resume at 4:21.)

Dates are but designations applied to the days.

Mankind lived without such designations for a much longer period than he has used them. Animals, without such designations, still know their position on the planet itself, and they are aware of the tides and the movement of the earth and planets.

(Long pause.) Karina has that same kind of orientation. At this point in her life, she has actually refused to concentrate upon languages, which would tend to tie her more tightly to the details of the world. *(Long pause, one of many.)* She does "return to the past," remaking it more to her liking. Her latest-present is beginning to show signs

of a deterioration. She wants a turning-off point from which to construct other realities, so it is not so much that the latest-present is deteriorating as much as the fact that she is purposely letting her attention wander, and <u>allowing</u> the latest-presents (with the hyphen) to diminish in strength and vitality. She will of course construct a new form from which to operate.

Now I may or may not return, but know again that I am present and approachable *(with humor.*

("Thank you very much."

(4:32 P.M. Jane had a cigarette. Yesterday had been one of Karina's bad days — her worst, in fact, as far as we could tell. She'd cried out unintelligible words steadily all afternoon, until finally her voice had begun to falter and crack by supper time. It had been more than a little disturbing. At the time I'd wondered if she was on the downgrade, for I didn't remember her calling out so steadily in weeks past. I'd thought her driving herself until she was hoarse was a late — or last — confrontation with a world that she might soon be leaving . . .)

JANUARY 14, 1984
4:31 P.M. SATURDAY

(The day is warm — 33 degrees — and the snow and ice are melting. This morning I worked on the final copy of our 1983 taxes, and will mail them to our accountant Monday morning. I brought Jane's eyebrow pencil to her at 330.

(3:15. Jane looked at herself in the mirror after she put on lipstick. She even smiled — "Since I'm supposed to" — and did well. I darkened her brows with the pencil, and she looked fine.

(3:25. I went down the hall to 307 to see Georgia, but she was asleep. I'd looked in while passing this noon; her bed had been empty, although two people had sat in the room talking.

(3:32. Jane finished her cigarette and I worked on mail.

(3:45. Jane began reading yesterday's session, and did very well indeed to start. Her reading was very fast. She was interrupted by people taking her vitals — temperature 97.3. By 3:57 she went back to the session — but now her pace wasn't as fast and sure. She said her eyes were changing.

(4:02. Jane stopped reading. She could hardly make out the session. A

little later she resumed reading sporadically. All of these changes were an excellent demonstration of the way Seth has said her eyes are behaving as they move up to a new plateau of improved vision.

(4:07. Jane took a break from reading for a cigarette. She resumed at 4:19, and finished the session, doing better at the end.

(4:25. Now she told me how earlier today she'd imagined herself visiting Enfield Glen.* She said she did very well thinking of herself walking and climbing around the park and the pool — but then she ended up blue, thinking of all she had to go through yet before she could do those things. "So it's tricky as hell to do all that stuff and not let yourself slide over the edge," she said. I said it was okay to slide over the edge, if you realized what was happening and took steps to not get carried away into a depressed mood by it. Nobody's perfect, nor do we even need perfection.

(Karina was mostly quiet today, although sounding off at times. Jane's Seth voice was stronger and more positive than usual, I thought, with considerable emphasis at times.)

Now, I bid you another fond good afternoon —

("Good afternoon, Seth.")

— and I am making myself known but briefly in order to accelerate those coordinates that are so beneficial for the progression of healing energy.

Ruburt did very well with his mental exercises — unusually well except for a few instances, when he did allow self-pity to grab ahold. It is extremely important that he concentrate upon those <u>pleasures</u> of life that he does enjoy. Eating good food, experiencing, again, the joy of reading, the joy of creative thought, the pleasure of friends, and so forth, for those benefits will then be increased more than a hundredfold.

All the improvements necessary are indeed happening at various levels of activity within his mental and physical experience. Following as he has been, he will indeed be able to stand on his own two feet, and to walk with some confidence. He must, however, <u>have faith</u> that this is so — and again, without worrying about how it will happen.

---

*Enfield Glen is the local name for Robert Treman State Park. It's located near Ithaca, New York, some 35 miles from both Elmira and Sayre. The Butts family spent many a happy summer camping there. Jane is from Saratoga Springs, in upstate New York. The beautiful Glen is the first place I took her to after our engagement in 1955.

The conscious mind can direct bodily activity *(long pause)*, but the body consciousness alone can perform those activities that bring forth life and motion.

I may or may not return, according to those rhythms of which I speak, but know again that I am present and approachable.

("Thank you."

(4:37 P.M. I told Jane the little session was excellent, as indeed it is. I thought it contained very positive and hopeful material — for some reason it really hit home. Jane was pleased too, and I reread it to her after supper.

(While we were eating the phone rang. It was John Bumbalo, our neighbor who lives across the street from our hill house. He invited me to a late supper with his girl, Lisa. I'm finishing typing this session now at 8:15 P.M., preparatory to going across Pinnacle Road. Sleep well, Jane. I love you.)

JANUARY 15, 1984
4:41 P.M. SUNDAY

(Last night had been very cold, and it was still only 18 degrees when I left for 330 this noon. This morning I finished the final statements for our 1983 taxes. The rest of the time I worked on Dreams. *Interruptions, though, leave me feeling that I'm way far away from what I want to do when I first return to a project.*

(Jane said Georgia Cecce was in to see her this morning, and to borrow another pack of cigarettes. A nurse by the name of Gaye washed Jane's hair this morning; I told my wife it looked good. Jane looked in the mirror and didn't agree, although she did admit that her hair wasn't white, but gray and white. Jane went through the motions of smiling into the mirror, after she'd put on lipstick. Gaye had darkened her brows with the eyebrow pencil earlier this morning.

(After lunch Jane told me that she'd had a new catheter inserted at about 3:30 this morning. No trouble. But she needed the new one after the new girl on the floor had pulled it loose several times while taking care of her. No hydro this morning.

(Jane, with Carla's help, tried to call me twice last night, but I didn't get back to the house from John Bumbalo's until about midnight. We had an excellent supper. I woke up stewing around 3:00, and got up for about

an hour before returning to bed. The pendulum told me I was fretting about losing time on Dreams.

(2:50. Jane began reading yesterday's session, and did quite well. She was done at 3:05 after a good read. She had a smoke while I tried to concentrate upon mail, but I didn't do well. I was sleepy.

(From 4:00 to 4:07 people came in to take her vitals — temperature 99, up a bit, but Jane felt okay. I was beginning to think she wouldn't have a session when she told me to get my paper.)

Now: I bid you another fond good afternoon.

("The same to you, Seth.")

I am announcing myself briefly once more in order to better activate those coordinates that are so important in the healing processes.

It is an excellent idea for Ruburt to tell his arms and legs that it is perfectly safe for them to straighten out, to stretch and flex, and to use their normal capacity for motion. The suggestion is highly valuable, and he is using it well. The hands are indeed beginning to accelerate their improvements — the right one in particular, so that the fingers begin to uncurl.

The rapid changes in the eye motions demonstrate the rapidity of muscular action and reaction that takes place in <u>all other</u> portions of the body as well.

It would be a good idea once or twice for him to remember the Jungle Gym *(in Webster, New York where my younger brother Bill and his family live)*, and the first time he remembered faltering in a physical fashion. If he can, then have him imagine himself <u>not faltering</u>, but continuing on. In that way he also repairs the past. If he has difficulty with the exercise, however, then let it go, but continue with the safety suggestions.

I may or may not return, again according to those rhythms of which I speak — but know that I am present and approachable.

("Okay. Thank you."

(4:47 P.M. Earlier this afternoon Jane had showed me how the curled-up fingers of her right hand had indeed loosened up to some extent. I'd applied Remedy Rescue Cream to the knuckles of both hands. I've also been aware, for some time, of changes taking place on the wrist and the back of her left hand. When I turned her before supper this evening, her right arm moved quite freely and loosely at the elbow. The right knee also flexes better and better. So these invaluable changes continue to happen.

(I left Jane at 7:07 after reading the prayer with her. I waved to Georgia in 307 on my way out. She had company so I didn't stop.

(Both of us instantly remembered the Jungle Gym at the lakeside park in Webster, where we'd first noticed Jane's faltering in physical movement so many years ago. Today when Seth mentioned it she hadn't seem distressed, though, so perhaps that memory can be put to good constructive use by us now.)

JANUARY 16, 1984
4:23 P.M. MONDAY

(It was very cold last night, and at 6:30 this morning it was still 5 degrees below zero. When I left for 330 this noon the temperature was barely 10 above. I'd typed a letter to our lawyer, regarding our taxes, and mailed it this noon. I told Jane later that I need information about accepting gift money, via Maude Cardwell. I suspect such funds are taxable, so to legally avoid having much of any funds lost through heavy taxes, Jane and I need advice as to what to do. It may be, I said, that we'll never see the money. Maude Cardwell may have to pay bills for us, and so forth. In any case, the donor can take deductions, I think.

(Jane ate a good lunch. Afterward she described a series of "experiences" she'd had after I left her last night. They happened at about 8:15, before staff people came in to turn her on her side. It's difficult to describe what she told me, and would take many words and much time. "I wish I could write it myself," she said. She was in various altered states during some of the experiences, I'd say, and a dreaming one in others.

(Jane began by finding herself as a young girl on a swing at the recreation field across the street from St. Clement's Catholic Church and School in Saratoga Springs, where she grew up. "I looked down and saw that I wore black shoes and white socks, like little kids do, like I look in some of those old photographs." At one time here she thought she was only four years old. She knew she was doing those things while at the field, she said.

(Then she found herself in a tub of warm water, and she was filled with sexual sensual feelings, especially in the vaginal area. "I suddenly realized I was hallucinating the water and stuff, that I was really in my hospital bed. Then I thought that anyway, I could have a kitten here. We have two rooms and Rob could hide the kitten, and keep a litter box hidden too — how I didn't know."

(Next, Jane said she was trying to find a radio and recorder here at our hill house in Elmira so that Sue Watkins, who lives an hour's drive to the north, could borrow it. While searching she suddenly found a lot of cubbyholes filled with trinkets that she knew were all hers, and she was very pleased at this knowledge. "Then the rest of the time I was involved with recorders." She found herself inside something like a boxcar that was also the inside chassis of a cassette-playing machine. In this chassis Jane and Sue were going up and down and around beautiful, jewel-like green hills. "It was fantastic." Then like a rising sun Jane saw her own enormous face looking down at it all — the jewel colors, Sue and herself, the vehicle.

(Jane didn't actually see Sue during the experience — she just knew Sue was there, talking to her. Then the trip "got much less clear," and she was trying to figure out what to lend Sue. She can't remember.

(3:10. I cleaned Jane's glasses. She put on lipstick, then looked in the mirror I held up for her. She even volunteered to do this herself. She smiled — briefly. I laughed, telling her her behavior reminded me of our cats this morning, when it was so cold: Both Billy and Mitzi had barely stepped out onto the picnic table from the kitchen window, when they reversed themselves and hopped right back into the house. I doubt if my wife thought the comparison was humorous.

(3:38. Jane tried to read yesterday's session, but had a lot of trouble. She read a little in spurts of clear vision. "Jesus, that's terrible," she said. "It scares me when I do that. It would scare anybody." She lay the session aside for a smoke. Carla took her temperature — 98.1. Diana took her blood pressure.

(4:00. Jane tried to read the session again. No go. "It makes me mad. Oh — and I forgot to tell you. They did blood work this morning. They took blood just for the thyroid, though, after breakfast. Other tests, they have to take blood before you eat, so maybe they'll be back tomorrow morning." This is the first blood work in several weeks, at least.

(4:05. Finally, I read the session to Jane. She had a cigarette before going into the session for today.)

Now: I bid you another fond good afternoon.

("Good afternoon, Seth."

(With many pauses throughout:) Ruburt displayed an excellent example of the mobility of consciousness in last evening's experiences.

Healing also takes place at many different levels of consciousness. *(Long pause.)* Ruburt's experience, all in all, touched many of those levels, facilitating the healing processes at each given level. The "boxcar" episode represented his living at one level of physical experience, even while he also existed as the giant-sized self that peered over the mountain top and watched his progress. An excellent portrayal — or portrait — of the infinite inner self watching and guiding the physical self's existence.

(It would make a great painting.

(4:28.) The sexual aspects of the earlier episode indeed represented the toning-up of the sexual capacities and their pleasurable aspects. In the very early episode, Ruburt experienced the healthy and joyful child's body, with its innocent spontaneity. This allowed him to come into touch with childhood's early vitality — and in a sensual manner, not just, say, as a memory.

The excellent glowing colors also helped remind him of the eyes' ability to perceive bright hues, and so activated the nerves and muscles of the eyes, reminding <u>them</u> of their natural capabilities.

The boxcar elements, beside the explanation already given, also represented the body as a vehicle, moving easily and swiftly. The entire episode shows the way that the mind derives new experience through using more than one level of consciousness at any given time. And the small trinkets that Ruburt discovered to his own delight represented the small but very valuable pleasures of daily life that he is now reclaiming.

Now I may or may not return, again according to those rhythms of which I speak — but know that I am present and approachable.

("Can I ask a question?")

You may.

("What's the connection with Jane finding herself inside a recorder? And with Sue?" Sue wrote the two-volume Conversations With Seth.)

Sue represents a certain portion of Ruburt — the writing self, signifying that the "psychic" portions of Ruburt's personality were helping out the writing portions, and letting them share in the psychic knowledge and experience.

("Is that it?" I asked after a long pause.

("Yes," Jane said.

(4:38 P.M. I was a bit surprised at the ending of the session at that point, I told Jane, because I'd been still waiting for Seth to answer the part

of my question dealing with her being inside a recorder. Jane was surprised also — since she hadn't heard me ask that part of the question. I hadn't spoken loudly. Maybe Seth can go into it next time. I told Jane that obviously the recorder was a communication device of a kind, so the connection may lie there.

(It would also be interesting to have Seth comment on the kitten, and its symbolism, in Jane's experience.

(I went out to the parking lot to run up the car at 5:00, it was so cold. After getting back and turning Jane and massaging her with Oil of Olay, she showed me how her right hand is still releasing the curled-up fingers, as begun yesterday. She had good movement in the right elbow, quite free as far as it will open up, and this is increasing. I told her that the changes in the nodules on top of her left wrist have now decreased in size considerably, as they have been doing very gradually for some time now. Sleep well, Jane.)

JANUARY 17, 1984
4:25 P.M. TUESDAY

(The day was much warmer — 30 degrees — at noon. I had no interruptions this morning while working on Dreams *— it seemed strange. Jane was okay in 330, already turned on her back when I got there. She did okay in hydro. No one came this morning to take additional blood. The curled-up fingers of her right hand continue to loosen.*

(I didn't see Georgia today. When I got to 330 Jane told me that Karina had been moved to a rest home in Wellsburg, a small community a few miles east of Elmira. I was surprised and in a way sad for her, wondering how she would make out, and what problems the new place would have with her. So for the first time in weeks, we didn't hear Karina cry out in Russian, or cry for Georgia in English.

(3:00. Jane started to read yesterday's session. It was hard going for her, but she stuck with it and finally finished at 3:30. I worked on mail, reading several great letters and answering a couple. One of them has potential — about a group of young actresses in New York City who want to read Seth on a series of radio shows. I plan to send their proposal and letter to Lynne Lumsden, our editor at Prentice-Hall.

(4:00. A new girl — probably a floater — took Jane's temperature — 98.4.

(Jane said she wanted to have a session even though it was getting late. She also said she wanted to read over some of the later sessions: "Because I need them." She repeated this several times during the afternoon.)

Now: I bid you another fond good afternoon.

("Good afternoon, Seth.")

In Ruburt's recent experience, he found himself inside the chassis of a recording device — signifying that instead of playing a cassette at several different speeds, he was instead, so to speak, playing his own consciousness at different speeds.

He was not just listening, then, to recorded material, but he was himself the recorded information and a <u>recorder</u> upon which the experiences played.

(4:28. A nurse came in to take Jane's blood pressure. She left the room door open when she left, so that hall noises intruded.

(4:31.) The analogy of the many <u>speeds</u> of consciousness actually fits in well with the actual neurological sequences upon which consciousness plays. As you know, everything alive is conscious — and even so-called dead matter possesses its own variety of self-awareness.

(Pause.) In your terms, the rhythm of some kinds of consciousness would seem exceedingly slow, so that a century might pass between one perception and the next. Other variations might seem amazingly quick — the perceptions following each other so swiftly that they would indeed escape <u>your</u> (underlined) perception entirely; yet in the wondrous marvels of inner nature, all of these rhythms are connected one to the others, and in a matter of speaking — excuse the pun *(amused)* — they each balance each other.

It is not so much the actual rhythms that are manifested that make the difference in perception, but the <u>absence of certain other rhythms</u> *(intently),* upon which perceptions ride.

Now I may or may not return, again according to those rhythms of which I have just spoken.

("Do you want to answer my question from the session yesterday, about the reason for the kitten in Jane's experience?")

The kitten merely represented wish fulfillment, in that Ruburt does plan to get a kitten as soon as he is home. In the experience the kitten was in the hospital room, and there seemed to be adjoining rooms, as at 458 *(the address of the apartment house we'd lived in on W. Water Street)*. This signified that Ruburt was building up similarities between present and past experience, so that the kitten, appearing in the dream's present and past also, would indeed appear in the future.

I am also accelerating those coordinates that are involved with Ruburt's healing, thus quickening those vital healing processes.

("Thank you."

(4:44 P.M. Jane had done well. I reread the session to her after supper. Also, it seems that Seth has answered all of the questions I'd thought of in connection with her experience of the afternoon before last. That is, without my going into more detail — then the questions could be endless.)

JANUARY 18, 1984
4:29 P.M. WEDNESDAY

(The day wasn't bad — 25 degrees as I headed for Room 330 — but a snowstorm was predicted for the afternoon. Jane was already on her back; her left shoulder had been bothering her. It was obvious that she was blue. I got the nurse to help me hoist her further up on the bed so she'd be more comfortable, and that seemed to help. I wasn't in any too great a mood myself.

(Then Jane told me that last night Shawn Peterson had dropped the bottle of Oil of Olay, and thrown away the dispenser along with the broken glass. The dispensers are hard to find. I asked Jane why she hadn't at once asked Shawn to save it, but when she remembered to some ten minutes later, it was too late; Shawn had cleaned up the mess and thrown it all out. For some reason this news served as a trigger to plunge me into a depressed mood of my own, which lasted for most of the afternoon. Maybe I was tired.

(Then as I was fixing the tray for lunch, Peggy Gallagher, our friend who is a reporter for the Elmira Star-Gazette, visited and stayed through most of the meal. I didn't feel like talking, but we had a good visit after we loosened up a little. At the same time, I couldn't help wondering why Peggy had chosen this day to visit us, of all days. She's been very busy.

(I worked with mail, but didn't feel like it, really. At 3:15 Jane started reading yesterday's session. She did pretty well — better than she had yesterday. She was interrupted by Carla and Shawn to check her vitals — temperature 99 — and finished the session ten minutes later.

(3:50. "I need to read some of the earlier sessions," Jane had said when I arrived, so at 3:50 she began reading the session for January 13, a good one, while I did mail. At 4:20 she gave up reading for a cigarette and a possible session, regardless of the late hour.)

Now: I bid you another fond good afternoon —

("Good afternoon, Seth.")

— and I am announcing myself again in order to quicken those coordinates that quicken the healing processes.

You both did fairly well in handling <u>unfavorable</u> moods. Do not bother now, but when you are momentarily "down," it is then particularly important that Ruburt look in the mirror, apply the lipstick, and smile in whatever fashion. Sometimes a humorous aspect will indeed show itself, and lift his mood automatically.

The eyes, again, show the swiftness of muscular response and neural activity. It is a good idea to remember that the neurological quickness happens in all portions of the body. The more healthy connections are being made in that regard, and it is true that Ruburt's body often feels exceedingly warm. That heat is the result of the body's activity <u>being</u> quickened. It <u>does</u> generate heat, and it is characteristic of many, if not most, healing experiences.

Once again, it is most important that Ruburt keep his goals in mind, and remember that <u>despite</u> any given mood the healing process continues. His right hand also continues to improve, and he is doing a good job of reminding himself that it is safe for all of his limbs to straighten out in a normal manner — to stretch and flex and express their true capacity for motion and action.

Now, I may nor may not return, again according to those rhythms of which I speak — but know that I am present and approachable.

("Thank you.")

One point I wanted to mention: Peggy Gallagher telepathically picked up your moods, and felt the impetus to visit.

(4:38 P.M. As noted, I'd wondered myself about the timing of Peggy's visit. Until Seth mentioned it, I'd forgotten all about asking Jane to look in the mirror today. She had coffee and a cigarette before I turned her. I read the session to her before leaving at about 7:05. It was still snowing. I made it up the hill okay, but with hints of sliding around. I'll probably go shovel at least part of the driveway after I finish this.)

JANUARY 19, 1984
4:13 P.M. THURSDAY

(The temperature was only 18 degrees when I got to 330. After a minor snow storm yesterday afternoon and last night, I'd shoveled the driveway late last night and early this morning. No calls this morning. I forgot to call our lawyer early, and when I did think of it I said to hell with it and continued work on **Dreams.** *On the way to the hospital I stopped at the post office to mail Lynn Lumsden a copy of a fan letter we'd received, offering us a year's free ads in a crossword puzzle magazine.*

(I never really know what to do about such offers, and have answered several such lately. Then today I opened a package that contained a book of trance material similar to Seth's. I guess I'm supposed to say thanks and that it's great, to the publisher and the medium. Actually, I think those two people removed their material — which talks about All That Is — too far from its human source, its everyday contact with human personality, and thus produced just another psychic book. You could take six of those books, I thought, shuffle the names of the mediums around, and never know who produced what. I can only think the mediums involved must be afraid of the emotions and implications involved.

(Jane ate a good lunch. Then she told me to get the mirror, lipstick, and eyebrow pencil. When she looked into the mirror she smiled briefly, and showed her teeth — a lot better than yesterday, when we didn't do it at all.

(3:00. Jane began reading yesterday's session, and did quite well. She was through in 10 minutes or so — quite good. I did mail.

(3:33. She began to read her second session for the day, of January 17, and again did well.

(It came to me that what bothers me about the kind of book I opened today is their limited viewpoint. As limited in its way as a book on geology or clothing or any of innumerable others. There's no questioning mind at work, no new ideas or theories — merely the familiar rehash about All That Is, love, reincarnation, and so forth. Valid enough, perhaps, but lacking original insight and individuality like the Seth material has.

(I told Jane of my dream of the night before last, in which she and I and Leonard Yaudes — who had been our downstairs neighbor at 458 — moved into an apartment together at 458. In the dream the rooms were larger and better kept than they really are. I told Jane I suspected the dream grew out of my meeting Leonard at the new Super-Duper market the other night, when he'd joked around and repeated several times how good he felt

physically, after his heart operation. Jane said she thought the dream meant that the three of us were all embarked on a journey into better health, a better outlook on life.

(3:42. After Shawn took her temperature — 97.2 — Jane began reading her third session for the day — that of January 14 — and did even better on this one, fast and easy, I felt. She was interrupted by staff giving her eyedrops and taking her blood pressure, and finished that session at 4:02. She said the type has been "as good as any I've ever seen — it cleared up amazingly at times." This after I'd realized she was indeed doing very well reading.

(4:05. She had a cigarette, and told me that both hands were still improving and changing. "I'd like it to be quicker, but I know they are.")

Now: I bid you another fond good afternoon.

("Good afternoon, Seth.")

(With humor:) Dictation. *(Pause.)* If any of you, my readers, are in poor health, or generally unhappy, no one is asking you to pretend that those conditions do not exist. I hope to show you that even those unfortunate situations were created out of a misdirected good intent. In this book we will keep reminding you, however, that exuberance and high spirits are a natural part of your heritage.

We also hope to allow you to recapture those feelings, if you have lost them *(long pause),* and to give other ways of keeping those emotions fresh and intact. Readers will benefit in various fashions, according to their own conditions and intents, but every reader will benefit to some degree or another — and <u>each reader</u> will become reacquainted with those inner springs of vitality and well-being that are so important in human experience.

(With a lilt:) End of Chapter One.

(4:19.) Comments.

It is because Ruburt now has more vitality that he sometimes becomes quite impatient with his progress.

He feels more energetic, and of course wants to become much more active. *(Long pause.)* His food is doing him more and more good. He assimilates it far better, and this <u>does</u> allow the healing process to quicken. At the same time there is often that unevenness, as all portions of the body <u>start up again,</u> so to speak. The eyes today showed what I mean, as on occasion he could <u>briefly</u> read far better than he has so far, then seemingly go back to a previous level, and then back and forth between various stages.

The advice I recently gave must particularly be followed — so that he concentrates upon the joys that he possesses, keeps his goals in mind, and trusts the infinite intelligence within him to bring about the desired results. This frees his mind and allows his improvements to continue without interruption.

I may or may not return, again according to those rhythms of which I speak — but know that I am present and approachable. My congratulations on the new edition of <u>Seven</u>.

(Seth meant the Pocket Book edition of The Further Education of Oversoul Seven, *which had arrived from Prentice-Hall last night — nine copies.*

("Can I ask a question?")

You may.

("What do you think of the dream I had, about Leonard, Jane and me moving back to 458 West Water Street?")

The interpretation you discussed is a good one. Leonard expressed his good health, and you are taking <u>good health</u> as a <u>neighbor</u>.

(Very well put, Seth, I thought. "I've got another question.")

Go Ahead.

(Seth spoke while I tried to catch up on my writing.

("I hadn't planned on asking about this this afternoon — but lately I've noticed that my closeup vision without glasses isn't as sharp as it used to be. I don't think the cause is physical. I think something's been bugging me lately, and it's coming out that way. It's nothing drastic, but enough to be bothersome at times. I haven't spent much time trying to figure it out — ")

Give us a moment . . . It's your version of <u>worrying</u> that desired effects may not be brought into the present — that is, will not come into your close vision. When you feel that way, close your eyes, if only for a moment, reassure yourself that you <u>can trust your vision</u> — mental and physical — and that indeed your goals <u>will</u> be brought into clear focus.

("Okay."

("It's me," Jane said as I wrote.

("Thank you, Seth," I said at 4:32 P.M. His advice was as excellent as always. I felt relieved, and will try the technique. I plan to type it separately where I can keep it in view in my writing room. Maybe on the desk itself. I told Jane I thought the question had been triggered by the session material today, especially that concerning Leonard.)

THE PURPOSE OF THIS BOOK

JANUARY 20, 1984
4:33 P.M. FRIDAY

*(Jane called me last night with Carla's help. The night was very cold —
it was still 6 below when I got up at 6:30 A.M., and only 12 above when I
left for 330. More bitter weather is predicted for the weekend.*

*(Jane went to hydro as usual this morning, but wasn't too happy about
the system. While she was eating a good lunch I thought of telling her the
typewriter repair service had called this morning, citing a bill for $90.00
for the repair and a box of a dozen cartridges, but I forgot to mention it as
we talked about other things. I'd also called our optometrist and asked his
secretary to have him return my call so I could ask him a couple of techni-
cal questions about a note I'm writing for Session 901 for* Dreams. *Since I
had to wait for his call — which never came — I couldn't leave the house
to get Jane's typewriter. I want to try it out to make sure it's okay before I
turn my own in for repair, which it needs.*

*(3:00. Jane began reading yesterday's session, getting through it much
more slowly than she did yesterday. She finally finished it at 3:25.*

*(At 3:43 she began reading the session for December 27, 1983, doing
better than she had earlier. She was interrupted by people taking her
vitals — temperature 98.3 — and finished the session finally at 4:20,
after resting from reading several times.*

*(Once again Jane talked about "watching my impatient moods." She
really wants improvements to take place much more quickly than they are —
really fast. I said I thought that maybe her impatience was meant to serve as
an impetus to her healing speed. "At least it shows your body you want to do
something," I said. "What if you* had no *impatience or impetus?"*

(She agreed, of course, and said she wanted a short session.)

Now: I bid you another most fond good afternoon —

("Good afternoon, Seth.")

— and I am announcing myself again to quicken those conditions that accelerate the healing processes.

You are correct about Ruburt's impatiences: He is to <u>use it</u>
(underlined) as a tool, however, and not let <u>it</u> use <u>him</u>. That is, the
impatience is indeed meant as an impetus, as a stimulus to further
activity and motion — so he must think of that impatience as a
friend, not as an adversary.

The remaining bedsores will be healing themselves at an even
quicker rate, since he is now assimilating protein so much better

than he used to. His mental exercises involving the inner "darning" *(which Jane had told me about earlier this afternoon)* of the sores with new tissue works well. Let it be done in a playful manner, however.

I may or may not return, again according to those rhythms of which I speak, but know I am present and approachable.

("Thank you."

(4:38 P.M. Jane said both her hands are still improving, and they seemed so to me as I massaged them with Oil of Olay after I'd turned her on her left side. She ate well after I'd had a nap, as usual, and read the prayer with me at 7:05. Sleep well, Jane. I love you.)

JANUARY 21, 1984
4:11 P.M. SATURDAY

(Last night had been very cold — it was still 5 below when I got up at 6:30 A.M. After breakfast I ran the car to do several errands, getting the budget bills ready to mail, and so forth. Monday I pick up Jane's typewriter.

(Jane told me that she'd had her catheter changed at 11:30 this morning, and had just finished having her dressings done before I arrived. She ate a good lunch. While she ate I described my reactions to and thoughts about Quest for Fire, *a well-known movie of a couple of years ago that I'd seen part of on television's* Showtime *channel while eating supper last night.*

(I said I was most curious that Seth comment, since what the movie showed was so at odds with his material on early man in Dreams. *I expected there to be a great difference, but watching our early history as shown in the movie made life seem impossibly grim 80,000 years ago. I didn't see how our ancestors had survived, were the movie accurate. It had to be wrong — for all it depicted was savagery, on the parts of animals, apes, dogs, man, cannibals, and so forth. "If anyone lived to be even 20 years old under those circumstances," I told Jane, "it would have been a miracle." There was no compassion, no intuition; little understanding revealed by the characters in the movie other than the emotions of bloodlust, survival of the fittest, and selfishness. It certainly offered no insights into how the human young were cared for over the long period necessary while they simply grew.*

(On my way to 330 Georgia called me in to her room and said she's to have some sort of back surgery next Monday or Tuesday. She's also being

moved to the first floor — Surgical 1. I have a toy unicorn I'll be giving her tomorrow, along with a verse Jane wrote. Both are clever and creative. Here is Jane's verse:

The unicorn said,
"Oh, pray take me
to see my good friend,
Georgia Cecce.

Oh, I'll jog and jig with glee
for one smile from my friend,
Georgia Cecce.

My magic powers will set her free,
my good friend,
Georgia Cecce."

(3:18. *Jane began reading yesterday's session, but had hard going at first. She did a little better as I worked on mail, then quite good as she read the last page.* "My eyes started coming in better," *she said at 3:22.*

(3:29. *She started the session for December 28, 1983 going slowly again. She gave up on it at 3:40 for a cigarette. Then minutes later Carla came in to take her temperature* — 98.5. "Almost perfect," *I said, joking.*

(3:55. *Shawn took Jane's blood pressure and pulse, then my wife went back to reading the session, doing a little better. Jane announced she was ready for the session at 4:10. She'd already told me she thought Seth would comment on the movie.)*

Now I bid you another fond good afternoon.

("Good afternoon, Seth.")

The picture of man, animals, and nature depicted in the movie of which you were speaking is the only possible portrayal of reality that could be logically shown, considering the beliefs upon which the premise rests.

The environment, man, and the animals were all characterized as ferocious, hostile to each other, each one determined to attain survival at the expense of the other. Man could not have existed under the conditions fostered in the moving picture — nor for that matter could any of the animals. Despite any other theories to the contrary, the world, all of its physical aspects, and all of its creatures, depends upon an inborn cooperation. The species <u>do not compete with each other</u> over a given territory, no matter how frequently that <u>appears</u> to be the case. *(Long pause.)* Period.

Science has promoted the idea that hostility is a constant attribute of nature and all of its parts, while it sees the <u>cooperating</u> characteristics of nature as rather infrequent or extraordinary — but certainly outside of the norm *(wryly amused).*

Even biologically on the most microscopic of levels, there is a vast inbred network of cooperating activity, and these unite the animal and mineral kingdoms with all the other aspects of earthly existence. Each organism has a purpose, and it is to fulfill its own capabilities in such a way that it benefits all other organisms.

(4:23.) Each organism is therefore helped in its development by each and every other organism, and the smooth operation of one contributes to the integrity of all. Men did not begin hunting animals until certain groups of animals needed a way to control their own population. As I have said before, men and animals learned from each other. They were immediate allies, not enemies.

Men also domesticated animals almost from the very first, so that men and animals both did each other a service — they worked together. The stability of planetary life depended above all upon this basic cooperation, <u>in which all species pulled together</u>.

Man's brain was always the size that it is now —

(4:28. A nurse came in to give Jane eyedrops. Afterward I read Jane what she'd given on the session. I mentioned that men and animals must have been cooperating even while still largely in the dream state. Resume at 4:37.)

— and the animals existed in the forms by which you know them today. No animal — or virus — is truly extinct. All exist *(long pause)* in an inner webwork, and are held in the memory of an overall earthly knowledge — one that is biological, so that each smallest microbe has within it the imprinted biological messages that form each and every other microbe. The existence of one presupposes the existence of all, and the existence of all is inherent in the existence of one.

I may or may not return, again according to those rhythms of which I speak.

("Do you want to say a word about how Ruburt is doing?")

Ruburt continues his improvements, and overall his strength grows daily. Certain conditions are happening within the body that will very soon now bring about very noticeable actual physical improvements in motion and overall coordination.

(4:43 P.M. "It's me," Jane said after a pause. She'd done well. I was particularly glad to get Seth's encouraging words about her own condition, for she's still impatient for more improvements to take place.

(With Carla's help, Jane called me at 9:47 P.M., just as I was finishing typing this session. I told her the temperature was already down to zero. Sleep warm and cozy, Jane.)

JANUARY 22, 1984
4:07 P.M. SUNDAY

(The temperature was 5 below when I got up at 6:30, but it was up to 15 when I left for 330 at 12:30. On the way to Jane's room, I stopped in Surgical 1 to give Georgia the unicorn we'd bought for her yesterday, and the poem Jane had written, which I'd transcribed onto the card we'd also bought. Georgia is to be operated on next Tuesday.

(In Georgia's room, I met a nurse who used to take care of Jane. She'd had the same operation, a myelogram, that Georgia is to get for a herniated disc. She gave Georgia plenty of negative suggestions while I was there: "You don't get over something like that very quickly," etc. Later this same nurse dropped in to say hello to Jane. "I sure hope I don't get her to take care of me," Jane said after she'd left. "I want to get out of here."

(Jane ate a good lunch. I told her about my very vivid and colorful dream of last night. She and I had been walking — hiking — along the banks of the Susquehanna River toward Sayre. We wore very bright and colorful clothing. The day was a beautiful balmy summer one. There were friends with us, and they offered us rides to our destination. We refused. Jane especially insisted on walking along the riverbanks. Her strides were perfectly normal and agile; she was in excellent health.

(I also told Jane that beside the dream I'd like Seth to comment on the fact that I'd awakened this morning with Maude Cardwell on my mind, including the letter I'd written her a couple of weeks ago. I'd almost forgotten about it. I wanted Seth to comment on Maude's reaction to the letter. I told Jane that I wanted her to know the question in case we heard from

Maude this week, say. I figured there was a reason I was thinking about her this morning so definitely. Jane agreed that we might hear soon.

(2:38. Jane put on lipstick, then looked at herself in the mirror — briefly.

(3:00. She began reading yesterday's session, not too easily — then quit at 3:20 for a cigarette. I worked on mail. I also gave myself the suggestions Seth had outlined in the session for January 19, concerning my eyes when they aren't seeing as sharply as I know they can. It helped. I'd also used the suggestion a couple of times this morning, with good results. It's a matter of worrying. I need to use the suggestion for a few days in order to give my creative self time to put it into effect; that's the way suggestion usually works with me.

(3:39. Jane did much better now when she went back to reading the session. Carla took her temperature at 3:45 — 98.1.

(Jane said she'd have the session early, so I could watch the Super Bowl, which was to begin at 4:30, but I said it didn't matter all that much. I'd be sitting in my chair and taking a nap during part of the game anyhow.)

Now: I bid you another fond good afternoon.

("Good afternoon, Seth.")

I am again announcing myself to quicken those coordinates that so favor the healing processes.

Once more, it is extremely important that Ruburt keep his mind on his goals, and not burden his conscious mind by trying to figure out circumstances and conditions that are best handled by the infinite intelligence that is within his own subconscious mind. The way and the means will be taken care of. They will indeed appear almost effortlessly — but he must let the <u>burden</u> of worry go.

(Long pause.) Give us a moment . . . Maude was pleased and also astonished by your letter. She did not realize your circumstances — the medical expenses, or their <u>extent</u>. She is a great organizer, and is at work at several plans.

It is, again, a good idea to review those portions of our sessions devoted to Ruburt's condition.

Now I may or may not return, according to those rhythms of which I speak — but know that I am present and approachable.

("What did you think of my dream about him last night?")

The dream accentuated Ruburt's determination to achieve normal motion, and his insistence in the dream that he depend upon his own mobility, rather than, say, a vehicle or conveyance. It also represented your joint determination to travel together, so that even friends could not deter you, or change your way.

(*"It's me. That's it."*

(*"Thank you."*

(*4:14 P.M. I read the session to Jane. "That ought to make you feel better, especially that part about the dream," I said. Jane agreed that she'd been stewing about getting better, getting out of the hospital, even more lately than I'd thought she was. She even wondered "if they have any kind of wheelchair I could use to get around in . . ." I said I doubted if she could fit in any kind of chair until her doubled-up right leg began to open up more. But the important thing is that that desire is now present, and will certainly bear results — good ones. She's now expressing serious desires about mobility that I can't remember her voicing for many years. The changes are in the works, and Seth has given many encouraging bits of information that they are having, and will have, an effect.*

(*To help reinforce positive attitudes about the great days of change that are coming, I read aloud to Jane the personal parts of the sessions from January 13 to date. They helped her considerably, reminding her of some points she'd temporarily forgotten. It's easy to let a good point slip away as the sessions pile up day after day — but those bits of information can always be retrieved through review. We're doing better at that than ever before.*)

JANUARY 23, 1984
4:24 P.M. MONDAY

(*Our dear friend, Frank Longwell, who has been a great help to us for many years, visited while I had lunch today; he's made his first sale of a hearing aid. We wish him well. The day was much warmer — 25 degrees — when I left for 330. I turned Jane on her back right away. She said that after I'd left last night two nurses had taken care of her, and that while they were doing so, they unloaded numerous negative suggestions about many things. Jane didn't say anything. Then when Steve and Tracy visited shortly afterward, they too had many negative things to say about many things — until finally Jane told Steve to quit dumping on her. Steve was also talking about the phases of the moon having influence on his behavior and actions, Jane said she didn't believe in that. He apologized.*

(*I described an excellent dream I'd had last night. Once again in brilliant color — one of those you keep returning to. Jane and I had moved back to 458 W. Water Street, only now the house was much bigger than it really is, had many more apartments in it — they were all in good shape, with numerous stairways connecting them on a split-level layout. They weren't closed off from each other as apartments usually are, so that the numerous tenants could have free interchange with each other if they chose to. But when I wanted to be by myself to paint, I had a corner studio I could retire to where I could work in privacy — a very nice room. Jane was very active and healthy, walking about normally. In the dream I was involved with painting, but not writing.*

(3:16. Jane started reading yesterday's session, and did fairly well, better than yesterday, I thought. I did mail. She began to have trouble getting through the session, but finished by 3:30, doing better towards the end.

(3:55. I began questioning Jane about her religious training in Catholic grade school. I'd started roughing out a note this morning having to do with Seth's statement in a session for Chapter 5 of **Dreams.** *In it he'd referred to early humans living for several centuries — the only time he's ever made such a reference. I planned to look up the ages of some Biblical patriarchs, and wanted to know what Jane might have been taught about such people, and their ages.*

(Carla interrupted our conversation to check Jane's vitals — temperature 98.4. During our talk I noticed that it didn't take my wife long to begin reacting emotionally to my questions, which I thought were innocent enough — but it was apparent that the subject matter of our conversation had an emotional charge for her. One of them, I thought, probably related to her symptoms if one traced it back. In fact, I was sure of it. However, after she realized what she was doing, Jane seemed to take my questions in stride, and even volunteered a lot of information I hadn't asked for.

(4:20. Jane asked me to rub a certain spot on her left temple. Finally, when I withdrew my finger, she suddenly cried out and her head dipped quickly to the right. Some kind of muscular release had taken place, quite unexpected. She cried out several times and appeared momentarily dazed. She asked me to rub the equivalent spot on her right temple, but before we got any results a nurse came in to say, "I'm making my 4 o'clock check a little late. Do you want anything?"

("And I got hot too, after that," Jane said, referring to her forehead reaction, This made me think that the warmth she felt was a sign of bodily healing, such as Seth had said recently was associated with warmth.

(After our talk about religious questions, I wrote a short note quoting Jane — one that I may use in the note for Dreams *— and got her okay on it.)*

Now: I bid you another fond good afternoon.

("Afternoon, Seth.")

In those early days men and women did live to ages that would amaze you today — many living to be several hundred years old.

This was indeed due to the fact that *(pause)* their knowledge was desperately needed, and their experience. They were held in veneration, and they cast their knowledge into songs and stories that were memorized throughout the years.

Beside this, however, their energy was utilized in a different fashion than yours is. They alternated between the waking and dream states *(long pause),* and while asleep they did not age as quickly. Their bodily processes slowed. Although this was true, their dreaming mental processes <u>did not</u> slow down. There was a much greater communication in the dream state, so that some lessons were taught during dreams, while others were taught in the waking condition.

There was a greater and greater body of knowledge to be transmitted as physical existence continued, for they did not transmit private knowledge only, but the entire body of knowledge that belonged to the group or tribe as a whole.

(Pause at 4:33.) Now: your dream represented the larger rooms of beliefs into which you are emerging. The many people, and connecting rooms, represented the new structure of vaster beliefs that are all interconnected while you are still, however, concentrating upon the private creative self, and from that viewpoint viewing the world — hence your private corner in which you painted, as from that corner of private creativity you viewed the large interacting structure of new beliefs.

Now I may or may not return, but know that I am present and approachable, and that I have again quickened those healing processes that are leading toward Ruburt's full recovery.

("What was that reaction he had when I rubbed his left temple?")

It was an excellent reaction. He knew instinctively what pressure points he wanted you to touch. These are important points in the body that accentuate energy, but can also absorb stress. Touching them as you did releases the stress — and Ruburt felt <u>lighter-headed</u> in response. Such events also release other portions of the body as the effect reverberates, so to speak.

(4:40 P.M. I thanked Seth for appearing. Jane had some ginger ale before I turned her on her side. I didn't note it in my dream account earlier here, but I'd described to Jane how I'd asked whoever owned 458 W. Water Street these days how much our rent would be. I did this several times, but received no answer. I expected it to be good, and was afraid it would be high. Seth hadn't commented, and I didn't ask him.)

JANUARY 24, 1984
4:27 P.M. TUESDAY

(The day was amazingly warm — over 43 — as I drove to 330 after leaving my own typewriter at the service franchise. As she ate lunch I told Jane about my very vivid and colorful dream of last night. I felt it was significant.

(First, I was hiking with her father Del along mountain trails in very deep snow. There were many other people about; it wasn't an isolated-type setting. Up and down and around we went. Then Del left me for some reason, and alone I tried to continue — but wound up clinging motionless to a very steep slope lest I slide way down into a deep ravine that would be very difficult to get out of. Then Del returned; he wore clean, modern, tailored hiking clothes, a wool jacket and a fedora with a feather in it — much sharper than he dresses in real life. He also looked much younger and more self-possessed than I'd ever seen him be.

(Then, I was in a lodge on the mountainside. Some of the walls were of floor-to-ceiling glass. There were many people about, sitting and eating at small round tables with white cloths. The setting was very posh. I was with Jean Longwell, the daughter of our friend Frank. We got up and began dancing, holding each other very close. I felt deep affection for Jean, a strange and surprising longing mixed with a strong sexual awareness of her attractiveness. I also knew she felt the same way about me. We talked. As we did my eyes were so close to her face that I could see the tiny pores in the skin below her eyes — very fine and smooth. The dream ended here, or faded into other levels.

(This dream stayed with me the whole day, so strong was its impact upon me. I kept feeling that strange affection for Jean, mixed with a regret

of some kind that nothing could really transpire between us — because of age and other factors. I told Jane I also felt that Jean was somehow dissatisfied in life, perhaps confused, perhaps caught between her artistic leanings and her upbringing to lead the more conventional life — working at the hospital, and so forth. I sensed, I think, that she wasn't too sure about her move to the city in North Carolina — Raleigh? — that she planned with her boyfriend. Yesterday Frank had told me that it wouldn't be as easy to see Jean now that it was a 15-hour drive instead of just running down to Washington DC.

(3:00. Jane began reading yesterday's session, but couldn't do it. She quit after a few minutes while I worked on mail. She tried again at 3:20 and did much better. I told her I've tried Seth's suggestions about enhancing my close-up vision, given in a recent session, and that they've worked very well. Jane finished the session at 3:35. At 3:40 she started reading the session for October 9, 1983, but didn't do quite as well — see the hospital and session chronology in my opening notes for the session of January 6, 1984. She laid the session aside again for a cigarette, then went back to it at 3:58. Finally she just gave up on it, and eventually decided to have a short session, since it was getting late.)

Now: I bid you another fond good afternoon.

("Good afternoon, Seth.")

Your dream was triggered specifically by Frank's visit *(yesterday noon)*, and his discussion about his daughter, Jean.

That led you, just below normal consciousness, to consider the relationship between father and daughter, and then to think of Ruburt's father, Del. He appeared younger and more vital than you had ever known him — indeed, transformed in a fashion. He was <u>redeemed</u> in your mind, and appeared as his ideal self. In that capacity he helped lead you along safe paths, out of danger.

This also signified your knowledge on other levels that Ruburt was becoming free of any negative beliefs that were the result of his relationship with his father.

Jean Longwell then represented Frank's feelings toward his daughter, and in a fashion you felt those as your own — a mixture of paternal love, sexuality, and sympathy. Those feelings were also representative of Del's redeemed love for <u>his</u> daughter — for Ruburt.

The dream signified your knowledge that Ruburt was being cleared of negative connotations in relationship to his father. On the other hand, the young Del was also a symbol for your own inner self, acting as a guide and companion.

This session, again, activates those coordinates that quicken bodily healing. Have Ruburt remind himself again that it is safe to let go, and trust his own spontaneous rhythms, his own motion.

I may or may not return, but know that I am present and approachable.

(4:38 P.M. I read the session to Jane. "I don't know why," she said, "but as you read that I got the feeling that my father is looking out for me . . . " I said that was certainly implied in the session, and that I'd wondered about it as Seth spoke. I also reminded her that in the October session I'd written in my notes about redemption. This is a subject I feel strongly about, yet we seldom if ever mention the word. I've also dealt with its implications in Dreams.

(We hadn't been interrupted during the session. In fact, we finally realized that no one had checked Jane's vitals or emptied her Foley all afternoon. A nurse showed up at 4:47 and did the vitals — temperature 98.3, blood pressure excellent.

(As we talked, something triggered Jane's memory of a time in her teens when she'd hiked all the way out to the garage where her grandfather had worked in Saratoga Springs — "way across town." She thought she could have been in the eighth grade. Jane remembered looking down into a puddle and composing a poem. She even remembered at least some of it:

> I looked in the puddle
> and what should I see
> but the stars in
> the heavens looking back at me . . .

(Strange: Later in the afternoon I finally made an important connection about the unexpected value of dreams. I told Jane that I suddenly understood that in the dream I'd experienced paternal feelings — genuine ones — that I'd never known in conscious life, or had access to. It followed that in the dream state, then, I'd actually enlarged upon my experience in this life, and in a most meaningful and strong way. Even as I write this account at 9:30 P.M. I still feel the impact of those feelings.

(I might as well add that in Chapter 5 of Dreams *I deal with a couple of my intense experiences with the "light of the universe" back in 1980. Frank had been involved in one of those, too, in the dream state, and Seth*

had explained how I'd picked up his concerns about age and sexuality and worth, and so forth. So last night's dream also involved elements based upon data I'd picked up from Frank. Evidently our psychic communication works very well . . .)

JANUARY 25, 1984
4:09 P.M. WEDNESDAY

(Once again the day was quite warm — 40 degrees by the time I left for 330. Jane was on her back. She'd just had her dressings changed before I got there. The staff had been very busy, and so had hydro.

(While she ate I told her I'd called our lawyer this morning. No news about Blue Cross — but he had said that we had no worries about gift taxes should anyone contribute to the fund Maude Cardwell is presumably organizing for us. There's a $10,000 starting point before taxes take effect.

(I also told Jane about the entertaining time I'd had this morning checking Biblical genealogies, preparatory to the note I want to write for Chapter 5 of Dreams. *Seth's elders would have lived long before those in the Bible — or would they? For Adam was the first man, at least according to the Bible. It would depend upon what terms one chose within which to view the situation.*

(Jane ate a good lunch. TV was on, advertisements for movies, and I asked her why our literature is made up of the bad in life — murder, mayhem, thievery, bribery, robbery, and so forth. I said our craving for such "entertainment" must reflect our basic social beliefs beneath our veneer of respectability — the conscious, negative fears of the unknown, meaning that we've created such a division in ourselves by shutting out our conscious awareness of our own true selves. We've now reached the point where our subjective lives are largely hidden, but continuously striving to show themselves against all pressures . . .

(3:00. Jane began reading yesterday's session — and doing much better than she had yesterday. She finished at 3:08 — quickly — and said that part of the time her vision was very clear. She had a smoke and I worked on mail while waiting to see if she wanted to do any more reading.

(3:18. She began the session for January 13, and did even better — very fast.

(Somewhere in here I'd gotten her lipstick for her, and after applying it she had looked in the mirror — again briefly. But she did it.

(4:00. Carla and Shannon took her vitals — temperature 98.3. Jane said she wanted to have a session. I mentioned to her my idea that Seth's elders must predate by far the elders of the Bible, and she agreed.)

Now — I bid you another fond good afternoon.

("Good afternoon, Seth.")

Once again, I quicken those coordinates that are so important in the healing processes.

There was additional improvement in Ruburt's eyes and vision, and those improvements specifically are connected with freer motions of the head and arm areas — the hands being included.

Many preparations are being made for motions that <u>will</u> be needed in the near future, to aid in balance and general locomotion.

(Long pause.) The Bible is a conglomeration of parables and stories, intermixed with some <u>unclear</u> memories of much earlier times. The bible that you recognize — or that is recognized — is not the first, however, but was compiled from several earlier ones as man tried to look back, so to speak, and recount his past and predict his future.

Such bibles existed, not written down but carried orally, as mentioned some time ago, by the Speakers. It was only much later that this information was written down, and by then, of course, much had been forgotten. This is apart from the fact of tampering, or downright misinformation *(long pause)* as various factions used the material for their own ends.

(Long pause at 4:16.) You mentioned the paternal feelings of your dream. They allowed you to expand your experience while in the dream state. This also presents you with an example of the ways in which early man expanded his own knowledge and experience in the dream state. In the same way, as mentioned in <u>Dreams</u>, man also had dream images of actual geographical locations to which he had not physically traveled.

Now I may or may not return, according to those rhythms of which I speak — but know that I am present and approachable.

("Yes. Thank you.")

(4:19 P.M. Neither of us had particularly thought that my dream-paternal feelings represented an analogy with the way early man had expanded his own knowledge while in the dream state — but we saw the connection as soon as Seth mentioned it. I read the session to Jane.)

(I thought, as soon as Seth had mentioned it, that the data regarding the Speakers and oral traditions went way back to when Jane produced Seth Speaks *in 1970–71. [See Session 558 for November 5, 1970, in the appendix of* Seth Speaks*]*

(Jane said that as I read to her, she picked up from Seth information that in those old days people most often insisted upon returning to the sites of their destroyed or damaged cities and towns and farms, even though such events had wiped those places out more than once. It was as though the people were psychically and emotionally drawn back to such places for reasons that made no sense intellectually. We talked about the well-known "tells" in Israel, for example.

(A note: I still feel the effects of my dream of two nights ago, involving Del and Jean Longwell.)

CHAPTER 2

BIOLOGICALLY VALID THOUGHTS, ATTITUDES, AND BELIEFS

JANUARY 26, 1984
4:08 P.M. THURSDAY

(The temperature was about 33 degrees as I left for 330. Jane had the window of her room wide open, and the place was still hot. I began peeling off clothes layer by layer. I told her about my dream of last night: I'd been in my writing room and I heard Jim Baker, our optometrist, in my studio. He was talking and using an occasional cuss word in a rather humorous way. I heard his voice clearly. I knew that Jane was in the house somewhere, that she was walking perfectly all right, and that Jim had come to see her, not me. I wasn't concerned or jealous.

(As we talked before lunch came, Jane shed a few tears. She wanted to get up and get out of bed and start walking — without waiting. I told her of the insight that came to me as she talked. It was that the body healed itself at a rate prescribed by its circumstances — that actually it could heal itself very rapidly if it was unimpeded. Thus, being in a hospital with all the negative suggestions could operate telepathically as well as overtly to slow down healing. The insight, which is hardly original, popped into my mind when I asked Jane why the healing was taking so long, in response to something she said. I hoped Seth would comment.

(After eating an excellent lunch, Jane told me of her own long and complicated dream of last night. She was with Ronald Reagan and one of his

daughters. She talked him out of his nuclear-arms policies, and out of the devil — and evil — idea. She was very pleased in the dream at her success. She also said there was more she couldn't remember.

(Then we had a discussion about some articles I've just read in the latest issue of Free Inquiry, *a magazine whose writers express a deep skepticism about anything having to do with the paranormal.*

(3:30. Dana took Jane's temperature — 98.6 — perfect. Jane had just started reading the session for yesterday. She resumed, doing pretty well, at 3:40. I did mail.

(3:58. I rubbed Jane's right temple at her request, and got a good reaction when I pulled my finger away finally: "I feel so light — it's great. I can even feel it in the crook of my elbow — there must be a nerve there." She said she wanted to have a session.)

Now: I bid you another fond good afternoon —

("Good afternoon, Seth.")

— and we will begin Chapter 2, to be titled: "Biologically Valid Thoughts, Attitudes, and Beliefs."

(Long pause.) When you are born you possess a group of attitudes toward yourself and toward life. These allow you to grow with the greatest possible impetus into childhood. They are also important in every period of your life. You can see *(long pause)* the results in life all about you, though in animals or plants these are experienced as a matter of feelings rather than, say, as thoughts or attitudes.

It may sound very simplistic to tell you that you must have sunny thoughts as well as rays of the physical sun in order to be healthy — but sunny thoughts are as biologically necessary to your well-being as are the rays of the sun that shines in the sky. Even as infants, then, you are predisposed naturally toward certain feelings, thoughts and attitudes that are meant to insure your healthy survival and emergence into adulthood. These are actually composed of inbred psychological information as necessary and vital to your life as the data transmitted by your genes and chromosomes. Indeed, these inbred, inner psychological predispositions are all-important if the information carried by your genes and chromosomes is to be faithfully followed.

(4:17.) It is difficult to translate such *(pause)* biological and psychological material into the words of any language, even though these inbred psychological prerequisites form a kind of language of

their own. It is a language that promotes growth, exuberance and fulfillment, and stimulates the entire organism of the body — signaling the proper responses that are required for health and growth.

Later we will discuss contrary feelings, thoughts, and emotions. I want to substitute beliefs for emotions —

(*"Yes."*)

— that greatly curtail the natural progression of health and vitality. Here, however, we will deal primarily with those inner predispositions that encourage life and vitality.

(*4:24.*) Now: Comments.

Ruburt has been feeling new, strong surges of desire — desire for normal health, normal motion, energy, and strength. Those feelings are also meant to be used as impetuses to lead him in the proper directions, so that indeed those desires are fulfilled. He must understand them as such. By themselves they can act to unlock additional energy, vitality, and quicken his sense of purpose.

Again, have him almost as <u>nonchalantly</u> as possible imagine himself behaving as normally as possible <u>in the future</u>. Now this is to be a <u>new</u> future, brought on as the result of healthier, wiser beliefs and attitudes. The "future" that he feared, he must understand, no longer exists — for it was composed of beliefs he no longer holds.

(*Long pause at 4:29, eyes half closed. I'd say the paragraph just above is extremely important.*)

The first chapter of the book can be called, quite simply: "The Purpose of This Book, and Some Important Comments About Exuberance and Health."

Now I may or may not return, again according to those rhythms of which I speak, but know that I am present and approachable.

I wanted to give you book material, and that is why I did not comment upon your dreams —

(*"Well, you can say something about the dreams if you want to . . . How about Jane's dream?"*)

Give us a moment . . . In Ruburt's dream, he is completely re-educating the part of himself that he once considered an authority. He convinced that portion that the old beliefs about good and evil, self-destruction, and the existence of the Catholic devil, were not valid. In the dream he triumphs over those beliefs.

Your dream represents Ruburt's more healthy attitude <u>toward his eyes and their vision</u>. It also represents his growing faith in his own psychic vision, and hence his return to his own natural rhythms and motion.

(*"Thank you."*

(*4:37 P.M. "Well, I'm glad I asked about those dreams," I said. Both of them were very good, and should reinforce Jane's progress and attitudes.*

(*"I knew he was going to do something on the book," Jane said. "I have the feeling that the book's going to be* The Way Toward Health," *she said.*

(*I told Jane that Seth's opening line for Chapter 2, about possessing a group of attitudes toward oneself and toward life, at birth, runs directly counter to establishment theory that the newborn is like a blank slate, to be imprinted through teaching and experience. This would be especially true of behaviorism. She laughed.*)

JANUARY 27, 1984
4:08 P.M. FRIDAY

(*Today was even warmer than it has been — an incredible 45 degrees when I backed the car out of the garage. Wouldn't you know it — the spring mechanism that governs the travel of the garage door broke as I was lowering the door, so that I couldn't close it all the way. So when I got to 330 one of my first acts was to call* Overhead Door *and ask them to have someone check the garage door this afternoon, if possible. I gave directions and asked that a bill be sent to me. I hoped to get service today, it being Friday.*

(*Jane had an excellent lunch. While she ate I told her several times that I had a feeling of anticipation, as though I had something I wanted to tell her, but couldn't recall it. Only I hadn't forgotten anything. At times the feeling was rather strong.*

(*We watched* In Search Of *from 2:30 to 3:00, and the program reminded me of a number of questions I'd thought of at various times. The program dealt with the atom-bombing of Hiroshima, Japan, and the after-effects, such as cancer. My questions had to do with the consciousness that must reside within, or make up, radiation, and why that type of consciousness was so virulent that we humans couldn't tolerate it. Yet we'd created it, in ordinary terms. The same with a disease like cancer, I told Jane. Why did we create it when we couldn't tolerate many forms of it?*

(I went on to tell her of my idea that arthritis, for example, bridged all historical gaps and cultures, and that its origin — I think — lay in the individual's reaction to fear of motion, for a multitude of reasons. Jane seemed a little surprised at this idea. I said I'd felt it to be true for some time, meaning years.

(I added that I hoped Seth would eventually discuss such questions in his book.

(3:00. Jane began reading yesterday's session — it wasn't her best effort by any means, but she managed to get through it with a little help from me. She finished at 3:20, doing better at the end. I worked with mail.

(Jane told me she was a little surprised that Maude Cardwell hadn't answered my letter of a couple of weeks ago by now — but I said I thought things were proceeding as all of us wanted them to, really. After all, I hadn't given Maude our phone number — though I plan to — and we've maintained a distance from her and others who have offered help. If we behave that way, we can hardly expect others to act differently toward us.

(By 3:55 Carla had taken Jane's temperature — 98 — and Shawn her blood pressure and pulse. At this relatively early hour, Lynn came in to give Jane her eyedrops after which my wife said she was ready for a session.)

Now: I bid you another fond good afternoon.

("Good afternoon, Seth.")

Dictation. These inborn leanings or attitudes can roughly be translated as follows.

1. I am an excellent creature, a valuable part of the universe in which I exist.

2. My existence enriches all other portions of life, even as my own being is enhanced by the rest of creation.

3. It is good, natural, and safe for me to grow and develop and use my abilities, and by so doing I also enrich all other portions of life.

Next: I am eternally couched and supported by the universe of which I am a part, and I exist whether or not that existence is physically expressed.

Next: By nature I am a good deserving creature, and all of life's elements and parts are also of good intent.

And next: All of my imperfections, and all of the imperfections of other creatures, are redeemed in the greater scheme of the universe in which I have my being.

Those attitudes are inbred in the smallest microscopic portions of the body — a part of each atom and cell and organ, and they serve to trigger all of the body's responses that promote growth and fulfillment. Infants are not born with an inbred <u>fear</u> of their environment, or of other creatures. They are instead immersed in feelings of well-being, vitality, and exuberance. They take it for granted that their needs will be met, and that the universe is well-disposed toward them. They feel a part of their environment.

(Long pause at 4:20.) They do not come into life with feelings of rage, or anger, and basically they do not experience doubts or fears. Birth is experienced in terms of self-discovery, and includes the sensation of selfhood gently rising and unfolding from the secret heart of the universe.

(During the last paragraph the fire alarm bell began sounding by the elevator door outside Jane's room. The strange ringing was most distracting, and I thought it would never stop, yet Jane remained in trance, and continued dictation around a few pauses.)

Many people believe that birth, to the contrary, is a time of trauma, or even of rage, as the infant leaves its mother's womb. Birth is life's most precious natural process. Even in births <u>that are thought of</u> (underlined) as not "normal," there is on the infant's part a sense of discovery and joy.

We will have more to say about the process of birth later on in this book. For now, I simply want to make the point that in the most basic of terms the human birth is as orderly and spontaneous as the birth of any of nature's creatures — and a child opens its selfhood even as a flower opens its petals.

The inborn leanings and attitudes that we have been discussing should <u>ideally</u> (underlined) remain with you for the rest of your life, leading you to express your abilities, and finding fulfillment as your knowledge expands through experience. The same feelings and beliefs should also <u>ideally</u> (underlined) help you die with a sense of safety, support and assurance. While these inbred psychological supports never leave you entirely, they are often diminished by beliefs encountered later in life, that serve to undermine the individual's sense of safety and well-being.

(Pause at 4:33.) Comments.

Again, I quicken those coordinates that benefit the healing processes. Have Ruburt read again the material pertaining to him in yesterday's session.

Now I may or may not return, again according to those rhythms of which I speak — but know that I am present and approachable.

("Can I ask a question?")

You may.

("It's just about what we were talking about early today — the consciousness in radiation, that's so powerful to us — or in cancer — ")

All of that material, and its like, will be covered in this book. Make a note, however, of such questions when they naturally occur.

("Okay. Thank you."

(4:35 P.M. Jane had some ginger ale and a cigarette. "Well, he's going to cover those questions in the book," I told Jane — "about radiation, the consciousness involved with it, and with things like cancer. It ought to be fascinating, unique stuff." And, I thought, I had to start a page of questions and keep it with each latest session so I didn't let them get away from us.

(After supper I read to Jane the passages from the session of the day before that Seth had referred to. They're very good.

(I also think it quite evident that Seth began to go into those attributes we're born with in light of my comments about current psychological dogma that the infant is born without any impetuses . . .

(And when I got home tonight, my feeling of anticipation was borne out: there was a communication from Maude Cardwell. Also, the garage door had been fixed.)

JANUARY 28, 1984
3:54 P.M. SATURDAY

(The day was much cooler when I left for 330 — only 29 degrees. I took Maude Cardwell's letter to show Jane. She'd gotten back from hydro pretty late. "You don't want to hear about all of that," she said when I asked her how come. "Talking about it makes me sound like I'm bitching all the time. It worked out all right."

(Jane didn't eat much lunch — the cheeseburger was badly overcooked, and quite tough. Neither of us had dreams to report. I read her Maude's letter, and her article in Reality Change, *saying we'd have to work out a response. We'll also have to figure out how to handle any money we receive,*

until the hospital and insurance questions are resolved. I plan to call our lawyer Monday morning to ask for advice. I imagine I'll be opening a separate account at the bank for the fund checks. I also told Jane I'd like something from Seth that Maude can send to contributors.

(Carla and Denise were through taking Jane's vitals — temperature 97.6 — by 3:40. And Jane said she was ready for the session much earlier than usual.)

Now — I bid you another fond good afternoon.

("Good afternoon, Seth.")

Dictation. *(Pause.)* All of this talk about exuberance, health and vitality may seem quite beside the point to many of you. *(Long pause.)* It may seem instead that the world is filled with unhappiness and disease.

I admit that this certainly seems to be the case. It may also strike you, my readers, as quite shocking when I tell you that there is no such thing, basically, as disease. There are instead only processes. What you think of as disease —

(3:56. There was a knock on the door. Someone darted into the room, left a pile of white underpads on the desk, and darted back out.)

— is instead the result of an exaggeration or overextension of perfectly normal body processes. You are not attacked by viruses, for instance, for all kinds of viruses exist normally in the body. There are no <u>killer</u> (underlined) viruses, then, but viruses that go beyond their usual bounds. We will have more to say about such issues later on in the book — for I hope to show you how certain feelings and beliefs do indeed promote health, while others promote an unfortunate extension or exaggeration of perfectly normal bodily processes, or viral activity.

This means, of course, that you do not fall victim to a disease, or catch a virus, but that for one reason or another your own feelings, thoughts, and beliefs lead you to seek bouts of illness. Period.

Certainly, such ideas will sound like medical heresy to many readers, but the sooner you begin to look at health and "disease" in these new terms, the healthier and happier you will become. *(Long pause.)* You are not one thing and illness another, for your thoughts and emotions are the triggers that lead to bouts of poor health. Once you know this, you can begin to take steps that will serve to promote exuberance and vitality instead of fear, doubts, and "disease."

(4:07.) You will discover that so-called diseases perform certain services. They fulfill purposes for you that you may <u>believe</u> you can achieve in no other way. The reasons for such illnesses are not deeply buried in the subconscious, as you may think. They are much closer to the conscious mind, and usually consist of a series of seemingly innocuous decisions that you have made through the years. Other illnesses, of course, may be caused by sudden decisions that are a response to a particular event in your life.

(Long pause.) People have been taught that their bodies are a kind of battleground, and that they must be in a constant state of readiness lest they be attacked or invaded by alien germs or viruses or diseases that can strike without warning.

Soon, we will begin to discuss other negative beliefs that cause poor health. For now, however, we will concentrate upon those inbred, positive attitudes, feelings, and beliefs that constantly improve our sense of well-being, strength, and fulfillment.

Take a break and we will continue.

(4:15. Jane said she thought that right away Seth was starting to answer my question of yesterday — not the portion about radiation and why that phenomenon is too strong for us to bear, but the part about the consciousness embodied in cancer, say, which is also too much for us much of the time. I saw what she meant.

(Resume at 4:26, with a touch of amusement:)

Now: a letter.

I wish to thank you for your help to Ruburt and Joseph, and in return I send you those blessings that are mine to give. We are presently working on a book to be called *The Way Toward Health,* and I hope the material in that book will benefit you in the most personal of terms, and allow you to experience the exuberance, joy, strength and good health that are your heritage. Though we have not met in physical terms, I am indeed aware of your presence, circumstances, and good intentions.

On behalf of the three of us, again I send you our sincere thanks, and our <u>heartiest</u> salute. To be signed simply, "Seth."

Now I may or may not return, according to those rhythms of which I speak — but know that I am present and approachable.

I hope that my letter meets with your approval.

("Yes. Thank you," I said, although I was wondering if it was a little short.)

It can be addressed to "Dear Friend."

("All right."

(4:31 P.M. "Oh," Jane exclaimed, "we did get the title of the book! He didn't say anything about me today, but we did get something on the book." I read Seth's letter to her right away.

(Then I also took down Jane's own letter to contributors, which was obviously triggered by Seth's. She dictated this quite as easily as Seth had done his own. A few minutes later:

Dear Friends:

Thank you so much for helping us out at this time of our need.

I have to admit that I am touched and embarrassed, because Rob and I have always made it on our own until now. It's always been easier for me to give than to receive. Now I'm learning to receive graciously and thankfully — a lesson that I had to learn. Ill or not, I do still feel full of life, and I'm still kicking — at least symbolically!

Many, many thanks.
Love, Jane.)

JANUARY 29, 1984
4:18 P.M. SUNDAY

(I went shopping at the Acme after I left Jane last night, got home about 8:30, and finished supper an hour later. I was typing the session at 10:00 when she called with Carla's help.

(This morning I wrote Maude Cardwell a short letter, promising more later, both from ourselves and via our lawyer. Tomorrow morning I check with him regarding tax matters and donations and what sort of bank account I should open for the hospital money.

(Jane told me she'd had to have a new catheter inserted at 3:30 A.M. That part went okay, though she was quite uncomfortable by the time I got to 330 — generally uncomfortable, that is. She ate a good lunch, and I brought home scraps for our cats, Billy and Mitzi. Jane mourns not being able to see those creatures.

(2:35. She applied lipstick and looked briefly in the mirror. I don't think she's missed a day since Seth suggested it.

(2:40. Jane began reading yesterday's session, but found it hard going. She had some bladder spasms, and finally laid aside the session to have a cigarette while I worked on mail. She went back to the session at 2:56, doing a little better, and finished at 3:09.

(3:20–3:55. Judy emptied Jane's Foley, or catheter bag, Dorothy took her blood pressure and pulse, and Carla her temperature — 98.2. I did some more mail until Jane said she was ready for a session. The hospital had been very quiet today, and we'd been left pretty much alone most of the time. Jane's Seth voice was a bit stronger than usual.)

Now I bid you another fond good afternoon.

("Good afternoon, Seth.")

Dictation. *(Long pause.)* All elements of life are optimistic.

The fetus, for example, is remarkably optimistic, carrying within itself the miniature pattern for an entire human adult, taking it for granted that conditions will be favorable enough so that the entire pattern of normal life will be fulfilled despite any impediments or adverse conditions.

This expectation to grow and flourish is addressed within each atom, cell, and organ, and all of life's parts contain this optimistic expectation and are blessed with the promise that their abilities will grow to maturity.

(Long pause.) Children spontaneously take it for granted that their acts will result in the most favorable circumstances, and that any given situation will have a favorable end result. These attitudes pervade in the animal kingdom also. They are embedded in the life of insects, and in fish and fowl. They are the directions that provide life with purpose, direction, and impetus. No organism automatically expects to find starvation or disappointment or detrimental conditions — yet even when such circumstances <u>are</u> encountered, they in no way affect the magnificent optimism that is at the heart of life.

(4:28.) Even when biological "failures" develop, as with stillborn infants, or malformed ones, the inner consciousness involved does not give up, and even though death results, the consciousness tries again under different conditions. In such cases death is not experienced by the <u>organism</u> as a failure, or as a biological mistake. It is

simply felt to be an experience, a discovery, <u>that went so far</u> and no further — but the events in no way impede the vitality and strength of the inner consciousness so involved.

(Pause at 4:32.) Comments.

Make sure, again, that you review portions of the sessions dealing with Ruburt's condition. Remind him to accept impatience <u>as a friend</u>, meant to lead him to the fulfillment of his desire. Once more, I activate those coordinates that so promote the healing processes. I may or may not return, according to those rhythms of which I speak — but know that I am present and approachable.

("Okay."

(4:35 P.M. Jane's delivery had been good, and I told her the session was excellent. She sipped ginger ale and had a smoke. "I do get feelings while delivering the stuff," she said, "wondering if I'm giving it the best way — like that material about the fetus not taking its death as a failure, but an experience. That would be hard for most people to understand . . . "

("Not once they get the idea," I said. "They'd have to learn to think in new ways, but they could do it. It would make a lot more sense to them then, than thinking in the old ways."

(A few minutes before I was set to leave at 7:00, after we'd read the prayer, Jane said she wanted to talk. It developed that she's feeling more impatient, and really wants to be able to sit up — say in a lounge chair like the people from the infirmary mentioned. Only her bent legs would prevent her from taking any position except the ones she uses in bed. She said she'd even thought of asking her doctor for help — "except that I stay away from doctors as much as possible," she said with a half laugh.

(I said I've been waiting for her legs to begin to move, so that she can move more, and get out of the bed into a chair of some sort, but since that hasn't happened yet there isn't much we can do. I'd expected leg movement before this, but we'll have to wait.

(I didn't realize it until I got home, but I forgot to read the session to Jane. However, she remembered that Seth had said she was to make a friend of impatience. But her impatience is growing, no doubt about it, and if it continues to do so I'm sure it will bring about — even force — changes in her behavior and attitude. I know it's coming. I hope — I expect — that the body will have prepared itself for the changes in routine and motion when they do finally arrive.)

JANUARY 30, 1984
4:35 P.M. MONDAY

(This morning I called our lawyer, and got the necessary confirmation on several matters — the $10,000 exemption limit on donations, and so forth. He agreed with my idea to open a separate account for fund checks. He also asked for our copy of Reality Change, *to copy for the file, and I added a copy of Maude's letter also. I worked on* Dreams *this morning, and also did some quick rough work on a first draft of my own letter to be sent to those who give us money.*

(The day was about 32 when I left for 330, although Jane's room was getting cold. There was no heat, and one of the staff had called maintenance, she said. She ate a good lunch. Snow, which had been predicted, began to fall around 2:30; there is a heavier storm south of us. I hoped it didn't get too bad by supper time.

(3:00. Jane put on lipstick, then looked briefly in the mirror. I worked on mail. A maintenance man came, but couldn't find out what was wrong with the heater. He left to get tools. Jane had to be covered while he was in the room, but for a long while I didn't hear her complaining about this today.

(Shawn took her temperature — 98.3, and pulse.

(3:55. Jane began reading yesterday's session, doing but a fair job. She was interrupted at 4:05 by Diana, who took her blood pressure — 102/64 — "just fine." She finished the session five minutes later, doing better at the end.

(4:15. Lynn gave Jane eyedrops. Ten minutes later Jane began the session. Just before she did, we were treated to the rather strong and tasty smell of liver and onions, coming up the elevator shaft across the hall from our door, from the kitchen in the basement. Food odors often waft up to us that way.)

I bid you another fond good afternoon.

("Good afternoon, Seth.")

A session, no matter how brief, does indeed help accentuate the healing processes.

Inner improvements are occurring, that have not as yet actually appeared in physical motion, but will indeed shortly begin to show themselves as easier motion. Again, it is important that Ruburt realize that his impatience is now a mental and physical, natural <u>aspect</u> of the healing processes themselves.

His overall improved condition leads him to anticipate even greater changes. This is mixed of course with strong surges of desire, and the release of that desire is all-important — for now he truly <u>wants</u> (underlined) to walk normally, and is willing — more than willing — to give up any fears or doubts that have stood in his way in the past.

That is why I emphasize a <u>new</u> (underlined) beginning, for it is from that viewpoint that he will be structuring his life from now on.

I may or may not return, again according to those rhythms of which I speak — but again, know that I am present and approachable.

("Okay. Thank you."

(4:41 P.M. Even though it's a brief one, I think the session is a very important one. It signals the incipience of a new way of life — most interesting. It also reminds me of something Seth said many years ago — that when Jane passionately wanted to get rid of the symptoms, she would do so. I've never forgotten that idea. I think today's session shows that Jane has either reached that point of passionate desire, or is very close to it.

(I should add that our dear friends, Bill and Peg Gallagher, visited Jane rather late last night, and brought with them a bottle of wine which the three of them proceeded to drain. Jane was surprised and touched.

(I should also add that Sue, one of the aides we've become acquainted with, showed us pictures of her two young sons. Those gorgeous children struck home with me for many reasons — partly because of Seth's material, and partly because I think at my own age [65] I've come to appreciate more and more the truly creative act that being a parent is. I told Sue that her children were great, and meant it. So did Jane. I wouldn't mind Seth commenting on my own evolving views of parenthood sometime.

(Perhaps two or three inches of snow fell this afternoon; now I'll probably shovel for a while in the driveway. No problem driving home.)

JANUARY 31, 1984
4:30 P.M. TUESDAY

(Jane didn't call last night. She said Debbie Harris visited. I shoveled quite a bit of snow in the driveway last night after I finished typing yesterday's session, and for the first time in a long while felt the old panic return. It was gone by the time I went to bed, but taught me that sometimes the old ideas and beliefs die hard. I shoveled the rest of the driveway this morning,

and felt much better — although traces of the same feeling in the throat returned for a time.

(Last night I had a rather vivid dream that I described to Jane before today's session. I dreamed that I bought a new red, sporty-looking sedan car at a dealer's. He wasn't a very nice or pleasant man, younger than me, who swore a lot. I believe I told him off once or twice. After picking out the car I wanted at the agency, I left to get the money. When I returned I saw that a family of five people — parents and three young children — were in the car, and ready to drive away. The obnoxious dealer told me that he'd sold the car to the family, and had set aside an identical <u>green</u> car for me.

(I got really mad at him, and told him off in no uncertain terms, threatening, I believe, legal action if I didn't get that car back that he'd promised me. I got it. I saw the family with children standing to one side, quietly waiting, wearing hats and topcoats, and so forth. They were nice-looking average people. I got in my red car. End of dream.

(I didn't eat lunch because Lynn had arranged a surprise birthday party for one of the nurses, and she invited me to share in the food. I got to 330 by 12:40, but still had to wait until the tray came at 1:30. The food was delicious. Jane and I shared it. The strawberry cake was impossibly rich and sweet, though.

(When I walked into 330 Jane was singing to herself in a low voice. She wanted to be turned right away, since she'd been on her side since 10:30, after getting back early from hydro. She said she had a whole bunch of old songs she sang to herself — not Sumari,* but the old standbys. I knew many of the melodies, but few words or titles. She ate a good lunch, and so did I. Jane gave me a bag of unshelled peanuts that I brought home for the squirrels.

(2:30. Jane had a cigarette. By 3:00 she began reading yesterday's session, doing fairly okay with pauses. I worked on mail while she finished at 3:14. I told her that yesterday I got a box of 64 letters from our publisher, Prentice-Hall.

(3:55. After another smoke, Jane started rereading the session for January 29 again — this time doing quite a bit better than she had earlier today. She finished well at 4:13.

---

*Both Jane and I belong to the family of consciousness that Seth calls Sumari. Jane can write, speak, and sing in Sumari — rapid, seemingly-nonsense words that she unhesitatingly translates into English prose and poetry of great beauty. (I can write in Sumari, but Jane has to translate it for me — and I'm always surprised at the results.) My wife has a powerful singing voice. See her material on Sumari in *Adventures in Consciousness.*

(While we talked, and as I wrote some of these notes for typing when I got home, I suddenly began to understand my dream of last night. The car stands for my travels through the psyche, and the family represented conventional America and its everyday beliefs, which I rejected. By demanding the red car that I wanted, I insisted that I go my own way, and in my own way. The dealer could possibly be me, voicing my own doubts and conflicts with society. Jane thought I was right. I've had much better results interpreting my own dreams in recent months, by the way. I now make intuitive connections that I seemed to be opaque to in previous years.

(Jane's Seth voice was good, as it had been yesterday. The heater in 330 was working again, for some mysterious reason, since Jane said no one had been in to check it today, and yesterday the fellow hadn't been able to get it going. The window was open a good foot, but the room was still warm.)

Now I bid you another fond good afternoon.

("Afternoon, Seth.")

Brief dictation. *(Long pause.)* This optimism is reflected in many other areas of life also.

Many birds in their fantastic migrations demonstrate an amazing optimism, traveling thousands of miles to distant shores, almost literally flying by faith, as it were, ignoring all dangers, unbesieged by doubts. There is no hesitancy, but the sure flight. Birds do not question whether or not the weather will be favorable, the winds fair or foul. They simply fly toward their destination. Even if some birds <u>do</u> fall or die, this in no way impedes or undermines the faith of the others.

Monarch butterflies, in their remarkable migrations, often fly toward land that they have never seen themselves — and yet they reach their destination.

In all such cases there is an inbred biological faith, that courage and vitality, that biological optimism. It acts the same in people, triggering the necessary bodily responses. Only when that optimism is severely tampered with do the physical mechanisms falter. Even then, however, all creatures are sustained by that innate gift, that inner sense of security that not only propels creatures toward life, but safely conducts them past physical life and past death's doorway.

(Pause at 4:40.) Comments.

You yourself did an excellent job interpreting your own dream, covering all of its main points and meanings. It signals your determination not to be curtailed by those conventional beliefs that pervade in your society.

Again, I accelerate those coordinates that quicken Ruburt's healing processes. I may or may not return, according to those rhythms of which I speak. But know that I am indeed present and approachable.

("Yes. Thank you."

(4:43 P.M. I read the session to Jane. I said I'd forgotten to ask Seth to comment on my feelings about parenthood these days, especially as I'd felt them yesterday when looking at the photos of the aide's children. Jane suggested I remind Seth to do so tomorrow.

(Then I told her about the article I'd just taken from Science News *last night, concerning the abilities of animals, birds and bees to carry maps of their terrain in their heads. Very interesting.*

(I remember also seeing an article not long ago on the migrations of the Monarch butterfly, but doubt if I'll be able to locate that one easily.

(Jane and I talked about her legs, motion, and so forth as I was getting ready to leave at prayer time. She then said that she'd picked up something from Seth — to the effect that we should live each day without worry as best we could, and let the future take care of itself. I'm probably not quoting her completely or correctly here, since I didn't write down what she told me. She can add information, if necessary, after reading this note, and I'll incorporate it in tomorrow's session. I'm curious.)

FEBRUARY 1, 1984
4:10 P.M. WEDNESDAY

(Jane didn't call last night. It was only 10 above when I got up. I took a shower, ate breakfast and fed the cats, put the trash out to be picked up by the service we subscribe to, and gave both Classie and "Black Dog" — whose name, Margaret Bumbalo told me, is Missy — snacks of dry cat food. Both dogs belong to a neighbor.

(Jane wanted to be turned at once when I got to 330, since she'd been on her side since returning from hydro at 11:00. I was late because I'd stopped at the post office.

(She was gloomy and afraid. She'd had a pain in her side lying there, and was afraid that it was something serious — but when I put her on her back she began to feel better, and thought the pain might only be from gas. Yet her mood persisted through lunch — of which she ate little, by the way.

When I asked her if she was up to her old tricks, she said, "I know what I'm doing — but that doesn't mean I can't goof up once in a while."

(2:45. She put on lipstick and looked quickly at herself in the mirror. After that she was still very quiet as she had a smoke and I did mail. At 3:30 she started reading yesterday's session, and did fairly well considering her mood. She was interrupted by Carla taking her temperature — 98.3.

(4:00. After finishing the session, Jane told me now that she'd also been very blue last night, and "really got scared" this morning at the pain in her side, "imagining all sorts of things." I couldn't say too much, considering my own panicky reaction when I shoveled snow yesterday, but I did remark that we'd slipped back into the old ways of dealing with events.

(Now Jane corrected the quotation she'd received from Seth as I was leaving last night, and that I'd tried to remember: "The way toward health is simplicity itself. You can make plans for the future, but do not worry about the future. Live each day." Besides being excellent advice, I'm citing the quote here because it triggered the opening lines of the session today.)

Now: I bid you another fond good afternoon.

("Good afternoon, Seth.")

Dictation. *(Long pause.)* The way toward health is simplicity itself.

It is the natural, easiest way to behave, yet this natural mental behavior is often quite difficult for the intellect to understand, since the intellect is apt to enjoy playing with <u>complications</u> and solving problems. Therefore, to the intellect it often seems ludicrous to imagine that the answer to a question lies within the question itself.

(Long pause.) All of nature demonstrates this almost miraculous seeming simplicity. Plants and animals and all of life's aspects take it quite for granted that the sun will shine and the rains will fall in the way best conducive to all creatures. Animals certainly do not worry about tomorrow's weather conditions. *(Long pause.)* It may be true that animals do not need to know tomorrow's weather, since they do not plant seeds or collect the harvest. It is perfectly fine to make plans for the future, yet each individual should live day by day, without <u>worrying</u> (underlined) about the outcome of those plans.

The physical body can only react in the present moment. Worrying about future events, or dwelling upon past unfavorable situations, only confuses the body's mechanisms, and undermines their precise activity in the present moment.

(4:20.) I am not saying that anyone should pretend that unfavorable circumstances do not sometimes exist, or that they may not be encountered in the past, present, or future. It is also true, however, that <u>advantageous</u> events occur with a far greater frequency than do negative ones — otherwise the world that you know simply would not exist. It would have disappeared in the throes of destruction or calamity.

In a basic way, <u>it is against nature's purposes</u> to contemplate a dire future, for all of nature operates on the premise that the future is assured. Nature is everywhere filled with promise — not only the promise of mere survival, but the promise of beauty and fulfillment. Once again, that keen sense of promise is innate within each portion of the body. It triggers the genes and chromosomes into their proper activity, and it promotes feelings of optimism, exuberance, and strength.

Again, sometime later we will discuss those conditions that can undermine such fine creativity. In the meantime, however, live each day as fully and joyfully as possible. Imagine the best possible results of any plans or projects. Above all, do not concentrate upon past unfavorable events, or imagined future ones.

(4:29.) Comments.

Your own touches of panic, and Ruburt's blueness and fear, were both remnants of old habits, as both of you understand.

You can, <u>and must</u>, trust the body's activity. It naturally seeks fulfillment, vitality, and the fullest possible expression.

(An extremely important observation.

(Long pause.) Ruburt had a dream with excellent connotations, in which he looked through a beautiful old house of lovely carved wood and spacious rooms, and decided to move into the house, even though it was in an area that had previously nearly been condemned — signifying that he was indeed rising from beliefs that he condemned into a larger, spacious area of expression.

("Last night?" Jane hadn't told me about the dream.

(Note: Just as Jane had had this dream, I'd read an article in the Star-Gazette *to the effect that a few blocks near downtown Elmira, including the apartment house we'd lived in at 458 W. Water Street, had been designated a Historical Preservation Area by New York State. I meant to save the article,*

but forgot to. I think the area is bounded by Walnut, West Water, and Church Streets, back toward downtown.)

Indeed. I may or may not return, again according to those rhythms of which I speak — but know that I am present and approachable.

(4:35. "Will you say something about the feelings I've had about parenthood lately?")

Let us take a break.

("Okay."

(Jane had ginger ale and a few puffs. "If you hadn't asked, he was going to say something about your parenthood thing," she said. We talked about how strange it was that no one had been in yet to take her blood pressure and pulse — not that it would have mattered if they weren't taken. Resume at 4:40.)

Now: If you examine your feelings about parenthood in general, you will see that they bear an astonishing similarity to your feelings about your <u>painting</u> and <u>our work</u>. Only the focus is different. You are indeed both parents of an amazing body of work, and the psychic parents of innumerable people of all ages. You have set aside, however, the <u>conventional</u> idea of a family, as symbolized by your *(car)* dream of the other evening. You are actually exchanging one kind of a family for another, vaster concept, that also involves parenthood, however — but a psychic rather than a physical parenthood. The letters you receive are often like letters children write to their parents.

("Well, I guess that's it," Jane said after a pause.

("Okay. Thank you."

(4:45 P.M. I read the session to Jane. I told her it was so good I was going to make an extra copy to keep before me in the writing room. I read it to her again at 6:55 P.M. I'd been thinking about it ever since it ended.

(I told Jane that we have to follow it — that we simply must dump all else and trust the body, that nothing else makes any sense any more, that it's the key to our futures. She agreed, of course. She said she's going to start with Day One tomorrow, and take it from there, trusting the body, not dwelling upon the past, and leaving the future open. It is simplicity itself, I told her, and we must never again forget it on a consistent basis. Slipping up once in a while won't mean anything then. But part of our success will depend on keeping these simple goals always in mind, before us.

(Jane called at 9:45 this evening, with Carla's help, as I was finishing this session. It's mighty cold out.)

FEBRUARY 2, 1984
4:02 P.M. THURSDAY

(Note: This is "Day 1," Jane reminded me.

(The temperature was only 5 above when I got up at 6:30 this morning, but was up to 25 degrees when I left for 330.

(Jane was good, had been back from hydro since 11:00 again. Yesterday we'd received our copies of the Bantam paperback issue of The Nature of the Psyche, *and I'd brought a book in to show Jane. She thought it was as terrible — as cheap and sensationalized — as I did. I hadn't even gotten mad, I told her. I wanted a word from Seth on what our reactions should, or could, be, in light of yesterday's session about living in the moment.*

(I also had two more questions for her boy, I said as I fed her an average lunch. One was what does the staff, the people we see every day at the hospital, think of us? The other was Seth's comments on a very vivid and long dream I'd had last night.

(In the dream, all of which was in brilliant color, I'd combined many elements, which I described in more detail to Jane than I'll give here. First, we'd moved back to 458 W. Water — which I seem to do several times a week — and looking out my old studio windows, I saw my father cutting hair like a barber out in the driveway in front of the garage. I invited him to come up and take over the studio for a barbershop. Laughing, looking younger than his years, he did so. Then I was working for Jake Ruppenthal, my old boss at Artistic Card Company, when he was art director. I had left Artistic in 1972, to concentrate upon helping Jane with the Seth material. In the dream I was drawing foot-high oval letters in black ink, but was worried about doing a good job because my hand was shaky. Then I realized I could cut out the letters from cardboard or some such, and ink them in that way. Next, Jake and I were walking down a street in a town, on our way to see Jane's mother. Midway in the trip Jake left me, saying I could go on alone from there.

(When I approached the room in which I knew Marie lay in bed, crippled by arthritis, I heard Jane and her mother inside. They were talking and laughing and crying all at once. I went in and saw them both in a double

bed, fully clothed, arms around each other, <u>forgiving</u> each other. Both were younger than their years, both had shining black hair. Marie was bedridden, but Jane was perfectly healthy, and had come to forgive her mother, or make up with her. Quite a scene. The entire dream had made an impression on me, I told Jane.

(I told Jane that I didn't think I'd figured out very much of it, beyond that I seemed to be remaking the past, and that all of the figures in it except her seemed to be figures of authority from that past. I also felt that the idea of authority was somehow connected with my shaky right hand, and since this aspect of the dream wasn't discussed today, I'd like Seth to comment on it tomorrow if he has a session. I seem to remember from old pendulum sessions, that my mother is involved with the shaky hand, although she wasn't in this dream. Stella Butts had died in November 1973, at 81.

(3:00. Jane began reading yesterday's session, which I think is an excellent one, but she didn't do well at all. She quit for a smoke at 3:12 while I worked on mail. She tried again at 3:20, doing just a little better. I kept thinking about the session, listening to Jane try to read it as I looked over mail. Finally at 3:29 I read the rest of the session to her.

(3:36. Jennifer emptied Jane's Foley. The staff is very busy.

(I mentioned the three questions for Seth: 1. What does the staff at the hospital think of us? 2. How should we react to the Bantam cover situation? 3. My dream.

("Oh, he'll never get to answer all three of them," Jane said. Her Seth voice was again good.)

Now: I bid you another fond good afternoon.

(No sooner had Seth spoken than Lynn came in to give Jane eyedrops. I told her I'd done it myself an hour ago.)

Dictation. In his own mind, Ruburt calls these ideas, taken together, "The New Way."

The ideas themselves are quite ancient, of course. They are expressed by many cultures and religions, esoteric groups and cults from the past, and continuing into the present. Their strength, vitality, and worth has been greatly undermined, however, by distortions, negative ideas, and some sheer nonsense.

In other words, these concepts, so natural to all of creation, have not been practiced by humanity in anything like their pure form. To that extent they do indeed represent a new way. They run directly counter to much of your official knowledge and contemporary thought as far as the mainstream of world culture is concerned. Where such ideas <u>are</u> practiced, they are frequently contaminated by fanaticism, superstition, and expediency.

The main point I want to make is that this "new way" *(long pause)* is the ideal and easiest complement to nature's own innate integrity —

(4:12. Shawn came in to do all of Jane's vitals. Temperature 98.6. Jane had a cigarette at 4:17. I read what she'd given so far to her while Shawn went for ginger ale. She was back with it at 4:21. I imagine the interruption cut short dictation.)

Now: Comments.

Yesterday's session should be read two or three times a week for now.

Your dream did indeed deal with changing the past and the past beliefs, and therefore with inserting a new present, and a newer future. Often hair is a symbol for strength, but in this case it represents the strength of old beliefs, and your father is a barber who cuts away those — whereas in the past he followed many quite negative beliefs and concepts. Jake also represented any beliefs of your own dealing with work in general that can carry you so far and no further. You correctly interpreted the affair between Ruburt and his mother — an excellent omen, by the way.

(Now Seth came through with a sentence I didn't think was correct:)

The Bantam cover in its own way offers in the most positive of ways, despite your natural objections to it . . . It suggests the most unfortunate sensationalism, of course, yet people attracted to it for that reason are precisely the people it is important to reach. The ideas in the book proper will quite change their negative, charged ideas of psychic activity in general.

This does not mean that you should not write a clear letter stating your own reaction against the cover, if you so choose.

It will take some time to discuss the staff's opinion of you both, so I suggest that we leave that for another time of your choosing.

I may or may not return, again according to those rhythms of which I speak, but know that I am present and approachable.

("I'd like to go over that first sentence of the Bantam material — I've made a mistake, or something's wrong somewhere."

(At Seth's request I reread the sentence twice.)

No, there is an error somewhere . . . The Bantam cover, despite your obvious dissatisfaction, aids our work in the positive of ways.

(Again at his request, I read back to Seth the sentence he'd just given.) You are clear.

(4:32 P.M. I told Jane that I didn't know whether or not I'd get involved in a controversy over the Bantam cover. I didn't even want to spend time thinking about it, especially in light of yesterday's session.

(I cite the verbatim transcript involving Seth correcting the sentence he'd given, because as far as I can remember, that's the first time it's ever happened. A pretty fair record over the years, Jane. Sleep well. I love you.)

FEBRUARY 3, 1984
4:03 P.M. FRIDAY

(Jane didn't call last night. The temperature was already up to 44 degrees when I left for 330. Jane was already on her back — she'd refused to go to hydro when they hadn't come by 12:30. I told her I brought Session 903 of Dreams *with me so I could ask her a couple of questions. She said okay.*

(Jane ate an average amount for lunch. Afterward she had trouble reading Session 903, and I tried to read portions of it to her. However, I didn't think our talk about mammals, animals, transmigration and so forth went very well. Jane said she got irritated at the questions, and I ended up feeling the same way. However, I did figure out the way to handle the few notes for the session, and decided to forget others I'd started struggling with. I already regretted the time I was spending on the session for Dreams.

(Jane said I was really saying that I was settling for second best. I agreed, adding that I saw no help for it if ever I was to finish the book. Above all, I want to get the job done so I can go on to other things. I added that I was trying to avoid projecting any hassles with Dreams *into the future, in line with the session for the day before [February 1], though I was aware that some of what I was saying contradicted elements of that session. However, I'll work those out. I do want to get* Dreams *done as soon as possible, and will not be getting into any fixes of a similar nature in the years to come.*

(3:15. Jane began reading yesterday's session. Not the best, but she got along with many halting attempts as I wrote these notes. She did better as she went along, and finished at 3:42. A couple of minutes later Carla took her temperature. It was 100.2. "Oh, you do have a fever," she said. Jane

looked puzzled, since she felt okay. Diana took Jane's blood pressure and pulse. "You do feel warm," she said. "I don't have any damn fever," Jane said when they'd left.

(Jane wants me to note that this is Day 2 of her new approach to life, based on the session for February 1. I do think the session is an excellent one, and I've copied it for use at the house, too.)

Now — I bid you another most fond good afternoon.

("Good afternoon, Seth.")

Comments.

In regard to your dream: The shakiness represented values and ideas from your mother, primarily about work — beliefs you always felt <u>were</u> shaky. In the dream you manage to circumnavigate their effects. In daily waking life the shakiness still represents leftover uncertainty, and it is more noticeable whenever any strong interruptions occur.

As far as the book passages are involved, it is indeed very difficult to write about complicated matters with a simple vocabulary. This is what we try to do, of course. We try to use words that have an overall meaning for the general reader, and then make any necessary —

(4:08. Lynn came in to give Jane eyedrops, then left to get some iced ginger ale. I read to Jane what she'd given so far.)

— distinctions to make certain that the passage is correct.

Your question about transmigration *(in Session 903 in Dreams)* was an excellent one, and did indeed make the matter clear. It is a temptation at times to use more specific scientific terms, but these would be as confusing as the various definitions and classifications *(with humor)* that you read in the dictionary, so overall we try to hit a "happy medium." *(With more humor.)*

Again, do review Wednesday's session often — and it is a good idea to designate Day 1 and so forth, as each of you try to make this a new beginning, and take each day as it is, <u>one day at a time</u>. Now I may or may not return, again according to those rhythms of which I speak, but know that I am present and approachable.

("Okay, Thank you."

(4:14 P.M. Seth, then, verified my own pendulum information about my mother's beliefs and my reactions to them being involved with my shaky right hand.)

FEBRUARY 4, 1984
4:26 P.M. SATURDAY

(Jane called last night with Carla's help. Before that she'd had visits from our friends Debbie Harris and Elisabeth — who were there at the same time. Elisabeth left her some yellow primroses, very nice, and a place mat made by a lady in Germany whom Elisabeth, being German herself, has written to for us.

(The day was again warm — 42 — when I left for 330 at noon. Jane had just had her dressings changed when I got there. She'd gone down to hydro at 10:30, and it had taken all that time to get through the routine. I told her to refuse to go if she thinks she's going to have to wait long periods, but I can't see her doing that, I guess.

(Today is Day 3 of Jane's new routine, following the session on February 1. She said she catches herself all the time getting off the track, then tries to remind herself of her new healthier goals — living in the moment, thinking positively, and so on.

(She ate an average lunch. I described my very vivid dream of last night. It was most exhilarating. I dreamed I was jogging along a country road beside the Chemung River on the way toward Sayre. The road was similar to the old river road we used to drive. I wore shorts and a sweatshirt and had white hair. I was amazed and delighted at the smooth, effortless way my body was performing as I ran, especially for one my age. I really enjoyed the freedom of motion, of strength, running in the sunny summer air.

(I knew I'd been imprisoned, and that I was now free. Also that behind me, not too close, ran a police van, with several cops in it checking up on me. Every so often they came closer, but didn't interfere. And across the river at one spot, I saw a large group of men romping or working on the bank — I think they were still incarcerated. I waved to them as I ran past, opposite them.

(I told Jane that I thought the police in the dream meant that I'd left behind me old imprisoning beliefs, that I was now running free of those beliefs. Also, the group of men across the river represented old beliefs of mine that I'd discarded. I added that if I had the time I'd like to do some jogging now, since I have an ability and love for running.

(Jane wasn't at her best. They had taken her temperature this morning, and it had been 100.1. I asked her why it was up again, but she didn't know. They take it each shift when it's high. I rang for some ginger ale and ice, since the girl who'd promised to bring it an hour ago never showed up.

(2:40. Jane read yesterday's session while I read mail, and did quite well. Much better than she had yesterday.

(2:55. She started reading the key session for February 1. Again she did well. After that we seemed to let time get away from us, watching TV and so forth. I did a little mail. We went over parts of a long letter from Sue Watkins, but Jane couldn't read it. She was discouraged, I could tell, and I wasn't at my best either. Jane spent a lot of time waiting for people to do her vitals, then finally decided on a session.)

Now: I bid you another fond good afternoon.

("Good afternoon, Seth.")

Comments.

Your dream was indeed an excellent "omen." You were escaping from the jailhouse of negative beliefs, and you were delighted with the new <u>easy motion</u> of your body, once you had been released.

The feeling of buoyancy is a delightful sensation that is experienced, of course, by <u>all</u> children. The dream was meant to remind you of that inner <u>and</u> outer buoyancy and freedom.

I may or may not return, again because of those rhythms of which I speak, but know that I am present and approachable.

("Okay."

(4:30 P.M. I hadn't expected the quick ending to the session, since I'd thought there were some rather important topics Jane could have discussed, such as the reasons for the temperature increase. She showed no signs of wanting to, though, so I didn't press the idea on her. On my way home at 7:10 P.M., I wished I had, and realized that I hadn't been much help to her at a time of pretty obvious distress. Once, when I'd been massaging her, she'd started to talk about the high temperature, but I'd been distracted by the tense way she was holding her body and had cut her off. Maybe we can do better tomorrow.

(4:33. A gal took Jane's temperature, and it was again at 100. "Oh Jesus," Jane muttered, but said little else, beyond saying that she didn't want antibiotics. I felt sure the temperature was connected to the session for February 1, though I couldn't say why.

(I did think of a couple of questions on the way home. What's the reincarnational background of Jane's symptoms; and why does she still hold her right leg so tight against her belly, after all this time following the break at the knee?)

FEBRUARY 5 , 1984
4:06 P.M. SUNDAY

(This is "Day 4" of Jane's new program.

(Jane didn't call last night. I spent the morning typing letters from Jane, Seth, and me for Maude Cardwell to send to donors. I also wrote Maude a letter of my own. I did no work on Dreams.

(The day was about 34 degrees. When I got to 330 Jane told me that Shawn Peterson had been admitted to intensive care last night with chest pains, but that the tests so far have been negative. "The nurses are sicker than the patients," Jane said she heard one of the nurses say this morning.

(Jane didn't go to hydro — just had her face washed. Her blood pressure never was taken yesterday. She had lots to tell me, and acted much better than she had yesterday. I felt better, too. Her temperature had been taken after I left last night, and early this morning: 99 and 97.8 — down both times. After I left she gave herself "a good talking to," about trusting her body, and so forth, and this helped a lot.

(Jeff Karder, Jane's doctor, visited her this morning. He was very pleased with her progress. "For him to say very good is something," Jane said. "I've been getting good reports about you," he told her. He also asked Jane about our insurance hassles. She explained as best she could, and about the infirmary. Jane asked him why her right leg was shorter than the left one, and Jeff explained that the break had healed but that the bones were out of alignment, hence the shortness. He said it would take a major operation to restore the leg, with no guarantees that it could be done. A "minor" operation could fix the leg well enough so she could sit up, he said, after Jane said she wanted to start sitting up.

(It's hardly a coincidence, then, that one of the questions I had for Seth today, and had added to yesterday's session, concerned her right leg and why she wasn't straightening it out. The negative part of Jeff's information is that he said she couldn't sit up until the leg was fixed to some degree, at least. I'd expected that sort of diagnosis for some time. "Shit," Jane said, "if my body can recover like it has, then it can fix the leg too." I believe it. Jane took the visit well indeed this morning, and I congratulate her for doing so. I wanted to ask Seth about the whole thing anyhow, since he's said several times that she'll be able to walk normally and with some confidence.

(Jane said Jeff was plainly surprised at her improvements, but that at the same time he was condemning her to staying in bed. I said that from his position he could do little else.

(Jane had eaten a better lunch today. She was obviously relieved that her temperature was dropping. At 3:15 she began reading yesterday's session, and did well, her best in some days. She said she tried to explain to Jeff how she was uncomfortable and impatient in hydro, but got nowhere. She could see he knew nothing of what she was talking about, so finally she just quit.

(I showed Jane the list of questions I've been acquiring, at Seth's own suggestion, and told her that one of them concerned the insurance situation — that I didn't want to mess it up by demanding action from our lawyer, say. Seth had said six weeks ago that the issue would be settled to my satisfaction, and our lawyer had said not to worry, and that's the last we've heard. I added that I couldn't imagine the hospital not demanding action before this — yet they haven't. Seth had said the question would be cleared up without any long wait.

(3:40. At my suggestion Jane began to try writing with one of my pens. She managed to do something, resting the pad against her right knee — which is sore to the touch. She even held the pen in her right hand. I'm to bring in the clipboard tomorrow. I'm sure she can make progress here. It might free her enough so she could write poetry at night, say, when she's alone.

(I explained to Jane my mental saying, "Sorry, Mom, but I don't have time any more for your shaky beliefs or ideas," as it had spontaneously grown out of Seth's comments about why my right hand is shaky, in a recent session. The suggestion is working fairly well. I think it's quite humorous and original, and so does Jane. It may have a cumulative effect, and I'd like Seth to comment.

(At 4:00 Lynn gave Jane eyedrops. Jeff had told Jane her eyes looked better, too. Jane wanted to get started on the session, which she felt might be longer than usual, so I told her not to wait for people to do her vitals.)

Now: I bid you another <u>most</u> fond good afternoon.

("Good afternoon, Seth.")

Comments.

You were each surrounded by some highly unfortunate beliefs, that were at least partially paranoid, but in any case unfortunate. They were beliefs that had to do with talent, ability, or genius —

(4:07. A nurse came in to take Jane's temperature. It was 98.3 — down again; she got Jane some ginger ale.

(4:12.) These were distortive offshoots connected with misinterpretations of ideas of equality, connected with a democratic government. These same ideas also had involvements with psychology,

dealing with "the norm," the average man, and so forth. People try to be as much as possible like their neighbors, hiding eccentricities, failings and even talents and abilities that might close them off from their fellows. The end result was a series of beliefs that ran as follows:

If you are highly talented in any way, play the talent down or be extremely humble in its performance or expression, because other people will envy you, or be afraid of you, or try to drag you down "to their own level."

(*Long pause at 4:16.*) The more unusual and original your gift, the more you must protect yourself from the distrust of others. This line of belief continues as follows: If your talent is extremely unique or original, it may be safer to deny it entirely, or to adopt some disability or handicap that will quell the jealousy or envy of others who might otherwise hunt you down.

Now both of you were saturated with those beliefs — Ruburt because of his poetry and writing, and you because of your art. You early went into commercial work, where your love of painting could be <u>sheltered</u> beneath the Average Joe's love of money. That is, you obviously were an artist in order to make a living. This was just another version of the American male's conventional role.

Ruburt, as a young woman, felt that writers were on the outskirts —

(*4:23. Carla took Jane's blood pressure and pulse. Jane had a smoke while I read the session to her so far.*

(*4:29.*) — of society. Period.

His beliefs about poets were contaminated by ideas that said that the poet was too sensitive, too vulnerable to life's experiences — that this sensitivity brought weakness instead of strength, and that true artists or true poets came to a tragic end for that reason.

Other personal beliefs held by both of you to some extent or another, with the usual cultural connotations, stressed a false humility over the rightful natural pride of ability. Such beliefs are often given to children, appearing in such forms as, "don't be a showoff," "don't be an exhibitionist," followed by, again, the dire warning that your fellow creatures suspect any neighbor who is different or who shows any superior abilities.

This entire belief system was detrimental enough, when you were devoted to writing and painting as these are generally understood. When Ruburt's psychic abilities began to show themselves, however, those same beliefs made both of you even more cautious than before, and more worried about reprisal from others — and as far as Ruburt was concerned, more worried about criticism or scorn. All of those beliefs existed along with many unfortunate ones that were sexually oriented — those that dictated, for example, the traditional roles of man and wife, or man and woman. Ruburt felt some guilt in expressing psychic abilities in such a marked fashion, when it seemed that the male of the relationship should be the most highly talented, and by far the most successful financially *(intently)*. So your roles in that manner upset both of you at times.

(4:40.) Ruburt, at one period, even feared that the young psychologist at Oswego was correct — that his psychic abilities were mere attempts to prove himself superior to you.* These are all beliefs that both of you have wrestled with over the years. You also had many <u>excellent</u> beliefs going with you also, so that you did indeed use your abilities and express your natures. You enjoyed your relationship with each other, the relationship with friends, and you did also enjoy some financial success.

(Long pause.) The effect of those old negative beliefs, however, was stronger in Ruburt than in yourself, for he certainly thought at one time that if he curtailed physical motion people would not attack him for his amazing psychic and mental motion. The inhibition of physical motion obviously took place little by little, until he began to learn the truth — that human beings are meant to express <u>all</u> of their abilities, mental and physical, and that life is an arena of expression. In fact, <u>life is expression</u>.

At one point, for a while, Ruburt did no writing or sessions, and was physically nearly immobile besides. Then he began to learn the lessons that were needed — that life is expression, and that it <u>is</u> safe for him to move mentally and physically, using both his psychic, creative, mental and physical abilities to their fullest.

(4.48. The aide brought the supper tray and left the door open. There was noise in the hall, but Jane continued:)

---

*In 1965, in response to my letter, an older and very respected parapsychologist — "Dr. Instream," Jane called him — invited Jane and me to attend the hypnosis symposium he was to conduct at a New York State college. Doctors, dentists, and psychologists attended. It was there that Jane and I had our most unfortunate encounter with the young psychologist. See chapters 6, 7, and 8 of *The Seth Material*.

This session will serve as a reminder, however, to both of you, and will help brush away the remainder of any old lingering beliefs. Earlier, Ruburt was <u>afraid</u> to trust his body, afraid to let his body heal him, for fear he would be attacked by others. You both also believed that you must protect your special abilities with all of your might — but you can see the road of contradictions that is constructed in such a fashion.

I am aware of Karder's visit, and your own conversations about Ruburt's walking, and so forth — and I intend to answer your questions, but I wanted to give you the preceding material as a necessary preliminary. I am also aware of the time limitations.

(*"Well, that's no problem."*)

I can say that overall I agree with your decisions, and with Ruburt's interpretation of Karder's visit. Some of the material that I have just given will help Ruburt find greater release. The body <u>can</u> remedy itself. You have only to allow it to do so. I hope that this session helps <u>siphon off</u> the edge of any lingering doubts or contradictions.

(*"It's very good."*)

Remind me tomorrow of additional questions, and we will continue. I may or may not return, et cetera (*with humor*), and I am present and approachable.

(*"Thank you very much, Seth."*

(*4:57 P.M. I read the session to Jane while she had a smoke. "There's a lot to think of — that's a powerful session," she said. Indeed. She'd alternately sighed and grunted and groaned as I read. I think it will help a great deal.*

(*Jane called, with Carla's help, at about 10:00, as I was typing this.*)

FEBRUARY 6, 1984
4:33 P.M. MONDAY

Georgia — disc, ulcers, surgery
Shirley — disc, surgery
Susie — knee, surgery
Shawn — chest pains
Robert — coronary unit
Judy — back
Rhonda — surgery, unknown

Hydro:
Steve — ulcers
Debbie — heel, surgery
Tom — leg
Mike — shoulder

(The above is a partial list of staff members who have had serious medical problems that we know about since Jane came into the hospital last April 20. These are people we have come into more or less regular contact with in our own small circle in the hospital. Magnify their number proportionally amid the 1,000 or so employees at the hospital, and what sort of percentage of sick employees would you have? A high one, I think.

(Jane was singing to herself when I got to 330 today. She'd called last night as I was finishing the session. I worked on Dreams this morning, and mailed our letters to Maude Cardwell on my way to the hospital this noon. The day was just above freezing. Jane went to hydro this morning. She said she was singing to herself down there too, while waiting, and an attendant came in to ask her what was wrong.

(After lunch, at 2:45 Jane put on lipstick and looked at herself in the mirror. She said she had some extra freedom of motion in her right thumb. Her temperature today was 98.3 — down again. I forgot to ask her what it had been this morning.

(3:36. Jane began reading yesterday's session, and doing quite well. I worked on mail.

(3:45. Diana came in. "You're a celebrity," she said, pointing to Jane. Diana had found an article about Jane, with picture, in a book on the history of Chemung County and Elmira. We'd forgotten about it, but an older retired individual had contacted Jane years ago about doing such a project. Neither of us could remember his name. I believe someone connected with the Star-Gazette.

(3:56. Jane resumed reading the session, did well, and finished at 4:10. She had another cigarette while I did mail. She suggested having a short session when the hour began to grow late.)

Now I bid you another fond good afternoon.

("Good afternoon, Seth.")

Comments.

There is one other point in particular I wanted to mention, though it has, of course, been discussed often before. This is the matter of self-approval.

Many of the contradictory beliefs and negative ones discussed in yesterday's session led to strong feelings of self-disapproval. The beliefs were so contradictory that in living up to any one of them you actually seemed to be denying others in which you also believed. Hence, no matter what you did you were both left with strong feelings of self-disapproval.

You are largely over that kind of reaction — yet it is still apt to return now and then when you fear that you have not done as well as you should have, or when you have momentarily caught yourself behaving in old ways. A feeling of self-approval is absolutely necessary for any true sense of well-being; it is not (underlined) virtuous in any way to put yourself down, or to punish yourself, because you do not feel you have lived up to your best behavior at any given time.

Do keep an eye out for that kind of reaction, however, so that you can nip it in the bud.

Tell Ruburt that the same energy that healed or mended his right knee can also straighten it out. The mental exercises he has been doing are excellent in that regard. Do not worry about the insurance situation. It is being solved, and to your advantage.

As much as possible, playfully (underlined twice) imagine your worries floating away. It might help if you imagine balloons, one labeled insurance, another health, and so forth — then imagine them floating away, or popping open, or whatever. Again, this should be playfully done. You might surprise yourself, and find yourself as delighted as a child with a new game.

I may or may not return again et cetera, but I do activate those coordinates that quicken Ruburt's healing processes.

("It's me," Jane said after a pause.

("Thank you."

(4:45 P.M. I forgot to tell Jane about a dream I had last night. Not very elaborate: I'd dreamed that I'd been visiting some friends, a married couple, I believe, and that they had a number of cats of their own in the place. Our Billy was there also. When it came time for me to leave, I started hunting around to find Billy. Each time I picked up a cat, I discovered that I didn't have Billy. All of the cats were marked more or less similarly, yet there were enough differences in color and pattern so that I could know Billy when and if I found him.)

FEBRUARY 7, 1984
4:04 P.M. TUESDAY

(Jane called last night. Today was cold — 22 degrees when I left for 330. I stopped at the bank to buy money orders to pay bills. No one had taken Jane's temperature this morning, since it had dropped back to normal range. After lunch Jane told me that Steve and Tracy had sent her a telegram Sunday night, saying they couldn't make it for a variety of reasons. She'd forgotten to tell me.

(A note: This is "Day 6" of Jane's new campaign to change her thinking.

(3:02. After lunch Jane began to read yesterday's session, and did quite well. I answered mail. Jane remembered the name of the retired newspaperman who'd written about us in his history of Chemung County — "Burs."And this triggered my own memory: Tom Byrne.

(3:15. Jane finished reading the session, and had done quite well. At 3:55 a student took her blood pressure, which was good. Jane was ready for the session early. She decided not to wait for temperature.

(The room had been warm, and I had the heat off and the window wide open. Traffic noise was a bother at times — and that effect reminded me of how often such racket had been a problem when we held sessions at 458 W. Water Street.)

Now I bid you another fond good afternoon.

("Good afternoon, Seth.")

Book dictation. *(Long pause, then quite slowly:)* All creatures are also born, then, with a keen sense of self-approval.

Each creature is born proud of itself, and loving itself. That same self-approval is also experienced in varying ways not only by creatures as you think of them, but also by atoms and molecules, and by all orders of matter.

Ruburt once wrote a poem about a nail on a window sill. He endowed the nail with consciousness and self-awareness. Now every nail is indeed in its own way responsive to stimuli. It acts and reacts. A nail may not choose to jump down from a window sill and dance about the room, but a nail is indeed aware of the room, of the window sill, and aware of the temperature on both sides of the window. The atoms and molecules that compose the nail possess their own lively consciousnesses. Their motion is directed by electrons, so that within itself the nail actually experiences constant motion. Indeed, a dance is executed of great symmetry and rhythm. The nail, then, is indeed filled with its own sense of self-approval.

I am mentioning this only to stress the fact that self-delight and self-approval *(long pause)* are natural characteristics — characteristics that actually make your entire physical world, and world of experience, possible.

It is very unfortunate, therefore, when adults inadvertently undermine a child's sense of self-approval. A small boy might be caught in a lie, for example, and therefore labeled by an adult in the angriest of terms as a liar. Instead, a distinction should be made: the child made an error — he lied — but he himself is not the error or the lie. He can then determine to change his behavior while still saving his self-respect.

(Long pause at 4:16.) All creatures are basically of good intent; even when they commit the most dubious of acts, these are usually caused by a misdirected good intent. Actually, many criminals are motivated by distorted versions of righteousness. We will have more to say about this later in the book, but for now I want to stress the importance of self-approval in connection with exuberance, health, and well-being.

End of dictation. I may or may not return, again according to those rhythms of which I speak, et cetera, but I do indeed accelerate those coordinates that quicken Ruburt's healing processes. I remind you also to read the session of the day before yesterday whenever possible.

("It's me," Jane said after a pause.

("Thank you."

(4:21 P.M. Jane told me that yesterday Mary Jean, who had changed her dressings, had remarked upon how well the remaining bedsores are healing.

(4:45. Dorothy took Jane's temperature — 99.3. After she left Jane said, "See, instead of trusting my body I'm mad because my temperature is up again like that . . . "

(She didn't read over the session from the day before yesterday. I'd read it this morning at the house.)

FEBRUARY 8, 1984
4:24 P.M. WEDNESDAY

(I worked on Dreams this morning. The day was cold — about 22 — when I left for 330 at 12:30. I'd just turned Jane when the phone rang. It was someone called Danny Olson, from a small town in Missouri. He'd

sent some home-canned jars of fruits and vegetables at Christmas time; for the past year he'd also written a string of long letters signed "me," meaning I couldn't answer him to say thanks for the stuff. He'd done the same thing the Christmas before last, also.

(With an early letter he'd sent some photos of himself, and asked that they be returned. I did so. After that he quit adding his address to his letters. In the meantime I'd put his address downstairs in storage among many others, and hadn't taken the time to find it so I could answer — another of the mail hassles that crop up often.

(Today he told me that he'd found out Jane was in a hospital from someone he writes to in one of the Carolinas, so he called our area hospitals until he learned which one Jane was in. A simple procedure, and one I hope others don't pick up from him. I don't think he'll call back, though he may. We ended up in a rather acrimonious conversation in which I hoped I'd alienated him enough so he'd not bother my wife or me.

(He had lots of energy, which I could sense, but seemed to me to be contradictory in many ways, and I took him up on several points. He seemed to be so taken with the Seth material that he'd stopped reading everything else, he said, yet when I said he shouldn't do that, he said he read widely of other material — that sort of thing. I could tell he didn't understand that to be a creative leader one didn't follow others, but went out on his own. I knew as we talked that his flattering opinion of me, at least, was being shattered.

(I also ended up with familiar feelings — to the effect that it's impossible for Jane and I to ever live up to the fantasy pictures others may build up of us. I'm quite aware of the contradictions in our own behavior, too, as I told Jane after the half-hour conversation was over: We put our work out into the arena where it's available to anyone, and hope they'll pay attention to it. Then when they do, sometimes it turns us off.

(People's reactions are too varied, I've learned, for us to expect them to behave as we want them to. We must be afraid of that. But I wasn't pleased when Danny exclaimed, "Damn you, Rob, I want you to be as open with me as I am with you." He quite forgot that he shouldn't project his own feelings upon someone else who could be quite different. It made me wonder, as I drove home, what some people did <u>before</u> they came across the Seth material, or my own thinking. Who did they emulate then — how did they fill their lives, with what heroes and heroines? One thing is certain: They didn't

write books or develop an original philosophy of their own. They're quite content to leap upon the work of others, and to get mad at them because they — meaning Jane and me — don't react the way we're supposed to. They also forget, or don't understand, that being the way we are led to the creation of our work. If we were different people, the work would be different — or might not exist at all.

(I also thought the call might force a change in what I tell correspondents — but then, with the information about us that I furnished for Maude Cardwell's article in Reality Change, what would be the point of changing my response to the mail? We have few secrets left. It's apparent that the idea of people giving us money may have a negative side. But I can't say that I didn't know that.

(While I was on the phone an attendant brought us a letter from Sue Watkins. When I opened it I found a check for $1,000 made out by Helen Granger Park. "What's Miss Bowman sending us money for?" I asked Jane. I was momentarily confused — for my art teacher in high school in Sayre, Pennsylvania had been Helen Bowman, until she married later in life and became Helen Bowman Park. I'd always called her Miss Bowman. It turned out that the Helen Park who had written had read Maude's article in Reality Change, and sent the check to Sue to forward to us, to make sure we'd get it safely. That Helen Park lives in Austin, Texas. I may call her tonight, and Sue also. I told Jane I didn't know whether to attach any significance to the two Helen Parks or not. Money was involved with both people, since my Miss Bowman had lent me the money to go through art school in New York City. I had repaid her during my three years of military service during World War II.

(At about 8:30 last night, Jane said she'd had a very vivid "experience that was pretty real," in which for a few seconds she found herself cavorting in very clear and shallow water, feeling really free and enjoying herself greatly. She could see the pebbles beneath the water, and so forth. She slept well afterward. No temperatures were taken last night or this morning. She went to hydro around 10:00 A.M. and was back by 11:00 for a change.

(I should add that when I realized what the check for the $1,000 meant, I had strange initial feelings of guilt and of rebellion, of being now in a pretty vulnerable position in some strange way, even though the money would help with hospital charges. I also thought that although Helen Park said in her letter that there were no strings attached to the donation, still *there must be attachments in some form — that it was natural that there would be. The only way out of that situation that I thought of at the moment was that the giving of the gift, and the personal contact it meant, constituted the attachment. I now think there will be a variety of strings, in some form or another, and I don't mean to be cynical in making this observation.*

(4:00. A new lady took Jane's blood pressure, which was normal.

(4:05. A student took Jane's temperature — and it was up to 101.

(Jane began reading yesterday's session at 4:06, and did so-so. I helped her at times. I began sorting mail. When Jane was finally through she said she wanted to have a short session.)

Now: Another fond good afternoon.

("Good afternoon, Seth.")

I am speaking to reassure Ruburt his temperature is a sign of healing as the body throws off what it does not need.

Please do lovingly remind him *(Jane sneezed)* to trust his body and its processes. You both can be of great help to each other, when one or the other is worried or upset. Trust in the body automatically quickens all healing processes, and this session can put Ruburt's mind at rest. He has only to take my words <u>to heart</u>.

I do indeed also quicken those coordinates that so aid in those healing processes. I may or may not return, et cetera.

("Okay. Thank you."

(4:27 P.M. Jane seemed to feel better for having the session.

(I was just getting ready to leave for the day when Shawn Peterson visited. She is much better, and is going home tomorrow. She seems to have no heart trouble, but must wear a harness at home for 24 hours, to detect any heart abnormalities — a monitoring device that, I believe, somehow records electrical heart activity.

(I went food shopping at SuperDuper, ate a later supper than usual, and called Helen Park in Austin. She answered on the second ring, and we had a fine talk. She was surprised to hear from me, and I thanked her for her contribution. The connection was rather faint, but clear enough.

(Then I called Sue in Dundee to thank her for forwarding the check, and we talked for at least half an hour. The upshot of all of the activity is that I was late getting to the typewriter, and it's now 11:20 P.M. as I finish this session. Sleep well, Jane.)

FEBRUARY 9, 1984
4:16 P.M. THURSDAY

(Debbie Harris visited Jane last night. Jane didn't feel well while Debbie was there. An aide took Jane's temperature during the visit, and it was normal at 8:30. My wife's temperature was checked again around 11:00 P.M. and it was 101. The next time, after 3:00 A.M., it was 102. But after breakfast this morning Jane's temperature was down to 95.5. This was after she'd been given a pill to lower her temperature artificially. I do not know the name of the medication.

(Jane threw up mucous at least three times during the night. She did so while on her side, and couldn't get help when she pressed the call button. The staff people had to change all of her bedding in the middle of the night. Jane had to yell for help. She didn't get her lower teeth back afterward because they'd become messed up, she said.

("But Seth was right," she told me. "The body was trying to get rid of things — the mucous — that it didn't want." She sounded weaker than usual. Also during the night, her feet began to turn a mottled red color, reminiscent of the way they used to be when she'd had much swelling in them. Only now there was no swelling. The reddish clots looked like circulatory changes. I noticed them as soon as I entered 330. Jane said they didn't hurt, except that her right heel in back, and the inside of her right ankle, bothered her a little.

(This morning in hydro the sole of her right foot had stung in the same manner. She drank iced ginger ale all through the night, and decided to stop doing that today and switch to plain cool water. No one knows why the feet turned blotchy, although I think we do. Jane said she wouldn't have known it had happened if others hadn't told her.

(She had tried to call me twice last night, but her attempts had been made while I was talking to Helen Park and Sue Watkins, evidently. As she ate a light lunch I told her that our lawyer's assistant had called this morning, and that I stopped on my way down to pick up our tax forms. Incredibly, we owe money on taxes this year — $26,000 in medical expenses notwithstanding. I can't believe it, I told Jane. I'm in no hurry to pay the bill, now that we owe money instead of getting a refund. I'd hoped we'd break even at least.

(3:00. Jane put on the new lipstick I'd bought her a couple days ago, then looked in the mirror.

(3:25. She explained that her right foot was bothering her a bit. This is when she remembered having the same feelings in hydro this morning. I did some mail. The mail is threatening to get the best of me again.

(3:30. Jane began reading yesterday's session — and did very well. She was through by 3:45, zipping right through the session. "I'd say my eyes are better than the best they've been so far, Bob," she said — which really surprised me. For although she'd done well, I hadn't realized the extent of her improvement. Excellent.

(3:50. Staff began coming in to check Jane's vitals. I'd done her eyedrops an hour ago. Jane's blood pressure was normal, her temperature was 97, pulse good. She let me know when she was ready for the session. This is Day 8 of her new regime. Her voice wasn't as strong when she spoke for Seth, and in the beginning she'd utter a couple of words at a time and then pause noticeably. This effect largely disappeared as the session progressed.)

Now I bid you another fond good afternoon.

("Good afternoon, Seth.")

The high temperature was indeed flushing out the entire circulatory system.

It also helped rid the body of excess fluids — the phlegm, and so forth. *(Long pause.)* The fever itself broke in the middle of the night. Ruburt did well with his attitude — especially since the hospital help are so prone themselves to negative suggestion. The high temperature was also the result of stoking the body's furnace, so to speak — and, again, getting rid of any leftover "poisons." Period.

The changes in the feet show the varieties of the circulatory system — an unevenness of circulatory flow as the system clears itself out. The improvements in the eyes today were partially the result of those processes, as the sinuses and so forth were flushed out, relieving the eye muscles, and also ridding the areas of some excess fluid.

The process of clearing the body out began when Ruburt started his Day 1, but with the great frequency of negative hospital suggestions, and general false beliefs connected with fever, the beneficial aspects indeed had to be taken on faith as largely (underlined) they were *(louder).*

The improvements shown by the eyes, therefore, will be demonstrated by other portions of the body. I may or may not return, et cetera — but I do again quicken those coordinates that hasten physical healing.

("Thank you."

(4:26 P.M. I got Jane some cool water. "Gee, that was good — just cold enough . . . " She's sipped at liquids all day. Small wonder that her body needs them, after the fever, and so forth. For several days just past, her sinuses have been full, causing her to sniffle and blow her nose often.

(4:32. Jane was ready to be turned early — most unusual. She wanted her right foot massaged with Oil of Olay. By 5:00 I began my nap — but Jeff Karder and a nurse came in ten minutes later. Jeff wanted to run a blood test tomorrow — "I'm not sure of the cause of the fever. We'll watch those feet." I told him the blotchiness had lightened since I'd been there today. Jeff didn't want Jane to get dehydrated. He seemed generally satisfied, although he said Jane's urine was "too concentrated." I asked him to see if the latest brand of liquid vitamins my wife is taking could be switched back to her old one, for she dislikes the new ones intensely. He said he'd try.

(Jane didn't eat much supper. She asked me to take some of it home so no one could tell she hadn't eaten much, but I told her no one checks the trays; there are no names on them, for one thing. I did bring home some goodies for Billy and Mitzi. Mitzi is going through one of her affectionate stages these days.)

FEBRUARY 10, 1984
4:12 P.M. FRIDAY

(This is Day 9 of Jane's new regime.

(When I drove up Coleman Avenue to the hill house last night, I became aware of a strange vibrating, shuddering noise in the car's underbody. It was more prominent in reverse gear by far. I thought it might be ice, and could see nothing wrong.

(In the mail I found a letter from Maude Cardwell — and checks totaling about $1100, to my considerable surprise. I called the two people whose phone numbers were on their checks — one of them had donated $1000. Both were quite surprised to hear from me, and I felt good talking to them and saying thanks.

(This morning after breakfast I took the car to Ron Traver's service station — but the noise, which I'd heard when I started it up — had disappeared by then. Ron and I could find nothing wrong. In fact, the car seemed to run better than ever. He told me to keep in touch if anything went wrong. It was, I hoped, one less hassle.

(Jane's temperature went back up last night: 101 around 10:30 P.M., and the same at about 3:00 A.M. She had blood taken before breakfast — we have no results. A sample of urine was also collected. While Jane was eating a light lunch Lynn came in to start procedures for collecting another urine sample. It would be cultured — for what, we don't know.

(Then, while she was still eating, two lab technicians came in to take more blood from Jane — this was for a culture that would be grown for a week, they said. They said the doctor had ordered the tests — we thought they meant Jeff Karder.

(Jane was actually a little chilly at times, and asked me to turn up the heat, which was working fine. Her blotchy feet looked much improved, I saw as soon as I got there. She said Jeff had been in that morning, and saw that her feet were better, "Your temperature is up," he told her. "We'll have to watch that."

(Jane said she'd "slept terrifically last night." She wasn't worried about her temperature, especially after yesterday's session. She did her own thing about creating her own reality. She got down to hydro at a decent time this morning, and was back by 11:00. Georgia Cecce visited briefly this morning, looking good. No work for at least a couple of months. A nurse came in to tell us the staff is having its Valentine's Day party next Tuesday noon, and for me not to eat lunch at the house.

(3:09. Jane began reading yesterday's session. She had a lot of trouble — perhaps caused by the increase in temperature affecting the sinuses, which in turn affected the eyes again? She did so poorly that she quit reading at 3:13, as I worked on mail. When Judy brought ginger ale Jane decided to quit drinking carbonated liquids. She has taken in considerably more liquid, yesterday and today, and the urine looked much better as a result, staff said.

(Then came the blows. At 3:20 a nurse came in to put a heparin lock in Jane's right forearm. The lock is a stable opening in a vein for medication: Jane was to go on antibiotics. No sooner did we find that out than one of the two aides returned to take <u>more</u> *blood — they "want all they can get," Jane swore. The aide apologized. "I'd refuse to take the antibiotic," Jane said, "if it wouldn't raise such a fuss." I didn't know how to respond. It seemed that once again the body's natural defense mechanisms were being interfered with, according to Seth — but then, why were we here to begin with? I didn't want to think about it. "I trust my body a hell of a lot more*

than I do that antibiotic," Jane said. Judy came in and told us Jeff hadn't ordered the antibiotic — his wife, Olivia, who is also a doctor, had.

(3:36. After the nurse had inserted the heparin lock, Jane went back to reading the session. She did considerably better as we waited for the antibiotic. I felt discouraged. Her head was stuffy again.

(3:50. Judy came in to take the urine sample. It's to be cultured like the last blood sample. Jane finished the session at 3:55. She had a smoke. "Then if nobody comes in, I'll start the session anyway. I suppose they'll want to take my temperature and blood pressure all over again, too.")

Now —

(4:12. No sooner had Jane spoken Seth's greeting than a student nurse came in to take her temperature, at 101.2. "Shit," Jane said. Dorothy came in to take her blood pressure and pulse. We might as well start over," Jane said after they'd left by 4:18.)

Now: I bid you again a most fond good afternoon.

("Good afternoon, Seth.")

— and I am speaking simply to reassure you both.

The body is indeed clearing itself out, stoking its furnaces — an idea quite foreign to the medical establishment.

Their answer, of course, is antibiotics. As long as Ruburt's attitude is good the antibiotics will do no harm, and will provide an explanation as the conditions are cleared. It is, of course, unfortunate that Ruburt <u>is in</u> that environment, but these are definitely indications of the body's own healing processes. It will help you both to reread the passages for Day 1 or Day 2, so that you can remind yourselves of those vital issues.

I have again adjusted those coordinates that quicken the healing processes. Remember that the body is a natural self-healer.

Now I may or may not return, et cetera — but whether or not I do, I am in my fashion "in the vicinity."

("Thank you.")

(4:38. Jane was ready for me to turn her on her side by then. By 4:53 I'd just finished massaging her with Oil of Olay when Linda, the RN, came in with the antibiotic. She said it was "a broad spectrum drug" that could kill many germs. Gentamicin 60 mg. in 50 ml NS. She said it would take Jane perhaps half an hour to take it all in, and that afterward Jane would be given a small amount of heparin, which would keep the lock open for

future doses. Jane is to get the drug every eight hours. She swore again. "But you've got a fever," Linda said gently. She agreed that some people are allergic to the medication — "there are always side effects."

(5:05. The tray for supper came as I started my nap. When I got up at 5:40 Jane had absorbed all the antibiotic. Linda came in just as I was on my feet, and helped me haul Jane toward the head of the bed after I'd turned her on her back. Jane showed no reactions to the drug.

(Jane called at about 9:20, with Carla's help. Her temperature had been taken again after I left — 100.1, or something like that — she said it was down "a few points" from earlier in the day. She sounded good.)

FEBRUARY 11, 1984
4:23 P.M. SATURDAY

(The day was very warm — 45 — as I left for 330. The car worked fine. Jane was upset when I got there — although her blotchy feet looked much better. The dark reddish patches are much less extensive. She didn't go to hydro this morning — with her fever, Jeff didn't want her to go. She hadn't slept well last night, and staff had been too busy to help her turn often enough. Yet Jane doesn't know whether she received a dose of the antibiotic during the night while she may have slept.

(Last night, she estimated, her temperature had been 101 at 8:00, 101 at 11:00, and 101 at 3:00 A.M. At breakfast time it had been 99.3. After lunch it was 102.1. "Not bad," the male aide who took it said.

(I had trouble getting the above information from Jane after lunch, because she seemed on the verge of dozing off several times. She said she got mad at Jeff and Judy this morning because of their negative beliefs. Jeff said maybe the splotches on her feet were infected, and Judy said the drainage from the small ulcer on each hip had increased. Jane finally told them to cut it out. Jeff said he'd like to know where the fever came from.

(2:45. Jane remembered to tell me that last night two students had watched as an aide checked her catheter and Foley. This in turn reminded her that Jeff had also said this morning that maybe she had an infection from the catheter, "since people always do." She'd heard nurses say the same thing.

(3:10. Judy said the cranberry juice mixture Jane is taking helps keep her urine acid rather than alkaline — why, we don't know.

(3:37. Lipstick and mirror.

(3:45. Carla took Jane's temperature. 102.4 — the highest yet. Jane swore again. She was worried about Jeff's reaction more than the temperature. She's been drinking a lot of juice.

(3:50. Jane started reading yesterday's session while I did mail. She didn't do well at all. Five minutes later Leanne came in to give her some Ascripton, or aspirin, in ice cream, for the fever. Then she hooked Jane up to a new bag of Gentamicin 40 mg., the antibiotic. It should be absorbed in half an hour, as usual. Jane went back to reading the session — still not good.

(4:15. I finished reading yesterday's session to Jane.)

I bid you another fond good afternoon.

("Good afternoon, Seth.")

— and I can really only restate yesterday's session.

(Long pause.) Ruburt is in no danger. *(Pause.)* We can use the situation, however, as an educational tool, so that he does indeed rise victoriously from these unfortunate medical beliefs.

Once again, it is perfectly natural for each cell in the body, for each organ and each portion of the body to heal itself, and in the same terms it is really "unnatural" <u>not</u> to trust the body, rather than looking at it with suspicion. In any case —

(4:27. Leanne swept in. The antibiotic was all taken in by Jane; I'd seen it still dripping a few minutes ago. She left to get the heparin to inject into the lock on Jane's wrist.)

— In any case, it is of course important for Ruburt to keep his mind as relieved as possible. That alone relaxes all other parts of the body, and lets the healing processes operate more easily and efficiently.

Now I may or may not return, but I will indeed keep Ruburt in the eye of my attention, and you also.

("Okay. Thank you.")

(4:33 P.M. I read the session to Jane. She had a smoke. It wasn't until I was home tonight that I realized that after massaging her I'd forgotten to exercise her right leg as she lay on her side. I'm up to moving it back and forth 250 times, and it does better and better.

(Carla and a student and Dorothy came in to turn Jane before I could read her the prayer, so I left at 7:00.

(I couldn't help noticing as I walked down the hall on my way out, how busy all the patient rooms were, the cacophony of sounds, the numerous

visitors, patients and nurses and aides. I might as well be downtown on a
busy street, I thought. The hall was a community in itself, accepted by all.)

FEBRUARY 12, 1984
4:28 P.M. SUNDAY

(When Jane called last night she said her temperature had dropped to
99.7 — breaking the 100-degree barrier. Today was warm again — 42
degrees — when I left for 330. Jane's feet looked much better, She didn't go
to hydro. She said that after I left last night she resolved to do what Seth had
said, no matter what. Then Debbie Harris had visited. After that, Leanne
said my wife's urine looked much better than it has been. Jane has been
drinking considerably more.

(Jane slept very well, and at 5:30 A.M. her temperature was 98.

(She had blood taken again before breakfast, from her left foot. More
was taken after breakfast. Her temperature at 11:00 A.M. was 97.8. I
found that Jane's menu for tomorrow was marked "Calorie Count" for each
meal. This means I won't get to save them, since I have to estimate how
much of each food she eats so dietary can figure the calories involved. Jane
didn't eat a lot of lunch.

(2:15. She tried to read yesterday's session, but couldn't at all. She laid
it aside as Judy came in to hook her up to another medicine bag. There was
some confusion, since Judy told us it was the same medication — Gentam-
icin — that she'd been getting, only it was in 100 cc's of liquid instead of
50. Yet after she left I discovered a different name on the plastic bag:
(Septra) Bactrim.

(2:45. Jane tried again to read the session, but couldn't. At 3:10 I
started to read it to her when Mary Jean came in to check the flow of the
antibiotic. It turned out Jane was being given a second medication without
being told. This was an antibiotic for a bladder infection. Mary Jean said
Jeff must have seen something on the report of her urinalysis this morning,
and ordered the Bactrim, which is quite powerful. Jane was mad. "I want
to make a formal protest for the record," she told Mary Jean, "that I wasn't
notified about this." Mary Jean said she'd relay it to the head nurse —
where I suppose it'll die. It takes an hour for this second dose to flow into
Jane's body, compared to the one-half hour for the Gentamicin.

(3:20. I read yesterday's session to Jane, and started mail.

(3:30. Carla took Jane's temperature — it was up again to 101.2. Judy came in to check the flow, and said Jane was to get the Bactrim every six hours, or four times a day. With the Gentamicin every eight hours, this makes seven medications Jane gets every 24 hours. Jane has let everyone know she's pissed off. What's happened? "It would be nice to know," I said when she expressed concern, and she replied that she was doing all she could. I had the feeling of being caught in a whirlpool of the medical profession's making, and being drawn in deeper instead of being able to extricate oneself. I wondered why the body couldn't heal itself except through fevers and infections. "Well, that's it, then," I said, and went back to the mail until Jane said she was ready for a session.)

Now, I wish you another most fond good afternoon.

("Good afternoon, Seth.")

The bacteria is naturally found in every bladder — but when you <u>collect it or isolate it</u>, the doctors then call it infected.

I repeat, Ruburt is in no danger, but I would also like some of the late sessions reviewed as reinforcement. Once more I adjust those coordinates that quicken Ruburt's healing powers, and both of you rest in my <u>attention</u>.

It is, again, vital that you trust the body, particularity in the light of the medical profession's <u>suspicions</u> of the body's natural processes.

I may or may not return, et cetera, and a fond early good evening.

("Thank you."

(4:32 P.M. I read the session to Jane. After I'd turned her on her side at 4:40, Leanne came in to hook up Jane to her next dose of Gentamicin.

(I was getting ready to leave at 6:50, after turning and feeding Jane, and so forth, when I discovered I couldn't find my glasses. I don't wear them too much any more, but thought I'd had them on at least once during the afternoon. Otherwise, I'd left them home — something I've never done before. I finally found the glasses in the bathroom. After reading the prayer with Jane, I left at 7:25. It was still warm and pleasant. There was fog on the way up Coleman Avenue toward the hill house.

(Before leaving I rubbed the sole of Jane's right foot, which has been itching a lot. As I did so her left foot moved in rhythm — and she said she's noticed more movement in it lately. But she hasn't done any motions of note in a long time now.)

FEBRUARY 13, 1984
MONDAY

(Day 12 of Jane's new regime.

(Jane called last night.

(I made two useless trips today. Because it's a holiday, I guess, the bank was closed, so I couldn't pay the IRS.

(My dentist wasn't there even though I had an appointment for today that had been given me three or four months ago. I left at 1:20 , after leaving a note on his desk at the office.

(I got to 330 late. Jane was on her side. Suzanne helped me hoist her up on the bed. She ate a little better than yesterday. I marked the menu for calorie count.

(Jeff was in — said results of all of the tests showed a blood infection. That there's no doubt they can clear it up. They're trying out two medications — Gentamicin and Bactrim — to see which will do the job best. [Though how they can know is beyond me.]

(Peggy Gallagher visited during lunch. After lunch I read yesterday's session to Jane, which she couldn't do.

(Lipstick and mirror. Mail. Letter from Danny Olson. Threw it away as insulting.

(4:00 — Dana. Blood pressure and pulse.

(4:25 — Carla. Temperature 98.7. Medication still dripping.

(4:35 — I pressed the button for aide. Medicine done.

(4:50–5:15 — Turn, massage, tray.

(5:15–5:45 — Nap.

(6:00 — Supper.

(6:20 — Cigarette. Dessert. Teeth.

(7:05 — Cigarette. TV.

(7:13 — Prayer.

(7:20 — Leave.)

FEBRUARY 14, 1984
4:32 P.M. TUESDAY

(This is Day 13 of Jane's new campaign.

(Jane called last night. The day was again very warm — over 50 — when I left for 330. The snow and ice are gone. I stopped at the bank to buy a check for the IRS and money orders to pay bills. This morning I'd written

two letters to people who had sent us donations, I told Jane. I plan to open the account for those checks later this week.

(I also told Jane that in a batch of fan mail that had been temporarily lost, I found a note from my dentist's secretary and nurse, Babs, changing the date of my appointment from Feb. 13 to the 23rd. I'd sat alone in the office yesterday, the date of my original appointment, with no one ever showing up. I wrote the dentist a note and left it on his desk.

(I do have a thing going with dentists. I told Jane that if she'd had her regular session yesterday in 330, so that I was busy typing it last night, I wouldn't have found Babs's note, because I wouldn't have had the extra time after supper to go through fan mail, clean out the paper bag I carry to the hospital each day, and so on. So, why did she not have a session yesterday, the day of my dental appointment? It's the first one Jane has missed in weeks, literally.

(Today I called Babs from the hospital and verified the new appointment. This experience follows, of course, the one I had for my last appointment, and which is on record — when I chipped a tooth and went to my dentist's office the same day to see if he could fix it — and discovered that I had an appointment I'd forgotten about for that very same time on that same day. When I walked in Babs thought I was keeping that appointment . . .

(Jane went to hydro this morning. Her temperature is in the normal range, and her menu is no longer marked for calorie count. She did not see Jeff this morning. She is still on the two antibiotics, Gentamicin and Bactrim. Her blotchy feet are even more improved — remarkably so, I told her. [She can't see them.]

(Jane didn't eat a whole lot of lunch. Afterward I gave her a Valentine's Day card, and a box of candy shaped like a heart. I hadn't eaten lunch today because a nurse had said to eat there at 330, since staff was having a party. No one showed up with food for me, though, so I ate what Jane didn't want off the tray — half a roast-beef sandwich, with mustard. Very good.

(Since she had no session from yesterday to read, Jane tried to read the session for February 1 — the one that led to her Day 1, 2, 3 program. She couldn't manage it, though, so I read it to her: "Health is simplicity itself." An excellent session. Then I read her the session for February 5 — equally good. They helped her. Jane seldom asks to read past sessions — behavior that is still protective, I think, and has been for many years. This, even though Seth has lately again suggested she reread certain material. To me this situation has always been a clear demonstration that one part of herself

*is still in opposition to another part, and that the fearful self is still domi-
nant though perhaps to a somewhat lesser degree these days, for we have
made progress.*

*(Jane's temperature was normal — 98.3, at 3:45. Frank Longwell vis-
ited. I tried to do some mail, but didn't get far. Because of the warm weather,
the window of 330 was open a foot, and the heat was off. Once again, when
Jane had the session I became aware of traffic noise from Market Street.)*

Now: another fond good evening.

("Good evening, Seth.")

Ruburt needed to hear the precise material that you read to him
today.

(Long pause.) The ideas are so very beneficial that it is too bad
you cannot have some kind of schedule that includes reading that
material more often.

("He seldom asks me to read it to him.")

That is simply because everything is now scheduled in a fashion,
with the time available. That material, however, is "excellent medicine," and can indeed be life-saving *(intently)*. It is indeed unfortunate
that those beliefs that show themselves so simply and effectively in
nature seem so mysterious to the usual line of official consciousness.

The official line does have its role, of course — but once again,
by itself it must remain isolated from the deep, creative, healing
functions of body consciousness. The official line of consciousness is
really the "worrier," because it recognizes that it can only go so far,
and usually it is not educated enough to realize <u>it is itself</u> sustained
and supported — and now I bid you a fond good afternoon, and I
do indeed adjust those coordinates that do quicken Ruburt's healing
processes.

(To me:) <u>You</u> are in my attention also, of course, and these late
sessions should also help you tone up your own body, and revive feelings of exuberance and understanding.

("Can I ask you a question?")

You may.

*("Just what do you mean when you say that you "adjust those coordi-
nates that quicken Ruburt's healing processes?"*

(Slowly at 4:44.) Give us a moment . . . When I am "present," this
also places Ruburt within a different kind of framework in relation

to himself, in which most negativity simply takes no hold. It is as if you set up a small healing station, or platform and from that vantage point the body is then able to use its healing abilities far more effectively than usual.

Now I may or may not return, et cetera . . .

("It's me," Jane said.

(4:47 P.M. Jane only vaguely remembered Seth's answer to my question. I'd thought of asking it before, and should have. "I was going to ask another one, but you came out of it too quickly," I said. I read the session to her. Then I explained that my next question was simply whether she could place herself in that state with Seth present, even though I wasn't there and Seth didn't speak. "If you can do it once a day, why not twice — or more?" I asked. "Make believe I'm there in the bathroom, just out of sight, or out in the hall." I hoped this might help accelerate her healing even more. Jane agreed to try it.

("I can't believe that we can't find ten minutes a day to go over that session for February 1," I said, "even if we have to give up watching some TV. Especially when we've seen the program before." We can hardly let a "schedule" interfere with such important activity. And once again I felt that it was up to me to take the initiative in such matters.

(Jane said I could ask Seth my second question tomorrow.)

FEBRUARY 15, 1984
4:32 P.M. WEDNESDAY

(There was some water in the cellar last night from the steady downpour of yesterday. I mopped some of it before the old mop went to pieces, so I must buy a new one. It rained part of the night, and a bit more this morning. It was very warm again — 42 degrees — as I left for 330.

(Jane had more blood taken this morning, during breakfast. She slept well and went to hydro. Her temperature is normal, and she's down to the one antibiotic, Bactrim. She ate a fair lunch. Rita brought in some potassium and vitamin C that Jeff wants my wife to take, evidently as the result of a test. Rita crushed it and Jane tried it with Hawaiian Punch, which she didn't like.

(After her lunch I read to Jane the same two sessions I'd read her yesterday — for February 1 and 5. I told her that my question for Seth is, why

did the fever business start after her initiation of Day 1 of her new program?
There must be many connections.

(Jane tried to read yesterday's session, but couldn't do it very well, so she
laid it aside for a smoke. She showed how she had considerably more motion
in her entire left arm and hand, especially at the elbow. She's mentioned
changes in the hands several times lately. Then she showed how she also
had more motion in the right hand and forearm. Her feet, both of them, also
moved, and felt freer, she said. The splotches on her feet are again much
improved. It appears that her body generally is showing signs of more
changes, as though it's getting ready for them. Seth has forecast this. Jane
hasn't moved much at all for a long time. I read her yesterday's session.

(It was 4:20 before either of us realized it. I tried doing mail, without
getting anywhere. At 4:30 I rang for an aide, since the medicine bag was
empty on its pole at the head of Jane's bed. As we waited, Jane decided to go
ahead with the session. "I'll try to keep my voice down," she said. The
window had just been closed: I'd been bothered by traffic noise as I tried to
read to her. Her Seth voice was indeed on the quiet side.)

Now I bid you another most fond good afternoon.

("Good afternoon, Seth.")

There are <u>styles</u> of thinking, just as there are various styles of dress.

The official line of consciousness is a certain mental stance, a
kind of convention. *(Long pause.)* When you were a child you
thought in a freer fashion, but little by little you were educated to use
words in a certain way. You discovered that your needs were met
more quickly, and you received approval more often, when you
thought and spoke in that particular manner. Finally it seemed to be
the only —

(4:35. Rita came in to do something — what I don't recall, since I
didn't note it down. I read what she'd given to Jane. Resume at 4:39.)

— natural mode of operation. Your entire civilization is built
around that kind of inner framework. The way of thinking becomes
so automatic as to be mentally invisible. With creative people, however, there are always intrusions, hints or clues from ways of thinking
that certainly appear foreign, and creative people use those hints
and clues to construct an art, a musical composition or whatever.
They sense a surge of power beneath.

You and Ruburt have had the feeling many times — but what
we are trying to do is change over completely from one mode of

operation to another, and to construct, say, new inner blocks of meaning that will give rise to the next era.

(Long pause at 4:44.) What you are involved in then is really, of course, a completely new educational procedure, so that you are at least able to distinguish one style of thought from another, and therefore be freer to make choices.

I did want to give you this material, and in a fashion —

(4:48. Carla came in with the supper tray, and we told her about the medicine bag being empty. I'd turned off the nurse's call light early in the session, hoping we wouldn't be interrupted.)

— this will help you understand about the platform that Ruburt imagines, and the inner procedure required for a session without a session.

Now I may or may not return, et cetera — and once again I do indeed adjust those coordinates that quicken the healing processes.

("Thank you."

(4:50 P.M. Jane said Seth "could have gone on and on." I regretted the lost opportunity. She said she'd tried to reach the platform Seth had described in the last session, and as I'd suggested she try to do, but with limited success. Yet she'd achieved <u>something</u>, so it was worth keeping on with for a while, I said.

(I also reminded Jane that we hadn't gotten an answer from Seth to my question about why all the fever business started right after Jane had put her Day 1, 2, 3 program into effect. She said we'd try again tomorrow. I pressed the call button again — and Leanne came right in to unhook my wife, and give her a shot of heparin in her heparin lock, to keep it open for the next IV.

(Jane had another excellent episode of increased motions in both arms and hands as I was getting ready to leave, and in her feet also. I encouraged her to keep it up even if she was alone, and if she called tonight, to give me a progress report. I love you, Jane.)

FEBRUARY 16, 1984
4:20 P.M. THURSDAY

(Jane didn't call last night to give me a progress report on the new motions she was enjoying when I left yesterday. Those motions are still mostly with her, as she demonstrated today. She slept very well last night.

(Jane had some other excellent news. The therapist in hydro this morning, who'd examined her last week, literally gasped when she examined the ulcer on each thigh: "I don't believe this." She told Jane the ulcers had diminished in size by at least half — and she went to get a measuring device like a micrometer to check the shrinkage. Yet another nurse had said the other day that the drainage had worsened, a statement Jane had taken exception to, as had I.

(Jane's temperature has been in the normal range. No blood was taken this morning. She ate a fair lunch.

(3:30. I read yesterday's session to Jane, after she couldn't do it. My throat was hoarse. I'd started coughing after eating half of one of the candies I'd bought Jane for Valentine's Day. I had trouble reading.

(3:45. Jeff Karder came in. He wants to keep her on the Bactrim for a couple more days. Jane had had a blood infection, now clearing up okay. Jeff wants her on the potassium and vitamin C to keep her urine on the acid side, since this inhibits bacterial growth.

(3:55. Jane's temperature was 98.9. I read her the sessions for February 1, 6, and 7. She said her eyes do bother her. They're very red. I suggested she have a session soon if she was going to, regardless of whether her blood pressure still had to be taken. Once again the window was open and the curtains closed because of the very bright sun. This is Day 15 of her new campaign, and I'd already reminded her of the question we wanted Seth to answer: Why had this fever and infection business erupted after Day 1?

(Jane's Seth voice was again on the quiet side, her delivery quite slow at times.)

Now — I bid you another fond good afternoon.

("Good afternoon, Seth.")

Ruburt began the new program with a sense of determination and faith.

That determination and that faith also let him see *(long pause)* how far from healthy, normal behavior he had come. Earlier, he had been afraid to realize that distance. This did arouse still more faith and determination, but he was then faced with that realization he had not encountered earlier, and he saw how long it had been since he <u>had</u> enjoyed anything like normal mobility.

Those feelings did frighten him, and led to several bouts of blueness. Those bouts, however, helped rid him of buried feelings, and his determination did indeed give the body's immune system a greater thrust. The improvements noted yesterday and today show the body's abilities, and demonstrate its own intent toward greater movement and flexibility.

(Pause at 4:27.) In the same way, Ruburt encountered the hospital surroundings from another viewpoint, seeing how apart that environment was from a normal situation. That (underlined) frightened him also.

Through all of this, however, the body is responding, and it is indeed quickening the healing processes. It is an excellent idea, again, that you are reviewing those sessions.

Now I may or may not return, et cetera.

("Can I ask you a question?"

(There was a long pause. Jane hesitated, and I felt that I'd caught her half out of trance. She later confirmed this — but she went back into trance and answered.)

You may.

(I described my dream of the other day, which I'd already told Jane about: I'd been sitting on our couch with Jane and our neighbor, Joe Bumbalo. Joe was living with us; the three of us were eating supper as we watched a program on TV. Margaret, Joe's wife, wasn't in the dream. Briefly, at the time of the dream, I'd wondered if it hinted at something happening to either of them — Joe or Margaret, that is.)

Joe has recovered from a serious heart condition, of course — and if you will excuse me, that was the heart of the matter. Here you saw Jane, or Ruburt, as well-recovered as was Joe. It was as if you had taken in your neighbor Joe to serve as a case in point. Joe also survived the hospital environment.

("Thank you."

(4:33 P.M. "That makes that a pretty good little dream, then," I told Jane, for in the dream she, too, had been fully recovered. Jane did remember my telling her about the dream earlier this week. Then she said, her voice breaking, "It wasn't until the other day that I really realized — felt — just how far I'd strayed from normal motion, or life, after all this time. Now I want to get back to it so bad. I just have to use it, instead of letting it — life — use me . . ."

(Whereupon I reminded her that she didn't have to use anything, as per the session for February 1 that I'd read her today. She only had to get out of

the way of her own body's natural ability to heal itself. I was amazed at the way her body was still trying to right itself after all of these years. How cruel we could be to ourselves, I thought, and this reminded me of my old questions about why the body consciousness itself didn't just rebel at times and refuse to let itself be so beaten down by erroneous beliefs. Seth has said a little about this in response to a question of mine, but we need much more. Nor has he ever referred to my question about whatever reincarnational influences might be operating with Jane.

(I told Jane that now that the fever business was on the way out, I expected to see her body continue its improvements, as obviously it was trying to do. Her new motions were a good sign of the body's incredible strivings to express itself.

(Before I turned her on her side, and then took a nap, I tried without success to locate my description of the dream with Jane and Joe in a previous recent session. No luck. I finally had to believe that in spite of my good intentions I'd literally forgotten to type it up. Nor had I written it up in my notes for the one day recently when Jane didn't have a session — the 13th, I found out when I got home.

(I read this session to Jane after supper. She then admitted that she'd become frightened today because she'd been coughing up mucous occasionally. And she became even more frightened after the session. I was frightened by her reactions — appalled that after all we were trying to do, she still reacted to something beneficial — the coughing — as something to be scared of. The implications took my breath away, and I became depressed with thoughts that I didn't see how she was ever going to make it, ever going to break that cycle of fearful response to the world and her place in it, her fear of being attacked, of life itself. I wondered what we'd been trying to do all of this time.

("Can I say something?" I asked. "I don't understand how you can be so frightened of a beneficial thing like the coughing, yet put up with the inability to walk all these years. The contradictions are beyond me. I don't care what Seth says about the extremes of poverty, say, I think your behavior is extreme. Within the context of our society, it's extreme . . . "

(Now for the little dream I had while napping. I told Jane about it while she ate supper. I dreamed that I received a call from a clerk at the bank. The girl told me that one of the checks I'd deposited for Jane's hospital fund wasn't for $1000, as we'd both thought — but was instead for $1 million.

I was totally surprised at the news. "Are you sure?" I asked. The clerk said she was, that we'd miscounted the zeroes before. "Hold that check," I said to her. "I'll be down there in 20 minutes."

(I told Jane I didn't expect that anybody was going to give us a million, but I did think it was a dream that meant well for our future . . .)

FEBRUARY 17, 1984
4:05 P.M. FRIDAY

(This is Day 16 of Jane's new campaign.

(She didn't call last night. A nurse called for her this morning, though — seems Jane was out of cigarette lighters, and wanted me to bring some to 330. We spoke briefly.

(I worked on answering Christmas cards for half an hour after breakfast, and will have to adopt some sort of system like that to get caught up on the fan mail. Although we are more than glad to get those precious letters — where would we be if people didn't care about what we're trying to do? — still answering them takes time away from Dreams.

(Jane went to hydro this morning, and did okay. She still has the new motion in her arms and hands. She also said there's a new kind of motion, "like a ball bearing," in her left foot at the ankle, even though it may not look like a different movement. She's still on the Bactrim. Eyes still quite red. She tried to read yesterday's session, but couldn't do it. I read it to her at 2:45, after she'd finished a good lunch.

(3:00. After I'd finished the session, especially the last portion and my notes about my own reactions, which upset Jane, she told me that yesterday she'd actually been very blue the last hour I was there. She'd also been very afraid that the coughing up of mucous meant she was getting pneumonia — something she hadn't told me. She'd picked up the suggestion from something a nurse had said that morning. I said it wasn't what others said so much, as her <u>reaction</u> to what they said. I'd hoped we were past that stage. I said I'd expressed myself plainly in the session yesterday so she'd know how I felt.

(Jane didn't comment today on my reference to any possible reincarnational connections with her symptoms. And the pneumonia idea was, I said, another example of an extreme. Yet Jane said that after I'd left last night her blueness had lifted almost magically, and she'd felt good and slept

well. I said that maybe by now she'd learned how to cut the blue periods shorter — a sign that we were learning something after all.

("I just had an ugly thought," I said. "That this concentration upon trying to avoid negative suggestions makes you even more sensitive to them." Jane said she'd had the same thought at times.

(She's been coughing a lot and blowing her nose heavily since I got to 330 today. The room had no heat — it wasn't coming through the register for some reason.

(3:08. Jane had a smoke while I read her the session for February 1, after she'd put on lipstick and looked in the mirror. Then I read her several other good and later sessions. Next, I described my vivid dream of last night: Jane and I were still driving our old yellow Cadillac convertible. She was walking normally. While we were in a local bar, two youths stole the car, which was parked nearby, and went for a joyride. I went outside to get the car to take Jane home, and found it gone. I called the police. I also found a young man in the bar who knew the two who had taken the car, but he was afraid to tell me who they were. Eventually the police found the car, abandoned some distance away, but unharmed. I was very angry about the whole thing and vowed to find out who had taken it. I told Jane the dream almost sounded like an exercise in exploring a probable reality.

(3:47. Temperature 99.1. Jane said that was the highest it's been since it started going down in recent days. She was getting a bit chilly. I suggested she have a session if she was going to, then I could have staff call a maintenance man about the heat. Jane was still coughing and blowing at times. I looked at mail but didn't accomplish anything.)

Now: I bid you another most fond good afternoon.

("Good afternoon, Seth.")

I wanted to remind Ruburt of some material given several times in the past.

When an idea for a book or a poem comes to him, he "tunes into it" immediately. It never occurs to him to wonder how many vowels or syllables, words and sentences, paragraphs or pages might be involved. He takes it for granted that his intent will be executed —

(Leanne came in with a new bag of Bactrim. We asked her to call maintenance about heat. I read to Jane what she'd given so far.

(4:11.) That is the natural, creative way to function, and it has provided him with many excellent books and poetry. When he is

writing he does not think in terms of impediments. What impediments there may be, he brushes aside.

Now his health can be handled in the same fashion, without wondering how many nerves or muscles or stages must be activated, without worrying about how much time will be involved. In a fashion the body is a living book, being produced in every moment.

Again, it may seem too simple — but by applying the same methods to the body, the body's health <u>will be written</u> with health and vitality, using blood and corpuscles, joints and ligaments and so forth instead of syllables, consonants, words and sentences.

I may or may not return, again according to those rhythms of which I speak — but know that I am present and approachable.

("Can I ask a question?")

You may.

("What do you think of my dream yesterday afternoon, about our receiving the million dollars?")

You both interpreted it correctly. It simply meant that far more benefits are being <u>added to your account</u> than you imagine — meaning abundance, and not just in financial terms alone.

("Yes. How about my dream of last night — about the old Cadillac being stolen?")

Take a break, and we will continue.

(4:18. Jane had a cigarette while I read her the account of my dream that I'd just written for my daily notes, since she didn't remember the dream all that well.

(4:24.) Now: The dream of the car represents beliefs that you had when you had the car. In a manner of speaking, those beliefs "took you for a joyride" — therefore the joys represented portions of yourself. In the dream you are quite angry simply because those beliefs <u>did</u>, in a fashion, take the vehicle of your life out of your own hands, since you did not recognize those beliefs as your own in the past. At the end, the car or the vehicle <u>is</u> (underlined) returned to you, and the dream shows that you understand, now, the process that the dream outlined.

("It's me," Jane said.

("Thank you," I said to the departed Seth.)

(4.28 P.M. I told Jane that Seth's analysis of the car dream was excellent. From its position atop the pole at the head of Jane's bed, the Bactrim still drips into the plastic tube, on its way into Jane's right arm. I felt chilly, but she didn't want anything over her yet. When I took my nap, she said a maintenance man came in and adjusted the thermostat, saying it would give us some heat, but it did no good. The problem still wasn't solved as I read the session to Jane after supper, nor was it solved by the time I left at 7:10.

(Jane can't know it yet, but in the mail tonight was another letter from Maude Cardwell, containing some $620 in checks for her hospital fund. I don't equate this figure with my dream. I think, and as Seth agreed, that the dream means far more than sums of money received alone. It's a very encouraging dream, and I'm very pleased to have had it. Not that the checks aren't welcome! Sleep well, Jane. I love you.)

FEBRUARY 18, 1984
SATURDAY

(Day 17

(Jane called me last night — forgot to tell me Debbie Harris visited.

(Day warm — 50.

(Finished typing Chapter 5 of Dreams *this morning.*

(Still on Bactrim. Heat working, but turned off. Window wide open. Jane ate fair lunch. Feet still better. Lipstick and mirror.

(2:49 — Jane asked to see yesterday's session, but didn't read it — I did. She's coughing a lot.

(3:14 — Read Jane letters sent by Maude Cardwell.

(4:00 — Bactrim still dripping.

(4:10 — Lynn, temperature — 98.

(4:45 — Turn. Massage.

(5:10–5:40 — Nap. Jane off Bactrim.

(6:00 — Supper.

(6:20 — Cigarette, Dessert. More coughing and blowing. I asked if she had a cold — a poor suggestion — but instead of denying it, Jane said she didn't know.

(6:45 — Cigarette, TV.

(7:00 — Prayer.

(7:05 — Leave. Shopping at Acme Supermarket.

FEBRUARY 19, 1984
4:23 P.M. SUNDAY

(Jane called last night. She said she'd dozed through most of her evening TV programs — something she hardly ever does. The day was again warm — 44 degrees — when I went to 330. She had the heat off in her room. Her coughing is better today. She said her "eyes are terrible," though the redness is largely gone. Her feet look much better again. She's still on the Bactrim, and her temperature has been normal.

(My suspicion is that her cold-and-other symptoms mean that we've set up some resistance on the part of her psyche since she initiated the Day 1 program on February 2. Today is Day 18 of the program. My feeling is that we ought to minimize the health aspects of the sessions for a while.

(Jane ate a better lunch than she did yesterday. She had a smoke afterward and I got out mail to answer. Jane put on lipstick and looked in the mirror.

(She did more coughing and blowing as the time passed. Carla took her temperature — 98.8. Five minutes later Penny hooked her up to another dose of antibiotic. I did mail until Jane had the session. By then most of the drug had been absorbed, but I didn't call anybody. Jane was coughing enough so that she remarked that she hoped she could get through the session. The window was closed by now and the heat was on. It had turned very windy, and I thought it might mean another cold spell.)

Now: I bid you another fond good afternoon.

("Good afternoon, Seth.")

The material given for Day 1 should definitely be reviewed today.

The body has many ways of accelerating its own defenses *(cough)*. The so-called common cold is a case in point. I will speak more about that kind of mechanism at another time. The body is now, then, going full steam ahead, so to speak. The head, neck, and shoulders are being worked on to further strengthen the arms and fingers — hence the transient condition of the eyes.

I am, in fact, announcing myself only to let you know that I am indeed present and approachable, and also that I am making those adjustments that quicken the healing processes. Ruburt is in no danger *(pause)* of blindness, or any other dangerous condition. A fond early evening.

(4:28 P.M. "I suppose that means I'm to read you the session for February 1 again," I said. She agreed. "I thought that session was the one that's

resulted in all the upsets since then," I added. I noted that it was now conceded by both Jane and Seth that she did have a cold, as I'd asked her yesterday.

("Remember what I used to say years ago?" I suddenly asked. "It came out of the private material back then — that when things got worse it meant they were getting better." Jane said she'd thought of that this morning. I'd forgotten all about the remark for some time, meaning years.

(When I read this session to her, I was struck again by Seth's use of the word "blindness," and Jane admitted that she'd been worrying about losing her sight because of her eye difficulty. I laughed, but out of incredulity, not humor, for the other day she'd feared she was getting pneumonia. Once more, I wondered when that cycle of fearful response would end. "Spare me," I said, only half joking. I'd been surprised today when Seth had said that things were going ahead full steam.

(Just before supper I told Jane about my dream of last night, involving Bill Gallagher: He'd been a white-haired stage performer, and I looked down on him from a box seat in the loge of an intimate, dramatically-lit theater. Bill had lost a shoe during his act, and had stopped performing out of frustration, his rhythm interrupted. He stood helplessly on stage in the spotlight, wearing brightly colored stage clothes like a comedian might. Someone may have helped him leave the stage. I believe that before this scene, he'd had another similar episode, where an accident had halted his performance and he'd ended up frustrated and confused, but I don't remember it clearly enough to describe.)

FEBRUARY 20, 1984
4:27 P.M. MONDAY

(This is Day 19 of Jane's new campaign.

(She called me last night. I told her that I'd called the two people who'd sent us donations. After breakfast I called to see if the bank was open today, since I wanted to open the account for Jane's hospital fund, but it was closed for Washington's birthday. I answered Christmas cards for half an hour, then worked on Dreams.

(The day was cooler — 39 — when I left for 330. Jeff was in to check Jane's bedsores after she got back from hydro. He took her off the antibiotic, and wants her to take extra vitamin C to get her urine even more on the

acid side. He suggested she start trying to lay on her right side also. Jane's feet look improved again. Her coughing and blowing has subsided somewhat, her temperature is normal.

(She ate a light lunch. Although her eyes looked better, she couldn't make out faces on TV at times, and later couldn't read yesterday's session at all. "That really upsets me," she said. "I thought that when you were getting better it showed," I said. "So did I," she replied. Both of us were still puzzled as to what's been going on since Day 1. I told her I'd had another dream last night about our moving back to 458 West Water, but that I couldn't recall it. This in turn triggered her own memories that she'd had several dreams last night that she couldn't recall either.

(3:26. I read Jane yesterday's session. My idea in it, that we should forget the concentration on health problems for a while, was one that she'd had herself this morning, she told me, in surprise. She was still quite upset about the eye business, and so was I, although I didn't think there was anything wrong with her eyes.

(3:45, Carla took Jane's temperature — 98.4. I read to Jane the session for February 17, concerning impediments in health versus her utter freedom in writing. I started on the mail.

(4:09. Shannon brought Jane some vitamin C in ice cream. Jeff wants her to take this four times a day.

(The heat was off in 330 and the window was open as Jane held the session.)

Now, I bid you another fond good afternoon.

("Good afternoon, Seth.")

Ruburt has been <u>trying too hard</u> *(pause),* and it is not unusual for a period of <u>new decision</u> to be accompanied by a period of worrisome doubts.

In such cases, relaxation is in order. The situation <u>is</u> (underlined) as I have given it. Have him imagine himself reading a session, or hearing you <u>exclaim</u> over how well he has read one. Otherwise, have him forget his vision as much as possible, and it will indeed right itself.

There is more material along these lines, and I will see that you get it — though right now is not the time. <u>In</u> the meantime, I do touch those coordinates that quicken Ruburt's healing processes. I may or may not return, but know that I am present and approachable.

("Thank you."

(4:32 P.M. I read the session to Jane while she had a smoke. Seth at least verified some of my ideas. I told Jane that his promise of giving more material doesn't usually work out — I'm aware of a number of such references he's made in this series of sessions. The additional material never comes through. I said I'd either have to keep a list, and keep bugging her for the information, or she'd have to keep the instances in mind. And I couldn't see her doing that, especially if often she never even sees the typed session, but hears me read it to her. So I've stopped pushing for continuances of the promised material. I know it's there, and that in certain cases at least, it would be very helpful if we could get it.)

FEBRUARY 21, 1984
4:40 P.M. TUESDAY

(Today is Day 20 of Jane's new campaign.

(She called me rather early last night. I told her I'd bought her a different brand name of liquid multiple vitamins. This morning I worked on Christmas mail and finished marking Chapter 5 of Dreams *for the printer.*

(I finished early so I'd have some extra time to open the account for Jane's hospital expenses — but wouldn't you know it, the phone rang at 11:50 A.M. It was someone from social services at the hospital. She wanted to know what the latest news was, and I told her we were doing the best we could. I didn't understand all she said, but something about the Infirmary, beds, and what she's been telling people. She said she was "getting frightened" at what she had to tell people. I told her Jane and I have been frightened for a long time, and she understood. I explained how I'd had to back off from worrying in order to save my sanity and get some work done. She did have a bit of news — that insurance has been asking for more records of Jane's care.

(I did stop at the bank and open the account for Jane.

(Jane went to hydro this morning. Her eyes don't look as red, but she said they're bothering her a great deal. She's trying to ignore it. She couldn't read the session after a good lunch, so I read it to her at 3:18. I'd forgotten to stick new mail in my envelope to work on this afternoon, though I did find a couple of other letters I'd forgotten. "If I didn't live so far from the hospital, [three miles] I'd go back and get some mail," I said in frustration.

"I thought you were thinking about that," Jane said. Her feet again look much better, and she's not coughing or blowing nearly as much.

(The first time I read her the session she fell asleep when I got to the Seth material, so after she came awake with a start I read it to her again. I figured she needed the rest after the bouts of infection.

(3:48. Lynn took Jane's blood pressure. Shannon took her temperature — 98.6 — perfect. Then Diana brought in the extra vitamin C Jane is getting four times a day.

(The window was closed but there was no heat again in 330, even though it had been "fixed" by changing the thermostat. Seth's opening remarks were undoubtedly in response to my own remarks at the close of yesterday's session, when I'd written that he often didn't follow through, as promised, on material.)

Now I bid you another fond good afternoon.

("Good afternoon, Seth.")

Apropos the material I mentioned yesterday *(about Jane's symptoms, particularly her eyes.)*

Most such material is indeed given at a later date, though not always under the same heading or category, and often wound into another body of material.

Specifically, I wanted to make the point that the body's actions are unfortunately often misread and misunderstood. The body often clears out, or tries out, its own processes — perhaps by being feverish for several days, and then by lowering the temperature once unwanted materials are burned out, so to speak.

It may store urine to retain minerals at one time, and urinate seemingly to excess in another. When the body is basically held in distrust, however, all such behavior is considered dangerous and suspect. Ruburt's "cold," the bothersome eyes, are all connected with unusual muscular activity of the jaws, head, shoulders, arms and hands. In your terms, the conditions will right themselves, with the eye muscles being both more flexible and more elastic as needed.

His temperature has returned to normal. His feet are returning to normal coloration, and his urine is cleansed.

Now I may or may not return, according to those rhythms of which I speak — but know that I am present and approachable.

("Thank you, Seth."

(4:47 P.M. Seth's material was reassuring, of course, and I believed it. So did Jane, I think, in spite of it all. "So if you followed his stuff," I said after supper, when I was getting ready to leave, "you wouldn't have taken the antibiotics, and the body would have taken care of itself." That also meant that in the interim Jane wouldn't have "been trying too hard," of course.

("But what do you do when you're faced with that kind of treatment in a place where you can't walk out if you disagree with it?" I asked. "That's when you're stuck . . . We're a long ways from having any medical profession think about the body like Seth does, or even like we do."

(And no matter what Seth says, I'd still like some material on the extremes of Jane's behavior to her fears of ridicule, guilt, being attacked — the whole bit. I guess I was thinking that it's even okay to have fears, even strong ones, without going all the way with them so that they end up rendering one helpless. In larger terms I even understand why one would choose to carry certain behavior to ultimate extremes. In the short run, it's still not easy to grasp, however.)

FEBRUARY 22, 1984
4:14 P.M. WEDNESDAY

(The day was 45 degrees and bright and sunny when I left for 330. Jane had been to hydro this morning. Her feet continue to improve. She ate a fair lunch. Afterward she tried the brand of liquid vitamins I'd bought on the way home last night; she said they tasted better than the hospital's brand — but I didn't see vitamin C or E listed on the label. I'll have the new brand checked out by staff people.

(After lunch Jane showed me the extra long motion she now has in her right arm — better straightening at the elbow. She said it was even more pronounced in hydro, when she lays flat and has room for the arms to reach farther down. I told her I hoped it was an early sign of the new healing and freedom Seth has been saying she's on her way to achieving through her latest bouts of fever, her cold, and so forth.

(3:20. She couldn't make out the session for yesterday at all, so I read it to her. She said that she wanted "to do book stuff, but I'm spending all my time trying to find out about my health." I said I was willing to forget about the health business for a while — a long while, if necessary. It wasn't helping all that much, as far as I could see. Perhaps any improvements she can

achieve can come about better if we simply leave the whole business alone and quit focusing on it. I can't think of anything else to do.

(3:43. I read Jane the last book dictation she'd given 15 days ago, actually, on February 7. Hard to believe. At 4:09 Jane was given her next dosage of vitamin C — Jeff had changed the hours for some reason.

(We had the window open and the curtains pulled shut against a bright sun as session time approached. I'd turned the heat back on, though — it was working again now, somewhat mysteriously, I thought, since no one has looked at it. Jane had already taken her glasses off, saying she could see better without them. Things weren't clear, she said, just less blurred. Maybe that too was a sign of improvement, I said. I don't wear my own glasses nearly as much as I used to. Jane's Seth voice was quieter than usual, and had a hoarse or rasping quality to a mild degree.)

Now I bid you another fond good afternoon.

("Good afternoon, Seth.")

Dictation. *(Long pause.)* In this book, we do want our readers to look at body and mind in a different fashion.

Do not think of the mind as a purely mental entity, and of the body as a purely physical one. Instead, think of both mind and body as continuing, interweaving processes that are mental and physical at once. Your thoughts actually are quite as physical as your body is, and your body is quite as nonphysical as it seems to you your thoughts are. <u>You</u> are actually a vital force, existing as a part of your environment, and yet apart from your environment at the same time.

It is obvious that you impress a room with your characteristics as you furnish it, but you also mark *(long pause)* what seems to be empty space in the same fashion — that is, you turn empty space into the living matter of your body without ever realizing that you do so. Your health and the daily weather interact with each other. This happens on a personal and mass basis. I admit that some of this material quite contradicts your usual ideas, but the health of your body is intimately related not only to the state of world health, but to the physical climate as well.

(Long pause at 4:25.) You do not "catch" a drought. You do not catch a cold, either. In a fashion a drought is partially caused by the emotional states of the people who experience it — yet a drought is not a disease. It is part of a process. It is a <u>necessary</u> portion of the

larger process of the world's physical stability. As unfortunate as a drought might seem, it is in its way responsible for the balanced proportion of moisture of the entire planet's surface. In the same way diseases in their fashion are also often parts of larger processes whose greater purpose is the body's overall balance and *(long pause)* strength.

(Long pause at 4:30.) You cannot see the wind directly — you see only its effects. The same applies to your thoughts. They possess power as the wind does, but you only see the effects of their actions.

Now I may or may not return, again according to those rhythms of which I speak, but know that I am present and approachable.

("Thank you."

(4:32 P.M. Jane wanted a cigarette, even though smokes make her cough. No one has done her vitals today, although her temperature has been normal. Jane had "no idea that he was going into that weather stuff." I read the session to her.

(Jane called just as I finished typing this session at 9:31 P.M.)

FEBRUARY 28, 1984
4:16 P.M. TUESDAY

Dictation: (Time, less than five minutes)

My thoughts go buzzing
through time's corridors,
winging their way
through the sunny hours,
dipping into shaded corners,
sipping sweet honeycombs
of desire, slipping through
golden keyholes
and flying free past
the meadows of eternity.
I bid them a safe journey
as they travel ahead
of me, for one day I will
surely follow.

(Note: March 1, 3:05 P.M. Jane read this poem, and the one for February 29, quite easily without her glasses. Surprised and pleased.)

FEBRUARY 29, 1984
4:00 P.M. WEDNESDAY

Dictation: (Time, about five minutes)

My thoughts go flying
backward into yesterdays,
fat honeybees
seeking fresh nectar
in hidden stores,
raiding cubbyholes of desire
and tasting honey saved
from the past's sweet moments,
each time growing better nourished
than before.
How wise I was
to save a portion of the past
untasted 'till now.

MARCH 1, 1984
3:28 P.M. THURSDAY

Dictation: (Time, 3:28–3:35 P.M.)

My history is filled
with kingdoms lost and kingdoms found,
with magic mirrors that open up
into brand-new cosmic maps,
and within my head (pause)
glittering worlds are spread
enough to fill
a thousand books. (long pause)
Multiple vision leads me on
over paths that form (long pause)
new worlds of fact.

Dictation: (Time, 4:45–5:00 p.m.)

A moment from the past
suddenly flashed before my eyes
and there I was, on all fours
watching a June bug
head toward the grass,
its body shining oval and hard.
I put my face down
as close as I could
and stared as it moved (interruption)
like a dark shiny live rock.
Its shadow fell wrinkled
upon the grass while its
body glittered in the bright sunlight. (interruption)
It made a crinkling sound
as if its joints needed oil. . . .

(Jane had had two interruptions by this point, from staff, and for what-
ever reasons couldn't finish the poem. "I hate to leave them like that," she
said several times, then finally added a couple of lines that she wasn't very
satisfied with:

. . . and it leapt on legs thin
as dry straw.

(Note: March 2 — Jane read her two poems again without glasses —
just as good as she had from my notes yesterday. Not perfectly, but she did
do it . . .)

MARCH 5, 1984
MONDAY

My mind's wings
fly into tomorrow's skies,
enchanting children who shout,
"Come see the lovely dragonfly."

(3:48–3:49 P.M.)

Sometimes my thoughts
go rolling downhill
like small stones.
Villagers below cry,
"Look out for the avalanche!"

(3:52–3:53 P.M.)

Sometimes my thoughts gather force
and roll down the beaches
of my mind.
Bathers cry, "Here comes
the ninth wave."

(3:54–3:55 P.M.)

My thoughts need
good straight legs.
I bet my thoughts can
send my legs racing
up and down stairs
or anywhere
with a quickness too fast
for me to decipher,
because my thoughts demand
locomotion.

(3:58–4:00 P.M.)

My dreams fall down
one after another,
melting into each other,
and other dreamers below
run for dry ground.

(4:02–4:04 P.M.)

MARCH 10, 1984
3:38 P.M. SATURDAY

(After today's session — the first since February 22 — I told Jane that my plan when she resumed sessions was to type the session material only, and not the daily notes about her physical condition, temperature, and so forth, unless there was something out of the ordinary to note. She agreed. I have a record of that incidental material in my daily handwritten notes. Someday that material may be transcribed and used, for some as-yet-unknown purpose.

(I do want to note, however, that I met Dr. Jeff Karder as I walked down the hall from the emergency room today, on my way to climb the stairs to 330. He asked how Jane was, asked about her work, and books, and commented quite positively on her recovery from the recent infection and fever. "She's very resilient, isn't she?" he said, and I could tell that he was very pleasantly surprised and pleased at Jane's performance. "My wife is an extremely strong-willed person," I said, and Jeff agreed. He said he'd be up to see her, but is keeping tabs on her through records.

(Jane was pleased to hear my account of the meeting. "I'll bet I can use that, about the resiliency," she said, meaning that she'd incorporate it in suggestions, attitude, and so forth. Both of us were pleased that the incident had taken place.

(Jane's Seth voice was a bit stronger than usual, and carried what seemed like extra energy.)

Now — I bid you a fond good afternoon.

("Good afternoon, Seth.")

Dictation. In any case, magic is everywhere in the operation of your body, and in the operation of the world.

My definition of magic is this: Magic is nature unimpeded, or magic is <u>life</u> unimpeded. It is true that your thoughts and emotions and beliefs form the reality that you experience — but it is also true that this <u>creative construction</u> is, in a manner of speaking, <u>magically formed</u>. That is, the construction of your body and the construction of a world *(pause)* are produced with the greatest combination of order and spontaneity — an order and spontaneity that seems hidden rather than apparent *(all intently)*.

You think, for example, without consciously knowing how you do so, and you speak long sentences without consciously being aware at the beginning of the sentence what the conclusion will be.

This does not mean that you must forever remain in ignorance, but it does mean that there are different kinds of knowledge, and that all of your information does not come by reasoning alone. You grew from a fetus into an adult, for instance, so obviously some part of you does know how to perform such an amazing activity as the growth and care of the physical body. The reasoning mind alone, however, cannot by itself grow even the smallest cell, or activate the life of even one molecule, yet the growth and maintenance of the body is constant.

The same hidden ability that promotes your body's health and vitality also fulfills and preserves the world in general. All of this is done playfully, and yet emerges with the greatest display of order and design.

When you become too serious you overwork your intellect and tire your body, for then it seems that your entire life depends upon the reasoning of your intellect alone. Instead, of course, your intellectual abilities are supported and promoted by that inner mixture of spontaneity and order that so magically combine to form both your reality and the reality of the world.

I bid you a fond good afternoon —

("Thank you.")

— and I do indeed actuate those coordinates that regenerate all aspects of your lives in general.

("Thank you," I said again.

(4:02 P.M. Jane said she was glad she'd had the session.

(I meant to add in the opening notes that Jane's resiliency was proving a learning experience for Jeff Karder as well as for her and me.)

MARCH 12, 1984
3:08–3:12 P.M. MONDAY

(Dictation.)

Winter birds sing
their winter song
while the chill wind blows
above the frozen lawn.
Where will the birds go
when evening comes?

Who will feed the winter birds
that sit on branches,
post or fence?
I feed them corn and crumbs of bread
and listen to their winter song
as the snowflakes fly
above the frozen lawn,
for the winter birds greet
the winter dusk and dawn.

(Note: Jane <u>sang</u> this poem as she read it on March 13 — quite good.
Said she'd originally thought of it as a song, but hadn't mentioned that to
me before.)

CHAPTER 3

DAREDEVILS, DEATH-DEFIERS, AND HEALTH

MARCH 13, 1984
4:10 P.M. TUESDAY

(Jane's Seth voice was a bit stronger than usual, more forceful, and with the usual pauses.)

Now — I bid you another fond good afternoon.

("Good afternoon, Seth.")

Dictation. Chapter 3 — you have the heading.

(Jane gave it to me yesterday afternoon: "Daredevils, Death-Defiers, and Health.")

At first thought, it certainly seems as if people love life and fear death — that they seek pleasure and avoid pain.

Yet this is not always the case. There are people who must feel themselves to be at the brink of death before they can fully appreciate the quality of life. There are people who cannot appreciate or enjoy the satisfaction of life or of happiness unless faced simultaneously with the threat of death or intense pain.

There are other people who firmly believe that the pursuit of pleasure must lead to pain, and there are also others for whom pain itself <u>is</u> pleasure. *(Long pause.)* There are also individuals whose beliefs cause them to feel very uncomfortable when they are in a state of health — and for these individuals poor health brings a sense of security and safety.

There are innumerable stages of health, from high, sheer, energetic exuberance *(long pause)* to dwindling lethargy and discomfort.
In that sentence, scratch out "dwindling." There are, in fact, an
almost infinite number of stages connected with the state of health.
You could invent a completely different way of regarding human
health by numbering and defining each of those stages. Instead, of
course, your society has chosen to recognize and define all of those
stages that are detrimental to health — stages that are recognizable
because of <u>health's absence</u> to one degree or another.

In this book, therefore, we will devote ourselves to ways of promoting health, and we will purposely avoid the specific naming of
dis-hyphen-eases. Period.

(4:22.) It should be noted before we begin that death itself is the
delivery — a deliverer — of your species and all others. It is not negative in itself, but instead is the beginning of a different kind of positive existence. It <u>prunes</u> the planet, so to speak, so that there is a
room and time for all, energy and food for all. Because of death, life
is possible, so these two seemingly opposite qualities are simply different versions of the same phenomena.

If death disappeared on your planet <u>even an hour</u> all of life
would soon be threatened. And if all life possible suddenly emerged
at once, then most surely all would be annihilated. We must admit,
then, that death is indeed a part of life — and even more, we must
say that death is <u>healthy</u>.

Take your break.

(4:28–4:36.)

Now: End of dictation.

A comment about your dream. It was, as you supposed, of a tele-
pathic nature. There is a cellular communication between or among all
of earth's living cells, as if the earth itself were one large physical body.

Your own knowledge, desire, purpose and intent tuned you into
some such communications, so your concern for Joe Bumbalo *(our
next-door neighbor on Pinnacle Road)* tuned you into his physical and
emotional state at that time.

Now I bid you a most fond good afternoon — and once again,
the sessions themselves do indeed set up excellent coordinates for
the improvement of health and healing.

("Thank you very much."

(4:40 P.M. "That reminded me of the old days," Jane said, pleased at the way the session had come through.

(On March 6, 1984 I wrote this in the daily notes I make each day at the hospital: "This afternoon I described to Jane my dream last night about Joe Bumbalo. I dreamed he was taken very ill with heart trouble — that all he wanted to do was lay on his back in bed — I think in a trailer environment. His wife Margaret was there, and myself. I'm not sure if this meant Joe's death or not, I told Jane."

(I then more or less forgot the dream. At 11:55 A.M., as I was waiting for a call from our lawyer, John Bumbalo, Joe's son, called. He wanted to borrow my car. His had just frozen up due to unsuspected overheating; he had to be at the Chemung County airport at 2:30 to pick up his sister Judy, flying in from the Midwest, then again at 5:30 to pick up Margaret and Joe. I was of course amazed, since the parents weren't due back from Florida 'till May.

(Joe, John said, has been taken very ill — pains throughout his body, in the bones, but also in the heart area. A test of fluid drawn from the heart area had shown free-floating cancer cells. A CAT-scan did not reveal where they came from. Joe had lain in bed in the trailer, and Margaret had resisted sending him to a hospital. His diabetes is out of control. As I drove John to the hospital, he said the date of my dream checked with developments Margaret had described. I may have tuned into the testing of the fluid around the heart, but I doubt if this can ever be confirmed. It doesn't matter. John took the car after leaving me at the hospital, and called at 6:45 to say "mission accomplished," that all were home now. He picked me up at 7:05. The weather is poor, and we had a couple of fairly close calls as he drove me home. I told him to have Margaret call me when I can visit them.

(Jane remembered my dream, and we recalled my saying at the time that we hoped it didn't work out. Evidently it has. On the way home, John said a later report showed that Joe does have cancer throughout his body.)

MARCH 15, 1984
4:06 P.M. THURSDAY

(Jane's Seth voice was stronger than usual — indeed, almost loud at times, with the usual pauses.)

Now: I bid you a fond good afternoon —

("Good afternoon, Seth.")

— and we will resume dictation.

Individuals who defy death time and time again are actually more frightened of it than most other people are. Trapeze performers, stunt men and women, race-car riders, and many other groups have a life-style that includes death-defying stunts on a very regular basis.

Trapeze performers may have several acts a day, for example. It seems that such individuals perform with great daring, even with a rashness that is unfamiliar to most people. Most such performers, however, are extremely regulated. They work with a carefully calculated eye, under conditions in which each detail, however minute, is of supreme importance. No matter how often certain trapeze acts may be repeated, for example, there is always the threat of instant disaster — of missed footing, a final plunge. Through testing "fate," death-defiers try each time they perform to prove to themselves that they are indeed safe, that they can overcome life's most dire conditions. Period.

Life, then, has the sweetest buoyancy, the greatest satisfaction, because it is contrasted with the ever-present threat of death. Many such people do not feel at all safe living under life's usual conditions. They protect themselves by setting up the <u>conditions</u> of such an encounter, and controlling those conditions, again down to the smallest detail.

(Long pause at 4:16.) Only when they pursue some death-defying career do such individuals feel safe enough to relax otherwise and live a fairly normal life outside of their death-defying careers.

I do not mean to pass any <u>moral judgment</u> upon such activities. Often they do permit an extremely keen sense of exuberance and vitality. It is also true, however, that such people may enjoy excellent health for years, not counting perhaps an assortment of broken bones and bruises — only to fall suddenly prone to some illness if they try to give up their activities.

This need not be the case, of course. Self-understanding and self-knowledge may be able to change the individuals' lives for the better, regardless of their activities or conditions of life. It is true that these individuals do choose for themselves a carefully planned and regulated style of life, in which the threat of death is encountered personally and regularly; each day becomes an odyssey, in which death and life are purposefully weighed. Period.

Children may come down with many childhood diseases, and still be very healthy children indeed. Adults may break a bone skiing, or indulging in some other sport, and still be very healthy. *(Long pause.)* People "come down" with colds, or the flu, or some other social disease that is supposed to be passed from one individual to another — yet overall these may be very healthy individuals. The body has its own self-regulating system. This is often called the immune system.

If people become ill, it is quite fashionable to say that the immunity system *(Seth's pronunciation)* has temporarily failed — yet the body itself knows that certain "dis-eases" are healthy reactions. The body does not regard <u>diseases as diseases</u>, in usually understood terms. It regards all activity as experience, as a momentary condition of life *(pause)*, as a balancing situation. But it possesses a sense of <u>wholeness</u> and of overall integrity, for it knows that it continues to exist, though under different conditions, and it realizes that this change is as natural and necessary as the change of seasons if each individual is to continue to exist, while the earth itself possesses the nutriments necessary to the survival of physical life.

End of dictation.

Again, I do indeed accelerate those coordinates that so promote overall vitality and healing, and I bid you a most fond good afternoon.

("Good afternoon, Seth."

(4:42 P.M. Jane had a smoke and a sip of water before I turned her over.

(When I got home from 330 I called Margaret Bumbalo. Joe is in the hospital, room 560, and has a sarcoma in or surrounding the heart area. He gets chemotherapy tomorrow, so I won't see him until the next day. He can come home between treatments. His diabetes isn't yet under control.

(In my dream I'd written that he had a heart attack, but this appears to be off the mark, although pinpointing the correct area of his trouble. At times I've even wondered if I recorded the dream accurately, since in it I didn't see him having a heart attack, only rubbing his chest area with Margaret helping him, and myself there as only a witness. Margaret thinks the dream remarkable, and is going to check details time-wise.)

MARCH 16, 1984
3:58 P.M. FRIDAY

I bid you another fond good afternoon.

("Good afternoon, Seth.")

We will resume dictation.

Before we can really study the nature of health or illness, we must first understand human consciousness and its relationship with the body.

You know that you have a conscious mind, of course. You also possess what is often called the subconscious, and this merely consists of feelings, thoughts or experiences that are connected to your conscious mind, but would be considered excess baggage if you had to be aware of them all of the time. Otherwise they would vie for your attention, and interfere with the present decisions that are so important. Period.

If you tried to hold all of those subconscious memories uppermost in your mind all of the time, then you would literally be unable to think or act in the present moment at all. You do more or less have a certain access to your own subconscious mind, however. It is perhaps easier to imagine a continuum of consciousness, for you have a body consciousness also, and that body consciousness is itself made up of the individual consciousness of each molecule that forms all parts of the body itself.

(Long pause at 4:06.) It is sometimes fashionable to say that men and women have conscious minds, subconscious minds, and unconscious minds — but there is no such thing as an unconscious mind. The body consciousness is highly conscious (underlined). You are simply not usually conscious of it. *(Long pause.)* Reasoning takes time. It deals with problem-solving — it forms an hypothesis, and then seeks to prove it by trial and error.

(4:10. Carla, temp. 98.5. I read the session to Jane so far. Resume at 4:15.)

If you had to use that kind of process before you could move a muscle, you would get nowhere at all, of course. The other portions of your consciousness, then, deal with a kind of automatic thinking, and operate with a kind of knowledge that takes no time in your terms.

You might say that the varying portions of your own consciousness operate at several different speeds. Translations between one portion of consciousness and another goes on constantly, so that information is translated from one "speed" to another. Perhaps you can begin to understand, then, that the whole picture of health or illness must be considered from many more viewpoints than you might earlier have supposed. Many of you have been saturated by conventional, distorted ideas concerning health and illness in general. You might think, for example, of the body being invaded by viruses, or attacked by a particular disease, and these ideas, then, may make you question. You might well wonder why the body consciousness does not simply rise up and cast off any threatening diseases: why would the body allow certain cells to go berserk, or outgrow themselves? The very concept of the immunity system suggests, at least, the disease invader against which the body's immunity system must or should surely defend itself.

That is the end of dictation.

I bid you another most fond good afternoon — and again, I activate those coordinates that accelerate the healing processes.

(*"Good afternoon, Seth."*

(*4:27 P.M.*)

MARCH 18, 1984
4:19 P.M. SUNDAY

Now — I bid you another fond good afternoon.

(*"Good afternoon, Seth."*)

We will resume dictation for now — but I always do keep your personal concerns in mind.

Dictation. You usually think of your conscious mind as your ego. It is directed toward action in physical life. Many schools of thought (*long pause*) seem to have the curious ideas that the ego is inferior to other portions of the self, or "selfish," and imagine it to be definitely of a lower quality than the inner self, or the soul.

In the first place, it is really impossible to separate portions of the self, and we make such distinctions only in an effort to explain the many facets of the personality. (*Long pause.*) It is generally understood, then, that you do have an ego, directed toward exterior activity, and in those terms (underlined) you also have an inner ego. It is also conscious, and is the director of all automatic interior activity (*emphatically*).

Most people do not realize that they can indeed have access to this inner awareness. This inner ego or inner self should not be thought of as superior to your ordinary mind. It should not be thought of, really, as something <u>separate</u> from your ordinary mind. Your ego and your ordinary consciousness bring into focus all of your physical experiences, and make possible the brilliant preciseness of physical experience.

It is true that physical life represents only one —

(4:30. Temperature: normal. Resume at 4:32.)

— condition of being. You have other kinds of existence, then. The conscious mind is one brilliant segment of your larger consciousness, but it is <u>composed of</u> the same universal energy and vitality that composes all consciousness. There are ways of communicating with the inner ego or inner self, however, and we will discuss some of these very shortly. It is important, again, to remember that this inner ego or inner self *(long pause)* uses a process that is far swifter than reasoning.

When such communications are made, therefore, they often consist of inspiration, intuition, impulses, and deal with feeling far more than with usual logical thinking.

End of dictation.

(4:38.) Your dream, Joseph, as you supposed, represented a state of mind and of confusion. It was not, for example, precognitive, but it did inform you — using images and feelings — of the picture that was sometimes painted in different terms by your conscious thoughts. Ruburt could have had the same kind of dream, for example.

His eyes are not deteriorating. I will have more to say concerning your fund later this week, I bid you both a fond good afternoon, and I do indeed quicken those coordinates that accelerate the healing processes.

("All right. Thank you."

(4:43 P.M. Jane had a cigarette. I read the session to her before turning her on her side preparatory to taking my own nap.

(Jeff Karder had been in to see Jane this morning, and had seemed pleased enough as he examined her bedsores, and so forth. He'd also agreed that she could forget the sleeping pill at night before sleep, and stick to just aspirin — a definite improvement. He hadn't, however, held out any hope that Jane could get to sit up, because of her broken right leg, and this had depressed her. She said she had decided to stick to book work and do the best

she can. I felt somewhat discouraged also, and agreed there was little else we could do at this time, since nothing else seemed to be working. She did read a little better today, without her glasses, but I still ended up reading the last session to her.

(Seth commented upon the fund, perhaps, because of the letter I took to read Jane, from Mary Newman. This most kind and generous lady offered substantial financial help if we need it. I've tried to call her twice so far. Jane suggested I send her a copy of Oversoul Seven. *If I can't reach her soon, I'll write her again. Through mutual friends Jane and I had met Mary several years ago: while on a business trip to New York City, we had stayed at her apartment for a number of days.*

(My dream Seth referred to took place yesterday morning, and was so vivid I lay awake for an hour after having it. It stayed with me all day. Because is was so vivid, it would make a great series of paintings. It obviously expressed my conscious fears about our situation, and in it I ended up lost amid old factory buildings, with the car gone. I was naked, saying, "I've lost my way," to a girl, possibly a nurse, seated at a desk in a cavernous, vacant, rust-red old room. I'd even found myself exploring the town dump of Elmira — only the landscape looked volcanic, beautiful in its own way, heaped with gray fine ash like the surface of the moon, almost.)

MARCH 19, 1984
4:21 P.M. MONDAY

(Jane had been blue and depressed yesterday, and she was that way again when I got to 330 today. There were tears before lunch. She'd called last night. I told her I'd talked with Mary Newman this morning, boosted our insurance coverage, and called Jim Baker, our optometrist. Jane is hoping that if he can give her new glasses her vision will improve, and this would help her spirits.

(She was still blue at session time, but her Seth voice was stronger than usual.)

Now I bid you another fond good afternoon.

("Good afternoon, Seth.")

We will resume dictation, and the following session should be particularly taken to heart by Ruburt *(intently)*.

Each person is a vital *(long pause)*, conscious portion of the universe. Each person, simply by <u>being</u>, fits into the universe and into universal purposes in a way no one else can. Each person's existence sends its own ripples throughout time. The universe is conscious at every conceivable point of itself. Each being is an <u>individualized segment</u> of the universe; then, in human terms, each person is a beloved individual, formed with infinite care and love, uniquely gifted with a life like no other.

No animal considers itself a failure, obviously. People, however, often identify with their seeming mistakes, forgetting *(pause)* their abilities in other directions, so that it seems that they are misfits in the universe, or in the world. The conscious mind can indeed have such thoughts because it so often tries to solve all problems on its own, until it begins to feel frightened, overburdened, and a failure in its own eyes.

The inner ego, however, always identifies with its source-identity as a beloved, individualized portion of the universe. It is aware of the universal love that is its heritage.

(Pause at 4:33.) It is also aware of the infinite power and strength that composes the very fabric of its being. Through being made aware of these facts, the exterior ego can begin to feel a quicker sense of support and nourishment. The knowledge can let it relax, let go, so that it feels its life <u>couched</u> and safe, and knows itself to be indeed a beloved child of the universe, both ancient and young at once, with an identity far beyond the annals of time.

It is of great value, then, that each person remember this universal affiliation. Such a reminder can often allow the inner self to send needed messages of strength and love through the various levels, appearing as inspiration, dreams, or simply pure bursts of feeling. The inner ego *(long pause)* draws instant and continuous support from the universal consciousness, and the more the exterior ego keeps that fact in mind, the greater its own sense of stability, safety, and self-esteem.

(4:41.) One of the attitudes <u>detrimental to good health</u> is that of self-condemnation, or dislike of the self. Such attitudes are unfortunately sometimes fostered by parents, schools, and religions. Feelings of self-worth, self-esteem, and pleasure with one's abilities promote feelings of well-being, health, and exuberance.

End of dictation.

(4:45.) Read this to Ruburt once a day for several days, and it will also be of help to you.

("Yes.")

The session should, on its own, clear up some of Ruburt's difficulties and increase his pleasures.

(4:46 P.M. It was time to turn Jane. I read her the session after supper. She called me, with Carla's help, at 9:20, as I was finishing typing the session.)

MARCH 20, 1984
4:25 P.M. TUESDAY

(Jane seemed to feel somewhat better today, and she described the way she was now attempting to look at the world in general and her own situation in particular. I told her her attitude was a great improvement. Her eyes looked better also. She tried reading yesterday's session, but got only halfway down the first page, so I read it all to her. It's an excellent session, and, as Seth suggested, I'll be reading it to her for at least several days.

(Once again, today her Seth voice was stronger than usual, with pauses.)

I bid you another fond good afternoon.

("Good afternoon, Seth.")

We will resume dictation.

The universe actively loves itself and all of its parts. The world loves itself and all of its parts. It is not true that energy is neutral or indifferent. Energy is active, positive, propelled by what can almost be called an <u>instantaneous pleasure</u> with itself and its characteristics.

Despite all concepts to the contrary, energy is indeed at its basis, love. *(Pause.)* It is also composed of highly charged consciousness that operates almost in a leapfrog fashion, with great bursts of exuberance and vitality. The great — the greatest creative force — that force that is the origin for all physical life — did not suddenly appear once in some distant past, sparking the birth of your reality, endowing it with an energy <u>that could only then</u> run down, or dissipate. Instead, ever-new virgin energy, so to speak, is created constantly, and appears at every conceivable point within your universal system.

Each new rose in the springtime is in truth a new rose, composed of completely new and unique energy, utterly itself, innocent, alive in the world.

(Long pause at 4:36.) In the deepest of terms, while each body has a history, each moment in the body's existence is also new, freshly emerging into the world, innocent and unique. While there is indeed pain in the world, it is the miraculous principle of pleasure that propels life itself.

End of dictation.

There are actually several new twists in this material, as you should see when you read it over. I bid you now a fond good afternoon.

("Good afternoon, Seth."

(4:41. Jane hadn't seen that it was so late, she said.

(There are indeed "new twists" in the material, some of which I cannot really put into words — but Seth's creative gifts have yet to be exhausted, I note.

(I should also note that today, with a bit of a struggle, I carried in to 330 a large vase containing long hollyhocks and irises. The gorgeous flowers are part of a package of flowers wired to us from a reader in Holland. Neighbor John Bumbalo took delivery of the package yesterday afternoon while I was at the hospital, and brought it over as soon as he saw me drive into the garage. There were so many flowers in the package that I ended up dividing them among three vases I found here at the house. I'll take another one — tulips this time — in to Jane tomorrow.)

MARCH 21, 1984
4:15 P.M. WEDNESDAY

(Jane didn't call last night. She felt better today. I told her I'd deposited $1200 in her hospital-expenses account on my way to 330. We're very grateful for the help readers are offering. She ate a good lunch. Afterward she read yesterday's session, and the one for the day before, in far better fashion than she's been able to do for many days. She wore glasses, and read in a good strong voice.)

Now — I bid you a fond good afternoon, and we will resume dictation.

("Good afternoon, Seth.")

Those who look upon physical life as inferior to some other more perfect spiritual existence do a great injustice to physical existence in general. Physical life is everywhere filled with the universal energy that is its source, so it can hardly be inferior to it's own composition.

Again, corporeal reality is a brilliant segment of existence. It cannot be <u>inferior</u> to existence. It is because you so often view your world through a system of highly limited beliefs that you so often misread the implications of temporal life. Period.

(Long pause.) Such beliefs serve to limit your comprehension, until it seems often that physical life consists of a frantic struggle for survival at every level of consciousness. Such ideas certainly do not foster feelings of security, health, or well-being, and they distort the nature of your physical environment.

That environment is not something separate from yourself, for you to control. Instead, you and the environment support, strengthen, and fortify each other in ways that often escape you. *(Pause.)* All portions of the environment contain their own kinds of consciousness. They are aware of their own parts in the body of the world, so to speak, and they are aware not only of their own conditions, but of their relationships to all other portions of the world. They add to the world's health, in other words, and your own vitality — and that of your environment — are everywhere interrelated.

End of dictation.

(4:33.) I bid you another fond good afternoon, and again I activate those coordinates that are so vital for healing and well-being.

("Thank you."

(4:34 P.M. "I felt that was sort of slow," Jane said.

("It was," I said. Seth had used many pauses. I was a bit surprised that he'd ended the session so quickly, given the slow pace. So was Jane.)

CHAPTER 4

THE BROKEN-HEARTED, THE HEARTLESS, AND MEDICAL TECHNOLOGY

MARCH 23, 1984
4:00 P.M. FRIDAY

Jane didn't call last night. She's still somewhat depressed — said she hasn't slept as well since taking the night medication prescribed by Jeff. With her glasses, Jane did fairly well reading most of the sessions for March 19 and 21.

(At 3:10 Jane said she'd just picked up from Seth the heading for Chapter 4 of the book — that she had to reach a certain level of well-being before she could get his material, obviously.

(Her Seth voice was good, but with many pauses.)

Now — I bid you a most fond good afternoon.

("Good afternoon, Seth.")

We will resume dictation.

Many psychiatrists and psychologists now realize that a disturbed client *(long pause)* cannot be helped sufficiently unless the individual is considered along with his or her relationship to the family unit.

The same idea really applies to physical illness as well. It is possible, however, to carry this idea even further, so that a person in poor health <u>should be</u> seen by the physician in relationship to the family, and also in relationship to the environment. Old-time family doctors understood the patient's sensitivity to family members and to the environment, of course, and they often felt a lively sympathy and understanding that the practitioners of modern medicine often seem to have forgotten.

I am speaking of a deeper relationship to the environment, however, and of the environment's symbolic as well as practical aspects in relationship to health and illness. Your ideas about your own body, your mind, the universe and your part in it, and your relationship to family, friends, and environment are all connected to your state of health, to your sense of well-being, or your feelings of dis-hyphen-ease. Period.

In the next chapter let us look more specifically at the importance of symbolism in your mind, your body, and your environment.

Chapter 4: "The Broken-Hearted, the Heartless, and Medical Technology."

Take your break.

(4:12. Jane had a sip of water. Seth's chapter heading is the same as the one she'd picked up from him earlier this afternoon, she said. Resume at 4:20, with many pauses.)

Now: Modern medical science largely considers the human body to be a kind of mechanical model, a sort of vehicle like a car that needs to be checked by a garage every so often.

As an automobile is put together at an assembly line, so the body is simply seen as a very efficient machine put together in nature's "factory." If all the parts are in their proper places, and functioning smoothly, then the machine should give as excellent service as any well-running automobile — or so it seems.

All of the automobile's parts, however, are alone responsible for its operation as long as it has a responsible driver. There are, however, hidden relationships that exist between various parts of the body — and the parts themselves are hardly mechanical. They change in every moment.

The heart is often described as a pump. *(Long pause.)* With the latest developments in medical technology, there are all kinds of heart operations that can be performed, even the use of heart transplants. In many cases, even when hearts are repaired through medical technology, the same trouble reoccurs at a later date, or the patient recovers only to fall prey to a different, nearly fatal or fatal, disease. This is not always the case, by any means, but when such a person does recover fully, and maintains good health, it is because beliefs, attitudes, and <u>feelings</u> have changed for the better, and because the person "has a heart" again, comma, in other words, because the patient himself has regained the will to live.

End of dictation.

(Resume at 4:36, again with many pauses.)

Many people who have heart trouble feel that they have "lost the heart" for life. They may feel broken-hearted for any of many reasons. They may feel heartless, or imagine themselves to be so cold-hearted that they punish themselves literally by trying to lose their heart.

With many people having such difficulties, the addition of <u>love in the environment</u> may work far better than any heart operation. A new pet given to a bereaved individual has saved more people from needing heart operations than any physician. In other words, "a love transplant" in the environment may work far better overall than a heart-transplant operation, or a bypass, or whatever; in such ways the heart is allowed to heal itself.

End of session. I bid you a fond good afternoon, and again I quicken those coordinates that are so important to health and vitality.

("Thank you."

(4:43 P.M. "I felt he was trying to make certain points," Jane said, "and I hope that I got it through clear enough — you know what I mean? I guess I said it right," she added, after hesitating in an attempt to say herself what Seth had said, if only briefly.

("I was also getting," she said, "that he wasn't saying that people didn't need those operations sometimes, but that when they did, they needed those other things in order to make the operations work."

(As we talked Jane impressed upon me that she'd definitely picked up that a household pet would help our neighbor Joe Bumbalo a great deal — she wants me to be sure to impress upon Margaret Bumbalo that this is the case; she felt it strongly, it wasn't just a generalized idea, Jane said.)

MARCH 25, 1984
4:13 P.M. SUNDAY

(Jane didn't call me last night. In the mail for yesterday I found the new cover design for the trade paper edition of The God of Jane *— a nice-*

looking job, we like it. And I found another check for $1000 in a letter, as a donation to Jane's hospital-expenses fund. I wondered if any of these events — or all of them — were tied in with the feeling of anticipation I'd been quite conscious of yesterday afternoon at 330. I'd told Jane about the sensations.

(I might add that yesterday I opened a letter from the BBC — the British Broadcasting Corporation — that was dated in January. I don't know how long it's been at the house. The producer wanted to know about doing a series on Jane's work. Maybe that was connected to my feeling of anticipation . . .

(Once again, Jane's Seth voice was good, with the usual pauses.)

Now — I bid you a fond good afternoon —

("Good afternoon, Seth.")

— and we will resume dictation.

Later on we will discuss more thoroughly distorted ideas about the self and the body in particular that stand in the way of natural exuberance and good health.

Without going more deeply into the reasons for such beliefs until later, let me discuss several of the ways in which they impede general well-being. Right now it is socially fashionable to take up some kind of exercise, gym work, or strenuous sport, so it seems obvious that the general populace must have a great regard for the physical body. Unfortunately, large segments of the population feel uncomfortable with their bodies, and do not trust the body's spontaneity, strength, or overall dependability. They have been taught that medical science knows more about bodies than any private individual knows about their own bodies and their ways and workings.

People have been taught to trust X-rays for a picture of what is happening within their bodies, and cautioned not to trust their own feelings. Period. Some public-service announcements stress the "fact" that the individual can be gravely threatened by high blood pressure, for example, even though he or she feels in excellent physical health.

The populace has embarked upon this strong exercise program because of a mixture of very unfortunate beliefs. Since they feel divorced from their bodies, many people suspect what is going on inside. Some religious beliefs suggest that the body is impure, and the heir to disease and infirmity. Often people exercise over-zealously to punish their bodies, or to force the body to respond at its best, since they do not trust it to do otherwise.

(4:27.) In many instances people exercise quite simply because they are afraid of what will happen if they do not. They may run to avoid heart disease, for example, while their own fear can <u>help</u> to promote the very eventuality they fear.

The body's health is the expression of inner well-being. Poor health is an expression also, and it may serve many purposes. *(Pause.)* It goes without saying that some people become ill rather than change their activities and their environments. They may also become ill, of course, to <u>force</u> themselves to make such changes.

End of dictation.

MARCH 27, 1984
4:12 P.M. TUESDAY

(Jane called last night. Margaret Bumbalo visited her just as I was leaving.

(At 11:00 this morning our lawyer called to tell me that Blue Cross has agreed to pay our insurance claim. I could hardly believe it, and barely reacted to the news. I did ask if he knew whether the company is paying 80% or 100%, and he didn't know. If it's the former figure, we'll still owe a hefty bill.

("Seth was right," Jane said with a smile as soon as I gave her the news. During the afternoon she said that she'd never worried about the insurance question. I think the good news may not have penetrated my psyche yet, not even as I type these lines at 9:00 P.M. After talking to our lawyer this morning I went back to work on Dreams *just as though nothing had happened. However, that mixture of dread and anticipation I've felt every day for months when I went to the mail box should now begin to dissipate.*

(I told Jane that last night I'd had another long, torturous dream in which I'd been pursued through rooms by unknown men who were after me for some unexplained reason. I always got away and hid, in room after room, but the dream was an upsetting one, like that I'd had a week or so ago, when I'd lost my way amid a series of deserted factory buildings on the edge of Elmira. I still recall that one vividly.

(I understood the import of last night's dream much better than its predecessor, however, having learned what that first dream meant — my own fears on a number of counts.

(Jane's sight has improved, as well as movement in both arms and other places. I read her two letters from female scientists in California that, I thought, would cheer her a great deal, since they both stressed the value of her work. And they did help. Jane also read a couple of recent sessions herself, and marched right along through them for the most part — better than she has been doing by quite a bit.

(After I'd told her about the insurance thing, and Jane had told me about her increased motions, she added that she now felt that everything would be fine, and that she would recover. What a treat that will be!

(Jane's Seth voice was good, with pauses.)

I bid you another fond good afternoon.

("Good afternoon, Seth.")

We will resume dictation. Congratulations after the long wait concerning your insurance. I understand that the wait seemed longer to you than to me, but I was not concerned.

(Seth was almost amused and understanding at once. After the session I told Jane that he'd said more than he realized — that in the case of predictions it would be wise of us to remind ourselves that his sense of time is indeed far different than ours, that much more time could be involved on our parts than on his. This in turn had reminded me of my dream of months ago, when from the elevator tower of the hospital I'd looked out a window to see checks from the insurance company lying on the asphalt at the side of the left front wheel of the car. I'd interpreted that dream to mean that a meaningful settlement was still far away from us, but there nevertheless. I do not recall the date of the dream without checking.

(Pause.) Now: Dictation. I do not mean to imply that exercise is <u>detrimental</u> to good health. It is true, however, that the reason that you exercise is actually more important than the exercises that you do perform. The reason can promote your good health or actually impede it.

Thus far in this book, we have barely begun to touch upon the multitudinous issues involved in good health or in its absence. Before we are finished we hope to give you a far greater framework in which to consider your own well-being and the many options that are open to any individual. We will discuss the aspects connected with a long, healthy, fairly happy lifetime, and those involved with early death, severe illnesses, and suicide — particularly with the suicides of fairly young persons.

Earlier we spoke about the incredible impulse on the part of all of nature toward exuberance and well-being. It is as if nature always tries to exceed itself, and certainly to increase the quality of its existence. The individual person is also involved in an ever-continuing process to increase the quality of life as it exists at all levels of personal experience. Reality is so constructed that each individual seeking such fulfillment does so <u>not</u> at the expense of others, but in such a way that the quality of life is increased for all.

(Long pause at 4:22.) Each person impulsively tries to <u>grow into</u> his or her sensed potentials — even when they are not immediately apparent.

In one way or another each segment of consciousness is aware of each other segment, through an instantaneous communication that exists on many levels. It is important that your <u>ideas</u> circulate freely, and that the ideas of the peoples of the world circulate freely, just as it is important that your individual body has good circulation. Your <u>ideas</u> about your own health are even more important than those steps you take to promote it.

Your ideas about foreign countries, allies and enemies, also have a vital role to play in how you handle your own bodily defenses. People who are afraid that their nation will be invaded by an enemy will often also consider viruses or diseases to be enemies, ever about to threaten their personal survival. Such attitudes will, of course, be detrimental to feelings of well-being, health, and exuberance. While it is true that medical technology has many serious defects, it is also true that many people <u>believe</u> in the medical profession to such a degree that it would be nearly impossible for them to survive in good health without it.

Later on in this book we will also discuss the ways in which you can use your own beliefs about the medical profession to reinforce your overall sense of health, rather than to undermine it.

End of dictation.

(4:34.) Overall, you have both activated Framework 2* sufficiently enough so that its effects are beneficially appearing in <u>all</u> areas of your lives — including the physical area.

I bid you now a fond good afternoon, and I do indeed activate those coordinates that quicken healing <u>and</u> exuberance.

("Okay. Thank you."

(4:36 P.M. I read the session to Jane. That's the first time Seth has ever said that we were doing that well with Framework 2, I'm sure. And in all areas, yet! Maybe we are learning some things, Jane. I love you. Sleep well.)

APRIL 2, 1984
3:58 P.M. MONDAY

(This is Jane's first session in six days — quite an unusual occurrence for her.

(I've made good use of the time. I have every letter in the house answered. I've paid bills and actually feel like I can relax and draw a deep breath at times, when I consider the improving state of our finances, work, insurance problems, and so forth.

(On March 29, last Thursday, I failed to get to the hospital to see Jane for the first time since she was admitted last April 20. The reason was simple: a late snowstorm of very deep and heavy wet snow the night before, and continuing on into the next day, had split the Chinese elms in the back yard and caused the one nearest the garage to fall across the driveway, so I couldn't get the car out of the garage. The trees are ruined. Insurance will not pay for them. On March 31, Frank Longwell came over with his power saw and helped clear the driveway enough so I could get the car out. The day before, John Bumbalo had taken me back and forth to the hospital.

(Jane now has over $7000 in donations through Maude Cardwell's efforts in Reality Change.

---

*In Jane/Seth's *The Individual and the Nature of Mass Events,* which was published in 1981, I wrote: "Seth maintains that Framework 2, or inner reality, contains the creative source from which we form all events, and that by the proper focusing of attention we can draw from that vast subjective medium everything we need for a constructive, positive life in Framework 1, or physical reality." Seth has a lot to say about Frameworks 1 and 2 in *Mass Events.* For example: "Those unique intents that characterize each individual exist first in Framework 2, then — and with birth, those intents immediately begin to impress the physical world of Framework 1."

(Jane did very well today, reading the last session, plus the one for March 19, which Seth wants her to review every so often.

(Her Seth voice was quite good, although she used a number of long pauses.)

Now — I bid you another fond good afternoon —

("Good afternoon, Seth.")

— and we will resume dictation.

There are many large issues that touch upon the circumstances involving the health of individuals, and these concern questions that we have not yet discussed.

They will indeed be covered later in this book, but for now we will only be concerned with them in a general way. They are more divorced from ordinary medical thought, and would indeed be considered sheer quackery in the majority of medical circles.

The fact is that each individual lives many lives, and that the inner self is quite aware of its own spiritual and physical dexterity. The body consciousness alone understands that its physical existence in any one life is dependent upon its physical death — and that that death will assure it of still another existence. The "drive for survival" is, therefore, a drive that leads to death and beyond it, for all of consciousness understands that it survives through many forms and conditions.

Reincarnation, therefore, also is part of the larger framework in which any individual's health and well-being must be considered. The reincarnational influences are most apparent in what would be considered bodily defects dating from birth, and these will be discussed later on in this book.

Reincarnational influences are not nearly as rigid as many believers in the concept think. That is, reincarnational influences usually leave many options open to an individual in any case. It is quite simplistic, for example, to say, as some people do, that any given particular event from a past life leads inevitably to a particularly matching effect in a present one. There are too many other elements that also apply to the human personality. No one is "fated" to have bad health. No one is punished in one life for "evil" activities in a previous one.

A person who has been cruel in one life may choose to experience conditions in the next life in which he or she understands the meaning of cruelty, but this does not mean that such a person would then necessarily experience an entire lifetime as a victim.

New learning would always be involved, and thus new options would always be open. There are, in fact, so many distorted ideas connected with the concept of reincarnation in general, that I think it far better to simply concentrate upon the idea of multiple existences. Period. Because of the true nature of time, and the interrelationships of consciousness, a future life affects a past one, for in actuality all of these existences happen simultaneously. All systems are open-ended, particularly psychological ones. In greater terms, you are working "at all levels" and at all of your own existences at once, even though it is useful sometimes to think of reincarnation as a series of lives, one after the other.

End of dictation.

(4:22.) You are indeed beneficially impressing reality at a Framework 2 level, and in ways that are becoming apparent at all of the <u>normal</u> levels of your individual and joint experience.

I do activate those coordinates that quicken the healing processes, and foster feelings of well-being and exuberance.

("Thank you."

(4:24 P.M. I read the session to Jane. While I did she had some thoughts of her own — that a person can choose illness, for example, in order to explore that reality, and to exert certain effects upon others around the ill person: thoughts I have had many times — my old idea of consciousness getting to know itself in as many ways as possible.

(She also had the idea that in our society we're so educated and used to condemning ourselves if we have anything wrong with us, that we blind ourselves to the real reasons we fall ill to begin with. Another idea I've mused about. I'm afraid I think that consciously we're a long ways from incorporating such ideas into our daily society.

(Jane added that when she listens to me read a session to her, she'll get glimpses from Seth sometimes of what he's going to say next time: "The thoughts are mine, but also a mixture, they have a tinge of Seth's ideas." She thinks that such was the case today.

(When I asked her if she believed we were operating within Framework 2, she said she did — that the insurance questions, the donations, and our current work, all show that we are doing things much better — and I agree.

(Jane called, with Carla's help, at 9:45 P.M., just as I finished typing this session.)

APRIL 3, 1984
4:03 P.M. TUESDAY

(The day was warm — 50 degrees.

(Jane did very well reading aloud the first two notes I'd written for Session 907 of Dreams, *as well as yesterday's session. In fact, her reading of the session was as fast, or faster, than any I've heard her do. Peggy Gallagher visited briefly in the middle of Jane's effort.)*

Now — I bid you another most fond good afternoon.

("Good afternoon, Seth.")

We will resume dictation.

The concept of the survival of the fittest has had a considerably detrimental effect in many areas of human activity — particularly in the realm of medical ideology and practice.

The whole idea was developed in the most mechanistic of terms, stressing competition among all aspects of life, pitting one life form against another, and using physical strength and dexterity, swiftness and efficiency, as the prime conditions for the survival of any individual or species.

It is quite true, however, that in the wild many animals protect and provide for wounded or disabled members, and that the wisdom that comes with age is indeed appreciated even in the animal kingdom. The survival of the fittest concept, however, has been exaggerated far above those of cooperation.

(Long pause at 4:12.) Politically as well as medically, such distortions have led to unfortunate conditions: the Aryan-supremacy biological ideas fostered in the second world war, the concentration upon "the perfect body," and other distortions. The idea of the ideal body has often been held up to the populace at large, and this often sets forth a stylized "perfect" physique that actually could be matched by few individuals. Any variations are frowned upon, and any birth defects considered in the most suspicious of lights. Some schools of thought, then, have it that only the genetically superior should be allowed to reproduce, and there are scientists who believe that all defects can be eradicated through judicious genetic planning.

As a result of such long-held theories, people have grown distrustful of their own bodies. The handicapped are often given messages, even by the medical profession, that make them feel like misfits, unworthy to survive. When people become ill, they often blame themselves in such a way that unnecessary guilt is the result.

In the past some religious groups have also promoted beliefs that illness is a sign of God's punishment, or vengeance for sins committed against his "goodness."

The same beliefs often spread to economic areas in which *(long pause)* people who met pleasure in God's eyes were therefore gifted with wealth and prosperity, as well as good health. Therefore God was seen to be on the side of those who competed most strenuously, so that to be poor or sick was almost seen as a sign of God's disfavor. All such concepts appear in one form or another at most official levels of thought and education. The whole idea of the esthetics of nature is forgotten — a subject that we will touch upon further as we continue our discussion.

(Heartily:) End of session. A fond good afternoon.

(4:40 P.M. "Good afternoon, Seth. Thank you.")

APRIL 4, 1984
4:14 P.M. WEDNESDAY

(This noon Frank Longwell visited briefly, and agreed to take down the damaged Chinese elms in the back yard, till the soil, and put in wild flowers. I told Jane about the plan and she more or less likes it, although she mourns the loss of the trees. "Maybe you can keep the sawed-off trunks in place to make bird feeders," she said.

(After lunch Jane read yesterday's session very well. The heat isn't working in 330 and we waited most of the afternoon for service.)

Now — I bid you another fond good afternoon.

("Good afternoon, Seth.")

We will resume dictation.

This chapter consists of a potpourri of different ideas — merely to hint at the multitudinous issues connected with health and well-being.

(Long pause.) Your ideas about yourself are, again, vital in the larger context of a healthy lifetime. The condition of your heart is affected, for example, by your own feelings about it. If you consider

yourself to be coldhearted, or heartless, those feelings will have a significant effect upon that physical organ. If you feel broken-hearted, then you will also have that feeling reflected in one way or another in the physical organ itself.

Obviously, as I mentioned earlier, each individual also has many options open. Everyone who feels brokenhearted does not die of heart failure, for example. The subject of health cannot be considered in an isolated fashion, but must be seen in that greater context that gives health itself a value and a meaning. As mentioned earlier, each person will also try to fulfill their own unique abilities, and to "fill out" the experience of life as fully as possible.

If an individual is hampered in that attempt strongly and persistently enough, then the dissatisfaction and frustration will be translated into a lack of physical exuberance and vitality. There is always an unending reservoir of energy at the command of each person, however, regardless of circumstances, and we will also discuss the ways in which you can learn to tap that source and better your own health situation.

(Pause at 4:25.) The sooner you can rid yourself of rigid beliefs about the survival of the fittest, the better you will be. All philosophies that stress the idea of the body's impurity or degradation should also be seen as detrimental to bodily and spiritual integrity. Such beliefs clutter up your conscious mind with negative suggestions that can only frighten the exterior ego and impede the great strength and vitality that is your heritage from lending you the fullest possible strength and support.

Later on we will indeed discuss various methods of healing, conventional and unconventional. Medical technology alone, however expert, cannot really heal a broken heart, of course. Such a healing can only take place through understanding and through expressions of love. In other words, through emotional transplants rather than physical ones alone. The emotional factors are extremely vital, both in the development and in the healing of all dis-hyphen-eases.

We will not stress particular diseases in this book, and mention symptoms only to identify the cases associated with such conditions. It is actually far more important that we stress the symptoms of health and those methods, beliefs, and healings that promote them.

End of session. I bid you a fond good afternoon — and I have activated those conditions and coordinates that quicken a sense of well-being and exuberance.

(4:37 P.M. "Thank you.")

APRIL 6, 1984
4:13 P.M. FRIDAY

(Jane called last night. I worked on Dreams *but an hour this morning, and once again, told her that I was concerned about lost working time on the book. She said she'd been very blue as I left last night, but that the period had passed after a while and she'd felt fine. I've also had a number of blue periods lately, but try to keep going anyhow.)*

Now: I bid you another fond good afternoon.

("Good afternoon, Seth.")

It is natural enough in your situation to have blue periods now and then.

(Long pause.) These can often serve as springboards, however, leading to greater understanding, and the feelings themselves do indeed help rid you of fears and doubts that are expressed through such a medium. I am sure that I mentioned this before, but I wanted to refresh your memory, and this applies, generally speaking, to all individuals. It is far better to express those feelings than to inhibit them.

At the same time, you both should — and do — try to turn your minds in other directions, so that the periods do not linger. Generally speaking, you have handled such situations well, and what I said about your activities in Framework 2 does still apply.

This will also be reflected in your concerns with books and [your publisher] Prentice-Hall — with <u>any</u> of your business concerns. It is a good idea, then, to remember that regardless of appearances at any given time, those issues are being settled to your satisfaction. Your letters have an effect, whether or not it seems that any given questions are being answered.

I bid you now a most fond good afternoon, and I do activate those coordinates that quicken healing, well-being, and exuberance.

("Good afternoon, Seth. Thank you."

(4:20 P.M. "I had the feeling it would be for us, instead of dictation," Jane said. I read the session to her. "That last part ought to make you feel better," she said. "Does it?"

(I had to stop and think, since I've been pretty angry and upset about communications with Prentice-Hall lately. "It's surprising," I said, meaning Seth's comments about our doing well in Framework 2, including the publishing angle. "I didn't think I was doing that well." I guess I still don't, but we'll see.

(I told Jane I'd had another one of those long, involved, being-pursued dreams last night, this time involving my brother, Linden, who is 13 months younger than I am. I can recall little of it. It worked out okay, yet it reflected my state of mind often these days — my fears, probably on a lot of subjects.

(I do think Seth offered an excellent insight when he said that the blue periods on both our parts were ways of expressing fears. Without thinking about such bouts particularly, I suppose I at least had taken it for granted that the blue periods reflected weaknesses on my part, say — times when I should have known better or wasn't doing well. I dare say Jane has the same ideas. Now we can appreciate that the blue periods are therapeutic.

(I went shopping at SuperDuper on the way home tonight, and ate a late supper. Jane called with Carla's help at 9:50, as I was typing this session. I love you, Jane.)

CHAPTER 5

Suggestion and Health

APRIL 8, 1984
4:30 P.M. SUNDAY

*J*ane was upset when I got to 330 this noon. Jeff Karder, her doctor, had been in. At first she didn't want to tell me what he'd said until after lunch, but I persuaded her to tell all. One of the nurses had evidently told Jeff that the open sores on Jane's right knee were draining. He told Jane that there could be an infection there, at the site of perhaps a bone spur — he wasn't sure. Jeff added that a small operation might fix it, or that perhaps nothing need be done.

("Well, that wasn't so bad, was it?" I asked my wife when she'd finished. Jane seemed to take it well, and recovered okay, I thought.

(I'd brought in Chapter 6 of Dreams, which I'd finished typing this morning, and ended up reading the whole thing to Jane except for a couple of notes. I had the time, being caught up on correspondence again. She liked the whole thing. She had the same feeling I'd noticed when reading sessions one hadn't seen for several years: that it was all brand new, and surprising, as though someone else had produced the work. I told her at the end of the day that the Seth material is an excellent example of her own direct cognition; this obvious description had come to me after I worked with Seth's material on direct cognition in Chapter 6 of Dreams. A very good point, though, and one I want to add a note on for the chapter.

(It was so late when I finished reading Chapter 6 to her that Jane wasn't planning on a session today, until I told her it was okay with me.)

Now I bid you another fond good afternoon —

("Good afternoon, Seth.")

— and we will resume dictation, with a new chapter, to be called: "Suggestion and Health."

(Jane had received this title yesterday, and told me.)

Suggestions are usually statements directed toward a particular action or hypothesis. To a large extent, suggestions are tied into conscious thought processes, following the dictates of reason. For example: "If thus and thus be so, then thus and thus must follow." There is no magic connected with suggestions — but repeated often enough, and believed in fervently, such suggestions do indeed take on a deeply habitual nature. They are no longer examined, but taken for literal truth.

(Long pause.) They are then handed over to the more automatic levels of personality, where they trigger the specific actions that are so strongly implied. Many such suggestions are "old-hat idioms." They belong to the past, and again they escape the questioning and examination that are usually given to new ideas. Period.

These suggestions may be remarkably long-standing, therefore, and consist of beliefs received in childhood. Period. Accepted now in the present, noncritically, they may still affect health and well-being. Such suggestions can be beneficial and supportive, or negative and detrimental. Here are some examples that should be quite familiar to many people. They consist of suggestions given to children:

"If you go out in the rain without your rubbers, you will catch cold."

"If you are too talkative or demonstrative, people will not like you."

"If you run you will fall down."

There are many variations, of course, such as: "If you go out in rainy weather, you'll get pneumonia," or: "If you tell a lie your tongue will turn to stone."

These suggestions and others like them are often given to children by their parents with the best of intentions. When they are young, the offspring will accept some such suggestions uncritically, coming as they do from a revered adult, so that the suggestions are almost interpreted as commands.

A suggestion like: "If you go swimming too soon after lunch, you will drown," is extremely dangerous, for it predicts behavior of a disastrous nature that would follow almost automatically after the first act is performed. Obviously, children who go into the water right after eating do not all drown. The suggestion itself can lead to all kinds of nervous symptoms, however — panics, or stomach cramps — that can persist well into adulthood.

Such suggestions <u>can</u> be removed, as we will explain shortly.

(4:47.) There are other kinds of suggestions that involve identification. A child may be told: "You are just like your mother; she was always nervous and moody." Or: "You are fat because your father was fat."

These are all statements leading toward a certain hypothesis. Again, the problem is that often the hypotheses remain unquestioned. You end up with structured beliefs unexamined, that are then automatically acted upon.

End of dictation.

(4:50.) Tell Ruburt not to worry. The leg question will work out, and without a needed operation.

I bid you both a fond good afternoon, having activated those coordinates that quicken your individual and joint well-being and healing qualities.

("Thank you." 4:52 P.M.)

APRIL 9, 1984
4:01 P.M. MONDAY

(I discovered considerable drainage on the foam rubber buffer between Jane's knees when I got to 330 this noon, and turned her on her back.

(At 2:50 Dr. Wilson, whom Jane likes, came in to examine the knee. He said a part of the bone at the break site, had become infected, and probably had been for a long time. It might go away, he said, as it evidently had once before when the ulcer there had healed. He agreed with us that it was okay to leave the area uncovered and free of cream, since it's thoroughly washed each day in hydro. He didn't advocate doing anything like an operation, and his advice was consistent with Seth's material yesterday. He'll check on the knee, he said.

(Jane said my parting words yesterday, that she shouldn't worry, that the leg will work itself out fine, cheered her quite a bit. I meant it, and repeat it now once again.

(At 3:15 she tried to read yesterday's session. She didn't do well, though, and I read it to her finally.)

Now — I bid you another most fond good afternoon —

("Good afternoon, Seth.")

— and we will continue dictation.

The suggestions we have given so far are predictives; they actually predict dire events of one kind or another, following a given original action.

There are many of these, dealing particularly with <u>age</u> also. Many people believe fervently that with approaching age they will meet a steady, disastrous deterioration in which the senses and the mind will be dull, and the body, stricken with disease, will lose all of its vigor and agility. Many young people believe such nonsense, and therefore <u>they set themselves up</u> to meet the very conditions they so fear.

The mind grows wiser with age <u>when it is allowed to do so</u>. There is even an acceleration of thought and inspiration, much like that experienced in the adolescent years, that suddenly brings a new understanding to the aged individual, and provides an impetus that should help the person to achieve greater comprehension — a comprehension that should <u>quell</u> all fears of death.

(4:08. Shannon took Jane's blood pressure. I read the session so far to Jane. At 4:13 Jane resumed with material she'd told me yesterday that Seth planned to cover today.)

Thoughts and beliefs do indeed bring about physical alterations. They can even — and often do — change genetic messages.

There are diseases that people believe are inherited, carried from one generation to another by a faulty genetic communication. Obviously, many people with, for example, a genetic heritage of arthritis do not come down with the disease themselves, while others indeed are so afflicted. The difference is one of belief.

The people who have accepted the suggestion uncritically that they will inherit such a malady <u>do then seem to inherit it</u>: they experience the symptoms. Actually, the belief itself may have changed a healthy genetic message into an unhealthy one. Ideally, a change of belief would remedy the situation.

People are not simply swung willy-nilly by one negative suggestion or another, however. Each person has an entire body of beliefs
and suggestions — and these are quite literally reflected in the physical body itself.

(4:19. Dana took Jane's temperature. I read Jane the last few lines.)

All practical healing deals with the insertion of positive suggestions and the removal of negative ones. As we mentioned earlier, each
smallest atom or cell contains its own impetus toward growth and
value fulfillment. In other words, they are literally implanted with
positive suggestions, biologically nurtured, so to that extent it is true
to say that in a certain fashion negative suggestions are unnatural,
leading away from life's primary goals. Negative suggestions could be
compared to static sounding on an otherwise clear program.

End of dictation.

I bid you both another fond good afternoon, and I have indeed
quickened those coordinates that lead to healing and well-being.

("Thank you.")

I am, of course, very pleased with your work on <u>Dreams</u>, and with
the notes that you read yesterday. I take it for granted that you do
understand my appreciation.

("Yes. Thank you."

*(4:28 P.M. I read the session to Jane. "As you read that I again got
what was coming up tomorrow," she said. "About the confusion that comes
when you start trying to change beliefs, 'cause they're all raveled in together.
But that's not right either," she added, meaning there was much more to be
learned.)*

APRIL 10, 1984
3:55 P.M. TUESDAY

*(The day was warmer — over 50 degrees as I drove down to 330. Jane
looked good. Not much drainage from her right knee. Georgia was taking
care of her today; she washed Jane's hair this morning. The nurses and
aides on the floor are full of hell today, telling explicit sexual jokes and playing tricks on one another.*

*(Jane described a very vivid and even exhilarating dream she'd had
last night, in which she'd been playing with her own collection of trinkets,
sitting on the floor, and so forth. I neglected to note down the details. Jane*

said she was really enjoying the dream, after supper, when Debbie Harris arrived for a visit and woke her up.

(Jane read yesterday's session, but found lots of it hard going. She did better toward the end, though, after several attempts, then did very well indeed reading rapidly through her favorite session — and mine — for March 19.)

Now, I bid you another most fond good afternoon.

("Good afternoon, Seth.")

We will resume dictation.

Worry, fear, and doubt are detrimental to good health, of course, and these are very often caused by the officially held beliefs of society.

Those beliefs paint a dire picture, in which any given situation is bound to deteriorate. Any conceivable illness will worsen, and any possible catastrophe be encountered.

Such beliefs discourage feelings of curiosity, joy, or wonder. They inhibit playful activity or spontaneous behavior. They cause a physical situation in which the body is placed in a state of defensive aggression. Under such conditions it seems only rational to look for the worm in the apple, so to speak, and to expect pain or danger in each new experience or encounter.

Play is a very important — indeed, vital — attribute in the development of growth and fulfillment. Children play naturally, and so do animals. For that matter, insects, birds, fish, and all kinds of life play. Even ants and honeybees play. Their sociability is not just a matter of constant work within a hive or an ant mound. This playful activity is, in fact, the basis for their organized behavior, and they "play" at adult behavior before they assume their own duties.

Creatures play because the activity is joyful, and spontaneous and beneficial, because it activates all portions of the organism — and again, in play youngsters imitate adult patterns of operation that lead finally to their own mature activity.

(5:09.) When people become ill, worried or fearful, one of the first symptoms of trouble is a lack of pleasure, a gradual discontinuance of playful action, and an over-concentration upon personal problems. In other words, illness is often first marked by a lack of zest or exuberance.

This retreat from pleasure begins to cut down upon normal activity, new encounters, or explorations that might in themselves help relieve the problem by opening up new options. Such a person becomes dejected looking — unsmiling and somber, leading others to comment upon such a dejected countenance. Comments such as these: "You look tired," or: "What's the matter, don't you feel well?" and other such remarks often simply reinforce the individual's earlier sense of dejection, until finally this same kind of give-and-take leads to a situation in which the individual and his fellows begin to intermix in a negative rather than a positive manner.

I do not mean to imply that it is always detrimental to make such queries as "Are you ill?" or "Are you tired?" Such questions do <u>indeed predict their own answers</u>. When a person is feeling in good health, exuberant and alive, such queries will be nonchalantly shoved aside — they will have no effect whatsoever. But constant questions of such a nature do not help an individual who is having difficulties — and in fact <u>too frequent</u> expressions of compassion can also worsen a person's state of mind, stressing the idea that he or she must be very ill indeed to attract such feelings of compassion. It is far better, then, to make no comment at all under such conditions. *(Long pause.)* I am not speaking of genuine questions of concern so much as rather automatic, unthinking, negative comments. Period.

On the other hand, it is an excellent practice to comment upon another individual's obvious zest or energy or good spirits. In such a way, you reward positive behavior, and may indeed begin a chain of positive activity instead of continuing a chain of negative reactions.

End of session.

Ruburt's dream was excellent, showing that he is now making the <u>best</u> of his past, rediscovering playful beliefs — the trinkets — and sources of pleasure and activity. Again, I quicken those coordinates that promote health and well-being.

("It's me," Jane said.

("Thank you."

(5:30 P.M. Jane had been interrupted at 4:14 by a nurse bringing vitamin C; then I'd read my wife what she'd delivered on the session so far. Now, after today's session I read the first session for Chapter 1 of Dreams *to her. I got the idea of reading the whole book to her because of her excellent response the other day when I'd read her Chapter 5. Again, today, she was quite impressed with that first session. "I think it important that*

you know what a great job you did on that book," I said. It's incredible to us that she gave that first session in September 1979, some four and a half years ago.)

APRIL 12, 1984
4:13 P.M. THURSDAY

(Jane called last night. The temperature was 60 degrees when I left for 330. Leaving the house, I picked up from the mailbox some $360 in contributions sent to us by Maude Cardwell. This morning I finished marking Dreams *for the publisher.*

(I'm beginning to get that harried feeling again, especially since another batch of mail arrived from Prentice-Hall today. Some of my teeth bother me at times, and tonight the pendulum told me they do so because I'm worrying about Jane.

(I stopped at a Convenient Market to buy potato chips to contribute to a party the staff is giving for one of the aides who's changing jobs at the hospital. Carla saved me a plate of food from the party, and I brought it home for supper. Very good. It was after 9:10 P.M. before I began typing this session.

(It was quite warm in 330 this afternoon, and Jane was often uncomfortable.)

Now — I bid you another fond good afternoon.

("Good afternoon, Seth.")

We will resume dictation.

I am not telling you to gush out a steady stream of positive suggestions, whether or not they bear any relation to the situation at hand.

I <u>am</u> saying that it is far better to look on the most hoped-for solution to any situation, and to voice that attitude rather than to expect the poorest outcome, or express the most dire of attitudes. *(Long pause.)* There are some issues highly vital to health and happiness, that are quite difficult to describe. They are felt intrinsically. They are a part of the <u>esthetics</u> of nature itself. Flowers are not just brightly colored for <u>man's</u> enjoyment, for example, but because color is a part of the flowers' own esthetic system. They enjoy their own brilliance, and luxuriate in their own multitudinous hues.

(4:20.) The insects also appreciate flowers' profusion of color, and <u>also</u> for esthetic reasons. I am saying, therefore that even insects have an esthetic sense, and again, that each creature, and each plant,

or natural entity, has its own sense of value fulfillment, seeking the greatest possible fulfillment and extension of its own innate abilities.

This sense of value fulfillment, once more, benefits not only the individual, but its species and all other species. In a manner of speaking, then, the picture of nature is painted by its own consciously vital, esthetic portions. Each portion of nature is also equipped to react to changing conditions, and therefore deals with its own kind of predictive behavior, so that it can grow today into tomorrow's condition.

Nature always works with probabilities. In human terms, this means that each person has a vast bank of avenues that lead to value fulfillment, and that individual abilities will ideally form their own boulevards of expression.

Poor health, or simply unhappy situations, arise only when the individual meets too many <u>detours</u>, or encounters too many blocks to the expression of value fulfillment.

End of dictation.

(4:30.) Once again, I activate those coordinates that quicken healing and well-being.

(Long pause, eyes closed. "Well, I guess that's it," Jane said.

(4:31. "Okay." I read the session to Jane after giving her a drink of water and lighting a smoke for her. "You ought to make a note," she said, "that because of our conditions in the hospital the sessions are a lot shorter. We have so many things to do, turning me over, feeding me, eating at a decent time so you can get home at a decent hour and have supper — "

(I said that the near-daily routine of sessions probably compensated for their brevity — but also that we let much time go by that we could use for sessions. "Right now, for instance," I said, "we're alone and no one's bothering us. You could go on for a little while longer."

(4:39.) Resume dictation.

With man's own exteriorized ego, this leads to the question of free will and the making of conscious choices.

The human individual is aware of large numbers of probable activities. Each individual person literally possesses far more abilities than can be adequately expressed <u>in any given lifetime</u>. This insures a large profusion of possible actions from which the individual can draw according to changing circumstances.

Each person can also intrinsically sense the direction in which he or she is most inclined. Inspiration will send nudges towards certain activities. It will be easier and more delightful for each person to move and grow in certain directions, rather than others.

In this discussion, I am not merely speaking in terms of exterior accomplishments, or goals, though these are important. Many people, however, will find they have a natural knack for relationships with others, in which the known value cannot be easily judged, as it can, say, in the works of an artist or writer.

Instead, such people will indeed perform a kind of artistry of relationships, composing, say, symphonic, emotional compositions that indeed play as masterfully upon the emotions as the pianist upon the keys. By looking at your own life, you can quite easily discover in what areas your own abilities lie by following the shape of your own impulses and inclinations. You cannot learn about yourself by studying what is expected of you by others — but only by asking yourself what you expect of yourself, and discovering for yourself in what direction your abilities lie.

End of dictation again.

("Thank you."

(4:56 P.M. "Boy, am I sweating," Jane said. The windows were wide open. I should have added that before the session Jane finally got through the session for March 19 by herself, after some hard going, and that I had to finish reading the last session to her myself.

(At her suggestion I'd brought in her old wire-frame glasses, but they didn't seem to make much difference. They looked good on her.)

APRIL 17, 1984
3:58 P.M. TUESDAY

(This is Jane's first session in five days — her longest recent break.

(Jane's been pretty blue lately, wondering whether she'll ever get home again. I said I didn't know how she would — or could — at this time. It's been very nearly a year — April 20. We had a discussion that wasn't very cheerful or helpful, and covered a lot of ground that we'd traversed before. I repeated my old comments that I'd have been more than willing to chuck the whole psychic bit years ago, if she wanted to, for I'd seen signs of trouble way back when she was producing Seth Speaks. *If the psychic work was at the base of her troubles — which I didn't really believe, and still don't.*

*(I think that whatever fears of life Jane has are the result of condition-
ing early in life, and that they have successfully resisted all attempts to dig
them out. My saying that such a course of bodily harm is pointless is beside
the point, when one considers how deeply they have ruled Jane for many
years. I told her I think the Seth material touches upon those fears, but
doesn't eradicate their emotional content and force. I don't know how to
help her any more. I myself have had little hope since last year, following her
burst of motion beginning in October, 1983. When I saw that she was
giving up on those movements after a couple of months, I took it as another
sign of resistance on the part of deeply entrenched parts of the personality.*

*(Then there followed the round of infections, the antibiotics, the broken
leg opening up, and so forth, and to me these meant that she had little hope
herself. But more importantly, that they, too, reflected a dogged resistance to
change on her part — of certain portions of the personality, that is. I
cannot conceive of my wife's situation being otherwise. Her body has not
been given permission to heal itself, otherwise it would be doing so. It has
that potential, undoubtedly. When Seth began saying that Jane would
resume walking in reasonable comfort, I at first believed him, but soon came
to not believe him, for I saw no sign of such a change even beginning.
Instead I saw the fevers and infections, and realized that those events meant
the time for healing and walking was not now.*

*(My own position may be too simple, but I do not believe a body can be
coaxed to good health by others, or sessions, or whatever. I told Jane that if
she ever improves, it will be because certain parts of her give permission. She
said through tears that she wants to get well, but that meant little to me, I'm
afraid, since her state flatly contradicts such protestations. I also said that
on a larger, more inclusive scale I can understand a person choosing a life
of illness, say, in order to learn and to explore consciousness in certain
ways. I think this is what she has chosen to do so far in life. In ordinary
terms her behavior is an extreme — and I added that when I asked Seth
about this, he countered by talking about the extremes of poverty in Africa,
say, but he said precious little about Jane per se. I took that as another sign
of resistance. Nor did Jane ever return to the subject. I concluded that my
asking questions was a waste of time, and stopped doing so. I have no plans
to resume, for I always ended up feeling that without my pushing, Jane —
either with or without Seth — just would never deal with them. And that's
been the case. Most of the private sessions we have in those 40 loose-leaf*

notebooks, about her symptoms, are the result of my pushing her for answers, not the other way around.

(Jane's Seth voice today was quiet, and I had to listen in competition with noises outside and in the halls.)

Now I bid you another fond good afternoon.

("Good afternoon, Seth.")

This is not book dictation.

(Long pause.) I will try to clear up several important issues. Of course, on one level Ruburt wants to be home, and you want him home also. On another level, he is afraid of going home, thinking it almost impossible <u>under current conditions</u>. This applies to you also.

He is afraid of going home because of current conditions — but that fear also prolongs current conditions. To some extent or another, you have both been afraid of making any plans at all concerning Ruburt's return home, because they seem impractical <u>at the present time</u>. Both of you do indeed think in terms of impediments that do indeed seem all too real: the responsibility of maintaining good health, the financial question — and on Ruburt's part, at least, the fear that he would not recover fully enough, but become ill again and require hospital attention once more.

In this confusion of thoughts and fears, the goal of Ruburt's recovery, or even of a considerable improvement within a foreseeable period of time, is lost. You have to eradicate as much of that fear and confusion as possible. See the goal as certainly possible. Begin to consider plans — for the plans themselves will help Ruburt's condition improve, and will begin to diminish those impediments that now loom so large in both of your minds.

I may or may not return this afternoon. I am doing my best, giving what information I can, at any rate. Take a break.

("That's it, right at this minute," Jane said.

(4:08 P.M. I read the session to Jane. Seth obviously didn't return.

(The session reinforced much of what I wrote in my notes before it was held — that fear rules, and whether by choice or not, has for many years. But then, ultimately it had to be chosen. I found myself thinking as the session progressed that what's needed is not the allaying of any current fears about going home, but the more basic ones that are "responsible" for the whole situation to begin with. Then the current fears would melt away, I

think. I even think that when Seth told Jane a few weeks ago that her broken right leg could straighten itself out, this generated more fears right there — that it couldn't do so, and so forth. I also think that when an individual wants protection or shielding from the world badly enough, he or she will go to any length to get it.)

APRIL 18, 1984
4:50 P.M. WEDNESDAY

(Jane didn't call last night. This morning I took the cats to the vet, with far less trouble than I had feared. Yet last night I'd slept poorly, waking up to wonder how I'd make out trying to get them into the carriers for the journey to the veterinarian in Horseheads, which is a small community very close to Elmira. To me, they already seem better tonight, although they've each had but one pill for the itching.

(At 11 P.M. as I was about to begin copying checks from Maude Cardwell, Frank Longwell visited, and we talked about how to fix the back yard when the trees are gone. Now tomorrow I should take the lawnmower in to get that put in shape, for the grass is turning green and soon will be growing. I haven't worked on Dreams *for what seems like days.*

(Jane seemed somewhat subdued, although she ate well. We discussed yesterday's session. She tried to read it while I did mail, but I ended up reading most of it to her. I'd feared it was too harsh, but as I read aloud I did see that it expressed my thinking. Jane seemed to agree with the thesis that basically a deep fear is in back of her troubles, and we went over some of the same ground we'd covered yesterday. She suggested trying dream suggestion to get clues as to the root causes of her fears, and I said that that was a good approach.

(Another approach we want to try is to play the tape a friend had sent us several months ago — a reading by someone whom he considers gifted psychically. Jane is now ready to listen to the tape, and so am I. Last night I couldn't find the tape, but now I did, just before beginning to type this session. So tomorrow I take the tape and recorder in to 330.

(So much time passed this afternoon that I thought Jane had passed up a session, but finally, after we'd talked some more, she said she wanted to have a short one. She'd become upset as the time passed, for our conversations more and more stressed the fact, without our overtly laboring the point,

that our situation is, in our minds at least, rather hopeless. She didn't know whether she could have the session, or dredge up anything that might help.

(The day was warm and rainy at times, and the windows were wide open. Once again, her Seth voice was quiet, and I had to pay close attention to hear it competing with other hospital sounds. This time, also, however, her delivery varied in a strange way, seeming to ride rhythms of emotion and resolve by turn. She took many long pauses, and sighed at times while speaking for Seth. I thought several times that she might stop speaking in mid-delivery, but she kept going. At a few spots I felt the tears in her voice, and that they were very close to breaking through.)

Now — I bid you a most fond good afternoon.

("Good afternoon, Seth.")

This session is obviously in response to this afternoon's troublesome discussion.

It is imperative that both of you realize that Ruburt's body has been constantly healing itself, though not with the thoroughness that you both desire. Otherwise it seems to him as if he is a physical failure <u>in that regard</u>. *(Long pause.)* He has not been as successful as he would wish — but even when fears brought about complications, the body has been successful in many ways in countering these.

At one level Ruburt did allow himself to participate in a very difficult health situation. There were many questions he asked himself about his mother's condition in particular *(Marie is a bedridden arthritic),* and about such situations in general, and he did indeed allow himself to go along on one level to provide an extraordinary impetus that he felt would be needed to conquer such extraordinary conditions.

The entire question is a deeply creative one, bringing about insights that he felt were highly vital. He felt himself adequate to the task. On the other hand, on the more usually understood human level, he also became extremely frightened.

(Long pause at 5:00.) I will have to take a break. I do not know whether or not he will continue today, for it is a hard session for Ruburt to give, while maintaining the necessary trance level.

(5:01 P.M. I could tell the session was a difficult one for Jane, especially when her voice wavered, and she almost halted her delivery several times. She said so too. "Yeah," I said, "but how tough can a session be, compared

to your daily situation laying in bed in the hospital? That's a lot worse. This session might lead to something important."

(I didn't say so because the time was speeding past and I felt dead tired myself, but the session seemed to offer some glimmers of hope. Earlier today Jane had remarked several times that on April 20th she'll have been in the hospital a year, and she didn't see how she was ever going to get out.

(My personal opinion, which I haven't even had the time to discuss with her, is that she ought to continue sessions in this vein, no matter how difficult they may be, simply to break the chains that keep her bedridden and hospitalized. Surely that goal makes them worth it. Earlier this afternoon I'd repeated my own grim assertion that putting oneself in Jane's condition because of a fear of others, or the world at large, was untenable, and that I'd never stand for it. I asked her if she'd done enough of that herself after the session, and she said she was ready to change. We'll see. At least I feel a small hope.

(And it's also obvious, I want to note, that we're both aware that in certain ways Jane's body is healing itself. If it didn't it would die. The point is that the healing we want, or a reasonable facsimile thereof, has to come from a deeper understanding and encounter with those powerful forces that brought about the situation to begin with.

(Yesterday I'd mentioned to Jane that I hope Seth, in his current book, will go into the real relationship between wellness and disease. That is, what purposes do diseases serve in our world, since they are so prevalent, and have always been with us? I feel that there must be reams of information there that may be quite new, or revolutionary. Certainly we aren't doing well as a species in coping with diseases. I also asked Jane about the question of diseases in wild animals — even those who have never seen a human being. If we create our diseases through our thoughts and lifestyles, how about animals? There must be similar reasons for the same results to occur, which would mean we are even more closely related to animals than we suspect. Or there are different reasons for animal diseases — reasons that yield the same results we have to cope with. Some of my questions grew out of my taking the cats for treatment of fleas and ticks, I told Jane, and I repeated the questions today.

(I'm quite aware that many of my own questions in this vein spring from insights gained through Jane's condition — just as Seth referred to such goals on Jane's part. But, I told her, there may be other ways to get the

same information. Meaning that Jane has carried her own situation far enough, and then some.)

APRIL 19, 1984
4:03 P.M. THURSDAY

(Jane called last night. This morning I took the lawn mower out to the shop a couple of miles outside town on Wellsburg Road. When I returned home I visited our next-door neighbors, the Bumbalos, briefly. They were getting Joe up to go to the doctor's office for blood work. He is very weak, and couldn't get up himself. I believe his death is near.

(Jane was okay, although as I got to 330, three nurses were trying to insert a new catheter. Jane had had spasms. The nurses had some difficulty, and we were late eating lunch. Afterward we played the tape of the psychic reading a friend had sent us last September. The tape was a copy, and the quality terrible — so bad we couldn't understand it all. I marveled that a scientist would send out a product like that.

(Some of the material from the tape is good, other parts not good — some right, some wrong, as might be expected. He said Jane could die, but obviously she didn't. He was correct in mentioning anemia, incorrect about liver and spleen problems, as far as we know. The problem with such readings is their generalizations. One can always cite energy blockages, and probably be correct, but this says little. Most of us have energy blockages of some sort. Also, one not only has to penetrate the reality of the person being read, but that of the medium doing the reading. The reading offered no specific insights into the causes behind Jane's troubles, although this would be difficult in such a short time span.

(The psychic reading was correct, I think, in saying that Jane had the creative potential to create a spectacular success, and recover. We thought the tape contained a number of negative suggestions, though how one deals with physical troubles without sounding negative at times may be a problem in itself. Specifics are vital, however, so once again we are on our own. I still think Jane carries within her her own solutions. She said she was "more unfavorably disposed toward the reading than favorably disposed toward it." Amen. So am I. But it's a valuable learning experience. I told Jane part of that value lay in the fact that we waited until now to play it, when she has decided to try to uncover her own causes and effects. Obviously, we didn't want to use the tape before.

(At 3:40 Jane began reading yesterday's session, and did very well indeed — her best yet with speed, and with both eyes open, whereas she usually has to close one or the other. She wore her glasses. "Maybe your doing so well today is an outcome of the session for yesterday," I said. She thought it possible. She was also eager to have a session today, and began it early.)

I bid you another fond good afternoon.

("Good afternoon, Seth.")

The following material is for dictation, but I am giving it here also so that Ruburt will take it specifically to heart. There are certain simple steps that can be followed, whenever you find yourself in a difficult situation, whether the condition is one of poor health, a stressful personal involvement with another, a financial dilemma, or whatever.

These steps seem very obvious, and perhaps too easy — but they will bring an immediate sense of ease and a peace of mind while your inner reserves are being released and activated. I have mentioned these steps many times, because they are so vital in clearing the conscious mind, and bringing some sense of <u>relief</u> to the frightened ego.

1. Immediately begin to live in the present as much as possible. Try to become as aware as you can of present sense-data — <u>all</u> of it. Often, while you are in pain, for example, you concentrate upon that sensation alone, ignoring the feelings of ease that may be felt by other portions of the body, and unaware of the conglomeration of sounds, sights, and impressions that are also in the immediate environment. This procedure will immediately <u>lessen the pressure</u> of the problem itself, whatever it is, and give you a sense of refreshment.

2. Refuse to worry. This fits in automatically with Step 1, of course. Tell yourself you can worry all you want tomorrow, or on some other occasion — but resolve <u>not</u> to worry in the present moment.

3. When your thoughts <u>do</u> touch upon your particular <u>problem in that present moment,</u> imagine the best possible solution to the dilemma. Do not wonder how or why or when the ideal solution will come, but see it in your mind's eye as accomplished. Or if you are not particularly good at visual imagery, then try to get the <u>feeling</u> of thanksgiving and joy that you <u>would</u> feel if the problem was solved to your complete satisfaction.

These steps will allow you breathing time, and actually help minimize the pressure of your situation, whatever it is. Then, quieted, you will be able to consider other suitable steps that may more directly address your particular solution.

We will take a break, and then resume.

(4:21. "He will come back, I guess," Jane said. She had been interrupted twice during her delivery: once to have her temperature taken — 98.7 — and once to be given vitamin C. I read the session to her. "I have the feeling this is like first aid," she said. Resume at 4:27.)

This is not dictation. Give us a moment.

(Long pause.) While you and Ruburt embark upon a resolved path of getting to the bottom of Ruburt's difficulties, it is highly important that Ruburt in particular increase his experience of pleasure, and his concentration upon it, so that pleasure can <u>counter</u> any other emotionally distressful feelings that may emerge along the way.

Again, we do not want <u>a concentration solely upon</u> deeply-felt fears. While these must be uncovered, they should be balanced by a new determination to seek out pleasure *(emphatically)* — the pleasure will help couch the fears.

We will not abandon book dictation, but the concentration for now will be largely devoted to bettering Ruburt's condition by releasing his own energies, health, and flexibility.

I suggest you start with a kind of free association on Ruburt's part. With your resolve in mind, almost any subject matter you begin with will start to lead in the proper direction. Again, we want, say, the release of painful thoughts or emotions somehow balanced by the steps I gave today, so that they provide a kind of supporting framework.

("You're talking about outside the sessions themselves.")

I am indeed.

I will interrupt whenever I can be of benefit — and I will also provide sometimes short but pithy session material *(with humor)* that can be used sometimes as subject matter for free association. You can begin of course by free associating with any appropriate subject — his mother, his father, your relationship, your individual or joint sexual feelings, his ideas about his psychic material, his writing, or whatever — and I will also provide guidelines.

The endeavor itself will also activate his own dream mechanisms, and you will find that both of you bring new creative understandings to the task.

Ruburt's *(session)* reading today also shows the body's own resiliency.

Again, I activate those coordinates so vital to healing, exuberance, and well-being.

("It's me," Jane said after a long pause.

(4:43 P.M. I read the session to her. It certainly would be a mistake to let book material go, for any reason. It would provide variety and a sense of accomplishment aside from any other more personal material Seth may give. The free association approach Seth suggests will be something different for us to try. I'll let an approach to handling the material work itself out.

(Jane called early — before 9:00 P.M., as I was getting ready to type this session. An insight concerning my questions about the role of diseases came to me after supper, before I began typing this session, and I want to note it for possible future discussion. Regarding my visit with Joe Bumbalo this morning: He has cancer. I found myself thinking about the cancer being a new, explosive growth within a body that was aging. That growth was fated to bring about not only the death of its host, but the cancer itself. So what was it doing, behaving in such a fashion? Was Joe Bumbalo giving birth to a new life form that upon death would be released to continue its growth elsewhere, just as we believe Joe will do after his death?)

CHAPTER 6

"States Of Health And Disease"

APRIL 20, 1984
4:12 P.M. FRIDAY

(J*ane called me last night with Elisabeth's help. Elisabeth, our German friend, left a lemon cake for me and had brought Jane an Easter basket.*

(As Seth suggested we do yesterday, we tried free association today. It worked well, and came about spontaneously when I dropped my notebook on the bed when Jane asked me to get her water. I was tired and somewhat exasperated, and she picked this up from me immediately. It set off a chain of associations for her, and she pursued them while saying she was half embarrassed to mention them. Here are the brief notes I wrote as she talked:

(When I seemed exasperated when Jane asked me to do something for her, and dropped my notebook on the bed, she at once felt a strong fear that she'd exasperate me beyond bearing — that she couldn't afford to get me mad at her. This at once led her to feeling that as a child it had been vital that she avoid the disapproval of others — her mother, Marie, especially. And even in college, the same thing. Jane feared that if she got Marie mad, Marie would get sick and die. Marie used to tell Jane it was her fault the mother was sick, and that it was also her fault that Jane's grandmother died, and the housekeeper. "If you didn't watch yourself," Jane said, "you could get hurt yourself or hurt other people."

(Jane also felt that the sessions could be responsible for more deaths, or hurting people. She'd been terrified holding sessions, way back in the beginning, for the woman in Louisiana who had MS. At the same time she'd felt a responsibility toward helping her. Jane basically didn't want anything to do with sick people — was afraid she could hurt them in sessions.

(Jane didn't think the sessions could hurt her, though she often felt she didn't get enough information through for herself. We talked about other similar situations and things, and she was near tears at times — so there definitely is emotion there. I don't actually think we said anything brand new, but it was good to review it all. I explained my position that she didn't need to make bargains with herself, as she used to tell me she did — that it was perfectly okay to be healthy and talented at the same time, using one's abilities as one chose. The world wasn't going to pass any sort of judgment if she didn't choose to deal with the sick.

(Afterward, she said several times that she wanted to have a session. I'd thought she might pass it up. Her Seth voice was somewhat louder than usual.)

I bid you another most fond good afternoon.

("Good afternoon, Seth.")

You have started the free association in a good and rousing fashion, so that Ruburt becomes consciously aware of some of his own attitudes that he has more or less become blind to. He has progressed far enough, however, tell him, so that he does not have to fear any <u>regression</u>. The framework we have set up will prevent that.

Now: Dictation.

Before we discuss the human situation more specifically in relationship to health and "dis-ease" — let us consider the so-called states of health and disease as they apply in planetary terms, and as they operate in all species. This will give us a far vaster framework in which to understand the ways in which each individual person fits into the entire picture.

Give us a moment . . . We will begin the next chapter, to be called: "States of Health and Disease" — the entire sentence in quotations.

I used quotation marks around the entire heading for this chapter to stress the point that the heading is written with your own ideas of health and disease in mind. Actually, however, regardless of appearances and misreadings of natural events, the very idea of disease as you usually think of it, is <u>chauvinistic</u> *(louder)* in health rather than in sexual terms.

Basically speaking, there are only life forms. Through their cooperation your entire world sustains its reality, substance, <u>life</u>, and form. If there were no diseases as you think of them, there would be no life forms at all. Your reality demands a steady fluctuation of physical and nonphysical experience. Most of you, my readers, understand that if you did not sleep you would die. The conscious withdrawal of mental life <u>during</u> life makes normally conscious experience possible. In the same way there must, of course, be a rhythm of physical death, so that the experience of normal physical life is possible. It goes without saying that without death and disease — for the two go hand in hand — then normal corporeal existence would be impossible.

(4:30.) For all of man's fear of disease, however, the species has never been <u>destroyed</u> by it, and life has continued to function with an <u>overall</u> stability, despite what certainly seems to be the constant harassment and threat of illness and disease. The same is true, generally speaking, of all species. Plants and insects fit into this larger picture, as do all fish and fowl.

I have said elsewhere that no species is ever really eradicated — and in those terms no disease, or virus, or germ, ever vanishes completely from the face of the earth. In the first place, viruses change their form, appearing in your terms sometimes as harmless and sometimes as lethal. So-called states of health and disease are also changing constantly — <u>and in those vaster terms</u> disease in itself is a <u>kind of health</u>, for it makes life and health itself possible *(all quite intently)*.

Later we will discuss what this means to you, the individual person, but for now I want to stress the fact that while it may seem natural enough to consider disease as a threat, an adversary or an enemy, this is not the case.

The subject matter of <u>suffering</u> is certainly vitally connected to the subject at hand, but basically speaking, disease and suffering are not <u>necessarily</u> connected. Suffering and <u>death</u> are not <u>necessarily</u> connected either. The sensations of suffering, and the pain, do exist. Some are indeed quite natural reactions, and others are <u>learned</u> reactions to certain events. Walking barefoot on a bed of fire would most likely cause most of you, my readers, to feel the most acute pain — while in some primitive societies, under certain conditions the same situation could result instead in feelings of ecstasy or joy.

We want to discuss "disease" as it exists apart from suffering for now, then. Then we will discuss pain and suffering and their implications. I do want to mention, however, that pain and suffering are also obviously vital, living sensations — and therefore are a part of the body's repertoire of possible feelings and sensual experience. They are also a sign, therefore, of life's vitality, and are in themselves often responsible for a return to health when they act as learning communications.

(Long pause.) Pain, therefore, by being unpleasant, stimulates the individual to rid himself or herself of it, and thereby often promotes a return to the state of health.

End of dictation.

(4:48.) Remind Ruburt — in the meantime — that he is indeed a <u>beloved</u> daughter of the universe, and that his parents are as much the sea and sky as his physical parents. Period. End of session. I also, however, look in rather often on your own situation, and send you my support.

(4:50 P.M. "I'm glad I had it," Jane said, "even though it's late, 'cause it's got information you wanted. I did all right. I was able to clear my mind enough to give it." She seemed to feel good, and I told her she'd done well. And the session had gone into the question I'd noted yesterday at the end of the session, about the roles of health and disease in our world. I was tired.

(Jane called with Carla's help at about 9:40, as I was typing this session. She said Carla had told her that she was on duty the night of the day Jane was admitted to the hospital April 20, just a year ago. I hadn't remembered this, nor had Jane.)

APRIL 22, 1984
3:35 P.M. SUNDAY

(No session was held today, April 21, 1984, but we did do some free associating, so I'll present a summary of that material here, and follow it with a session and more free association whenever they come through.

(I had several questions resulting from Jane's material of yesterday. A remark that I'd made, to the effect that her illness has probably cost us at least half a dozen books over the years, elicited a response from her; she

brought it up today, in fact. Now, she said, she wasn't doing anything except a little bit each day. She'd picked up the idea of discipline from me, in a most unfortunate way, I thought, considering her most spontaneous nature. We talked about why her psyche had done so. She agreed that she is protected from life in the hospital. She also thought that she personally couldn't live up to the high quality of the Seth material — her own "mental work," a good way of putting it. The symptoms, then, served to keep her at her desk over the years because she was afraid that if left alone she'd fly off somewhere and wouldn't do anything.

(The symptoms — and now the hospital — protected her from criticism, eliminated book tours, the whole bit. Jane got scared with Sumari in the beginning, just as she had at the start of the sessions in 1963, but she was also very curious and turned on. She was also frightened at the tests in sessions, of being wrong, and of the seance. Thought she'd be called a hysterical woman, an exhibitionist, and so on. <u>Being right didn't carry the weight that being wrong did</u>. Very good. There were tears at various times with today's material.

(I talked about the first session for Jane's symptoms — the private portion of Session 208, for November 15, 1965 — yet she said that for her the whole thing really started the day before we went to a party in June 1966 regarding How to Develop Your ESP Power. *Our friends wanted to celebrate the publication of her first "psychic" book, her first mention of Seth, but she read poetry at the party and wouldn't talk about the ESP book — too embarrassed. A strange, protective way to behave.*

(At 4:40, she was near tears when I asked why her psyche hadn't risen up to protect her when it became obvious that she was heading for deep trouble with the symptoms. She said her psyche <u>did</u> rise up to protect her many times — otherwise she'd have died, of course. She mentioned various periods of improvement — her work on her unfinished and unpublished autobiography, From This Rich Bed; *her published novel,* The Education of Oversoul Seven, *and so on. But each time a new book came out she got worse. Near tears, she said that she didn't have to get any worse when a new book comes out — what's left? She agreed with me that she now has the ultimate protection of the hospital.*

("I'd better get some good out of this," she said. "It's no fun dredging up those feelings, so boy they better pay off."

(A session obviously was held the next day, however, on April 22, 1984. It took place on Easter Sunday, a chilly, gray day. Jane had read the free-

association material for yesterday; she got through it okay, but had to strug-
gle a bit. After we'd talked about the material, she announced a session.)

Now — I bid you another most fond good afternoon.

("Good afternoon, Seth.")

The following material is for Ruburt, and can be used as material for free association. Give us a moment.

(Long pause.) Ruburt felt that his writing, and writing abilities,
justified his existence — that it, the ability to write should make up
for all other deficiencies. His mother helped make him feel unlike-
able, but his abilities seemed to be his saving grace — and therefore
to be encouraged and protected at all costs.

It will help, as you did once some time ago, if you compose a list
of Ruburt's good qualities and excellent personal characteristics.

Then use this brief session itself as a starting point for free association. I may or may not return this afternoon, but I do activate
those coordinates that quicken understanding, exuberance, and
well-being.

("All right," Jane said.

(3:43 P.M. I read the session to her.

*(Afterward we tried some free association. Jane began talking of her
attempts to get people to listen to her poetry, and her early fears that she was
considered odd because of her talents. This led her into talk about my
mother's opinion of her — though I tried to show that Stella's opinion had
changed and that she really liked Jane in later years. Jane agreed. I said it's
easy to judge the past, whereas one should instead simply try to learn from
it and understand it, and go on from there. We seemed to arrive at an
impasse of understanding today.*

*(Jane was afraid of others as a young girl, and even in college — that
she wouldn't get their approval — whereas, I said, the others should have
been afraid that they wouldn't get her approval, since her abilities tran-
scended theirs. So why should she sink to the common denominator? Jane
said she'd never thought of that. I said it's too bad the young don't have the
insight to stress their capabilities regardless of the opinions of others — but
such thinking comes with age, usually, I'm afraid.*

*(Even those at the writer's conference in the summer of 1957, at Mil-
ford, Pennsylvania, told her she'd outgrow her urge to write — that she
should have a baby. And Jane felt that her body could betray her by getting
pregnant. She even thought I felt that way. It's true that I had no urge for*

parenthood, but I didn't think of betrayal, or bargains. Jane was afraid getting pregnant would ruin my career because I'd have to work full time. I could have reacted better than that, I'm sure.

(I think the important thing today was that as we talked we saw how with each category Jane described <u>negative</u> beliefs and reactions — an excellent point. It's a thought we've had before — but it seems that each thing we've accomplished has been in the face of, or in spite of, a barrage of negative thoughts, feelings, and beliefs.

(Yet she finally admitted that she knew she'd succeeded with my mother — not with my father, though. As to her own mother, Marie, I said it was perfectly okay to admit that she didn't succeed there, or chose to withdraw or admit failure. Jane thought her mother hated her as a child, and still did even now. The mother's hatred, Jane said, led to her need for protection — perfectly normal, I said. Jane said that when he was drunk her father told her that Marie was her enemy. Evidently she believed this.

(I read parts of the session for April 18 to Jane — wherein Seth had said she'd become extremely frightened. It's an excellent session. "But that's it," Jane said mournfully. "I'm afraid I've gotten in so deep I can't get out." A good, up-to-the-minute fear, out in the open. I've had the same fear many times. "But I've decided that enough is enough," Jane said, after I'd speculated about why her psyche hadn't put the brakes on her symptoms before this. Emotions were expressed after all, today, and the session was a success.)

APRIL 25, 1984
3:10 P.M. WEDNESDAY

(No session was held. Here is a summary of the free-association material we discussed yesterday, April 24:

(Jane was blue and uncomfortable this morning: "What a way to live," she said. She'd thought of death, but didn't want to do that to me. She's looking for a sign of something better — some improvement that will lift her spirits. She felt better after I read her the session for March 19, and a great Sumari poem I used to close out the essays for Dreams *with.*

(Jane has even thought of having Debbie Harris take dictation at night, for another children's book. Perhaps an autobiography also. The nurses and aides were raising hell this morning with their jokes and tricks. This usually helps cheer up Jane, though she gets nervous if they don't keep their minds on what they're doing when they lift her, say.

(We talked about differing opinions regarding Prentice-Hall. These are to be expected, but all seem trivial now, given our present situation.

(Jane thinks her work, her poetry, is good. Before he did Seth Speaks, *she was scared Seth couldn't write a book. I'd had no such worries. Jane had felt that I was disappointed by the publication of her novel,* The Rebellers — *and correctly so. Both of us had been upset at the poor-looking, cheap, double-novel presentation.*

(I kept trying to get at events — before and at the time the sessions began — and Jane's symptoms. "I can't even go home for an hour, without it costing two hundred dollars," Jane said, and started to cry. "But I'm not ready to reconcile myself to the spot I'm in." But she said she was often careful about what she said to me, so that she wasn't always dumping on me when I came to the hospital. But if not me, I said, who could she talk to? Besides, I knew her moods and feelings much better, evidently, than she realized. She surprised me when she said, "I realized that I used to really dislike women." There was more.)

I bid you a most fond good afternoon.

("Good afternoon, Seth.")

We will resume dictation.

Even in situations that involve a so-called host-and-parasite relationship, there is a cooperative process. Fleas, for example, actually help increase circulation, and constantly comb animal's hair. At minute levels they also consume some bodily wastes, and creatures even smaller than they are. They also keep the immune system active and flexible.

Many diseases are actually health-promoting processes. Chicken pox, measles, and other like diseases in childhood <u>in their own way</u> "naturally inoculate" the body, so that it is able to handle other elements that are a part of the body and the body's environment.

When civilized children are <u>medically</u> inoculated against such diseases, however, they usually do not show the same symptoms, and to an important extent the natural protective processes are impeded. Such children may not come down with the disease against which they are medically protected, then — but they may indeed therefore become "prey" to other diseases later in life that would not otherwise have occurred.

I am speaking generally here, for remember that your individual beliefs, thoughts, and emotions cause your reality, so no person dies ahead of his or her time. The individual chooses the time of death. It is true, however, that many cancers and conditions such as AIDS result because the immunity system has been so tampered with that the body has not been allowed to follow through with its own balancing procedures.

Again, however, no individual dies of cancer or AIDS, or any other condition, until they themselves have set the time.

There are many other conditions to be taken into consideration, for such diseases certainly do have strong social connections. They occur in social species. This does not mean that they are necessarily contagious at all, but that they do bear an overall relationship to the give-and-take between individuals and their social and natural frameworks.

(3:27.) A city might be overrun by rats, for example — a fine situation for the rats if not the populace — but the entire picture would include unrest in the populace at large, a severe dissatisfaction with social conditions, feelings of dejection, and all of those conditions together would contribute to the problem. <u>Rat poison</u> may indeed add its own dangers, killing other small birds or rodents, and contaminating animal food supplies. Nor are insects invulnerable to such conditions, in such an hypothesized picture (long pause). Actually, all forms of life in that certain environment would be seeking for a balanced return to a more advantageous condition.

You may wonder why so many forms of life would be involved in what might seem to be self-destructive behavior, often leading to death — but remember that no consciousness considers death <u>an end or a disaster</u>, but views it instead as a means to the continuation of corporeal and noncorporeal existence.

I may or may not return this afternoon, but in any case I have activated those coordinates that so encourage self-healing, faith, and well-being.

("Thank you."

(3:35 P.M. Jane had been interrupted once for nursing care. "I don't know when, but sometime earlier — quite a bit earlier — I felt that that would be the subject today," she said. "It's more on your own questions, too." Then she added, "I know he's going into at least two other things in this chapter, too: that at certain times people mostly died in their 30's, say, at one period, and usually lived to be very old in another. Also, that we've *gotten out of touch with our own feelings about death, and are afraid of it. And he isn't going to tell people not to get vaccinated otherwise they'd end up totally confused."*

(I thought the session very interesting. Seth's comments about fleas made me wonder about using the flea bombs in the house that Frank Long- well had gotten for me a few days ago. These would kill every flea in the house, supposedly. And the vet had given me flea powder to use on the cats themselves. Would this actually deprive them of a valuable symbiotic rela- tionship? I began wondering how to compromise about the flea situation this summer, now that the rugs in the house are all clean.

(I told Jane that Seth's material on childhood inoculations leading to later diseases might be vulnerable to statistics. Enough records certainly exist, that such connections might be found — if they were looked for dili- gently enough on a long-term basis. Such a discovery could lead to revisions in medical treatment, though I'm not sure what or how. I told Jane that the material made me speculate about Joe Bumbalo: He's had many operations in his life, and has been shot full of drugs often. Could such repeated dosages have anything to do with his having cancer now? And even now Joe is taking powerful chemotherapy treatments. He's losing his hair, I believe.

(Today Jane said she'd talked it over with Debbie Harris, and that the latter would be coming in three nights a week while Jane tries some sponta- neous dictation. Fifty cents a page for finished copy, they agreed upon. Jane didn't know about trying an emotional subject like an autobiography with someone else, though. I said let it work itself out.

(Jane and I were both impressed that we received checks totaling more than $900 from Maude Cardwell yesterday. I deposited them in the special account on my way to the hospital this noon.

(I got no work done on Dreams *this morning. It's been over a week since I've worked on the book.)*

APRIL 27, 1984
4:20 P.M. FRIDAY

(The day was brilliant and very warm — almost 80 degrees when I left the house for 330. Jane's room was pleasantly cool, though. Later I turned on the fan. She showed me how the large scab on her right knee, over the site of the broken bone that had become infected, had peeled off partially in hydro this morning. It's now half its former size. Underneath the missing portion

I saw the fresh pink flesh of new growth. There is still a large hole in the leg at the drainage site. Both of us felt good about the improvements, though.

(On the way to 330 this noon I stopped to give the hospital the check for $18,000-plus that I'd received the day before yesterday from Blue Cross. A couple of weeks previously a check for some $3700 had arrived; the two go together to make one payment as billed by the hospital to the insurance company. I'm afraid that when I opened the letter and saw the check for the $18,000, I felt no reaction at all. I wondered then at my lack of feeling. I put my neutral state down to the long wait involved, my decision not to worry if at all possible, and probably other factors I haven't even bothered to examine. Anger must be involved. Nor did I feel anything when the check for the $3700 came. I confess the lack of feeling here has caused me periodic concern.

(It appears that the payments will be for 100% of the bill, rather than 80% — but here again I'm waiting to see, suspended in a kind of cocoon of inaction or non-reaction . . .

(The windows were wide open and a refreshing breeze filled 330 as Jane went into trance. The fan was on also.)

I bid you another most fond good afternoon.

("Good afternoon, Seth.")

The obvious improvement in Ruburt's knee is a fine example of the body's self-healing processes.

It could not be accomplished by the conscious mind — though the conscious mind can indeed will the process to occur. *(A most important point to remember.)* The knee will continue to improve, and the finger also *(on the left hand)*.

Now give us a moment . . . dictation.

<u>I am not</u> advising my readers to refuse to have their children vaccinated, since you now have to take vaccination into consideration because of the prominence of it in society. It is very possible, however, that science itself will in time discover the unfortunate side effects of many such procedures, and begin to reevaluate the entire subject.

It is true that some native populations — particularly in the past — were free of many of the childhood diseases that are considered natural by western medicine. It is also true, of course, that some primitive societies have lost large numbers of their populations to disease. Some of those instances, however, were caused precisely by the <u>sudden</u> introduction of western medicine.

I am not condemning western medicine per se, however, but merely pointing out its many detrimental aspects. Medicinal science is also in a state of transition, and it is just as important — if not more so — that it examine its concepts as well as its techniques.

The idea of using animals for experimentation has far more drawbacks than advantages; there is the matter of one kind of consciousness definitely taking advantage of another kind, and thus going counter to nature's cooperative predisposition.

In the distant past some ancient civilizations did indeed use animals in such a fashion, but in a far different framework. The doctors or priests humbly stated their problems verbally and through ritualistic dancing, and then <u>requested the help</u> of the animal — so that the animals were not sacrificed, in those terms, nor taken advantage of. Instead, they united in a cooperative venture, in which animals and man both understood that no consciousness truly died but only changed its form.

Animals have indeed often been quite helpful to man in various healing situations and encounters, but in all such cases these were cooperative ventures.

(4:36.) This leads me of course to at least mention here the cruel methods used in the slaughtering of animals and fowls for human consumption. The creatures are treated as if they possessed no feeling or consciousness of their own — and such attitudes show a most unfortunate misreading of natural events. As a direct result, at least as many diseases develop through such procedures as would exist in a highly primitive society with unsanitary conditions. Period.

In <u>that</u> kind of setting, however, balances would right themselves because the basic understanding between living creatures would be maintained. You cannot divorce philosophy from action, and the cruelty in slaughterhouses would not be perpetrated if it were not for distorted philosophies dealing with the survival of the fittest on the one hand, and the egotistical assumption that God gave man animals to do with as man wished.

End of dictation. *(4:43.)* Take to heart what I said about Ruburt's knee, so that he realizes <u>in fact</u> that the healing processes are indeed operating within him all the time. That realization will help change conditions enough so that the two of you can be home together sooner than you may think possible. Again, I activate those coordinates that quicken high spirits, strength, and vitality — and I bid you a fond good afternoon.

(4:45 P.M. "Good afternoon, Seth.")

APRIL 30, 1984
4:11 P.M. MONDAY

(Here's a summary of the free association material we discussed on Sunday afternoon, April 29:

(Jane had had thoughts of death when she came into the hospital a year ago. She was on morphine and had hallucinations, too. Frank Longwell's father had just died, and she feared she might take the same road. She really did dislike women when she was younger. She'd been afraid of her body, and sex. Took it as a compliment when told she had a mind like a man. Also thought women disliked her — feared that she was after their men, and all kinds of things.

(We talked about her home environment, and how in 1965 the young psychologist at Dr. Instream's hypnosis symposium had rearoused her fears, and my own upsets. Jane recalled being called a fraud by a fellow student in college, and by my mother. We talked about religion. All of this engendered some emotional reactions, but no tears. I kept trying to go back to what had happened before Jane got her symptoms, before she became well-known, and so forth. I told her I remembered Seth saying once that her symptoms "were amazingly stubborn." Many things spoke of a great fear of spontaneity, reinforced again and again after the sessions had started, and the symptoms.

(Jane began to cry when she recounted the time at home a few years ago when she couldn't get up and on her feet — finally reaching that point of helplessness. I got mad at her and yelled, saying I'd leave her sitting there if she didn't get up — thus displaying my own deep fears that we had reached a sad and desperate point in the course of the symptoms. She remembered my crying at times. I told her I'd cried at times when she hadn't known it.

(We tried more free association on the afternoon of April 30:

("Years ago in the 1960's," Jane said, "I thought I loved you a lot more than you loved me, and that you could get along very well all by yourself." I said that was a total misconception on her part, that I'd never had such ideas, nor wanted to do any such thing. It had never entered my head. I knew things bugged me — working, being an artist, or trying to, and so

forth — but not anything to do with her. I didn't even fear fatherhood as much as she feared becoming pregnant. Not that I wanted fatherhood.

(We talked a lot about our early days together — work and our arts, prestige, money, and the opinions of others. I said that much of what we talked about would be considered the normal hassles in life, but that we had put negative connotations on those things and ignored the positive. Our told troubles now seem minute in retrospect. I added that each person is so different from each other person that it's useless to make judgments, so each person might as well do their thing and let the chips fall. Who's to say it's right or wrong, as long as one doesn't injure another, or steal, and so on.

(Jane said she thought that if I'd had to choose between painting and her, I'd have chosen painting. Not so, I said — after all, I worked at commercial art four years full time at one stretch, and part time a number of other times. She agreed that she needed much approval — something I hadn't fully understood at the time we married. I added that I'd always been proud of her as my wife, and considered myself very lucky to have her. I'd never once questioned her loyalty or love, and I'd taken it that she felt the same way. I discovered today that I could have been wrong at times — strange.

(She'd even thought I disapproved of her way of dress at times, whereas, if memory serves me correctly, I'd almost always liked the way she dressed, fixed her hair, and so on. I made no such judgments. She said she'd brooded a lot.

(At 4:03 she said she was getting upset by our talk. I asked her to have a session on Seth's remark about her symptoms being "amazingly stubborn." She decided to have a cigarette and see if she could go into trance. I'd always thought the sessions themselves were a form of self-hypnosis. We'd talked about self-hypnosis as a way of breaking through today.

(When Jane spoke for Seth her voice was rather quiet, since it was still sort of raspy from yesterday's laryngitis, or whatever she'd had. She thought the loss of voice volume was due to free-association material. A strong wind — very strong at times — had sprung up this afternoon, and at times I had trouble hearing Jane above its noise. Her eyes were often closed, and she took many long pauses. The day was alternately bright and sunny, and very gloomy and cloudy.)

I bid you another fond good afternoon.

("Good afternoon, Seth.")

This is not dictation.

Above all, Ruburt must not concentrate upon what is <u>wrong</u>. In the deepest of terms, if you understand my meaning, <u>nothing is wrong</u>.

You have instead a conglomeration of severely conflicting beliefs, so that there is no clear single road to action.

(I understand Seth's declaration that in the deepest of terms there is nothing wrong. It's a perception I've used often in the past year as I've tried to understand what's going on.)

<u>You want to clear the road</u>. The free association is valuable because it helps to point out those conflicting feelings and beliefs, brings them into consciousness, and into the present moment, where they can indeed be understood in the light of knowledge that has been acquired since — but not been allowed to act upon the old conflicting beliefs.

The expression of emotions in itself is an expression of action, of motion. To move requires first of all the expression of feeling, and the expression of any feeling makes room for still further motion. Self-hypnosis can indeed be invaluable in terms of accelerating bodily motion and healing. Expression, rather than repression, is vital.

Often Ruburt has not been in touch with his own feelings, but would try to intellectualize many away. He needs to realize that it is safe to express himself — and that expression will not bring about abandonment.

(4:24. Jane had also said today that she'd felt that she had to be careful how she approached me so I wouldn't get mad and leave her. Those feelings gradually dissipated over the years, yet they must have had a part to play in the onset of symptoms.)

People who wrote books against the Catholic Church were excommunicated. Ruburt transferred those fears to society at large. There was a conflict between creative work and the church even when only poetry was involved. He should indeed give himself suggestions that the <u>necessary insights</u> will come to him, and that the proper connections be made whether consciously <u>or</u> unconsciously. But the idea is that it is safe to express himself, and that the true purpose of his life is indeed to express those characteristics that compose his personal reality.

(Very long pause.) He should also realize that pleasure is indeed a virtue. By all means express your emotions to each other as they naturally occur. Ruburt was not taught to love himself as a child, and thought of his talents as a way of justifying his existence — an existence of <u>somewhat suspicious nature</u>, he felt, since his mother told him often that he was responsible for her own poor health.

These issues do all fit together, but they can be unscrambled, brought into the present, and reconciled. The body is more than agreeable, and more than able, to bring about an extraordinary recovery.

(Hear that, Jane?)

I do indeed activate for you both those coordinates that quicken insight, wisdom, peace of mind, and the healing processes. Again remind Ruburt of the steady improvement in his knee, and of his body's capabilities.

A fond good afternoon.

("Good afternoon. Thank you."

(4:33. "I did pretty good," Jane said as I lit a smoke for her. "I didn't know whether I could do it or not. I almost came out of it a couple of times, but I did it." I'd noticed the instances she meant. I read the session to her. She had a couple of thoughts as she listened to me. One: She transferred stuff about excommunication into the loss of companionship — that nobody would want anything to do with you if you crossed them up. Two: She'd tried to be more like me — cooler, not expressing so many emotions, more in control. And that had been a mistake on her part, a serious one, born, I said, out of her desire for protection and love.

("Well, you can see how they fit together," I said. As we talked she began to feel Seth around again. She was reluctant to do more because it was getting late. I told her to forget that.)

(4:45.) In other words, Ruburt was given strong creative abilities that he was determined to express — but at the same time early in his life he was given the idea that it was highly dangerous to express the very uniqueness <u>that was inherent in his creativity</u>. This is a part of the main issue.

He is to realize <u>that if he has any duty or purpose in life</u>, it is indeed to express those very abilities *(all very emphatically)*, since those abilities are so natural in his makeup, they also possess their own protective mechanisms. He must realize that he is free to express his poetic, psychic nature, and to follow wherever it leads — since it is indeed his natural pathway into existence, and his most intimate connection with the universe, and with All That Is.

This session does tie issues together quite well — and can be used to advantage for free association also.

End of session.

("Thank you."

(4:50 P.M. Jane had been interrupted once during her second delivery. "That was very good," I told her. "It contains excellent suggestions in itself." I've already planned to read it to her every day for a while. It can serve well as a basis for self-hypnosis, but I also plan to help my wife here, and we can see what we can accomplish in the afternoons.

(I hardly had time to discuss it with her, but I think the session is a breakthrough one that's most valuable. It also showed me that even Jane's poetry was suspect, where I'd been under the impression that the poetry was the one aspect of her creative abilities that was essentially free, or unconta-minated by fears or doubts. For years I'd thought that if Jane had done only poetry, she'd have had minimal troubles, if any.)

MAY 2, 1984
4:29 P.M. WEDNESDAY

("The mountains have fallen fathoms into the sea, and still I am I," wrote Jane in a poem when she'd been quite young.

("I became a priest of God to learn what sin is," she also wrote. The priests she saw while she was living with her mother hadn't liked those works, and castigated her for writing them. Jane rebelled. She refused to get a dispensation from the church so she could read certain works. She told me again about the book-burning a priest had conducted in her back yard, when she was a teen-ager. This is some of the free-association material we discussed on May 1.

(Jane has kept the session for April 30 in mind, but hasn't tried any self-hypnosis yet. One of us has to see that she either reads or hears it each day. I'd had the idea of starting right in trying to hypnotize her, but thought better of it. I decided it was better to let her think over the session for a while, then lead into the hypnosis thing. I think the session in itself is a form of hypnosis, and an excellent one.)

(When I got to 330 today I found that the call light in Jane's room hadn't been working properly this morning, and now saw that it hung out of its fixture, half dismantled. People were coming and going in the room often — at one time there had been four nurses and aides there, laughing and joking. I tried to read the session for April 30 to Jane after lunch, and it seemed we were interrupted every few lines. In addition, a nurse had unintentionally gotten Jane's medications mixed up this morning.

(Jane finally became quite angry and vexed, and burst out talking about the lack of privacy in 330 today. This was all part of our free-association material today, May 2. She vehemently expressed her feelings, with tears, that if she wanted privacy, being in the hospital wasn't the way to get it. She'd always wanted privacy, she added. "It's pretty dumb, because I sure as hell don't get any privacy this way," she exclaimed — and I thought she was clearing a road, as Seth had suggested last session.

(Jane reiterated that she hadn't trusted her female body, and that she thinks she's now paying for not having kids — after all, she'd been told that's what women were supposed to do. She also thought the church's teachings about motherhood were ambiguous. A sonnet by Shakespeare that she'd read in high school had also given her the idea that her role in life was to bear children, and forget everything else. She hadn't liked the sonnet and hoped it would shrivel away. She thought the church meant that a woman should be either a nun or a mother.

(A repairman finally came to fix the call light, which meant Jane had to be covered while he was in the room. This too bothered her. She'd started out trying to read the session, but did poorly, so I finished reading it to her by 4:25. We'd had many interruptions by then. "Well," she said, "I got pretty damned upset this afternoon, and I'm not comfortable, but maybe if I have a smoke and calm down I can have a brief session. I feel Seth around and he's got a couple of comments, so I should get them."

(Indeed, she'd been quite uncomfortable, lying on her back, most of the afternoon. The same yesterday. I thought her expressions of anger very beneficial, though. Her Seth voice still wasn't as clear as it usually is, nor was her "regular" voice, but both voices today were much improved over their condition yesterday. Her delivery today was faster, but her voice still wasn't very strong. The day outside was quite bright by now, so we had the heavy blue curtains pulled. And we got through the session without any interruptions.)

I bid you a fond good afternoon.

("Good afternoon, Seth.")

The expression of emotion is excellent, particularly the release of anger and frustration.

This does not mean those emotions should be concentrated upon, but acknowledged and expressed. This allows new feelings to take their place — and again, accelerates motion at <u>all</u> levels.

Some of the material may be difficult initially for Ruburt to express, but it is well worth the effort and the momentary outbursts.

Such experiences should be followed, however, by reassurances, both on your part, and by self-reminders on Ruburt's part that his being and experience are indeed couched and held securely in safety and love.

The free association is indeed then operating as it should, and that expression will clear the mental and emotional roads, so that Ruburt's natural, innate high spirits can begin to show their faces again. You are both handling the situation well, then.

I do activate those coordinates that quicken your individual and joint understanding, and the natural healing processes that do indeed promote a resurgence of natural exuberance and pleasure.

("Okay," Jane said, "it's me."

("Thank you."

(4:35 P.M. "I'm telling you, I didn't know whether I could have it or not," Jane said. Her voice had become somewhat ragged and muted. I read the session to her. She'd really gotten upset shortly before the session. I reassured her, saying to let the session penetrate. Then, I said, "You can write your own book about all of this, like God of Jane.*"*

("If I ever felt high spirits I wouldn't know what to do."

("You could enjoy them, though — after you'd questioned them," I joked.

MAY 6, 1984
4:23 P.M. SUNDAY

(Jane called last night. Her mattress felt better, she said. She's had a lot of difficulty with it for the past few days, and has been blue and quite uncomfortable while trying to lay on her back.

(I did no work on Dreams *yesterday while picking up the lawn mower, and only an hour and a half this morning because of writing letters. A couple of days ago 49 letters arrived from Prentice-Hall.*

(This morning Dr. Wilson visited Jane, and suggested that he'd like to clean out the site above her right knee where it's open and draining. There is a large hole there, although signs of healing are apparent. He also said that even if Jane had an operation, he didn't know if it would help straighten the leg. Jane and he discussed some sort of chair in which she could sit up, and he mentioned a type of vehicle like a wheel-chair-lounge of some sort, that perhaps could be adjusted for her to use.

("That terrible bout of the blues that I had for the last two or three days is gone," she said. "It just went away." I should have realized those feelings were contributing to her overall discomfort, for watching her I'd been positive that much of her trouble was caused by her own reactions. Yet she'd also been very uncomfortable today while lying on her back. Indeed, when I tried to position her for supper, she fell off to one side of the bed at such a severe angle that I had to call for help to get her straightened up again.

(My own exasperation had shown through clearly at times, for it seemed that no matter what I did myself, or what anyone else did, my wife was just not going to be comfortable — not then, anyhow. Her right leg, doubled up as it is, keeps pushing her toward her left, tipping her awkwardly.

(After she'd eaten and I was getting ready to leave, Jane said, "I really feel guilty at making your life so hard," and added more words to that effect. I think this is the first time — at least that I remember — that she's made this statement in such a simple, direct way. At once I thought it was excellent material for free association, and that we should pursue it. I replied that we'd better forget that and try to focus on the future — yet such guilt feelings could be playing a significant role in her daily life, and we should find out if this is so.

(My own pendulum sessions lately have told me that I was feeling my own guilt because I thought I should have helped her more in the past. Just this morning my pendulum* for the first time said that I no longer felt guilty. This is an accomplishment for me, and one I must continue to explore. I've taken to using the pendulum in the morning after breakfast and last thing at night before going to bed. It appears to be working well. I haven't gone into this material with Jane yet. Now may be the time.

(The windows were wide open in 330 when she had the session, and at times the traffic noise was quite bothersome. The room had turned a little chilly, and Jane had asked me to turn off the fan.)

I bid you a most fond good afternoon.

("Good afternoon, Seth.")

---

*In 1974 I wrote in Jane/Seth's *The Nature of Personal Reality:* "The pendulum is a very old method. I use it, with excellent results, to obtain ideomotor — 'subconscious' — responses about knowledge that lies just outside my usual consciousness. I hold a small heavy object suspended by a thread so that it's free to move. By mentally asking questions, I obtain 'yes' or 'no' answers according to whether the pendulum swings back and forth, or from side to side."

Dictation. Remember that each segment of life is motivated by value fulfillment, and is therefore always attempting to use and develop all of its abilities and potentials, and to express itself in as many probable ways as possible, in a process that is cooperatively — correction: in a process that takes into consideration the needs and desires of each other segment of life.

The very existence of certain kinds of viruses provides safety against many other diseases, whether or not those viruses even exist in an active manner. It is obvious, of course, that the overall physical stability of the earth is possible because of the ever-occurring storms, "natural disasters," and other seeming calamities. Yet such events promote the earth's great, bountiful food supplies, and serve to redistribute the planet's resources. Period.

In the same fashion, diseases also, in the overall picture, promote the health and well-being of life in all of its aspects. Value fulfillment operates <u>within microbes and nations</u>, within individual creatures and entire species, and it unites all of life's manifestations so that indeed creatures and their environments are united in an overall cooperative venture — a venture in which each segment almost seeks to go beyond itself in creativity, growth, and expression. In a smaller, individual framework, each man and woman, then, is motivated by this same value fulfillment. Period.

You will shortly see how some diseases are caused by the detriments <u>set up</u> against value fulfillment, often because of fears, doubts, or misunderstandings — and how other diseases may actually lead to instances of value fulfillment that are misread or misinterpreted.

I also want to stress here that <u>all</u> aspects of life experience not only sensations <u>but emotional feelings</u>. Therefore, there is a kind of innate gallantry that operates among all segments of life — a gallantry that deserves your respect and consideration. You should have respect, then, for the <u>cells</u> of your body, the thoughts of your mind *(pause)*, and try to understand that even the smallest of creatures shares with you the emotional experience of life's triumphs and vulnerabilities.

I bid you, then, another fond good afternoon.

End of dictation — and once again, I activate those coordinates that so quicken your vast energies, powers, and abilities.

("All right." 4:45 P.M.)

MAY 9, 1984
4:29 P.M. WEDNESDAY

(Here is a summary of our free-association material for Monday after-noon, May 7, 1984:

(I described to Jane my recent use of the pendulum to study my guilt feelings about her having her symptoms and losing her teeth. We went into considerable detail here. At the time we talked my gums were bothering me considerably in the lower front, and I've been having more than enough tooth trouble. I explained in some detail my feelings of guilt because Jane has her troubles. There was some emotion involved. Jane thinks I can regenerate my teeth and gums.

(We then discussed her reaction to her early religious home environment, especially to the priests in her life. She agreed that her own behavior was compulsive, in her fastening upon religion, say, and later on me. Some of this may have been due to her lack of a normal home environment, without a father, we said, yet I felt there were strong independent elements in her personality that encouraged such behavior anyhow. Of course all extremes aren't acceptable, as say, a life of crime. Jane lacked a countering influence to the priests. She also felt "betrayed" by Father Darren when he made advances to her when she was in her earlier teens. The book burning didn't help, either. The religious ideas really took hold, and I think we still only partially understand why.

(This is important to note: after we'd had our talk, I suddenly realized that <u>my gums had stopped bothering me</u>. I told Jane I'd forgotten about the situation. The lesson is obvious, as I wrote when I got home: <u>Sharing the challenge</u> with those others who are involved helps a great deal, and may be vital. The others can, it seems, help minimize the negative aspects of a situation while enhancing the positive. Have I helped Jane in this manner, or hindered her by reinforcing joint negative beliefs? But the event helped me get first-hand experience with the therapeutic benefits that can stem from simple communication. It reminded me of the therapist's classic couch. I want to discuss this more with Jane.)

~

(This is a summary of our free-association material for Tuesday, May 8, 1984 — Jane's 55th birthday:

(Jane tried using the pendulum I carry in my wallet; this followed from our discussions about my using the pendulum of late. Since I've been

achieving considerable relief with my gum challenges the last few days, Jane has become increasingly interested. She's also somewhat intimidated, saying that I get better results than she does — whereas I think her own attitude gets in her way and that comparisons shouldn't be made. We also had trouble with it today because, it being her birthday, several extra interruptions took place as various staff members came in to sing to us, and so forth. They brought cards and foil toys. I gave Jane a card and candy, and brought in forsythia, which moved her to tears. The yellow-flowered shrubs grow in the front yard of the hill house.

(Because of the interruptions by staff, Jane didn't stay long with the pendulum. She said she also felt that she should cover up her use of the pendulum, that "people will really think I'm nuts." I said that the truth of the matter is that no one paid the slightest attention to the pendulum lying on her belly, nor even understood what she was doing. I added that she had to be true to herself, that her troubles came from her not being so, and that if she wanted to use the pendulum then she should do so.

(Jane did get a few answers, and was able to hold the pendulum better in her left hand than she'd thought she could. First she received no answer when she asked if she had a clear road to using her abilities. Then came the answer, "No." The pendulum said it could help her open a clear road to motion. She did get the feeling of weight or motion while using the pendulum, which she said was a good sign. Mostly she decided to talk, though.

(Thoughts of her birthday at once led her to Mother's Day and her own mother, Marie. Jane talked at length about the welter of conflicting events surrounding Marie and herself. She realized that as a youngster she had <u>loved</u> her mother, and tried hard to do things for her, even when Marie had rejected her efforts say, in buying a nightgown of the "wrong" color.

(Then we talked about her grandparents in connection with Jane and Marie; her grandmother's death; the lawsuit against the town, which I don't think I'd heard about before; welfare; Jane's grandfather, Joseph Burdo, and her feelings for him, and so forth. She told me how a traffic light was installed at the corner of Lake Street and Nelson Avenue, as a result of the suit Marie won against the city, concerning her grandmother's death. Jane recalled no details about the suit, the time it took, the money involved. She'd been perhaps five or six years old. I said that once again Jane had been presented with extremes of behavior in the family. There hadn't been any middle ground, it seemed. She talked about her grandfather's death at the age of 68,

when she was 20 years old. I was surprised to hear her say that she'd never read any of her poetry to him.)

~

(May 9: Jane read the free-association material for the two previous days, and did quite well indeed. She read portions of it very rapidly. As we discussed it a little she reminded me that she still experienced feelings of isolation at times. I said they might be normal enough, that everyone was essentially isolated, or at least alone, since no one else could live their life for them. They couldn't be born for them or die for them. At the same time I knew what she meant — that she needed pretty steady or even constant reinforcement in the world.

(On the TV program, In Search Of, *we watched a presentation of Cleve Backster and his work with plants reacting — or not, as the case was sometimes — to human emotions. Very interesting, we thought.*

(After her lunch and reading of the free-association material, Jane said she didn't really know what to do with herself. I started work on fan mail, which has begun to pile up again. At 3:45, Jane said she sensed or felt a "larger you" — meaning me — about her. It was a hard thing to describe, she said, and echoed my question about it being my own entity, or a portion thereof. She felt a great love from the entity. If it could be described at all, she said, it could be "circular," though really it had no form in that sense.

(The aftereffects from the "form" lingered as we talked about it and I made these notes. Jane hadn't been consciously thinking about psychic matters. Earlier I'd read her the verse from the birthday card I'd bought her yesterday, and she had enjoyed that as much as she had yesterday, when I'd read it to her for the first time. Both of us had felt emotion at the reading, both times. She didn't know if that might have triggered her experience. But our feelings engendered by the reading of the card were valuable events in themselves.

(It was getting late when Jane said she felt Seth around after all. We had one interruption right after she started: A young girl delivered a bowl of flowers from Steve and Tracy Blumenthal. Jane lay quietly in trance while I took the gift from the girl and set it on the stand beside my chair.)

I bid you another fond good afternoon.

("Good afternoon, Seth.")

This is not book dictation.

(Pause.) Ruburt's experience this afternoon was a response to your own notes concerning communication and its importance.

(See my note at the conclusion of the free-association material for May 7, at the beginning of this session.)

In this case, the notes allowed Ruburt to see the vaster and yet even more intimate kind of communication that unites you, and that unites all of life.

The television program, about the communication of plants, also served as an impetus, so that Ruburt was able to sense the continuous "inner world" flow of love and cooperation within which all of life is couched. Ruburt had spoken about feeling isolated at times, and the experience was meant also to show him that isolation itself is an illusion.

(Long pause.) Such communications exist at all levels, but for his own personal reasons, and because of your relationship, Ruburt in particular tuned into your own greater personality with those attributes of love, deep understanding, and respect that often seem so difficult, it seems, to express adequately.

Once again I accelerate those coordinates that activate healing, exuberance, and well-being — and therefore touch the <u>source</u> from which, indeed, the spirit of life itself springs.

("Thank you."

(4:35 P.M. "It wasn't terribly vivid," Jane said about her experience, after I'd read the session to her, "but it was noticeable enough to be noticed — you know what I mean?" I said that in the session she'd effectively answered her own questions about the experience. I suggested that perhaps she could have it again when she was alone — at night, say.)

MAY 12, 1984
3:37 P.M. SATURDAY

(Jane was again very uncomfortable today when she lay on her back. This pattern has persisted for a number of days now. "How can you be more uncomfortable now, when the bedsores are healing, than you used to be?" I asked some time ago. She didn't know. My own eventual conclusion was that more was involved — that it had to do with her attitudes and beliefs.

(At least when I've been there in 330, Jane's appetite has gone downhill, and she's slacked off on free-association material and the sessions. I thought of requesting of staff that she be given some Darvoset, or something like it,

in the afternoons, but I hadn't mentioned this because I felt my wife would reject the idea. Then yesterday Jane promised to hold a session today, after I'd said that a session might help.

(The day was warm — in the 60's — and rainy at times. The windows were wide open so that traffic noise hit us. Down the hall somewhere a woman was shouting periodically — a display that took a lot of work and energy after a few hours. One of the nurses called her "a pain in the ass," then laughed when she added that the woman did have hemorrhoids. But to me her unintelligible shouting signaled more than a physical affliction.)

Now, I bid you another fond good afternoon.

("Good afternoon, Seth.")

This is not dictation.

Ruburt's recent discomfort is partially caused by the fear that his body will not be able to completely heal itself, even if he does uncover all of the reasons for his predicament.

The fears <u>have been there</u>, of course, and your latest efforts simply brought them into prominence, or cast a spotlight upon them. This can be countered if Ruburt stresses the idea that he is indeed <u>couched safely</u>, and that his existence is automatically, spontaneously held. That idea of safety and reassurance counters the fear, and opens the passageways again for free association.

This session should help to minimize that discomfort, which is often so apparent during your visits — precisely when he <u>wants</u> to be at his best. In other words, he is trying too hard. Each of his activities can indeed flow easily one into the other, and he should remind himself that the inner intelligence within him is indeed <u>on its own</u> always seeking his best interest, and always of itself working on his behalf.

If he wants to, have him imagine this inner intelligence as a beloved parent. This will also dull the edges of any resentments he may have regarding his own parents.

I may return briefly, but in any case I do now activate those coordinates that do increase feelings of self-love, exuberance, and well-being.

(3:45. I read the session to Jane twice. I worked on mail acknowledging the $650 we'd received in contributions through Maude Cardwell's efforts. Of course, we noticed that Seth had said that Jane's discomfort was only partially caused by her fears that she cannot heal herself. What about those other reasons, then? Jane said later that she thought Seth would indeed return. Resume at 4:16.)

The other reason for his discomfort has to do with his birthday, coupled with the idea of Mother's Day, which is tomorrow.

The idea of Mother's Day made him half resentful and half sorrowful because of the poor relationship between him and his mother *(long pause)*, and he had hoped for further improvements in time for his birthday.

Certainly he does believe that his body can begin to feel better and better — and that suggestion is a good one to use, for it implies continuance of input, without getting involved in absolutes.

(4:20. I read the session to her. She felt Seth around again. 4:23.)

He does not have anything new "wrong" with his body. Such fears show that the distrust of the body is still to some extent present, so he should refresh his memory on the connections between femininity, his physical body, and health.

I did want to mention that the circulation of our books is definitely increasing, and will continue to do so.

Once again I bid you a fond good afternoon.

("Good afternoon, Seth."

(4:26 P.M. I read the last half of the session to Jane. "I got the feeling there was something definitely involved in the increase in the circulation of our books," Jane said when I was through. The mail has picked up quite a bit, and at the moment I'm falling behind again.

(I felt depressed after today's session, for it seemed to me that Jane still hasn't shaken her fears, especially her distrust of her own body and its processes, after all this time. I saw the birthday/Mother's Day hassle as only the latest wrinkle in a 20-year cycle of reasons for the symptoms. The question isn't why she's so uncomfortable these days, but why the body, the psyche, has chosen to endure those symptoms for so long.)

CHAPTER 7

THE STATE OF CHILDHOOD IN
RELATIONSHIP TO HEALTH, AND
HINTS FOR PARENTS

MAY 13, 1984
3:10 P.M. SUNDAY

Jane called last night with Carla's help. Today was warm — about 63 degrees — as I drove to 330. It was also rainy, and rained heavily later in the afternoon. I got no work done on Dreams, *and may not get much done tomorrow. If the weather is decent I'll have to mow grass. I would also like to do some painting, but this seems impossible at this time.*

(Jane read yesterday's session for herself, and I helped her; she said nothing about my own notes for it. She didn't eat well for either lunch or supper. And this morning she did ask for Darvoset to ease her discomfort. She was already on her back when I got to 330 today. Georgia had put her there, and had also washed Jane's hair this morning. It looked good.)

I bid you another fond good afternoon.

("Good afternoon, Seth.")

Dictation.

We will begin the next chapter, which is to be called: "The State of Childhood in Relationship to Health, and Hints for Parents."

(Long pause.) For adults, ideas of health and illness are intimately connected with philosophical, religious, and social beliefs. They are even more entangled with scientific concepts, and with science's views of life in general. Children, however, are far more innocent,

and though they respond to the ideas of their parents, still their minds are open and filled with curiosity. They are also gifted with an almost astounding resiliency and exuberance.

They possess an innate love of the body and all of its parts. They also feel an eager desire to learn all they can about their own physical sensations and capabilities.

At the same time, young children in particular still possess a feeling of oneness with the universe, and with all of life, even as they begin to separate themselves at certain levels from life's wholeness to go about the delightful task. Seeing themselves as separate and apart from all other individuals, they still retain an inner comprehension and a memory of having once experienced a oneness with life as a whole.

(3:21.) At that level even illness is regarded simply as a part of life's experience, however unpleasant it might be. Even at an early age, children joyfully explore all of the possibilities of all sensations possible within their framework — pain as well as joy, frustration as well as satisfaction, and all the while their awareness is propelled by curiosity, wonder, and joy.

They pick up their first ideas about health and disease from parents and doctors, and by the actions of those people to their own discomfiture. Before they can even see, children are already aware of what their parents expect from them in terms of health and disease, so that early patterns of behavior are formed, to which they then react in adulthood.

You may take a break. I may or may not return, but I do activate those coordinates that accelerate your own healing processes and well-being.

(3:26. I did a few letters, thanking people who have contributed to Jane's hospital fund. Carla took Jane's temperature — 98.4. I read the last sentence to my wife. Resume at 3:44.)

For now we will speak of children who possess ordinary good health, but who may also have some of the usual childhood "diseases." Later we will discuss children with exceptionally severe health conditions.

Many children acquire poor health habits through the well-meaning mistakes of their parents. This is particularly true when parents actually reward a child for being ill. In such cases, the ailing child is pampered far more than usual, given extra special attention, offered delicacies such as ice cream, let off some ordinary chores, and in other ways encouraged to think of bouts of illness as times of special attention and reward.

I do not mean that ill children should not be treated with kindness, and perhaps a bit of special attention — but the reward should be given for the child's <u>recovery</u>, and efforts should be made to keep the youngster's routine as normal as possible. Children often know quite well the reasons for some of their illnesses, for often they learn from their parents that illness can be used as a means to achieve a desired result.

Often parents hide such behavior from themselves. They deliberately close their eyes to some of the reasons for their own illnesses, and this behavior has become so habitual that they are no longer conscious of their own intent.

Children, however, may be quite conscious of the fact that they <u>willed</u> themselves to become ill, in order to avoid school, or an examination, or a coming feared family event. They soon learn that such self-knowledge <u>is not acceptable</u>, however, so they begin to pretend ignorance, quickly learning to tell themselves instead that they have a bug or a virus, or have caught a cold, seemingly for no reason at all.

Parents frequently foster such behavior. Some are simply too busy to question a child about his own illness. It is far simpler to give a child aspirin, and send a child to bed with ginger ale and a coloring book.

Such procedures unfortunately rob a child of important self-knowledge and understanding. They begin to feel <u>victims</u> to this or that disorder. Since they have no idea that they themselves caused the problem to begin with, then they do not realize that they themselves possess the power to right the situation. If they are being rewarded for such behavior in the meantime, then the pressure is less, of course, so that bouts of illness or poor health can become ways of attaining attention, favorite status, and reward.

Parents who are aware of these facts can start helping their children at an early age by asking them simply the reasons for their illness. A mother might say: "You don't need to have a temperature in order to avoid school, or as a way of getting love and attention, for I love you in any case. And if there is a problem at school, we can work it out together, so you don't have to make yourself ill." Again, the reasons for such behavior are often quite clear in the child's mind. So if the parents begin such questioning and reassurance when the child is young, then the youngster will learn that while illness may be used to attain a desired result, there are far better, healthier ways of achieving an end result.

Some parents, unfortunately, use the nature of suggestion in the most undesirable way, so that a child is often told that he or she is sickly, or weak or overly sensitive, and not as robust as other youngsters. If that kind of behavior is continued, then the child soon takes such statements as true, and begins to act upon them, until they do indeed become only too real in the youngster's everyday experience.

End of dictation.

End of session. I bid you a most fond good afternoon.

("Good afternoon, Seth.")

(4:13 P.M. For some reason I didn't read the session to Jane. She was still uncomfortable, so I turned her on her side earlier than usual. She called, with Carla's help, around 9:25, as I was typing this session, and said she felt better.)

MAY 14, 1984
3:32 P.M. MONDAY

(The day was much cooler and rainy. Jane was on her back again when I got to 330. The fan was on part of the time because of the exceptional humidity, though. She seemed to be a little more comfortable, now that her birthday and Mother's Day are past — factors, Seth said, that contributed to her discomfort.)

Now — I bid you another most fond good afternoon.

("Good afternoon, Seth.")

We will resume dictation.

(Very long pause.) Good health is closely related, of course, to a family's beliefs about the body. If parents believe that the body is somehow an inferior vehicle for the spirit, or if they simply view the body as unreliable or weak and vulnerable, then children will at an early age begin to consider good health as a rarity, and learn to take depression, poor spirits, and bodily aches and pains to be a natural, normal condition of life.

If, on the other hand, parents view the body as a healthy, dependable vehicle of expression and feeling, then their children will look at their own bodies in the same fashion. It is very important that parents express a fond affection toward each other, and toward their children. In this way most children are assured of their parents' love, and hence need not resort to illness as a way of gaining attention or testing a parents' love and devotion.

There is no natural reason for children to feel a sense of <u>shame</u> concerning any bodily part. No portion of the body should be spoken about in secret, hushed tones. Each child should be told that his body, or her body, is a precious private possession, however, so that it is easy to build up a desirable feeling of bodily privacy, without any hint of shame or guilt.

It goes without saying that parents should hold the bodies of their male and female children in equal favor, so that one is not considered inferior to the other. Each child should be educated as early as possible by their parents, so that the youngsters are repeatedly reminded of the body's natural resources and healing abilities.

(Long pause.) Parents who are actually quite worried about their children's susceptibility to illness often go overboard, stressing all kinds of sports and sports-related projects, but the children sense their parents' unspoken fears, and they try to reassure their parents through achieving high goals or merit in sports programs.

There is no area of thought or belief that does not touch upon the subject of health in one way or another. Therefore, throughout this book we will be devoted to many ideas that may at first <u>seem</u> unrelated to the topic at hand.

End of dictation.

(3:51.) Again, it is a good idea for Ruburt to remind himself of the connections between his idea of his body and its relationship to his sexuality and to health. This will help him uncover the reasons for his distrust of the body, so that he can begin to feel a new sense of the body's <u>reliability</u>, resourcefulness, and powerful healing abilities.

I may or may not return this afternoon, but I do again accelerate your own healing abilities, and quicken those coordinates that accelerate your own sense of well-being and safety.

("Thank you."

(3:55. I read the session to Jane. She had been interrupted twice by hospital staff while delivering it. It should be noted that before today's session, she read yesterday's session very well, indeed — fast and easily.)

MAY 15, 1984
4:32 P.M. TUESDAY

(Jane was a bit more comfortable lying on her back today, though not a great deal. She ate little lunch — or supper, for that matter. But she did very well reading a couple of sessions. I said I was seriously considering giving up answering most of the fan mail, which has increased considerably lately. I'm having more and more trouble getting free time to concentrate upon getting Dreams *done.*

(The ulcer on Jane's right knee is showing definite signs of healing, and closing up on the inside — more so than on her knuckle on the left hand.

(We had the fan on and the windows wide open, although it wasn't that hot outside. Jane's Seth voice was stronger than usual. I might add that I had my "eye thing" throughout the session — those bright, jagged patterns moving across my field of vision. I described the effect, and added a drawing of it, in Jane's Adventures in Consciousness, *which was published in 1975. Today's episode was the first in a long while, triggered I believe by stress, yet it didn't last long. I didn't take the time to use the pendulum to learn more.)*

Now — I bid you another most fond good afternoon.

("Good afternoon, Seth.")

This is not dictation.

It will help considerably if Ruburt discusses his mistrust of the body with you — thus expressing those feelings within the framework of your relationship.

The feelings should not be treated with disapproval, for it is, of course, because Ruburt disapproves of such feelings that he often keeps them hidden. Expressed in such a manner, they may indeed elicit tears on Ruburt's part — and perhaps on your own as well.

Ruburt should actually address those feelings sympathetically, explaining to them where they came from. This allows the emotions some clear resolution. He may even refer to those feelings of distrust as a dear frightened part of himself, and then, again, address that part of the self sympathetically — telling it why it need no longer be frightened, and vocally and emotionally stressing the fact that the frightened portion of the self no longer needs defenses, but can now allow itself free and natural expression.

These suggestions, carried out, can be of more than considerable value. Tell Ruburt I will begin book dictation again at our next session, including the material on "better and better pills."

I bid you both then a fond afternoon, and again I accelerate your own healing abilities, and quicken your own sense of well-being and peace of mind. The suggestions I have given are quite potent.

("Thank you."

(4:40 P.M. "Well, I'm glad I did that," Jane said. "I'll have a smoke while you read it to me." She'd been interrupted right after the start of the session by a nurse bringing her vitamin C. Recording the session, I'd been quite amazed that a certain frightened portion of Jane's self could exert such power over the rest of her mental and physical personality. Then I thought that perhaps I wasn't amazed at all — that such things could be old stuff to therapists following various psychological disciplines. Once again, I ended up depressed.

(Jane picked up on this, for she said that I would disapprove. I said it would be useless to deny the existence of her symptoms. And she replied that she could already feel the emotions connected with the Seth material today. I thought that tomorrow we could do something about that, then realized that Jim Baker, our optometrist, was due after 2:00 P.M. to deliver the two new pair of glasses he'd examined Jane for some time ago. That was prime time for us to try free association, yet Jane had to have the glasses.

(Just as I turned Jane on her side after the session, our neighbor Joe Bumbalo — who is very ill with cancer — called to invite me to share Chinese food and rhubarb pie with him and his wife, Margaret. I didn't get to their house until after 7:30 because I'd been trying to help Jane get more comfortable. The food was delicious — until two pieces of chicken became lodged in my throat as I talked. Joe, lying on his couch, saw me trying to swallow, and called Margaret from the kitchen. I could still breathe, but with difficulty as my throat muscles kept trying to down the meat. I knew the situation could get very serious, but none of us panicked. Margaret, who had been a school nurse, used the Heimlich maneuver: she wrapped her strong arms around me from the back and squeezed. On the third squeeze, one portion of the chicken popped out of my mouth. I could talk hoarsely while feeling the second portion work its way down my esophagus. To the Bumbalos' surprise, I finally was able to finish the meal. In a flash I'd been prepared for Margaret to use all force necessary, even to the point of one or

more broken ribs, as I'd read could happen. And in bed that night, I wondered what would have happened to Jane had I not survived . . .)

MAY 18, 1984
3:48 P.M. FRIDAY

(Last night when I got home, I saw that the young fellow Frank Longwell has put me in touch with to do the lawn had done his job; the place looked great. This afternoon he was to come back and do the raking.

(Jane was on her back again when I got there. She seemed to feel a little more comfortable. After an average lunch she read the last two sessions to me, wearing her new close-up glasses, and zipped right through them. I told her I think that now she can read aloud faster than I can.

(The mail from Prentice-Hall is increasing considerably, whether or not this is in line with Seth's recent statement that an increase in sales of the books is under way. Batches of fan mail have arrived the last three days. Already I'm way behind, and feel that I'll never get it answered. In fact, today was the first day in 330 that I didn't answer at least a few letters from readers. It gave me a strange feeling of freedom; the afternoon seemed stretched out, or longer. I believe I'm on the point of renouncing the fan mail, or most of it. Perhaps I'll take the time from Dreams *to work out a final fan letter — including Seth's — to send folks who write. One I can sign, and that's it.*

(This material is free-association stuff, following Seth's suggestion in the private session for Jane on May 15. We're to discuss her mistrust of her physical body, and related subjects. We'd have tried it yesterday, except that Jim Baker brought her the new glasses. What follows is obviously simplified and shorter, since I couldn't record every spoken word between us. We wanted to tap into the hidden emotions behind the words.

(Much of this we've gone over before, at various times. Jane began by talking about how her mother, Marie, told her at puberty that she had bad blood in her from her father [Delmer], that he had syphilis. Jane was frightened at having her periods and talked to a nun about all of it — and the nun would have her own hangups, probably; Jane didn't say, or perhaps remember.

(She also recounted how she didn't have to take gym in school because of her periods, and how Marie said Del had bad eyes because of the syphilis and couldn't read. Jane remembers all of those feelings, yet doesn't feel them,

she said. She was very afraid to get pregnant, and never fooled around. After our marriage she was afraid of being pregnant, thinking it would wreck our careers. I reminded her that when she did get pregnant, I hadn't been terribly upset, and accepted it. She felt the men didn't pay her serious attention at the science-fiction conference 27 years ago because she was a woman. The same with the psychic stuff: a hysterical woman. She felt that men were superior to women.

(She identified with writing poetry very early in life. "I believed what I wrote, but people said I'd grow out of it and have kids, and I was determined not to." Had trouble sharing poetry with most boyfriends; smarter to play dumb, she discovered. Marie had always encouraged her poetry, and the two women shared it for a number of years. Jane used to write poems to get back in Marie's good grace: "At the same time I felt like I was betraying myself for doing it. I remember that quite well." I didn't remember Jane telling me this before, though she might have.

(Jane was terrified a couple of times that she might be pregnant by me. Yet except for one time in a passionate moment she never had any urge to have a child. "But I certainly felt the feminine part of you was the part you couldn't trust," she said. As we talked about these things she said she was getting edgy and nervous, and wanted a cigarette, so we were getting close to buried feelings.

(I asked her about Seth, a male, speaking through a woman. She said she suspected that as a woman she'd have more authority if she spoke as a male. She "sensed a feeling of duplicity" in the beginning of the sessions. I don't remember this either. Again she was getting nervous, her voice almost teary. She recalled that once Seth said that if he'd come through as a woman she wouldn't have stood for it. All of this male business is related to the male priests in her childhood years.

(About the envelope tests — Seth had to be almost omnipotent — because she transferred the authority of the church to him. An important point, and a new one, I think. Again Jane was nervous and edgy, near crying. But the church wouldn't approve of Seth, I said. Enter the idea of she starting a false church — heretical indeed — with a false god, Seth. The Catholic idea of penance was mixed in here. I added that since she wanted to use the abilities instead of denying them, as the church would want her to do, she chose to continue her mental rebellion and so had to pay penance physically, through the symptoms. The creative part of her poetry

had always been trying to go beyond where the church wanted it to go. A neat circle, with no way out, I said. Jane said she felt like she could chew nails. She was very uncomfortable, but no tears.

(We talked a lot about the priests in her life, and the conflicts her work set up with their early teachings, and their personal behavior, good and bad. Jane remembered no reaction from her mother when her poetry came into conflict with the church, or when Father Rakin burned her books. I thought this strange.

(3:35. She was again nervous and edgy, and had another smoke. She talked about having a session to put it all together. She described again all those visits from Father Trenton. She talked about how the one priest who put her to bed when she was but 3 or 4 years old would "play" with her sexually, and how Marie finally figured that out. This was the one who called her up while we lived together; he was old and living in a retirement home south of Pennsylvania, I believe. She described how Father Trenton sat with his back to Marie when he was mad at the mother, and how Father Rakin made advances to her. She grew up in a male-dominated world. The first time they met, Jane said Father Rakin said to her when she was but 13: "You're just too forward." A nice greeting, and one Jane obviously still remembers. She realized today, while talking, that her grandfather had no love for women either. And Marie said to her: "You were a nice kid until you turned about sixteen — then you turned into a bitch." Several times in Florida she thought I was going to leave her. I wasn't.

(Jane was frightened when her mother read cards or tea leaves. She remembers mother making predictions that came true — but how many did she make, I asked, that <u>didn't</u> pan out? Probably hundreds.

(All of the above is free-association material for Thursday, May 17, 1984.)

~

(Here is the session for May 18, 1984:)
Now I bid you another fond good afternoon.
("Good afternoon, Seth.")
This is dictation.

I have mentioned before that play is essential for growth and development. Children learn through play-acting. They imagine themselves to be in all kinds of situations. They see themselves in dangerous predicaments, and then conjure up their own methods of escape. They try out the roles of other family members, imagine themselves rich and poor, old and young, male and female.

This allows children a sense of freedom, independence, and power as they see themselves acting forcibly in all kinds of situations. It goes without saying that physical play automatically helps develop the body and its capabilities.

To a child, play and work are often one and the same thing, and parents can utilize imaginative games as a way of reinforcing ideas of health and vitality. When a child is ill-disposed or cranky, or has a headache, or another disorder that does not appear to be serious, parents can utilize this idea: have the child imagine that you are giving it a "better and better pill." Have the child open its mouth while you place the imaginary pill on its tongue, or have the child imagine picking the pill up and placing it in its mouth. Then give the child a glass of water to wash the pill down, or have the child get the water for himself or herself. Then have the youngster chant, say, three times, "I've taken a better and better pill, so I will shortly feel better and better myself."

The earlier such a game is begun the better, and as the child grows older you may explain that often an imaginary pill works quite as well — if not better — than a real one.

This does not mean that I am asking parents to substitute imaginary medicine for real medicine, though indeed, I repeat, it may be quite as effective. In your society, however, it would be almost impossible to get along without medicine or medical science.

While I want to emphasize that point, I also want to remind you that <u>innately</u> and ideally the body is quite equipped to heal itself, and certainly to cure its own momentary headache. You would have to substitute an entirely different learning system, at your present stage, for the body to show its true potentials and healing abilities.

(4:05.) In other cases of a child's illness, have the child play a <u>healing game</u>, in which he or she playfully imagines being completely healthy again, outdoors and playing; or have the youngster imagine a conversation with a friend, describing the illness as past and gone. Play could also be used even in old peoples' homes, for it could revive feelings of spontaneity and give the conscious mind a rest from worrying.

Many ancient and so-called primitive peoples utilized play —
and drama, of course — for their healing values, and often their
effects were quite as therapeutic as medical science. If your child
believes that a particular illness is caused by a virus, then suggest a
game in which the youngster imagines the virus to be a small bug
that he or she triumphantly chases away with a broom, or sweeps out
the door. Once a child gets the idea, the youngster will often make
up his or her <u>own</u> game, that will prove most beneficial.

Instead of such procedures, children are often taught to believe
that any situation or illness or danger will <u>worsen</u>, and that the least
desirable, rather than the most desirable, solution will be found. By
such mental games, however, stressing the desirable solution, children can learn at an early age to utilize their imaginations and their
minds in a far more beneficial manner.

Take a brief break, and we will continue.

(4:16. Jane had a smoke. Resume at 4:23.)

One of the most disastrous ideas is the belief that illness is sent as
a punishment by God.

Unfortunately, such a belief is promoted by many religions. Children who want to be good, therefore, can unfortunately strive for
poor health, in the belief that it is a sign of God's <u>attention</u>. To be
punished by God is often seen as preferable to being ignored by
God. Adults who hold such views unwittingly often let their children
in for a life of turmoil and depression.

In all cases of illness, games or play should be fostered whenever
possible, and in whatever form. Many dictatorial religions pointedly
refuse to allow their congregations to indulge in any type of play at
all, and frown upon it as sinful. Card-playing and family games such
as Monopoly are actually excellent practices, and play in any form
encourages spontaneity and promotes healing and peace of mind.

End of dictation.

(4:29.) Some playful behavior on Ruburt's part would be of considerable benefit — and this would be even better if the two of you
could possibly indulge in some kind of play together, even if only
mind games were involved — games with no particular purpose,
except fun.

Some version involving you two and the French book, for example.

Again, I activate those coordinates that quicken health, healing, and that revive high spirits. I bid you then a most fond good afternoon.

("Good afternoon, Seth."

(4:32 P.M. It was getting windy outside, and cooler, and was clouding over. "To tell you the truth, I was so uncomfortable I didn't think I could have a session," Jane said. She had a cigarette before I turned her. We thought of games involving the French book, or even crossword puzzles. In the ash tree just starting to get leaves beside the windows of 330, I saw a tiny yellow bird flitting about among the branches. I pointed it out to Jane, but she couldn't quite see it, except for a flash of color. I'd seen the same bird, I think, yesterday afternoon also.

(The book referred to is a French-English textbook from Jane's days at Skidmore College, in Saratoga springs, New York. Several years ago Jane had started reviewing her knowledge of French, and I had asked her to teach me a bit about the language. Fun, but neither one of us had stayed with our ideas.)

CHAPTER 8

CHILDRENS' PLAY, REINCARNATION, AND HEALTH

MAY 22, 1984
4:24 P.M. TUESDAY

(H*ere is a brief summary of free-association material given at 4:20 P.M. on May 20, 1984:*

(Jane discussed a positive, energetic dream of last night, which isn't recorded here. She said that last night's dream sequences were her celebration of her bodily abilities — her insistence on the excellent workings of the body. She thinks she hasn't used the abilities of her body. "I asked it to forgive me for not doing that. I gave it the freedom to move — and here I am uncomfortable as hell all afternoon."

(Could her uneasy state be a sign of the body's responding? She used to think that "if I used my body all the way, I wouldn't work — which is hysterical, because now I do hardly anything." She doesn't know if her body can fully recover, yet she really believes that she can straighten out her broken leg. I suggested that instead she realize that her good left leg is now in a position to straighten out. She hadn't thought of that. She does now think that it's safe to recover physically.

(Jane felt with some emotion — she refused to think about it — that she's embarked on some project involving her entity at this later time in her life. This was as a result of my question. She thinks it's possible.

often feel as if you are in another location entirely, and all of your senses seem pivoted in <u>that</u> location. Your experience is separated from your usual <u>living area</u>, in other words. You may dream that you are running or walking or flying, yet those activities are divorced enough from that area where imagination, motion, and physical actuality meet, so that your body remains quiet, relatively speaking, while you seem to be moving freely somewhere else.

(4:40.) In a fashion, reincarnation can partially be explained using the same kind of analogy. You have many existences at once — but each one has its own living area, upon which that portion of you focuses. In fact, that portion has its own name and selfhood and is master of its own castle, so to speak.

Each self has its own inviolate point where imagination, motion, and physical actuality intersect. Like the child play-acting, however, events occur within events, all dramatically real and vivid, all eliciting specific responses and actions, and each one possessing its own private <u>living</u> area *(intently)*.

End of dictation.

(4:44.) I did want to begin the chapter. Again I activate those coordinates that encourage your own healing abilities, peace of mind, revelations, and understanding — and I bid you a fond good afternoon.

("Thank you.")

(4:45 P.M. Jane has again been very uncomfortable today, especially lying on her back. She took Darvoset this morning and again this afternoon when I was there.)

MAY 23, 1984
4:31 P.M. WEDNESDAY

(This morning I finished making the portable reading stand for Jane to use in bed, and took it in to 330 this afternoon. Jane could use it after a fashion, but not as well as I'd hoped. It will help, though. She's still very uncomfortable at times, and is now on four-hour doses of Darvoset.)

Now I bid you another fond good afternoon.

("Good afternoon, Seth.")

We will resume dictation.

On any given day a youngster may take a ride on a merry-go-round. The same little boy or girl might also sit astride a toy horse, and pretend that the horse is part of the merry-go-round. The same child might see the image of a merry-go-round on the television screen, or be told about another youngster's visit to a playground, and a subsequent ride on a merry-go-round.

The child will be completely absorbed in the merry-go-round ride that was directly experienced. He or she may indeed be just as engrossed — or even more so — in the imaginary ride on the rocking horse. There will be some involvement, of course, as the child watches the images of the merry-go-round horses on the television station, while the story about another child's visit to the playground will not take nearly as much of his interest.

In <u>somewhat</u> the same way, events appear and are reflected in reincarnational existences. All the lives are actually occurring at the same time, as the hypothetical youngster's merry-go-round experiences happened all in one day.

In the reincarnational terms, however, the merry-go-round events might be experienced directly in some existences, or appear in a dream in another existence, or turn up simply as an image in another, or happen in an event involving <u>real horses</u> instead of merry-go-round horses. In other words, in one way or another the events of one living experience are reflected in each other living experience.

(4:42.) I am not saying that the events in one life cause the events in another, but that there is an overall pattern — a bank of probable events — and that in each life each individual chooses those that suit his or her overall private purposes. Yet those lives will be connected. An individual may have a serious illness in one life. That event may turn up as one uncomfortable nightmare in another existence. In still another life, the individual might have a dear friend who suffers from the same disease. In still another existence the individual might decide to be a doctor, to seek a cause and a cure for the same disease.

No one is <u>fated</u>, however, to suffer in one life for any crimes committed in another. The reasons and purposes for one's own existence in any life can be found directly in the life itself.

(Long pause. The last sentence echoes what I wrote in one of the essays for Dreams.*)*

End of dictation.

(4:48.) I bid you a most fond good afternoon. I wanted to continue dictation, even though the session was brief. Once more I activate

those coordinates that quicken your own healing potentials, and promote well-being and peace of mind.

(4:49 P.M. "Well, I guess that's it," Jane said. She had a cigarette before I turned her on her left side. She was uncomfortable.)

MAY 26, 1984
4:03 P.M. SATURDAY

(Yesterday I received in the mail a copy of a long article that Sam Menahem, a psychologist in Fort Lee, New Jersey, has written for a summer issue of Reality Change. *I took the article in to 330 today so that Jane could read it. Dr. Menahem very favorably compares the Seth material with a number of psychological disciplines, and I told Jane I hoped his feature would show her that the general validity of her work would continue to grow. She liked the article, and agreed that her work would continue to grow in influence.*

(As I was doing mail today she said she'd put off having sessions lately because she'd picked up from me that I wanted the time off to catch up on other things. True. But I told her that I was ready for a session today if she wanted to have one.)

I bid you another most fond good afternoon —

("Good afternoon, Seth.")

— and I will resume dictation.

Many proponents of reincarnation believe most firmly that an illness in one life <u>most frequently</u> has its roots in a past existence, and that reincarnational regression is therefore necessary to uncover the reasons for many current illnesses or dilemmas.

There is also a rather conventional stereotype version of karma that may follow such beliefs. Therefore, you may be punished in this life for errors you have committed in a past one, or you may actually be making up for a mistake made thousands of years ago. Again, all of a person's reincarnational existences are, indeed, connected — but the events in one life <u>do not cause</u> the events in the next one.

I must remind you once more that all time happens simultaneously, so the confused belief about punishment <u>now</u>, in retaliation for past action would actually be meaningless, since in simultaneous time <u>all</u> actions would be occurring at once.

(Long pause.) You may have overall reasons for a particular illness, however, that have nothing to do with crime or punishment, but may instead involve an extraordinary sense of curiosity, and the desire for experience that is somewhat <u>un</u>conventional — usually <u>not</u> sought for — exotic, or in certain terms even grotesque.

Each life, regardless of its nature, possesses it own unique vantage point, and an individual may sometimes take an obscure or a long-lasting disease simply to present himself or herself with experience that most others would shun. An individual might seek such a vantage point in order to look at the universe in a different fashion, asking questions that perhaps could not be answered if asked from any other position.

(4:16.) Another life, for example, might deal with exquisite health and vitality, and as mentioned, still another life might be devoted to the arts of healing — but overall, few people take health problems <u>per se</u> as frequent reincarnational themes, though they may be implied strongly in situations where one is born into a large populace of poor, underprivileged people.

If you do have health problems, it is much better to look for their reasons in your immediate experience, rather than assigning them a cause in the distant past. The reasons for maladies are almost always present in current life experience *(long pause)* — and even though old events from childhood may have originally activated unhealthy behavior, it is present beliefs that allow old patterns of activity to operate.

Give us a moment, and we will continue.

(4:22. Jane had a sip of coffee and a cigarette. Resume at 4:28.)

If you are concerned about any given problems — mental, emotional, or physical — there are certain facts you should hold in mind. I have mentioned most of them elsewhere, but they are particularly vital in this context.

New paragraph. You must realize that you do create your own reality because of your beliefs about it. Therefore, try to understand that the particular dilemma or illness is not an event forced upon you by some other agency. Realize that to some extent or another your dilemma or your illness <u>has been chosen by you</u>, and that this choosing has been done in <u>bits and pieces</u> of small, seemingly inconsequential choices. Each choice, however, has led up to your current predicament, whatever its nature.

If you realize that your beliefs form your experience, then you do indeed have an excellent chance of changing your beliefs, and hence your experience.

You can discover what your own reasons are for choosing the dilemma or illness by being very honest with yourself. There is no need to feel guilty <u>since you meant very well</u> as you made each choice — only the choices were built upon beliefs that were <u>beliefs</u> and <u>not facts</u>.

We will continue dictation at our next session. For you both again, I activate those coordinates that quicken your own inspirations, revelations, and self-healing.

(*"Thank you."*

(*4:44 P.M. Jane had been interrupted twice within three minutes since last break. "Gee, I felt these great big chunks of material there," she said. "And he's got even more, but it's getting late and the supper tray will be here and you have to turn me and stuff . . . " I could tell she was able to continue. "I think he was also answering some of the points that psychologist made in his letter," she said. I'd had the same feeling.*

(*She'd felt better today, which probably was one of the reasons for the longer session. She hasn't taken any Darvoset since this morning, which is an improvement. Jeff Karder has her on another vitamin supplement — a pungent colorless liquid that to me smells like orange peel. This since the blood test a few days ago. Jane dislikes the taste mightily.*)

MAY 28, 1984
4:08 P.M. MONDAY

Now I bid you another most fond good afternoon.

(*"Good afternoon, Seth."*)

And we will continue dictation.

If you are in serious difficulties of any kind, it may at first seem inconceivable, unbelievable, or even scandalous to imagine that your problems are caused by your own beliefs.

In fact, the opposite might appear to be true. You might have lost a series of jobs, for example, and it may seem quite clear that you are not to blame in any of those circumstances. You might have a very serious illness that seemed to come from nowhere, and it may strike you as most unlikely indeed, that your own beliefs had anything to do with the inception of such a frightening malady.

You may be in the middle of one or several very unsatisfactory relationships, none of which seem to be caused by you, while instead you feel as if you are an unwilling victim or participant.

You may have a dangerous drug or alcohol problem, or you may be <u>married to</u> someone who does. In both instances the situations will be caused by your own beliefs, even though this may at first seem most unlikely. For the purposes of this particular chapter, we will discuss illnesses or situations that have arisen since childhood, so we are not including birth defects or very early life-endangering childhood accidents, or most unfortunate childhood family situations. These will be discussed separately.

(Long pause at 4:19.) In most cases, even the most severe illnesses or complicated living conditions and relationships are caused by an attempt to grow, develop or expand in the face of difficulties that appear to be unsurmountable to one degree or another.

An individual will often be striving for some goal that appears blocked, and hence he or she uses all available energy and strength to circumnavigate the blockage. The blockage is usually a belief which needs to be understood or removed rather than bypassed.

In this book we will be involved with the nature of beliefs and with various methods that will allow you to choose those beliefs that lead to a more satisfying life.

Though this book is entitled *The Way Toward Health*, we are not speaking of physical health alone, but of mental, spiritual, and emotional health as well. You are not healthy, for example, no matter how <u>robust</u> your physical condition, if your relationships are unhealthy, unsatisfying, frustrating, or hard to achieve. Whatever your situation is, it is a good idea to ask yourself <u>what you would do</u> if you were free of it. An alcoholic's wife might wish with all her heart that her husband stop drinking — but if she suddenly asked herself what she would do, she might — surprisingly enough — feel a tinge of panic. On examination of her own thoughts and beliefs, she might well discover that she was so frightened of not achieving her own goals that she actually encouraged her husband's alcoholism, so that she would not have to face her own "failure."

Obviously this hypothetical situation is a quick example of what I mean, with no mention of the innumerable other beliefs and half-beliefs that would encircle the man's and the woman's relationship.

End of dictation.

(4:36.) Once again, however, I do accelerate those coordinates that quicken your own healing abilities and inspirations and revelations.

I do indeed look in on both of you frequently, and now I bid you a most fond good afternoon.

("Good afternoon, Seth."

(4:37 P.M. "On those days when I don't feel like having a session, you can rest," Jane said as we talked, "but on those days when I feel like having a session, I think I should do it —"

("You feel like you should do it, or when you want to do it?" I asked.

("Well, both," she said. "The two go together. I want to do it when I want to do it," she laughed. She had a cigarette while I read her the session. I think it's an excellent one, and contains much that applies to our own situation, I'm sure.)

CHAPTER 9

You, You, You, and You. Living at Cross Purposes

MAY 29, 1984
4:00 P.M. TUESDAY

I bid you another fond good afternoon.

(*"Good afternoon, Seth."*)

The next chapter, to be headed: "You, You, You, and You. Living at Cross Purposes."

(*Long pause.*) Each person is so unique that it is obviously impossible for me to discuss all of the innumerable and complicated strands of belief that form human experience — yet I hope here, some way, to present enough "specific generalizations" so that you the reader can find many points of application as far as your own life is concerned.

In fact, you may discover not just one you, but several you's, so to speak, each pursuing certain purposes, and you may find out furthermore that some such purposes cancel others out, while some are diametrically opposed to each other. Such cross purposes, of course, can lead to mental, spiritual, physical and emotional difficulties.

Many people believe that it is dangerous to make themselves known, to express their own ideas or abilities. Such individuals may be highly motivated, on the other hand, to become accomplished in some art or profession or other field of activity. In such cases you have two cross-purposes operating — the desire to express oneself, and the fear of doing so.

If both beliefs are equally dominant and vital, then the situation becomes quite serious. Such individuals may try "to get ahead" on the one hand, in society or business or in the arts or sciences, only to find themselves taking two steps backward for every step they take forward. In other words, they will encounter obstructions that are self-generated. If such a person begins to succeed, then he or she is forcibly reminded of the equally dominant need for lack of success — for again, the person believes that self-expression is necessary and desirable while also being highly dangerous, and thus to be avoided.

(4:14.) Dilemmas result in many ways. The person might succeed financially, only to make a serious or faulty business judgment, thus losing the financial benefits. Another person might express the same dilemma through the body itself, so that "getting ahead" was equated with physical mobility — so that it seemed that physical mobility, while so desired, was still highly dangerous.

Such reasoning sounds quite outlandish, of course, to most individuals, but the person in question, say with a disease like arthritis, or some other <u>motion-impairing</u> ailment, might ask themselves the question: "What would I do if I were free of the condition?"

Like the alcoholic's wife mentioned earlier, such a person might suddenly feel struck by a sense of panic, rather than relief, thus experiencing for the first time the fear of motion that underlay the problem.

Yet why should motion be feared? Because so many individuals have been taught that power or energy is wrong, destructive, or sinful, and therefore to be punished.

Often playful, rambunctious children are told not to be showoffs, or not to express their normal exuberance. Religions stress the importance of discipline, sobriety, <u>and</u> penance. All of these attitudes can be extremely detrimental, and along with other beliefs are responsible for a goodly number of spiritual, physical, mental, and emotional problems.

Unfortunately, there are also some particular teachings that are sexually oriented, and that therefore show their effects often on one sex rather than the other. Boys are still taught to "be cool," unemotional, aggressive, and assertive — as <u>opposed</u> to being emotionally warm, cooperative, gregarious but without fake bravado. Boys are taught that it is unmanly to be dependent in any way. They become embarrassed in late boyhood when kissed by their mothers, as a rule — yet it is quite natural to be both independent <u>and</u> dependent, cooperative <u>and</u> competitive.

Such young men grow up with the desire to be independent, while at the same time they also experience the natural drive for cooperation and dependence upon others. Many end up punishing themselves for any behavior they consider dependent or unmanly. They are often afraid to express love, or to accept <u>emotional nourishment</u> gracefully.

As a result some such people become severely afflicted with ulcers, so that their stomachs become sore and ulcerated at the acceptance of physical nourishment.

I may or may not return, but I do indeed again accelerate those coordinates that lead to peace of body and mind.

("Thank you."

(4:33 P.M. Nobody, Jane noted as soon as she was out of trance, interrupted us for anything. I told Jane the session was again very good, like yesterday's; it's obvious that much of it fits our own situation. I heard a nurse pushing the medicine cart outside our door as we talked. After she'd taken her aspirin and Darvoset, Jane had a cigarette before I turned her.

(Joe Bumbalo came back into the hospital this afternoon in preparation for his fourth dose of chemotherapy. I visited him after leaving Jane at 7:00 P.M. He looked and talked much better. Joe expressed concern about how long he would live with his cancer. He also described a dream he's had often during the last three months, but hasn't told Margaret about. To me it sounded obviously symbolic of his fear of death and his battle against surrendering to it. He agreed with my explanation, which I offered quite diplomatically. In any case, I can hardly be all that sure that I'm correct.)

MAY 30, 1984
4:15 P.M. WEDNESDAY

(At the close of yesterday's session I wrote that I visited Joe Bumbalo after leaving Jane at 7:00 P.M. While I was up in his room, 522, Margaret went down to say hello to Jane. Joe is due to go home Thursday morning.

(Last night Jane was extremely uncomfortable lying on her back; the bedsore on her left hip bothered her endlessly, she said. She took Darvoset

and aspirin, but these didn't help. She was on her back when I got to 330
today, and felt much better, although not at ease. I told her that at lunch
time John Bumbalo had called and said that his father wouldn't be going
home for a while: the doctor has found an infection in a lung. No one knew
about this yesterday.)

Now I bid you another most fond good afternoon —

("Good afternoon, Seth.")

— and we will resume dictation.

(Long pause.) Epilepsy is a disease often experienced also by
people who have strongly conflicting beliefs about the use of power
or energy, coupled with a sometimes extraordinary amount of
mental and physical energy that demands it be used.

In many such cases the individuals involved are highly intellectual, and possess obvious gifts that are, however, seldom put to full
use. Such people are so frightened of the nature of personal power
and energy that they short-circuit their nervous systems, blocking
the ability for any <u>purposeful</u> action, at least momentarily.

Because they realize that they do indeed innately possess strong
gifts and abilities, these people often seek attention <u>for their disease</u>,
rather than for their abilities. They may become professional patients,
favorites of their doctors because of their wit and repartee in the face
of their affliction. These persons, however, again, are living at cross
purposes. They are determined to express themselves and <u>not</u> to
express themselves at the same time. Like so many others they believe
that self-expression is dangerous, evil, and bound to lead to suffering — self-inflicted or otherwise.

This particular group of people are also <u>usually</u> possessed by an
extraordinary anger: they are furious at themselves for not being
able to showcase their own strength and power — but "forced"
instead into a kind of behavior that appears sometimes frightening
and humiliating.

(Long pause at 4:28.) Individuals who suffer from epilepsy are
also often perfectionists — trying so hard to be at their best that they
end up with a very uneven, jerky physical behavior.

In some instances, stuttering is a very mild example of the same
kind of activity. On the one hand some epileptic patients feel a cut
above the usual run of humanity, while on the other they perform far

more awkwardly than normal persons. Again, many also believe that those with special talents or gifts are disliked by others and persecuted. Period.

This brings us into a conglomeration of beliefs unfortunately connected with romanticism.

Take a break and we will resume briefly.

(4:34. Jane had a sip of coffee and a smoke. "Sometimes I feel like there's a chunk of material there, then other days there's nothing," she said. Resume at 4:41.)

These beliefs are centered around artists, writers, poets, musicians, actors and actresses, or others who seem unusually gifted in the arts or in various other methods of self-expression. The beliefs lead to the most dire legends, in which the gifted person always pays in one way or another for the valued gifts of self-expression — through disaster, misfortune, or death.

End of dictation.

(4:44.) Ruburt's unfortunate evening was the result of his own fears about the body — related to the fact that he then picked up Joe's own dire fears, and these fueled his own.

Margaret's visit was somewhat involved, as was your visit to Joe's room.

It will be a good idea, even if it is not pleasant, for Ruburt to do some more free association in relationship to his fears about his body's performance — and those fears should not then be treated impatiently. They can and should be reasoned with, even if this means going over counter beliefs time and time again.

I will also try to give you some further hints along those lines at our next session, and I bid you both now a fond good evening, and a comfortable and pleasant evening.

("Thank you."

(4:49 P.M. Joe discussed his fears with me last night when I visited him, but I didn't get a chance to tell Jane about them until I saw her in 330 this afternoon. In other words, she picked up Joe's fears herself, unless Margaret might have referred to them when she visited Jane last night after I'd left.

(Note: Margaret didn't — instead, she told Jane that Joe felt so much better that the family planned to take him home Wednesday night, instead of Thursday morning.)

MAY 31, 1984
4:15 P.M. THURSDAY

(On May 28, a nurse in hydro dropped an empty pan on Jane's left instep, making one of those depression cuts in the flesh. It hurt, Jane said. The spot is still sore, but is healing. This morning, Georgia and another aide banged Jane's right shin hard against the metal frame of the stretcher they put my wife on to take her to hydro. Jane screamed in pain, and Georgia cried. Jane at once began telling herself it all would be all right, and that appears to be the case. Although she has some pain in the lower leg and foot, and the area is tender to the touch, there are no wounds or discolorations. I noticed no signs of swelling when I got to 330 this noon.

(Jane ate a quicker lunch than usual because I had to leave at 1:45 to go to the dentist. When I got back I told her I'd try free association with her, or a session. She said she didn't know if she was up to any free-association efforts — "though I do intend to try it, as Seth says." She had a better night last night, but is still quite uncomfortable on her back, and is on Darvoset and aspirin too.

(I called Margaret Bumbalo in room 522 to see how Joe is. He was having a bone scan at the time. Margaret said he's grown considerably weaker than when he came into the hospital, though evidently the prognosis is okay.)

I bid you another most fond good afternoon.

("Good afternoon, Seth.")

We will resume dictation.

These concepts have many cousins, so that we actually have an entire family of beliefs that are all in one way or another related.

Foremost, connected with the distortions about creativity and expression, is the belief that knowledge itself is dangerous, evil, and bound to lead to disaster. Here, innocence is seen as synonymous with ignorance. What you actually have behind such a belief is a fear of free will and of making choices.

The more extensive your knowledge, the more aware you are of probable actions, and of the conglomeration of choices that then become available. There are also people, then, with an intense thirst for knowledge who believe that knowledge is indeed good and beneficial, while on the other hand they believe just as fervently that knowledge is forbidden and dangerous.

All of these instances lead, of course, to severe dilemmas, and often pull an individual in two directions at once. They are the cause, also, of many spiritual, emotional, and physical difficulties.

It should probably be noted here also that this suspicion of knowledge is intensified when the female sex is involved, for the legends quite erroneously give the impression that knowledge is twice as disastrous if possessed by a woman. This should be kept in mind whenever we discuss beliefs that are specifically sexually oriented.

It must seem obvious that behind all such beliefs lies the distrust of nature, man, and life itself.

(4:28.) We must also remember, however, that in a fashion <u>beliefs themselves are tools</u>, and that in some situations beliefs that seem quite negative can also clear the way for more beneficial ones. With all of this discussion of negative beliefs, therefore, it is a good idea not to call any beliefs <u>bad</u> or evil in themselves. They are no more bad or evil in their own way, say, than viruses are in theirs. If you look upon them in that manner, you will avoid being overwhelmed by what seems to be an endless parade of negative thoughts and beliefs that can only lead to destruction. Instead, compare the negative beliefs, for example, with the <u>storms</u> that sweep the country: they have their purposes — and all in all those purposes tend to promote and support life itself.

While we are still in the middle of such discussions, however, remind yourself that any situation <u>can be changed for the better</u>. Remind yourselves constantly that the most favorable solution to a problem is at least as probable as the most unfortunate "solution." Remind yourselves also that despite all of your worrying, the spirit of life itself <u>is</u> continually within your experience, and forms your physical body.

(Long pause.) In this session, again I accelerate those coordinates that encourage well-being and peace of body and mind. Have Ruburt pay particular attention to the last several sentences.

("Good afternoon, Seth.")

(4.38 P.M. Again, we had no interruptions during the session. Jane's delivery had been good. She had a cigarette while I read her the session before turning her.)

JUNE 1, 1984
4:12 P.M. FRIDAY

Now I bid you another most fond good afternoon —

(*"Good afternoon, Seth."*)

— and we will resume dictation.

(*Long pause.*) Large numbers of the population do indeed live unsatisfactory lives, with many individuals seeking goals that are nearly unattainable because of the conglomeration of conflicting beliefs that all vie for their attention. They are at cross purposes with themselves.

This leads not only to private dilemmas, illnesses, and seemingly futile relationships — but also to national misunderstandings, entanglements, and world disorders. There are indeed ways of breaking through such conflicts, however, and those broader avenues of expression, peace, and satisfaction <u>are</u> available to each individual, however unfortunate the entire picture seems to be.

It is possible, therefore, to improve your health, and to deepen the quality of all of your experience.

In terms of earthly life as you understand it, it is overly optimistic to imagine that eventually all illnesses will be conquered, all relationships be inevitably fulfilling, or to foresee a future in which all people on earth are treated with equality and respect. For one thing, in that larger framework mentioned earlier in this book, illness itself is a part of life's overall activity. Disease states, so-called, are as necessary to physical life as normal health is, so we are not speaking of a nirvana on earth — but we <u>are</u> saying that it is possible for each reader of this book to quicken his or her private perceptions, and to extend and expand the quality of <u>ordinary consciousness</u> enough so that by contrast to current experience, life could almost be thought of as "heaven on earth."

(*Long pause at 4:28.*) This involves a reeducation of the most profound nature. All of the conflicting beliefs that have been mentioned thus far are the end result of what I have called before the "official line of consciousness." Certainly people experienced disease long before those conflicting beliefs began — but again, <u>that is because</u> of the part that disease states play in the overall health of individuals and of the world.

What we are going to have to do, then, is start over. It is indeed quite possible to do so, for you will be working with material with which you are intimately familiar: your own thoughts, emotions, and beliefs.

You must start from your present position, of course, but there is no person who cannot better his or her position to a considerable degree, if the effort is made to follow through with the kind of new hypotheses that we will here suggest. These ideas are to some extent already present, though they have not predominated in world experience.

Take a break, and we will briefly continue.

(4:35. At break Linda brought in Jane's aspirin and Darvoset; my wife has still been uncomfortable while lying on her back. At the same time there was a great clangor outside: Three firetrucks and another vehicle, all with sirens, turned the corner just outside our third-story window, evidently heading toward the temporary entrance to the emergency room. Then a moment later there came a "Doctor Blue" emergency summons over the hospital's loudspeaker system. Resume at 4:44.)

This alternate way of thinking is biologically pertinent, for it should be obvious now that certain beliefs and ideas serve to foster health and vitality, while others impede it.

These ideas are translations of the emotional attitudes of all portions of nature and of life itself. They are better than any medicine, and they promote the expression of value fulfillment of all kinds of life, whatever its form.

End of dictation.

(4:47.) A note: This will be the last chapter of the <u>first part</u> of the book — which is to be called "Dilemmas." The beginning of the next chapter when we start it, will be the first chapter of the second part, to be called "Starting Over."

I want to remind you both that what I am saying is indeed possible, and more possible than not. Period.

Ruburt can start at his present position, as each person must begin with the situation at hand. The point of power <u>is</u> in the present.

Now I bid you a most fond good afternoon.

("Good afternoon, Seth. Thank you." 4:50 P.M.)

PART TWO

STARTING
OVER

When my father, Robert Sr., photographed Jane and me on our wedding day, December 27, 1954, and then in 1957, did any of us know that his work would be published almost half a century later?

Yes, I think that in our separate ways each one of us chose to create this probable reality out of the many available.

Within Seth's concept of simultaneous time, the treasured images in this gallery are fine examples of how the "past" lives in the "present" and in the "future."

Jane's mother, Marie, died in 1972.

Jane at less than 2 years old; at 7; and at 12 in 1941 — all in Saratoga Springs, New York. Her childhood was difficult.

Jane's parents divorced when she was 3, and she and her angry, bedridden mother lived on welfare. Jane also spent a year in an orphanage when her mother was hospitalized.

Jane's father, Del, photographed her in 1951, when she was 22. I met her three years later.

Jane and I had been married for three months when my father photographed her in March 1955.

With much humor, Jane as Seth made a point during a session in 1969. She was 40 years old. Photo by Rich Conz.

My friend, Laurel Lee Davies, photographed me in 1986, two years after Jane's death.

My parents, Robert Sr. and Estelle, supported the choices their three children made — and so they wholeheartedly welcomed Jane into the family. She in turn came to love them deeply. They died in the early 1970s.

Jane felt psychically connected to her "Little Daddy" — Joseph Burdo, her maternal grandfather. She was 20 when he died in 1949, at 68.

Delmer and Marie Roberts married in March 1928. They were each 23. Jane was born on May 8, 1929.

Jane liked this trance shot: In a quiet moment during a hilarious session in 1969, Seth contemplates Rich Conz, a photographer for the Elmira Star-Gazette. Rich had many questions.

Over the years I helped Jane while marvelling at her great creativity and trying to understand its source. Why was she doing the sessions? They were her way of contributing to understanding ourselves, and to peer into the great mystery of All That Is.

Robert F. Butts (1919 -): *Jane Roberts*. 1987. Oil on panel, 13 x 17 in.

The same year I painted my self-portrait, I painted Jane as I saw her in my dream of March 10, 1987. She had died in 1984. I knew that in the dream Jane was reassuring me that she still lived.

Robert F. Butts (1919 -): *Self-portrait.* 1987. Oil on panel, 16 x 14 in.

I painted myself when I was 68 years old. It's quite a psychic, psychological, and physical education to stare at oneself in a mirror over a period of three months!

Robert F. Butts (1919 -):
Seth 1968. Oil on panel,
27 x 21 in.

I painted Seth, that ageless
"energy personality essence,"
from a vision I had of him
five years after Jane began
speaking for him in 1963.
Their very creative relationship lasted for 21 years.

Oil on panel, 36 x 26 in.

Oil on panel, 24 x 30 in.

In 1965, at the age of 36, Jane had posed for the two conventional
portraits shown here.

CHAPTER 10

A New Beginning. Instructions, Suggestions, and Resolutions — and When to Ignore These

JUNE 3, 1984
3:11 P.M. SUNDAY

(A nurse and an aide met me at the door to 330 this noon and told me that they'd spent half an hour trying to get Jane comfortable. She was on her back when I arrived. She's still on Darvoset and aspirin, and the two drugs are beginning to affect her hearing. I've noticed for the last week or so that she's getting hard of hearing again — I have to speak louder, turn up the TV, and so forth.

(Jane ate well, however, and reread the last four sessions afterward, while I did some mail. I told her that Frank Longwell visited this morning. We agreed on the location of the Crimson King red maple in the back yard; Frank is to plant it tomorrow afternoon, and bring the young fellow with him to mow the grass, which is some six inches high. It rained again last night and this morning.)

Now I bid you another fine good afternoon.

("Good afternoon, Seth.")

First of all, a note to Ruburt: tell him not to put off free association in regard to his fear about his body's performance, but to discuss this as openly as possible with you.

This does also allow you to give him some comfort, and help alleviate any feelings you have of not being able to help enough. The feelings should be aired, however — and <u>then</u> not concentrated upon.

We will begin now with Part Two of the book: "Starting Over." The next chapter to be called: "A New Beginning. Instructions, Suggestions, and Resolutions — and When to Ignore These."

The thoughts and beliefs that we want to rearouse are those that were often predominant in childhood, as mentioned earlier in this book. They are spiritual, mental, emotional and biological beliefs that are innately present in the birth of each creature. Children believe not only that there will be a tomorrow, and many tomorrows, but they also believe that each tomorrow will be rewarding and filled with discovery.

They feel themselves couched in an overall feeling of security and safety, even in the face of an unpleasant environment or situation. They feel drawn to other people and to other creatures, and left alone they trust their contacts with others. They have an inbred sense of self-satisfaction and self-appreciation, and they instinctively feel that it is natural and good for them to explore and develop their capabilities.

Take a break.

(3:23. Jane called for a break because I'd been coughing and sniffling, trying to sneeze. I told her I'd felt something in my throat. I didn't know what had set me off, really, though.)

They expect relationships to be rewarding and continuing, and expect each event will have the best possible results. They enjoy communication, the pursuit of knowledge, and they are filled with curiosity.

All of those attitudes provide the strength and mental health that promotes their physical growth and development. However simple those ideas may sound to the adult, still they carry within them the needed power and impetus that fill all of life's parts. Later, conflicting beliefs often smother such earlier attitudes, so that by the time children have grown into adults they actually hold almost an opposite set of hypotheses. These take it for granted that any stressful situation will worsen, that communication with others is dangerous, that self-fulfillment brings about the envy and vengeance of others, and that as individuals they live in an unsafe society, set down in the middle of a natural world that is itself savage, cruel, and caring only for its own survival at any cost.

Take a break, and we will continue.

(3:33. Robert came in to take Jane's blood pressure. The day was cold and cloudy. Resume at 3:42.)

Your body actually lives on large quantities of joyful expectation.

The fetus is propelled by the expectation of future growth and development. It is bad enough to anticipate that most unfortunate situations will worsen rather than improve, but it is foolhardy indeed to believe that mankind is bound to destroy itself, or that nuclear destruction is nearly inevitable.

Many people no longer believe in life after death, and so large numbers of the population are philosophically denied a spiritual <u>or</u> a physical future.

This deprives body and mind of the zest and purpose needed in order to enjoy any pursuits or activities. Such beliefs make any human endeavor appear futile. There are ways of reacting to the dangers of nuclear energy that are far more healthy and beneficial, and we will discuss these later in the book.

For now, I simply want to suggest that all such beliefs should be understood and dismissed as soon as possible. We hope to show how most natural health-promoting beliefs can be applied to all mental, physical, or emotional illnesses or difficulties. I want to assure you that regardless of your circumstances, age, or sex, you can indeed start over, rearousing from within yourself those earlier, more innocent expectations, feelings and beliefs. It is much better if you can imagine this endeavor more in the light of children's play, in fact, rather than think of it as a deadly serious adult pursuit.

In other words, we will try to instill a somewhat playful attitude, even toward the most severe problems, for the very idea of play encourages the use of the imagination and the creative abilities.

This starting over —

(3:56. Leanne came in with the mixture of aspirin and Darvoset that Jane's been taking lately. It left a bitter taste. I read the session to her, and once again had to speak louder for her to hear me. Resume at 4:10.)

Again, because of the simultaneous nature of time, beliefs can be changed in the present moment.

There is no need to search <u>endlessly</u> into the past of this life or any other, for the "original" causes for beliefs. Making a change in the present of a certain kind will automatically alter all beliefs "across the board," so to speak. It is important, however, that you do not strain too hard to achieve results, but allow yourself some leeway. You react to your beliefs habitually, often unthinkingly, and in usual ideas of time, and in your <u>experience</u> of it — you must allow yourself "some time" to change that habitual behavior.

As you do, you will discover yourself reacting to the desired beliefs as easily and automatically as you did to the <u>un</u>desirable ones. As you do, keep the idea of child's play in mind, however. This will allow you to keep the entire affair in a kind of suspension.

The child plays at being an adult long before he is one, and so you can play with more desirable beliefs while you are still growing into that more beneficial picture.

End of dictation.

Again, I accelerate those coordinates that lead to peace of mind and body, and promote the healing processes. And I bid you a most fond early evening.

(*"Good afternoon, Seth." 4:19 P.M.*)

JUNE 4, 1984
3:19 P.M. MONDAY

Now I bid you another most fond good afternoon.

(*"Good afternoon, Seth."*)

We will resume dictation.

One of the issues I want to discuss in depth is that of spontaneity in relationship to health and disease.

Your very physical existence itself is dependent upon the smooth functioning of many spontaneous processes. Your thinking, breathing, and motion are all guided by activities that are largely unconscious — at least from the standpoint of what you usually think of as the conscious mind.

Your body repairs itself constantly, and your mind thinks — all without your normally conscious attention. The same applies to all of those inner processes that make life possible. Your thoughts are conscious, but the process of thinking itself is not. Spontaneity is par-

ticularly important in the actions of children, and in the natural
rhythmic motion of their limbs. Feelings also seem to come and go
in a spontaneous fashion.

It is indeed as if some inner spontaneous part of the personality
is far more knowledgeable than the conscious portion of which we
are so rightfully proud.

Many people, however, <u>fear</u> spontaneity: it evokes extravagance,
excesses, and dangerous freedoms. Even people who are not so fervently opposed to spontaneity often feel that it is somehow suspect, dis-
tasteful, perhaps leading to humiliating actions. Spontaneity, however,
represents the spirit of life itself, and it is the basis for the will to live,
and for those impulses that stimulate action, motion, and discovery.

In the truest regard, <u>your life is provided for you</u> by these spontaneous processes. As I've mentioned in past books, at one time the
human personality was "more at one with itself." It accommodated
unconscious and conscious experience more equitably. Man was
more aware of his dreams and so-called unconscious activity.

It is only because civilized man has somewhat overspecialized in
the use of one kind of knowledge over another that people fear the
unconscious, spontaneous portions of the self. The fear alone causes
them to block out still more and more unconscious knowledge.
Since the spontaneous portions are so related to bodily activity, they
are very important in facilitating good health, and when people feel
divorced from their spontaneous selves, they also feel divorced to
the same extent from their own bodies.

(3:43.) Such individuals become frightened of freedom itself, of
choices and of changes. They try desperately to control themselves
and their environment against what seems to be a raging, spontaneous mass of primitive impulses from within, and against a mind-
less, chaotic, ancient force of nature. In the physical world, such
behavior often leads to compulsive action — stereotyped mental
and physical motion and other situations with a strong repressive
coloration. Here any expression becomes almost taboo. The conscious mind must be in control of all actions as much as possible, for
such a person feels that only rigid, logical thought is strong enough
to hold back such strong impulsive force.

(Long pause.) These attitudes may be reflected in rather simple
compulsive actions: the woman who cleans the house endlessly, whether

it needs it or not; the man who will follow certain precise, defined routes of activity — driving down certain streets only to work; washing his hands much more frequently than other people; the person who constantly buttons and unbuttons a sweater or vest. Many such simple actions show a stereotyped kind of behavior that results from a desperate need to gain control over oneself and the environment.

Take your break.

(3:52. Jane had coffee and a smoke. It was getting cloudy; I told her I hoped Frank Longwell was at the house, planting the red maple while the young fellow from school was mowing the grass. Resume at 4:00.)

Any excessive behavior may enter in, including oversmoking, overeating, and overdrinking.

It will be difficult for some people to believe that spontaneity is to be trusted, for they may be only aware of feeling destructive or violent impulses. The idea of <u>expressing</u> impulses spontaneously will be most frightening under those conditions.

Actually the people involved are <u>repressing</u> not violent impulses but natural <u>loving ones</u>. They are afraid that expressions of love, or the need for dependence will only bring them scorn or punishment. Therefore, they hide those yearnings, and the destructive impulses actually serve to protect them from the expression of love that they have somehow learned to fear.

Science itself, for all of its preciseness in some areas, often equates instinctive, impulsive —

(4:06. Leanne came in to give Jane medications. She told us she's leaving the hospital to be a supervisor in Painted Post, a small community some 17 miles west of Elmira. We wished her well. I read the last sentence to Jane at 4:14.)

— chaotic, <u>destructive</u> activity as one and the same.

Nature and the inner nature of man are both seen to contain savage, destructive forces against which civilization and the reasoning mind must firmly stand guard.

Science itself often displays compulsive and ritualistic behavior, to the point of programming its own paths of reasoning, so that they cover safe ground, and steadfastly ignore the great inner forces of spontaneity that make science — or any discipline — possible. As I have said before, spontaneity knows its own order. Nothing is more highly organized than the physical body that <u>spontaneously</u> grows all of its own parts.

(All intently:) As your life is provided for you, so to speak, by these spontaneous processes, <u>the life of the universe</u> is provided in the same fashion. You see the physical stars, and your instruments probe the distances of space — but the inner processes that make the universe possible are those same processes that propel your own thinking. It is erroneous, therefore, to believe that spontaneity and discipline are mere opposites. Instead, true discipline <u>is the result of</u> true spontaneity.

(4:24.) Value fulfillment of each and every element in life relies upon those spontaneous processes, and at their source is the basic affirmative love and acceptance of the self, the universe, and life's conditions.

End of dictation.

Again I activate those coordinates that quicken your own peace of mind and self-healing processes — which are, remember, spontaneous.

("Thank you.")

(4:26 P.M. Jane had done well, I told her. She'd had a slightly better day, and ate well. As I drove up the road to the hill house, I held my breath — then saw that the grass had indeed been cut; it looked great. As I pulled into the driveway in back, I saw that Frank had planted the red maple. Not only that, he'd brought his tiller back, and had once again plowed up the back yard, preparatory to sowing the wildflower seeds.)

JUNE 5, 1984
3:05 P.M. TUESDAY

Now I bid you another most fond good afternoon.

("Good afternoon, Seth.")

We will resume dictation.

(Long pause.) Since ancient times religion has tried to help man understand the nature of his own subjective reality — but religion has its own dark side, and for this reason religion unfortunately has fostered fear of the spontaneous.

Instead of promoting the idea of man's inner worth, it has taught people to distrust the inner self and its manifestations. Most churches preach a dogma that stresses concepts of <u>the sinful self</u>, and sees man as a creature contaminated by original sin even before birth.

This distorted picture depicts a species of sinners innately driven by evil, sometimes demonic, forces. In this dogma man needs to apologize for his birth, and the conditions of life are seen as a punishment set by God upon his erring creatures. Unfortunately such concepts are also reflected in fields of psychology, particularly in Freudianism — where, say, slips of the tongue may betray the self's hidden, nefarious true desires.

The unconscious is understood to be a garbage heap of undesirable impulses, long ago discarded by civilization, while again much religious theory projects the image of the hidden self that must be kept in bounds by good work, prayer, and penance.

Amid such a conglomeration of negative suppositions, the idea of <u>a good and innocent</u> inner self seems almost scandalous. To encourage expression of that self appears foolhardy, for it seems only too clear that if the lid of consciousness were opened, so to speak, all kinds of inner demons and enraged impulses would rush forth.

(Long pause at 3:20.) Again, people who have such views of the inner self usually project the same ideas upon nature at large, so that the natural world appears equally mysterious, dangerous, and threatening.

In political terms such persons also look for strong authoritative groups or governments, stress law and order above justice or equality, and tend to see the poorer, less advantaged members of society as impulse-ridden, dangerous, and always ready for revolution. It is quite frequent for persons with those beliefs to discipline their bodies overmuch, take positions as police guards, or set themselves up in one way or another in control of their fellows.

I am not here stating that <u>all</u> police guards, members of the military or whatever, fall into that category. Such people will, however, tend toward a strongly disciplined life. Many of their health problems will deal with <u>eruptions</u> — interior ulcers, skin eruptions, or in very definite mental and emotional eruptions, and great outbursts of force and temper all the more noticeable because of the usual disciplined patterns of behavior.

Take your break.

(Resume at 3:50.)

In most such cases there is a lack of the normal range of emotional expression. Such persons often find it extremely difficult to express love, joy, or gratitude, for example, and this lack of expression is taken for granted by others, who do not see it in its true light, but think instead that the person is simply reticent.

Secondary personalities and schizophrenic episodes are also somewhat characteristic — again appearing as sudden explosive behavior when conflicting beliefs are <u>damned up</u> and held back. And when it is believed that the inner self is indeed a bed of chaotic impulses, then it becomes less and less possible for an individual to express normal ranges of activity. The person then feels lethargic and out of touch with work or family.

Expression is a necessity of life, however. Each person feels that drive. When one set of rigid beliefs threatens to make action appear meaningless, then another set of buried, repressed beliefs may surface, providing new impetus precisely when it is needed — but also forming a secondary personality with characteristics almost opposite to those of the primary self.

We will have more to say on all of these issues — but now I want to discuss spontaneity, or its lack, in relationship to sexuality and health.

All of the negative beliefs just mentioned touch upon sexuality in one way or another. Those with the beliefs just mentioned often think of sexuality as bestial, evil, and even humiliating.

These attitudes are intensified where the female sex is concerned. You have, of course, a strong drive toward sexuality, and if you believe that it is to be shunned at the same time, then you are in a very ambiguous position. Women with such beliefs and conflicts often wind up having hysterectomies, performed incidentally by male doctors, who hold the very same beliefs.

Many men look forward to having sons, while at the same time they revere marriage as a necessary part of respectable family life, and also feel that marriage is somehow degrading — particularly to a male — and that the sex act itself is only justified if it brings him an heir.

Such a male will seek sex with prostitutes, or with women he considers beneath him. In a strange fashion, he may even feel that it is wrong to have sex with his own wife, believing that the sex act so <u>degrades</u> the both of them. In many cases these people will be great sportsmen, follow conventionalized male pursuits, and perhaps express contempt for the arts or any interest considered remotely feminine.

End of dictation.

(4:33.) Once again I quicken those coordinates that energize your own peace of body and mind, and facilitate the use of your own intuitive abilities.

I bid you a fond early evening.

("Thank you.")

(4:34 P.M. Jane's rather slow delivery had been interrupted three times by staff. I told her that the session was very good, as all of them have been in this recent series. She was pleased.

(The day was hot — over 80 degrees — and felt something like summer for the first time. Jane had felt better today. She ate well for lunch and supper, and turned easily. She is still on the Darvoset-aspirin regime, plus the calcium and the other extra vitamins — we don't know what they are. Peggy Gallagher visited at about 6:40, so I got ready and left for the evening without Jane and I reading the prayer.)

JUNE 6, 1984
4:09 P.M. WEDNESDAY

(I brought Jane a chicken sandwich — the third in a series, and the last one made from the barbecued chicken I'd bought at a Convenient Market. She enjoyed it again. She's still uncomfortable, but felt a little better today. I told her that I'd be leaving early to go to the dentist. I'd broken a tooth last night, and feared I'd lose it.

(I suggested to Jane that she could have a session before I left. She didn't feel anything at first, and I did some mail while I waited. Finally she said she felt Seth around. Her delivery was a bit on the slow side, but steady.)

Now I bid you another most fond good afternoon —

("Good afternoon, Seth.")

— and we will resume dictation.

Many schools of religion and so-called esoteric knowledge have promoted the idea that sexuality and spirituality were diametrically opposed to each other.

People in the sports arena also often encourage the concept that sexual expression is somehow debilitating to the male, and can weaken his constitution. Priests take vows to ensure sexual abstinence.

The fact is that sexual expression is, again, an important element in the entire range of human experience, encouraging mental and physical health and vitality.

Some people may have a stronger or weaker sex drive than others, and yet that drive is a strong part of any individual's natural rhythm. Damned up, such sexuality still keeps trying for expression, and it is often men of habitual "sexual discipline" who suddenly break out in bouts of sexual promiscuity or violence.

In actuality, the combination of a philosophical stress upon discipline, physical and mental, with the belief in the sinful self, often brings about the most unfortunate human dilemmas. These ideas usually ride along with feelings that power is desirable but dangerous. To abstain from sexuality then means to store up one's own power. People with such beliefs often have severe problems with constipation, and have retention symptoms — retaining water, for example, or salt or whatever.

(4:21.) They may also suffer with stomach difficulties, many being overly fond of extremely spicy foods. Some have unusually heavy appetites, even though these may be regulated by a series of diets — which are then broken by overeating.

There are so many other elements involved in human nature that I do not really want to point out any culprits, yet male-segregated communities are obviously notorious for encouraging that kind of behavior. Every individual in such institutions or societies is not affected in the same fashion, of course — yet you do have these kinds of closed societies, relatively speaking, and they can indeed serve as cradles for fanaticism and rigid stereotypes of behavior. Again, here you find that discipline, rather than free will, is stressed, so that the opportunity for choices is drastically reduced. The more open a society, the more healthy its people.

End of session.

("Thank you." 4:30 P.M.)

JUNE 7, 1984
3:21 P.M. THURSDAY

(The day was very warm — over 90 degrees — when I left for 330 this noon. Jane was better today, and 330 wasn't bad at all, with the air

conditioner going, the fan on, and the windows wide open. I'd brought
shorts with me and changed into them; I already had sandals there. The
weather had a luxurious, lush feel, as though our globe had finally turned
from an adversary into a nurturing, supportive parent. I worked on mail
after helping Jane eat lunch, until she said she was ready for a session. I
told my wife that I had indeed lost the tooth.)

Now I bid you another most fond good afternoon.

("Good afternoon, Seth.")

We will resume dictation.

What I have said also applies to organizations segregated along feminine lines, though to a lesser degree.

In both cases the sexes are denied any true communication, and an extremely artificial framework is maintained, in which the sexes literally become strangers to each other. This also encourages various kinds of hysterical reactions, as well as a larger frequency of "contagious diseases" than is experienced by the normal population.

These conditions also occur in some varieties of religious cults, whether or not strict sexual segregation is enforced. If human relationships are highly regulated and supervised, or family members encouraged to spy upon their relatives or friends, then you have the same kind of curtailment of natural expression and communication.

People in such societies often suffer from malnourishment, frequent beatings, an excessive use of the enema, and often indulge in physical punishment. The children are strictly raised, and a lack of normal spontaneity is the rule rather than the exception. Members of such organizations often suffer maladies in which their bodies do not utilize nutrients. They are often food faddists of one kind or another, but because they do fear spontaneity to such a degree they will often become afflicted with diseases or maladies associated with the body's unconscious processes.

(Long pause at 3:34.) You can also find single families, of course, that <u>operate like</u> cults — or an entire nation — that are given over to repression with its resulting violence.

The ideas that you have, then, play a large role in the way the body handles its nutrients, and utilizes its health and vitality. If you believe that the body is somehow evil, you may punish it by nearly starving to death, even though your diet might be considered normal by usual standards. For it is possible for your ideas to cause chemical reactions that impede your body's ability to accept nourishment. If you believe that the body is evil, the purest health-food diet will or may do you little good at all, while if you have a healthy desire and respect for your physical body, a diet of TV dinners, and even of fast foods, may well keep you healthy and nourished.

If we are talking about health, it is to your beliefs that we must look. You have the most efficient and beautiful physical organs, the most elegant joints and appendages, the most vibrant lungs and the most exquisite of senses. It is up to you to form a body of beliefs that is worthy of your physical image — for you are nourished by your beliefs, and those beliefs can cause your daily bread to add to your vitality, or to add to your cares and stress.

Take a break.

(3:45. Leanne came in to check Jane's vitals — they were all normal — and to give her Darvoset. A new aide asked for tomorrow's menu, which I'd left on the medicine tray in the hall, as usual. Resume at 4:04.)

The weight of unfortunate beliefs perhaps falls heaviest on the older segments of the population, for the beliefs have had a longer period of time to operate relatively unimpeded.

Those particular beliefs actually take hold in young adults, so that it seems that <u>all</u> of life is meant to come to its fullest flower in young adulthood, and then from that prestigious position fall quicker and quicker into disuse and disarray.

These ideas do not only inflict severe difficulties upon older members of the population, but they also have a vital part to play in the behavior of many young people who commit suicide directly or indirectly. It seems to such youngsters that the pinnacle of life is just at hand, to last only briefly, and then to be snatched away. Undue stress is laid upon youthful beauty and youthful achievement, so that it appears that all of the rest of life's activities must suffer by contrast.

Knowledge through experience is not considered a practical-enough method of learning, so that the skills and understanding that come with age are seldom taken into consideration.

Again, to a certain degree, religion and science — and the medical sciences in particular — seem devoted to encouraging the most negative beliefs about human nature. It is taken for granted that all mental, physical, spiritual and emotional satisfactions become lesser with advancing age. It is taken for granted that memory fails, the body weakens, the senses stagnate, and emotional vividness dims. It is often considered scandalous to even imagine sexual activity after the age of even 40 or 50.

Faced with that kind of a projected future, no wonder many adolescents prefer to die before catching sight of the very first hint of deterioration — the first wrinkle or touch of gray in the hair. What forerunners of disaster such natural signs must seem (exclamation point)! And at the other end of the scale, older parents are treated by their grown children as if they themselves were falling into a grotesque version of a second childhood. Many people actually <u>speak louder</u> to older persons, whether or not they have any hearing difficulties at all.

Your entire world of commerce and advertisements, of competition and of business, prolong such attitudes. This is aside from the impact of the entertainment industry, which reflects that same glorification of youth, and that fear of growing old.

There are very definite, excellent side-effects of growing older, that we will also discuss in this book — but here I want to assure the reader that basically speaking there are no diseases <u>brought about by old age alone</u> (*intently*).

The body often wears out because it has been used less and less — and that is because little study has been given to the true capabilities of the healthy physical body in the later years of life. That period also contains certain <u>rhythms in which normal healing processes</u> are highly accelerated, and the life force itself does not wear out or lessen within a body. Its expression may be impeded at any time, but the unique energy of each individual <u>is not drained away</u> because of age alone.

We will have more to say concerning older people and their ways of life, and also discuss the many beliefs and ideas that can come almost immediately to their aid. The subject of suicide will also be discussed in a different context, and when I invite my readers to start over, I want it understood that you can indeed start over regardless of your age or circumstances.

End of dictation.

Again I accelerate those coordinates that encourage your own peace of body and mind, and accelerate your own healing processes.

(*"Thank you."*

(*4:35 P.M. It was getting late, and I didn't read the session to Jane.*)

CHAPTER 11

STARTING OVER FROM THE BOTTOM UPWARD.
THE WILL TO LIVE

JUNE 8, 1984
3:14 P.M. FRIDAY

(The day was once again very hot — at least 90 degrees — but room 330 was pleasant once more. There was a good breeze, which was quite noticeable up on the third floor. Jane and I read the prayer together after lunch. I did a little mail until she said she was ready for the session. She seemed to feel a bit better than she has been lately. Her delivery was on the slow side, but steady.)

Now I bid you another most fond good afternoon —

("Good afternoon, Seth.")

— and we will continue dictation.

Starting over — changing one's beliefs, is a bold endeavor. It is quite possible that along the way you may become discouraged or disillusioned.

At such times it is a good idea to give yourself time to relax. Turn your attention to something else entirely, and mentally say, "To hell with it all for now." The entire idea involves a process in which you <u>try and not try</u> at the same time, in which you do not <u>strain</u> to achieve results, but instead gently begin to allow yourself to follow the contours of your own subjective feelings, to uncover those spiritual and biologically valid beliefs of early childhood, and to bring to them the very best wisdom that you have acquired throughout your life so far.

So when you do become discouraged, a playful diversion should give you refreshing release. An escapist movie or novel, or the purchase of some small frivolous item may also serve to relax your conscious mind. We are actually involved in changing a way of life, in altering our very view of the self and the world in the hopes of acquiring a new sense of harmony with our bodies, our minds, our fellow creatures, and the environment.

Indeed, there is no more exciting adventure, and it will bring about more surprises and discoveries than any expedition to alien landscapes. Your beliefs are indeed alive in their own fashion. Now, instead of taking them for granted, you will begin to notice both their uniqueness and their variety.

(3:28.) If we are talking about starting over, however, we may as well begin at one of the lowest points and work upward. This way you can see beliefs in their darkest form, and then little by little watch them begin to show energy, vitality, and fresh impetus.

End of chapter.

The next chapter is to be entitled "Starting Over From the Bottom Upward. The Will to Live."

In nearly all matters of poor health, or unfortunate living conditions or mental or physical stress, there exists a strong tinge of denial, fear, and repression.

These are seen at their most severe and their most obvious where suicide is involved — particularly in the suicide of the young. Later we will discuss some special cases of reincarnational influence connected with suicide, but for now we will be concerned with the increasing numbers of suicides by young adults.

At one time or another most people consider the possibility of their own death. That is a quite natural reaction to the conditions of life. With some people, however, the idea of death seems to grow obsessive, so that it is felt to be the one escape from life's problems. It may even achieve an <u>allure</u> in some people's minds.

The propelling force in all of existence is the desire <u>to be</u>, however — the impetus toward expression, development, and fulfillment. Some people who consider suicide believe in life after death, and some do not — and in the deepest of terms all deaths <u>are</u> somewhat suicidal. Physical life must end if it is to survive. There are certain conditions, however, that promote suicidal activity, and the termination of one's own life has been held in great disrepute by many religions and societies, though not in all.

Individuals innately want to cooperate with their fellow human beings. They have a need to help other people, and to contribute to the common good. Many people who commit suicide feel to the contrary that they are no longer needed, or in fact that their very existence stands in the way of other people's happiness. Young adult suicides are not necessarily from the poorest or the lowest stratas of society at all. In fact, poverty often serves as a strong impetus, leading the individual to fight for his or her daily needs.

Such a person's days may be so crowded with desperate activity that there is no <u>time</u> with which to even contemplate suicide, because the struggle for life itself is so intent.

Again, the desire for value fulfillment, development and purpose is so strong that <u>if those</u> seem denied, life becomes — or seems to become — less precious. In many cases it is the son and daughter of the upper middle-classes, or the well-to-do, who run into such life-endangering dilemmas. Some youngsters are so overly provided for by their families that it seems that there is no way for them to achieve any more than they have.

(*Long pause at 4:00. Jane had been interrupted once during her delivery.*) If their parents are overly indulgent, then the youngsters may actually feel as if they were adjuncts to their parents, or possessions alone. On the other hand, some upper-middle-class families stress competition to such a degree that it seems to the children that they are only valued for their <u>achievements</u>, rather than being loved for simply being the people they are.

To most people, none of these situations seem particularly drastic, and certainly there are far worse cases of human disillusionment in the world. Yet many such youngsters literally see <u>no future</u> for themselves as adults.

They do not visualize themselves as future parents, or as having certain careers. It is as if their whole lives accelerated to the brink of adulthood — yet they could see nothing beyond. Along the way, whether or not it was obvious to parents, such youngsters begin to feel that life is meaningless. Often such individuals are highly gifted, yet they feel as if that promise will never blossom.

In most cases these youngsters are actually quite secretive — though the self they show to parents and friends might appear to be lively and gregarious.

Take your break and we will continue.

(4:11. I read the session so far to Jane, but it wasn't easy: because of the lost tooth I had trouble enunciating clearly. Resume at 4:34.)

Such persons <u>can</u> help themselves, however, and they can be helped by others.

First of all, let me make it clear that no one is "damned" for committing suicide. There are no particular "penalties."

Would-be suicides, for all their secrecy, usually do mention the subject to a friend, relative, or close family member. The subject should not be ignored or condemned, but honestly examined. Part of the mystique of the suicidal impulse is indeed the secretive aspect — so the very expression of the feeling is beneficial, and leads to better communication.

Indeed, part of the would-be suicide's dilemma may be caused by a lack of communication with others, a misinterpretation of the motives of friends or family members, and a difficulty in expressing one's own needs and wishes.

End of dictation.

Once again I accelerate those coordinates that activate your own peace of body and mind, and accelerate all of your bodily processes. A most fond early evening.

("Thank you, Seth." 4:42 P.M.)

JUNE 9, 1984
3:38 P.M. SATURDAY

Now I bid you another most fond good afternoon —

("Good afternoon, Seth.")

— and we will continue dictation.

(Long pause.) If you are a person who contemplates suicide often, you should indeed talk to a confidante about your problem.

This communication on your part will help clear the air to some extent. Such a person is considering an irreversible step — one certainly that should not be taken lightly. Often such people are in a very depressed state of mind, so that they have already closed their thoughts to the reasons <u>for</u> living, and only keep reminding themselves of the availability of death.

Often other people can make some small, seemingly innocuous comment that suddenly opens the disturbed person's mind to new possibilities. Because the entire mental, physical, emotional, and spiritual portions of the self are always stimulated to seek further growth and development and satisfaction, then it is quite possible for the mind to seize upon even the smallest event that will spontaneously release the person at least momentarily from depression, or even despair.

If you are in such a situation, do remind yourself that it is far more natural and probable for any problem to be solved, and that every problem has a solution. Death is not a solution. It is an <u>end</u> in a very basic manner.

No matter how depressed you may feel, you do still want to live, or you would be dead by now — so there is a part of you that seeks life and vitality, and that portion also deserves expression. It is a good idea to put off <u>making</u> any decision for a while. After all, if you do choose suicide, you can always kill yourself. If you commit suicide, however, your choices for this life are over.

Tell yourself you will make no decision until after your birthday, or after the holidays, or that you will put off any decision for a month, or even a week — whatever you feel most comfortable with.

Any therapist can also follow through by making such suggestions, thus gaining the client's cooperation at the same time by letting the individual choose the time period for which such a decision will be delayed.

(3:54.) It is futile to tell such a person that he or she <u>can not</u>, or <u>must not</u>, commit suicide — and indeed, such a procedure can be quite dangerous, hardening the person's leaning toward a death decision. The idea of making choices should be stressed: to live or to die is indeed each person's choice.

Some people might say, "I have a right to die," when they are arguing the case for suicide. And while this is true, it is also true that

the people on your planet need every bit of help and encourage-
ment they can get from each person alive. In a certain sense, the
energy of each individual does keep the world going, and to commit
suicide is to refuse a basic, cooperative venture.

It is also true that persons in ordinary good health who often
contemplate suicide <u>have</u> already closed themselves away from the
world to an important extent. Even their physical senses seem
blurred, until often they seek further and further stimulation. These
same attitudes are apparent in a lesser degree to varying extents in
periods of mental or bodily illness or in unsatisfactory life situations.
If you are such a person, however, there are also other steps that you
can take. Project yourself into a satisfying future. Remind yourself
that <u>the future is indeed there</u> if you want it, and that you can grow
into that future as easily as you grew from the past into the present.

Many depressives concentrate almost devotedly upon the miseries
of the world — the probable disasters that could bring about its end.
They remind themselves that the planet is overpopulated, and project into the future the most dire of disasters, man-made and natural.

Such thoughts are bound to cause depression. They are also
painting a highly prejudiced view of reality, leaving out all matters
concerning man's heroism, love of his fellow creatures, his wonder,
sympathy, and the great redeeming qualities of the natural world
itself. So such people must change their focus of attention.

The other creative, positive, achieving portions of life are ever
present, and thoughts of them alone can bring refreshment and
<u>release</u> from tension.

Take a break.

(*4:11. Jane had a smoke. The day was hot and gorgeous. A good breeze
moved outside the windows of 330, making the new green leaves of the
mountain ash tree dance. Resume at 4:23.*)

The point is that all of the world's problems also represent great
challenges. Young people in particular are needed to work for the
promotion of peace and nuclear disarmament, to take up the tasks
of deregulating and redistributing food sources, and of encouraging
nations to join in such a creative venture. Those are indeed worthy
and stirring causes, as noble as any that faced any generation in the
past. The world needs every hand and eye, and cries out for expression of love and caring. To devote oneself to such a cause is far more

praiseworthy than to steadily bemoan global problems with a sorrowful eye and a mournful voice.

If you are lethargic, resolve to take the first small steps toward action, however small they might be. Remind yourself that life implies action and motion, and even the activity of the most despondent thought flows in great bursts of rhythm.

All of the suggestions given here will also help in lesser situations, in ordinary bouts of worry, stress, or poor health. Even those with very serious diseases can always hope for improvement, so even if an individual is considering suicide because of a severe health dilemma, the matter should be carefully weighed.

The most seemingly irreversible physical situations <u>have</u> changed even drastically for the better, so each tomorrow does offer that possibility. Again, however, the individual must make his or her own choice, and without facing the additional burden of worrying whether or not the soul itself will be condemned for such an act.

Nature does not know damnation, and damnation has no meaning in the great realm of love in which all existence is couched.

Once again, I activate those coordinates that promote your own peace of body and mind, and quicken the healing processes — and I bid you a fond good early evening.

("Good afternoon, Seth."

(4:40 P.M. I read the session to Jane before turning her. She had been interrupted at 4:28 by a nurse bringing medication.)

JUNE 10, 1984
3:02 P.M. SUNDAY

(Jane seemed to be a bit better — not a lot — and I did mail until she said she was ready for a session. She's been starting considerably earlier recently.)

Now I bid you another most fond good afternoon —

("Good afternoon, Seth.")

— and we will resume dictation.

Unless physical pain is involved, drugs should be avoided — particularly for those in depressive states.

(Long pause.) The so-called uppers soon require downers for mood regulation, and the mind ends up in a state of confusion, and

often a stupor. Such drugs should also literally be considered dangerous for use in old-peoples' homes, for those considered senile, or even demented. With some variation these drugs are actually sometimes given to overactive children, where their effects can be very unpredictable, and result in moods that encourage suicidal tendencies, even in those so young.

Many people who use drugs socially <u>are</u> playing a kind of psychological Russian roulette. Their feelings can run something like this: "If I'm meant to live, these drugs won't hurt me, and if I'm meant to die, what difference does it make what I take?" They are taking a certain kind of chance with their own lives, however — those who indulge in such activities — and the stakes can be high.

It is true that some schools of knowledge almost glorify the use of some drugs as encouraging the expansion of consciousness and the release of repression. In some ancient cultures, drugs were indeed utilized in such a manner, but their use was well understood — and more importantly, their use was socially acceptable. Those societies were, however, highly ceremonial, and quite as stereotyped in their ways as your culture may seem to you.

(Very long pause at 3:14.) Doctors should be extremely cautious in the prescription of mind-altering drugs of any kind, and certainly not encourage their use for people in depressed states. Under drugs, choices become limited, and certainly people have committed suicide while under the influence of drugs — who may not have otherwise. I am not saying that drugs alone will cause suicide, but that the psychology of drugs already includes an attitude that promotes a Russian-roulette kind of mentality, that can only add to the problem.

People use drugs also in order to "let go." It seems as if some drugs permit an individual to let down barriers of fears and repressions, and to emotionally transcend the problems of daily life. The fact is, however, that many such people use drugs instead as a kind of chemical blanket that has a tendency to smother rather than relieve.

To "let go" is to trust the spontaneity of your own being, to trust your own energy and power and strength, and to <u>abandon</u> yourself to the energy of your own life. The word "abandon" itself may strike some readers as particularly strong, but each element of nature <u>abandons</u> itself to the lifeform. So does each atom of your body. To abandon yourself, then, to the power of your own life, is to rely upon the great forces within and yet beyond nature that gave birth to the universe and to you.

One of the very first steps toward mental, physical, emotional and spiritual health is precisely that kind of abandonment, that kind of acceptance and affirmation.

(Long pause at 3:26.) The will to live is also inbred into each element of nature, and if you trust your own spontaneity, then that will to be is joyfully released and expressed through all of your activities. It can also quite literally wash depression and suicidal tendencies away.

Take your break.

(3:28–3:36.)

Those feelings do indeed encourage expression of consciousness, and release intuitive information that may otherwise be buried beneath tensions and fears.

Such realizations have their own biological effects, stimulating all of the healing properties of the body — and also easily propelling the mind toward "higher" organizations, in which all of life's seeming inadequacies are understood to be redeemed.

This feeling of abandoning oneself to the power and force of one's own life does not lead to a mental segregation, but instead allows the self to sense the part that it plays in the creative drama of a universe. Such understandings often cannot be verbalized. They are instead perceived or experienced in bursts of pure knowing or sudden comprehension.

The natural world itself is a gateway to other realities. You do not have to try and blot out the physical world, or your ordinary consciousness, in order to achieve the necessary knowledge that leads to vibrant health or experiences. In fact, the natural world is itself a part of other realities, and the source of all realities is as present in your existence as in any other.

The more fully you learn to live, the more the seemingly hidden "mysteries of the universe" begin to appear. They do not necessarily make themselves known with great clamor or fanfare, but suddenly the most innocuous, innocent birdsong or the sight of a leaf might reveal knowledge of the profoundest nature. It is ironic, then, that many people who seek to discover the "hidden" mysteries of nature ignore nature itself, or consider the physical body as gross or somehow composed of lesser vibrations.

In the case of the suicide, however, we see the opposite attitudes at their most drastic. To a strong extent, such individuals reject their own lives, and often the conditions of life in general. Many of them object that they did not want to be born in the first place, and they feel that way because they have so thoroughly repressed the will to life within them. They also often express a strong feeling of alienation from their parents, friends, family and their fellow men in general. Along the way they have forgotten the cooperative, playful ventures of childhood, and the expression of love itself becomes most difficult.

All of the suggestions in this chapter can indeed help break down those habitual thought patterns, however, and if such a person is seeing a therapist, it is an excellent idea if the entire family join in the therapy.

Oftentimes this is financially impossible, but the inclusion of such an individual in some kind of a group situation is an excellent procedure. Communication between several people, all of whom have contemplated suicide, can also set up an excellent supportive situation, particularly with some direction set by a therapist. All would-be suicides do not follow through, and many end up leading long and productive lives, so that even when negative ideas are present in their most severe forms, there is still hope for improvement and accomplishment.

Those same unfortunate beliefs, feelings, and attitudes are also present to a lesser degree, and in different mixtures, in the cases of life-endangering diseases. However, those beliefs may not be nearly as observable, and many people may deny that they are present at all. They are often triggered, finally, by a traumatic life situation — the death of a spouse or parent, a major disappointment, or any experience that is particularly shocking and disturbing to the particular person involved.

These attitudes are often present in certain cases of cancer, severe heart problems, or other diseases that actually threaten life itself.

In such instances, an understanding of one's beliefs, and a generation of newer, more biologically vital ones, will certainly serve to better the situation, and help relieve the condition.

(4:16 P.M. This proved to be the end of the session, though we didn't realize it for a while. Jane stopped speaking when we heard a nurse pushing the medical cart to a stop outside our door to 330. A few moments later we heard her begin to pound away as she pulverized a vitamin C tablet in its packet. "I didn't know you could hear vitamin C," Jane said. I turned her on her side at 4:45.)

JUNE 11, 1984
4:08 P.M. MONDAY

(I told Jane that I woke up at about 4:00 A.M., worrying about all the things I had to get done this week. I was ready to start on another session for Chapter 7 of Dreams, *but realized I'd have to let that go. I had to go to the bank to get checks and money orders to pay taxes and bills, hook up the garden hose, and learn how to work the new sprinkler I'd bought to spray the flowers out back. Then Wednesday morning I'm scheduled to see our lawyer regarding taxes, Jane's social security, and so on. Later this month I should apply for my own social security benefits. There will doubtless be other things to do.*

(So I didn't get to work on Dreams *this morning, but hope to tomorrow. Trying to finish that book makes me feel like my feet are in quicksand up to my knees. I'm continually losing my sense of involvement, of creative application on a daily basis that is so indispensable, and I'm continually searching for ways to recapture it and keep it going on a daily basis. Jane suggested I get a checking account. It would help a little, but I need much more than that. I'm pruning away as much as I can, including a lot of business mail and projects we could get involved in. I no longer answer certain business or fan mail.*

(One thing I've learned above all else: I'll never again create a situation like this, where years pass before a book is delivered to the publisher. Something has to give, somewhere. I would like to get back to painting at least a little each day. This may be necessary — even vital — to my own well-being, although I must be careful about giving myself negative suggestions over it.

(The day was again extremely warm.)

Now I bid you another most fond good afternoon.

("Good afternoon, Seth.")

We will resume dictation.

The would-be suicide's problem is usually not one of suppressed rage or anger, it is instead the feeling that there is no room in his or her private life for further development, expression, or accomplishment, or that those very attributes are meaningless.

The will to live has been subverted by the beliefs and attitudes mentioned earlier.

People with life-threatening diseases also often feel that further growth, development, or expansion are highly difficult, if not impossible to achieve at a certain point in their lives. Often there are complicated family relationships that the person does not know how to handle. To numbers of such individuals crisis points come and are conquered. Somehow the person learns to circumnavigate the unpleasant situation, or the conditions change because of other people involved — and presto: the disease itself vanishes.

In all cases, however, the need for value fulfillment, expression, and creativity are so important to life that when these are threatened, life itself is at least momentarily weakened. Innately, each person does realize that there is life after death, and in some instances such people realize that it is indeed time to move to another level of reality, to die and set out again with another brand-new world.

Often, seriously ill people quite clearly recognize such feelings, but they have been taught not to speak of them. The desire to die is considered cowardly, even evil, by some religions — and yet behind that desire lies all of the vitality of the will to life, which may already be seeking for new avenues of expression and meaning.

(4:20.) There are those who come down with one serious disease — say heart trouble — are cured through a heart transplant operation or other medical procedure, only to fall prey to another seemingly unrelated disease, such as cancer. It would relieve the minds of families and friends, however, if they understood that the individual involved did not "fall prey" to the disease, and that he or she was not a victim in usual terms.

This does not mean that anyone consciously decides to get such-and-such a disease, but it does mean that some people instinctively realize that their own individual development and fulfillment does now demand another new framework of existence.

Much loneliness results when people who know they are going to die feel unable to communicate with loved ones for fear of hurting <u>their</u> feelings. Still, other kinds of individuals will live long productive lives even while their physical mobility or health is most severely impaired. They will still feel that they had work to do, or that they were needed — but the main thrusts of their beings still reside in the physical universe.

Each person's purposes are so unique and individualistic that it is quite improper to try to make any judgments in such matters. There is also the overall picture, for each family member plays a certain part in the reality of every other member.

A man might die very shortly after his wife's death, for example. Regardless of the circumstances, no one should judge such cases, for regardless of the way such a man might die, it would be because the thrust and intent and purpose of <u>his</u> life was no longer in physical reality.

End of dictation.

Once again I activate those coordinates that quicken your own peace of mind and body, that accelerate your healing processes.

("Thank you." 4:33 P.M.)

JUNE 12, 1984
2:58 P.M. TUESDAY

Now I bid you another most fond good afternoon —

("Good afternoon, Seth.")

— and we will resume dictation.

Many cancer patients have martyr-like characteristics, often putting up with undesirable situations or conditions for years.

They feel powerless, unable to change, yet unwilling to stay in the same position. The most important point is to arouse such a person's beliefs in his or her strength and power. In many instances these persons symbolically shrug their shoulders, saying. "What will happen, will happen," but they do not physically struggle against their situation.

It is also vital that these patients are not overly medicated, for oftentimes the side effects of some cancer-eradicating drugs are dangerous in themselves. There has been some success with people who imagine that the cancer is instead some hated enemy or monster or foe, which is then banished through mental mock battles over a period of time. While the technique does have its advantages, it also pits one portion of the self against the other. It is much better to imagine, say, the cancer cells being neutralized by some imaginary wand. Period.

Doctors might suggest that a patient relax and then ask himself or herself what kind of inner fantasy would best serve the healing process. Instant images may come to mind at once, but if success is not achieved immediately, have the patient try again, for in almost all cases some inner pictures will be perceived.

Behind the entire problem, however, is the fear of using one's full power or energy. Cancer patients most usually feel an inner impatience as they sense their own need for future expansion and development, only to feel it thwarted.

The fear that blocks that energy can indeed be dissipated if new beliefs are inserted for old ones — so again we return to those emotional attitudes and ideas that automatically promote health and healing. Each individual is a good person, an individualized portion of universal energy itself. Each person is meant to express his or her own characteristics and abilities. Life means energy, power, and expression.

(Long pause at 3:13.) Those beliefs, if taught early enough, would form the most effective system of preventative medicine ever known.

Again, we cannot generalize overmuch, but many persons know quite well that they are not sure whether they want to live or die. The overabundance of cancer cells represents nevertheless the need for expression and expansion — the only arena left open — or so it would seem.

Such a person must also contend with society's unfortunate ideas about the disease in general, so that many cancer patients end up isolated or alone. As in almost all cases of disease, however, if it were possible to have a kind of "thought transplant" operation, the disease would quickly vanish.

Even in the most dire of instances, some patients suddenly fall in love, or something in their home environment changes, and the person also seems to change overnight — while again the disease is gone.

Healing can involve help on many levels, of course. The world of normal communication I call Framework 1, while Framework 2 represents that inner world, in which indeed all time _is_ simultaneous, and actions that might take years in normal time can happen in the blinking of an eyelid in Framework 2.

Take your break.

_(3:22–3:36.)_

Briefly, Framework 1 deals with all the events of which you are normally conscious.

Framework 2 involves all of those spontaneous processes that go on beneath your conscious attention. When you are very young your beliefs are quite clear — that is, your conscious and unconscious leanings and expectations are harmonious. As you grow older, however, and begin to accumulate negative beliefs, then your conscious and unconscious beliefs may be quite different.

Consciously you might want to express certain abilities, while unconsciously you are afraid of doing so. The unconscious beliefs are not really unconscious, however. You are simply not as aware of them as you are of normally conscious ones. Negative beliefs can block the passageways between Framework 1 and Framework 2. It is an excellent idea for those in any kind of difficulty to do the following simple exercise.

Relax yourself as much as possible. Get comfortable in a chair or on a bed. Tell yourself mentally that you are an excellent person, and that you want to reprogram yourself, getting rid of any ideas that contradict that particular statement.

Next, gently remind yourself again: "I am an excellent person," adding: "It is good and safe for me to express my own abilities, for in doing so I express the energy of the universe itself."

Different phrases with the same meaning may come into your own mind. If so, substitute them for the ones I have given. There are endless exercises that can be used to advantage, but here I will only mention a few that appear most beneficial.

For another exercise, then, relax yourself as much as possible once more. If you have some disease, imagine it as particles of dirt. Tell yourself that you can see inside your body. You may see streets or boulevards instead of muscles and bones, but go along with the image or images that appear. You might see streets lined with dirt or garbage, for example. Then mentally see yourself sweeping the debris away. Order trucks to come and carry the garbage to a trash heap, where you may see it burn and disappear in smoke.

(Long pause at 3:49.) Instead of the drama I just outlined, you may instead see invading armies, attacking home troops. In such a case, see the invaders being driven off. The pictures you see will follow your own unique leanings and characteristics.

The unconscious levels of the self are only unconscious from your own viewpoint. They are quite conscious in actuality, and because they do deal with the spontaneous processes of the body, they are also completely familiar with your own state of health and well-being.

These portions can also be communicated with. Once again, relax yourself as much as possible. Sit comfortably in a chair or lie on a bed. A chair is probably preferable, since it is easy to fall off to sleep if you are lying down. You can refer to these portions of the self altogether as the helper, the teacher, or whatever title suits you best.

Simply make a straightforward request, asking that some picture or image be presented in your inner mind, that will serve as representative of those portions of your own inner reality.

So do not be surprised, for you may see a person, an animal, an insect, or a landscape — but trust whatever image you do receive. If it seems to be that of a person, or angel, or animal, then ask it to speak to you, and to tell you how best to rid yourself of your disease or problem.

If the image of a landscape appears instead, then ask for a series of such images, that will again somehow point the way toward recovery, or toward the resolution of the problem. Then follow through with whatever reply you receive.

In all such cases, you are opening the doors of Framework 2, clearing your channels of communication. Since your physical body itself is composed of the very energy that drives the universe, then there is nothing about you which that energy is unaware of. Simply repeating these ideas to yourself can result in release of tension, and an acceleration of the healing process.

These exercises may suggest others of your own. If so, follow through on them — but to one extent or another each reader should benefit from some of them.

End of dictation.

Once again, I bid you a fond early evening, and I accelerate those coordinates that bring about peace of body and mind, and quicken the healing processes.

("Thank you."

(4:25 P.M. Jane's speed of delivery had steadily increased as she progressed with the session. I told her she had done well.)

JUNE 13, 1984
3:13 P.M. WEDNESDAY

(It's been a very hot, very busy day. I worked on Dreams *for half an hour before going down to see our lawyer at 10:00 this morning. As I left the house, I was greeted in the driveway by Frank Longwell, who was checking up on whether I was watering the back yard and the new tree the way he told me to.*

(Frank left right away, but I was still late getting to the lawyer. We talked about many things, and he's to get back to me regarding Jane's social security, disability payments, income, and so on. He's also ordered a birth certificate for me from Harrisburg, Pennsylvania and is to check with social security about what benefits I may be able to get while still working.

(On the way home I bought a barbecued chicken at Convenient, and made Jane a sandwich for lunch. It was good, almost still warm. She ate a good lunch. I did some mail until she told me she was ready for a session.)

Now I bid you another most fond good afternoon —

("Good afternoon, Seth.")

— and we will continue dictation.

Again, every effort should be made to insert humor into the living situation as much as possible.

The patient might begin to collect jokes, for example, or funny cartoons from magazines and newspapers. Watching comedies on television will help — and so, in fact, will any distraction that is pleasing to the patient.

Crossword puzzles and other word games will also benefit, even if only done mentally. It might also be advisable for the patient to take up some completely new field of knowledge — to learn a language, for instance, or to study whatever books possible in any field to which he or she is attracted.

The more actively and fully such a diversion can be indulged, the better, of course, and yet the mental playing of games can be quite fruitful, and serve to give the conscious mind a needed rest.

Everything should be done to insure that the patient is given a hand in whatever physical treatment is involved. He or she should be enlightened enough through doctor-patient discussions to make choices about the treatment. In some cases, however, patients will make it clear that they prefer to hand over all responsibility for treatment to the doctor, and in such instances their decisions should be followed. It is a good idea for the doctor to question the patient sometimes, to make sure that the decision is not one of the moment alone.

Whenever possible, it is far better for the patient to remain home, rather than live steadily at a hospital. When hospitalization is required, however, family members should try to act as honestly and openly as possible. It is a good idea for such family members to join other groups of people who are in the same situation, so that they can express their own doubts and hesitations.

Some family members, in fact, may be quite surprised by a barrage of unexpected reactions. They may find themselves furious at the patient for becoming ill, and then develop unfortunate guilt feelings over their own first reactions. They may feel that their lives are being disrupted through no cause of their own, yet be so ashamed of such feelings that they dare not express them.

A therapist or a group of other people facing the same problem can therefore be of great assistance. The patient may also feel abandoned by God or the universe, and may feel unjustly attacked by the disease, thus arousing a whole new tumult of anger, and it is most important that the anger be expressed, and not repressed.

(Through the early afternoon of a very hot day — over 90 degrees — a storm had been trying to manifest. Gradually the sun disappeared behind heavier and heavier clouds, yet the rain seemed most reluctant to show itself. I hoped we'd get a heavy rain for the backyard at the house. A strong breeze kept whipping up the airy branches of the mountain ash outside the windows of 330, and the room began to cool down a bit.

(Then there came a stronger wind, and thunder in the distance, and the start of a meager rain. Traffic sounded louder. Doors slammed in the hospital corridor, and at the bathroom entrance to 330. Through it all Jane kept speaking in trance — and I gave up on expecting a real rain.)

Such a person might imagine his or her anger or fury filling up the inside of a gigantic balloon that is then pricked by a needle, exploding in pieces from the pressure within, with debris falling everywhere — out over the ocean, or caught up by the wind, but in any case dispersed in whatever way seems agreeable to the patient.

It is also vital that such people continue to receive and express love. If the person is mourning the death of a spouse or close family member, then it would be most beneficial for the individual or the family to purchase, or otherwise provide, a new small pet. The patient should be encouraged to play with the pet as much as possible, and to nourish it, to caress and fondle it.

Often such a procedure will reawaken new stirrings of love, and actually turn around the entire affair. This is particularly true if one or two beneficial changes simply seem to happen in other areas of life.

The rearousal of love might well activate Framework 2 to such an extent that the healing energies become unblocked, and send their threads of probable actions into the person's living situation as well — that is, once the channels to Framework 2 are open, then new possibilities immediately open up in all of life's living areas. And many of these, of course, have a direct bearing on health and the healing processes.

Take your break.

(3:42. There was a thunderclap not far away. Getting up to stretch, I saw that I'd been mistaken earlier: it hadn't actually started to rain yet. But it did now, fairly good. We decided to turn Jane on her side early, so I could feed her before leaving for the dentist's at 5:45. I'd saved a plate of food from lunch for this, in case the supper tray didn't show up in time. It __did__ come early, though, just as though we'd asked for it, so Jane had eaten most of her supper before I left.)

JUNE 14, 1984
3:20 P.M. THURSDAY

(The day was considerably cooler. At least some rain had fallen last night. Jane seemed to feel a bit better today.)

Now, I bid you another most fond good afternoon —

("Good afternoon, Seth.")

— and we will resume dictation.

In these, and all situations, it should be remembered that the body is always trying to heal itself, and that even the most complicated relationships are trying to untangle.

(I felt a great sadness when Seth delivered this sentence.)

For all of life's seeming misfortunes, development, fulfillment, and accomplishment far outweigh death, diseases, and disasters. Starting over can be done — by anyone in any situation, and it will bring about some beneficial effects regardless of previous conditions.

Behind all maladies, in the most basic manner lies the need for expression, and when people feel that their areas of growth are being curtailed, then they instigate actions meant to clear the road, so to speak.

Before health problems show up there is almost always a loss of self-respect or expression. This loss may occur in the environment itself, in changing social conditions. In the matter of the disease called AIDS, for example, you have groups of homosexuals, many "coming out of the closet" for the first time, taking part in organizations that promote their cause, and suddenly faced by the suspicions and distrust of many other portions of the population.

The struggle to express themselves, and their own unique abilities and characteristics drives them on, and yet is all too frequently thwarted by the ignorance and misunderstanding that surrounds them. You end up with something like a psychological contagion. The people involved begin to feel even more depressed as they struggle to combat the prejudice against them. Many of them almost hate themselves. For all their seeming bravado, they fear that they are indeed unnatural members of the species.

(3:35.) These beliefs break down the immunity system, and bring about the symptoms so connected with the disease. AIDS is a social phenomenon to that extent, expressing the deep dissatisfactions, doubts, and angers of a prejudiced-against segment of society.

Whatever physical changes occur, happen because the will to live is weakened. AIDS is a kind of biological protest, as if symbolically the homosexuals are saying: "You may as well kill us. We might be better off than the way you treat us now," or as if it were a kind of suicidal drama in which the messages read: "See to what ends your actions have led us!"

I am not saying that AIDS victims are outright suicides — only that in many instances the will to live is so weakened and a despondency so strong sets in that such individuals often acquiesce, finally, to their own deaths, seeing no room in the future for their own further growth or development.

The attitude even of doctors and nurses toward the handling of such patients shows only too clearly not only their fear of the disease itself, but their fear of homosexuality, which has been considered evil and forbidden by many religions. Emotions run at top pace in such cases, and the AIDS patients are often shunted away, out of human society. Often even their friends desert them. Yet AIDS can be acquired by those who are not homosexuals, but who have similar problems. *(Long pause.)* It is a great error to segregate some individuals, like some modern colony of lepers.

Luckily, the disease will run its course as sociological conditions change, and as man's inhumanity to man becomes clear even to the most prejudiced.

Take your break.

(3:47–4:00.)

Homosexuals can benefit from the ideas in this book, particularly if small groups get together, examining their own beliefs, and reinforcing their will to live, their <u>right</u> to live, and the basic integrity of their being.

Any anger or hostility should also be expressed, however, while not being overly concentrated upon.

Many other diseases that seem to be spread by viruses or contagions are also related to the problems of society in the same manner, and when those conditions are righted the diseases themselves largely vanish. It should be remembered that it is the beliefs and feelings of the patients that largely determine the effectiveness of any medical procedures, techniques, or medications.

Unfortunately, the entire picture surrounding health and disease is a largely negative one, in which even so-called preventative medicine can have severe drawbacks, since it often recommends drugs or techniques to attack a problem not only <u>before</u> the problems emerges, but simply <u>in case</u> it may emerge.

Many of the public-health announcements routinely publicize the specific symptoms of various diseases, almost as if laying out <u>maps</u> of diseases for medical consumers to swallow. There are many techniques apart from medically conventional ones, such as acupuncture, the laying on of hands, or the work of people who may be known as healers. The trouble is that these other techniques cannot be monitored sufficiently so that their benefits can be honestly appraised.

The body's own healing processes <u>are</u> forever active, however — which is why I so strongly advise that they be relied upon along with whatever medical help seems appropriate. But the individual, even as a patient, must always have a choice, and have the right to refuse any treatment being suggested.

(4:14.) The main issue is always the vital importance of the individual's belief systems, however, and the sense of worth he or she places on body and mind.

We have been dealing with quite drastic diseases, but the same concepts are true in other areas also. There are people who undergo a series of highly unsatisfactory relationships, for example, while another person might experience a series of recurrent diseases instead. In spite of all problems, the life force operates continually in each person's life, and can bring about at any time the most profound, beneficial changes. The idea is to clear the mind as much as possible from beliefs that impede the fine, smooth workings of the life force, and to actively encourage those beliefs and attitudes that promote health and the development of all aspects of healing experience.

(4:25.) End of dictation.

Once more, I activate those coordinates that encourage your own peace of mind and body, and quicken your own healing processes.

A fond good evening.

("Good afternoon, Seth.")

(4:26 P.M. No one had shown up to do Jane's vitals — which meant that the staff was behind schedule. In fact, no one appeared to do the vitals for the rest of the time I was there — until 7:10. For a change we didn't say the prayer together. Lately she's wanted to do it after lunch. "I get too blue when you're getting ready to leave," she said, "to want to do it then any more."

(Carla, the aide who used to help Jane call me late at night, has been on vacation. This afternoon we were speculating that she's about due to return. Maybe when she can call me again, Jane will feel better.)

CHAPTER 12

EARLY INSTANCES OF DEATH OR DISEASE
IN RELATIONSHIP TO FURTHER
REINCARNATIONAL INFLUENCES

JUNE 15, 1984
3:12 P.M. FRIDAY

Now I bid you another most fond good afternoon —
(*"Good afternoon, Seth."*)

— and we will continue dictation.

Before we discuss other varieties of health and illness as they more ordinarily appear, I want to bring up the subject of more or less extraordinary conditions — dilemmas of body or mind in early life that often seem to have no cause or meaning.

The universe is meaningful or it is not. Since the universe <u>is</u> <u>indeed</u> meaningful, then there must be a reason and a cause even for conditions that appear chaotic, cruel, or grotesque. Even in such cases, however, at some extent or another the individual can indeed start over — or at least those closest to the person in question can begin to see a larger framework of existence in which even the most dire of physical circumstances are somehow redeemed.

In many cases, it is the parents of such offspring who suffer more than their children, since it seems as if such families were unjustly saddled with the most unfortunate woes.

We hope to explain this larger framework of existence still further, for indeed it also affects the human condition in all of its aspects.

Next chapter: "Early Instances of Death or Disease in Relationship to Further Reincarnational Influences."

(3:23.) As I said before, the reasons for most physical, mental, spiritual, or emotional problems can be found in this one lifetime, and because of the nature of simultaneous time, new beliefs in the present can also affect those in the past.

In a basic way, it is possible for present beliefs to actually modify the beliefs of a life that is seemingly a past one. I must explain again that all lives are lived at once — but in different kinds of focuses. Your conventional ideas of time make it simpler, however, to speak of one life as happening before or after another.

Again, no one is punished for crimes committed in a past life, and in each life you are unique. The inner intelligence within you that gives you each life also gives you the conditions of each life. It certainly seems to you, or to many of you, that most people would always choose to be born healthy and whole, in an excellent environment, of parents with loving natures and genetic excellence — and in other words to grow up healthy, wealthy, and wise.

Life, however, is far too profound and multitudinous, and requires great depths of emotional response and action that could never be satisfied adequately by any given set of circumstances, however favorable.

(3:34.) The species is filled with a powerful sense of curiosity and wonder, and the need for exploration and discovery, so that even a man born as a king through several lives would find himself bored and determined to seek out a different or opposite experience.

In some lives, then, you are born in fortunate circumstances, and in others you may find an environment of poverty and want. You may be born in excellent health in one life, with a high intelligence and great wit, while in still another existence you may be born ill or crippled or mentally deficient.

It also seems that each fetus must naturally desire to grow, emerge whole from its mother's womb, and develop into a natural childhood and adulthood. However, in those terms just as many fetuses want the experience of being fetuses without following through on other stages. They have no intention of growing into complete human development. In fact, many fetuses explore <u>that element</u> of existence numberless times before deciding to go on still further, and emerge normally from the womb.

Those fetuses that do not develop still contribute to the body's overall experience, and they feel themselves successful in their own existences. An understanding of these issues can greatly help throw light on the question of early deaths and diseases, and spontaneous abortions.

Take your break.

(3:45–3:52.)

These are all part of the continuous undercurrents of life, and the same issues apply to many other species whose offspring are lost in very early life.

This is not <u>an uncaring universe or nature operating</u>, but portions of consciousness who choose at whatever levels certain experiences that nourish the living environment, and bring satisfactions that may never show on life's surface.

In the case of human beings, however, many questions certainly rise to the fore. I do not want to generalize, for each living situation is too unique for that. I do want to point out that all fetuses do not necessarily intend to develop into normal babies, and that if medical science, through its techniques, ends up in directing a normal birth, the consciousness of the child may never feel <u>normally allied</u> with physical experience.

The child may go from one illness to another, or simply display an odd <u>disinclination</u> for life — a lack of enthusiasm, until finally in some cases the child dies at an early age. Another individual, under the same circumstances, might change its mind and decide to go along with the experience of normal life.

It seems unnatural to some people to hear of animals' mothers who refuse to nurse one offspring, or sometimes even attack it — but in those instances the animal mother is instinctively aware of the situation, and acts to save the offspring from future suffering.

I am not advising that malformed infants be killed, but I do want to point out that even in those most severe cases there is meaning in such conditions, and the consciousness involved then chooses another kind of experience.

There are also perfectly healthy, normal children who have determined ahead of time that they will live <u>only to the threshold</u> of adulthood, happy and flushed with dreams and promises of accomplishment, yet not experiencing any disillusionment or regret or sorrow. Such young people die of sickness or accident, but go to their deaths like children after a splendid day. In most instances they choose quick deaths.

In one way or another, such children may try to describe their feelings to those closest to them, so as to cushion the shock. Usually these people are not suicides in conventional terms — although they may be.

(4:12.) Perhaps the greatest variances in human behavior show in mental states, and so parents are apt to feel most crushed and despondent if any of their children prove to be what is generally regarded as mentally deficient. In the first place, the term is a judgment cast by others, and a particular personality may feel quite comfortable in his or her own perception of reality, and only become aware of the difference when confronted by others. Most such persons are quite peaceful rather than violent, and their <u>emotional</u> experience may indeed cover nuances and depths unknown to normal persons.

Many simply perceive reality from a different focus, <u>feeling</u> a problem out rather than thinking a problem out.

(4:17. Jane took a break when we heard someone pushing what we thought was the medicine cart out in the hall toward our room. Then all became quiet. When I looked, no cart was in sight. Nor was any aide or nurse. It was as though we were alone on the floor.

(I suggested to Jane that she end the session anyhow, since it was getting to be about as long as I could get typed this evening, and I also had to go food shopping.)

I bid you a fond good evening — and once again I activate those coordinates that encourage peace of body and mind, and quicken the healing processes.

("Thank you."

(4:20 P.M. It was still very quiet. No one ever did come in to do Jane's vitals. They hadn't yesterday either, Jane said. A new policy? A nurse had brought in Jane's Darvoset and aspirin, and that was it.)

JUNE 16, 1984
3:23 P.M. SATURDAY

Now I bid you another most fond good afternoon —

("Good afternoon, Seth.")

— and we will continue dictation.

In actuality all of the seemingly erratic genetic variances that often crop up in human development are vital to the elasticity of the entire genetic system.

It would not be beneficial, for example, to try to "breed out" those seemingly unfortunate, divergent genetic traits. The physical system would become too rigid, lose the power of its natural diversity, and eventually bring a dead-end to human survival.

There is hardly any danger of that possibility, however, since it would be nearly impossible to perform such a task even with the most developed of technologies — and indeed, the very attempt to do so might well immediately trigger a response on the part of the whole genetic system, so that new divergences appeared with even greater frequency, as compensation.

There are individuals who do choose ahead of time — in one lifetime or another — to accept such a divergent genetic heritage for their own reasons — often to experience life from one of its most unique aspects, and sometimes in order to encourage the growth of other abilities that might not otherwise occur.

Human consciousness normally experiences wide sweeps of rhythms, varying states of awareness, and its amazing flexibility is partially dependent upon its lack of rigidity, its own spontaneous inclinations, and its capacity for curiosity, wonder, discovery, and emotion.

(Long pause at 3:35.) It is not too frequently noticed, but many so-called mentally deficient people possess their own unique learning abilities — that is, often they learn what they do learn in a different manner than most other people. Many possess abilities that are not discovered by others, that are most difficult to explain. They may utilize chemicals in a different way than other people do in the learning process itself. Some may even have superior understanding of physical and psychological space. Their qualifications emotionally are also quite advanced, and it is quite possible that they are gifted in

terms of mathematics and music, though these gifts may never come to fruition, since they are unsuspected.

Many deficient individuals in their way are as vital to the development of humanity as geniuses are, for both preserve the elastic nature of human consciousness, and promote its coping qualifications.

Each person makes his or her own reality, again, but each family member also shares the reality of the others. Often, therefore, instances of unusual genetic differences may also serve to bring out qualities of understanding, sympathy, and empathy on the part of family members — and those qualities also are vital to human development. Because the reasons for any such conditions can be so diverse, then life should be encouraged even in the face of deformities. If the consciousness involved has its own reasons for living, then it will make the most of even the most dire conditions. If instead the consciousness has been kept alive despite its own intents through medical procedures, it will terminate its own physical life in one way or another.

(Long pause.) It would seem that infants have no belief systems, and therefore could not be in charge of their own realities in any way. As mentioned earlier, however, the cells of the body themselves possess an equivalent in those biological leanings toward health and development. Even in cases where physical survival might seem pointless, it is also possible for the organism to alter its course to an extraordinary degree.

Children who are labeled mentally deficient or even called idiots, can often grow and develop far beyond medical science's suppositions — particularly if they are aided by loving parents who constantly provide stimulation and interest.

This is not to say that all such children should be cared for at home, or that parents should feel guilty if they are forced through circumstances to place their offspring in an institution. The intuition of the parents, however, will often direct the most proper course in each individual case. If it is understood that there is indeed a reason behind such circumstances, then that realization alone can help ease the parents' burden, and help them decide which course to take in their own particular case.

(Very long pause, eyes closed.) End of dictation.

Once more, I accelerate those coordinates that quicken your own peace of body and mind, and encourage your own healing processes — and I bid you a most fond early evening.

("Good afternoon, Seth."

(4:16 P.M. As I was leaving for the day Jane asked me what I thought of the sessions. I said they were very good — and meant it. It's what I expected, I told her. She said that she and Seth had been trying to handle some pretty heavy stuff in a certain way so that it wasn't too grim, and ended up with upbeat interpretations. I'm not quoting her exactly here by any means, however.

(Jane was interrupted twice during her delivery. She said staff isn't going to take her vitals regularly anymore, especially when they're busy.)

JUNE 17, 1984
2:41 P.M. SUNDAY

(It was a cold, cloudy day as I drove down to the hospital. It had rained some last night and this morning. Room 330 was on the chilly side to me, but Jane was comfortable.

(Carla was back from vacation, and I thought she might help Jane call me tonight. As I was taking my nap in 330 this afternoon, Margaret Bumbalo called, inviting me across the street for supper this evening.)

Now I bid you another most fond good afternoon —

("Good afternoon, Seth.")

— and we will resume dictation.

Each life influences each other life, and some portion of the personality retains memory not only of past lives, but of future lives also.

When reincarnational studies are embarked upon, on occasion people remember some instance of past-life experience, but conventional ideas of time are so strong that so-called future memory is blocked out.

The inner self is aware of all of your existences, in other words. It sees where and how your many lives fit together. It is only because you are so oriented outward from birth that this inner self can sometimes seem alien or distant and <u>un</u>related to the self that you know. It would be impossible to be consciously aware of all of the infinitesimal details that exist in even one life; your consciousness would be so full and cluttered up that you would be unable to make choices, or to use free will.

It would be even more difficult to try to handle the information of many lives at one time. In your terms, "it" takes time to think, and you would be so caught up in thinking itself, that action would be impossible. The inner knowledge of all of your lives, from your point of view, is in the same category as those automatic processes that underlie your existence.

That is, you know about your other lives, basically, in the same way that you know how to breathe or digest your food. A different kind of knowing is involved.

This does not mean that all conscious knowledge about your own reincarnational existences is forever beyond you — for through various exercises you can indeed learn to recall some of that information. It does mean, however, that you are innately aware of all of your existences, and that the knowledge gained in one life is automatically transferred to another, whether that life be present, past, or future.

(2:54.) You may therefore be trying out many different kinds of experiences, sometimes endowing yourself with super attributes and strength, relying upon the body's powers above all other considerations, while at the same time in another life you use and develop unusual mental abilities, enjoying the triumphs of creative thought, while largely ignoring the body's agility and strength.

I do not mean to imply that you necessarily deal with opposite kinds of behaviors, for there are endless variances — each unique — as consciousness expresses itself through physical sensation, and attempts to explore all of the possible realms of emotional, spiritual, biological, and mental existence.

I want to stress that within each life <u>full free will operates</u> once the <u>conditions</u> of that life are set.

Take your break, and we will continue.

(2:59. Jane had a smoke while I did some mail. A fine rain fell. Resume at 3:36.)

That is, if you have been born in poor or depressed circumstances, then free will will not alter the conditions of that birth.

It <u>can</u> help you become wealthy in adult life through the choices that you make. It should be helpful, and certainly somewhat comforting, to realize that even unfortunate birth conditions were not forced upon you by some outside agency, but chosen at inner levels of your own reality.

The same applies to almost any situation. Religion holds some ideas that are in complete opposition to each other in regard to the nature of suffering in general. Some believe that suffering is a punishment sent by God for past or present sins, or even omissions, while other religious schools insist that suffering is sent by God as evidence of his particular love for the individual involved: "God must love you very much, because he sent you so much suffering." *(As Jane has been told by several nurses.)*

That remark, and similar ones, are often made to ill persons. The idea is supposed to be that suffering is good for the soul, is a way of atoning for one's sins, and in some fashion the implication is made that such suffering in this life will be more than compensated for in heaven.

Such concepts encourage individuals to feel like victims, with no control at all over the conditions of their own lives.

(It also arouses my sense of irony and dismay — for the nurses who told Jane such things are presumably in better health than she is. Their implications were that God loved Jane more than he loved them, and would reveal this in heaven. What kind of heaven does this leave those healthier individuals to look forward to, then? Surely a lesser one, in perhaps unknown ways? This ought to give such people pause . . .)

Instead, it should be realized that as uncomfortable as suffering is, it does somehow have a meaning in the context of your entire existence — again, that it was not thrust upon you by some unjust or uncaring exterior force or nature.

To some degree, that kind of understanding can help alleviate suffering itself to some extent. I am not advocating a <u>fatalistic</u> approach either, that says more or less: "I have chosen such and such an unfortunate condition at some level I do not understand, and therefore the entire affair is outside of my own hands. There is nothing I can do about it."

For one thing, again, almost all situations, including the most drastic, can be changed for the better to some extent, and the very attempt to do so can increase a person's sense of control over his or her own circumstances. This does not mean that those adverse situations can be changed overnight in usual terms (though <u>ideally</u> that is also possible), but that the sense of control over one's life encourages all of the mental and physical healing properties.

(3:52.) In terms of "starting over" at such a point, the main thing to remember is not to expect too much too fast, while recognizing that instantaneous cures are indeed probabilities.

Again, mind games, the insertion of humor and diversion, are extremely valuable, so that you are not trying too hard. Some people try too hard to be spontaneous, while others are frightened of spontaneity itself. The knowledge of reincarnational lives <u>is</u> spontaneously held, and you can receive profound insights from that knowledge. This occurs when you are not looking for it, but when you are familiar enough with the entire concept, so that you realize such knowledge is available.

I may or may not return. Once again I do activate those coordinates that quicken your own peace of mind and body, and accelerate your healing processes.

("Good afternoon, Seth."

(3:58 P.M. Jane did call this evening — at about 10:00, just as I was sitting down to begin typing this session. I'd stayed much longer at the Bumbalos than I'd planned. The supper was delicious, and afterward John and I had an interesting conversation ranging over a number of subjects. He'd read Jane's latest book, The Education of Oversoul Seven, *and liked it very much.)*

JUNE 18, 1984
4:02 P.M. MONDAY

(We had a heavy rain at times last night and this morning.)
Now I bid you another most fond good afternoon —
("Good afternoon, Seth.")
— and we will continue dictation.

The reincarnational heritage is rich, however, and it can have a tendency to assert itself under certain conditions.

I am not speaking of usual, but fairly <u>unusual</u> events, when, in one fashion or another, reincarnational memory seems to bleed through to the present life. Again, this is not usual experience. It happens infrequently. On some occasions — sometimes in periods of poor health or seeming senility — such instances may occur. They are more apt to happen in adolescence, though I do want to stress that we are speaking of extraordinary cases.

Old people often begin to exercise their own consciousness in ways that they had not done earlier. There may be less diversions to take up their thoughts. They may be lonely, and then quite surprisingly find themselves casting about for different kinds of experience — experience seemingly most difficult to achieve in the physical world under their present circumstances.

Since they are often frightened and unsure of the future, they are more apt to cast their thoughts backwards into their early childhoods, reaching for their earliest memories, and mentally try to gain comfort from the remembered sounds of beloved voices, only to mentally glimpse other images than they expected, or to hear other voices than those for which they yearned.

In fact, fragments of many episodes from many other lives may rush into their consciousness, and in most cases they are, of course, quite unprepared for the experience. On the other hand, usually such episodes are highly reassuring, for along with them rides the inner assurance that life has been lived before, many times.

The individuals involved may then return to normal consciousness, but if they talked or muttered while the affair was happening, any observers might take it for granted that delirium was involved. Drugs should not be prescribed under those conditions, unless the patient becomes highly restless and confused, and requests them. In most cases, however, the experiences do not leave any detrimental side effects.

The same kind of event may happen in periods of poor health, or in over-drugged states. They are less easily handled, however, under drugged conditions, since the consciousness does not have the full agility to depend upon in periods of stress — unusual stress. The same can occur in adolescence, and easily be misinterpreted as a schizophrenic episode.

This happens perhaps more frequently than the other cases mentioned, but usually such events are not repeated. They remain only as memories, having opened up the person's mind to larger visions of life than he or she may have entertained before.

End of dictation.

Once again I activate those coordinates that quicken your peace of body and mind, and so reinforce your own healing processes.

("Thank you." 4:32 P.M.

(Hospital staff caused Jane to break off the session twice. Her vitals were taken, though. Temp up to 101.4 — Jane was angry. Shannon said the reading was up because it was a hot, muggy day.

(A light rain had begun just before I left 330, but it quickly turned into a downpour as I drove home. The rainfall was so dense at times that I could hardly see where I was going. It was both refreshing and exhilarating.)

JUNE 19, 1984
2:41 P.M. TUESDAY

(The hospital was hardly a quiet place, what with fire trucks and police cars pulling up beneath our window with sirens screeching and wailing, and with people in the hall outside 330 pushing carts that rattled and sounded like a bushel of pots and pans jouncing around — all of this as Jane was ready to begin the session. I couldn't help wondering what any patient would do who really needed a little peace and quiet.)

Now I bid you another most fond good afternoon —

("Good afternoon, Seth.")

— and we will resume dictation.

Thus far we have been dealing with conflicting beliefs, however — and most of those can be tackled in the context of this life alone.

These beliefs may have physical or mental repercussions, though in most cases the two do not occur at once. We have dealt with some of the numerous physical dilemmas than can result. In other instances the individual encounters the difficulties on mental or emotional levels. One portion of the personality might be whole-heartedly in favor of good expression of personal power, and be stimulated to express and use his or her energy and strength. Another portion of the personality may be just as terrified of power or its uses as the other segment exults in it.

Instead of developing physical complications, in usual terms, sometimes one portion of the personality actually does act with assurance, power, and energy, while another equally valid portion refuses to use energy or power in any way whatsoever. The ideas are so opposing, and such equal adversaries, that the conscious personality can hardly bear to be aware of both at once —

(2:50. Georgia, Mary Jean, and Jan came in to kid around, eat chocolate-covered graham crackers, and drop veiled references to the birthday party they're planning for me tomorrow. I pretended innocence — I think. They asked what my favorite cake was while telling me theirs — and I said chocolate with chocolate icing.

(I read the last line of the session back to Jane. 2:58.)

In such cases, while one portion of the personality is expressing itself, and in command of the usual conscious abilities, the other portion lies acquiescent, latent, and unexpressed.

The individual may act purposefully, with power, energy, and strength, for varying lengths of time. Then <u>sometimes</u> without warning the frightened, inactive portion of the personality will take over the normal abilities of consciousness — acting depressed, taciturn, and communicating very poorly with others.

One portion of the personality will carry on conscious behavior — go to work, shop, or whatever, while the other portion of the personality will not remember performing those acts at all.

Take a hypothetical case. Call Norma A the assertive part of the personality, and Norma B the passive partner. Norma A may go out dancing, go to a bar, then turn the entire proceedings over to Norma B, who finds herself in noisy surroundings, surrounded by people she does not remember, and with no idea how she reached her present destination.

<u>Her</u> trend of memory will go back to the last time that <u>she</u> was in charge of consciousness, and she will have — or may <u>not</u> have — any idea of the existence of Norma A at all. Norma A may enjoy action, sports, dancing and bodily activities, while Norma B may prefer reading, walking, or painting.

Such personalities may even have <u>separate sets of friends</u> — Norma A and B each having their own companions. Though these personalities may seem so divergent, they are connected with each other, however, and they may on occasion set up their own rather bizarre kind of communication. They may write mysterious notes to each other, leaving them where they are bound to be found — yet notes using a special code or symbols or drugs, because <u>too clear</u> a communication would disrupt the entire relationship.

People may actually carry on such existences for years, until some event or another shows that something is amiss: one of Norma A's friends might meet a friend of Norma B, for example, or the gaps in memory might finally become so frequent that it is obvious something is wrong.

Norma A and B represent fairly simple examples of schizophrenic behavior, and indeed I have kept the story simple to keep the issues clear. Norma A may actually grow into a more and more assertive or belligerent personality, even displaying violent tendencies at times, while on the other hand Norma B might become even more timid, depressed, and solitary.

On other levels, however, each one is well aware of the other's presence, and on <u>those</u> levels they do react to each other's activities. This means, of course, that the entire amnesia process, regardless of how perfect it seems, is a surface one. I have used the different beliefs about power as an example, but any belief may be involved if it and its opposite are held in nearly equal weight.

(3:20.) One portion may believe that sex is natural and good, while the other portion believes vehemently that sex is evil and depraved. Here we will use a man for a hypothetical case. Joe A may be an excellent husband, bread-winner, and father, a church-goer who believes in the beauty and goodness of sex. Joe B may hold the opposite viewpoint most intently — that sex is at least evil, perhaps sent by the devil, and below or beneath the dignity of a good man.

On topside Joe A may go to church frequently, be kind and considerate to his family, and, say, come home from work every night for supper. He may carry on a fruitful accomplished existence for varying lengths of time.

Then, however, perhaps with no warning, he may suddenly refuse to make love with his wife, become hostile with his children, stop off for a few drinks after work, before supper, or even begin seeing a prostitute, or begin an affair — often with a woman he considers beneath his own station.

Joe A may be quite startled to discover bottles of whiskey lying around in his dresser drawers, when he hardly drinks liquor himself at all. Joe B may suddenly "come to" in a strange bedroom, in a compromising position with a woman it certainly seems to him he has never seen before in his life.

CHAPTER 13

"Messages" from Gods, Demons, Heroes, and Other Prominent Persons — or, More Conflicting Beliefs

JUNE 20, 1984
3:50 P.M. WEDNESDAY

(T*oday I'm 65 years old, but certainly don't feel it. I guess it's supposed to mark a milestone in one's life — especially that of the male of the species — but I have no plans to retire, quit working, or give up the creative life. I feel I'm doing better than ever.*

(The crew at the hospital did have a birthday party for me, and even though I knew what they were up to, it was still a delightful surprise, what with their obvious good will and cheers, the cards, and the food — more than we could eat, at least Jane and I. Mary, the head nurse, made the chocolate cake with chocolate icing. I showed them my fancy patterned undershirt as a joke, and received the appropriate ooh's and ah's. Even some strangers in the hall outside 330 saw it and laughed. I also blew out all of the candles on the cake — perhaps 25 of them — in one breath, which I don't think staff expected I could do.

(I had a distinctly full feeling along about 2:30, and we still had food left over. I nibbled at it throughout the day, until I felt I'd better stop. Various people stopped in to wish me a happy birthday.

(Margaret Bumbalo called before I left Jane and invited me to supper, but by then I was full. I stopped at their house to get the spaghetti for tomorrow's supper. Joe is almost bald from the chemotherapy, and very weak, his

son John said. They had a package of books for me also. John made me a scotch and soda, like I'd had there the other evening, and I began to feel its effects in no time. By then I was actually half bombed, so I didn't get down to typing this session until 9:50 P.M.)

I bid you another most fond good afternoon —

("Good afternoon, Seth.")

— and we will resume dictation.

Before we continue, I would like to remind the reader that in the middle of these or any of the other problems we have been discussing, there may be a period of depression, or the feeling that one's own problem <u>has</u> no solution after all.

Whenever this occurs, the steps I have given before should be followed. Briefly, immediately refuse to worry about the future or the past. Tell yourself you can worry another time if you want to — but for the moment you will not be concerned about the past or the future.

Remind yourself that for all you might have read, or heard, or deduced earlier, it is certainly not inevitable that all unfortunate situations take the darkest of tones, and that indeed the opposite is true; for if such were the case, the world and all of life would have literally been destroyed through disasters and calamities.

Concentrate upon the present moment — but more, concentrate upon <u>the most pleasant aspects</u> of the present moment. If that moment has distracting, unfavorable aspects, then resolutely bring into your mind whatever images delight or please you at the moment. These may be very simple. Remember the smell of lilacs, for example, or try to hear the crisp crunch of snow, or try to visualize an ocean or lake. All of these procedures will serve to quiet your mind and body, and build up your own reserves.

(4:00.) This is an excellent policy to follow, because you can start it wherever you are. It will help alleviate fears and doubts at least momentarily, so that then you can pursue the entire issue later, with more assurance.

End of chapter. Take your break.

(4:02. We heard the medicine cart in the hall. A young nurse brought in Jane's Darvoset and aspirin. All was quiet and peaceful in the hospital now. Resume at 4:13.)

We will begin the next chapter. The heading, as given earlier, is correct.

Conflicting beliefs about the nature of reality can bring about dilemmas in almost any form, for the individual will always try to make sense out of his or her surroundings, and try to at least see the world as a cohesive whole.

Some of the most complicated ways of trying to put conflicting beliefs together are often mental or emotional ones. The more <u>inco</u>hesive the individual feels the world to be, the greater his or her efforts will be expended in an attempt to put the world back together.

Some people possess beliefs that are so in opposition to each other that they are forced into some of the most complicated mental or emotional footwork. Their problem will seem so gigantic that only some interference from an outside source will be sufficient to give the individual a sense of wholeness and sanity. A person may become so frightened of using his or her own power of choice or action that the construction of an artificial superbeing is created — a seemingly sublime personage who gives orders to the individual involved.

(*Long pause at 4:25.*) Again, let's use a hypothetical case — this time of a man named Donald.

Donald may be so terrified of making choices, so indecisive, that he constructs an imaginary superbeing who orders him to do thus and so. If a decision comes up on a job, for example, then the superbeing will order Donald to take one course or another. Donald has given up accepting responsibility for his actions. This imaginary personage may say that it is God, or a famous hero from the present or the past, or Jesus Christ, or Mohammed, and the personality involved will be quite certain that such is the case.

Donald, for example, may hear the hallucinated voice of the god or hero. The voice may be so frequent that it becomes highly distracting, or it may only appear in times of undue stress.

Again, we are starting out with a fairly simple picture. Our friend might also be convinced that he himself is evil, unworthy, or even depraved, the lowest of men or women. In such circumstances an individual might then construct an artificial devil or demon who annoys him constantly, and even orders acts of a highly destructive nature.

The individual, like Donald, has also given up the responsibility for his own choices, and feels that he or she cannot be held responsible for any destructive acts that might be committed.

(Long pause at 4:37.) Any of the two kinds of personalities mentioned might also begin to feel persecuted, chased, or harassed by some outside agency. Among the agencies chosen, of course, are the FBI, the CIA, the Russian Secret Police, the Ku Klux Klan, or any controversial group given to acts of violence for whatever purposes.

Sometimes such episodes last for long periods of time, but they can also appear for just several days, clear up spontaneously, and return again perhaps years later.

End of dictation.

Once again, I activate those coordinates that accelerate your own peace of body and mind, and quicken the healing processes.

("Thank you.")

(4:41 P.M. Jane said, "I have the feeling that whenever Seth gives exercises like that, that he's giving them just when I need them, and the reader too. Some of the stuff he advocates I do real well, and others I don't.")

(Very true, I think. I've often had the feeling that Seth's material parallels Jane's own situation, whatever that may be at that moment. I think it's especially true with this book. Large portions of it could be Seth's material for her alone.)

JUNE 21, 1984
4:03 P.M. THURSDAY

(I'd just gotten yesterday's mail sorted out this morning when another, lesser batch arrived today, both from Prentice-Hall and independently.

(Going through the mail was rewarding, though — for in various letters I found checks adding up to more than $375. We are both grateful and touched. Now when a batch of mail arrives I have to open the letters at once to see if money has been sent. Otherwise the letters may lay there for some time before I investigate them. I used to keep them unopened until I picked them up to answer. A California resident called Maude Cardwell in Texas, to tell her that he has our permission to market the audio tapes of Jane's ESP class, which ended in 1975. We haven't given anyone permission to do that, so I'll have to investigate the whole thing.)

Now I bid you another most fond good afternoon —

("Good afternoon, Seth.")

— and we will resume dictation.

Some people may seem completely normal in behavior unless certain subjects are brought up in the course of a conversation, or unless some stimulus in the environment arouses them.

For instance, the individual might be talking along normally enough when he or she hears the sirens of a police car in the distance. Instantly the person might leap up, convinced that that was evidence of the pursuit of the FBI or other agency.

The car with the siren might disappear, yet the alarmed person's attitude and actions may very well instantly cause his or her companion to realize that something was clearly amiss. The disturbed person may immediately begin a long tirade, describing previous episodes in which he or she was hunted from city to city. There may be further complications, in which the person insists that phones were bugged, letters opened, and privacy was constantly invaded.

This might be the very first sign to the person's companion that anything was wrong at all. In most such instances the tirade will continue for some time, while in other far lesser episodes it might instead simply leap to disordered, confused thoughts about being so pursued. Or instead, the individual might embark upon a rather heated discussion of police forces in general.

In actuality, people in those circumstances are often so frightened of the use of power that the idea of being under constant surveillance actually lends them a sense of protection.

Take your break.

(Resume at 4:25.)

The point is, that in such circumstances the person will try to use evidence from the outside world to prove that he is indeed being pursued.

In the same fashion, the person who hallucinates the voice of God or a demon actually does so to preserve the idea of sanity in his own mind. As long as he or she believes that a god or demon is involved, then the person can consider the entire affair most extraordinary, decidedly apart from usual experience, <u>but</u> valid.

If the therapist tries to convince such a person that the hallucinated personage does not exist, then this threatens the person's concepts of personal sanity.

End of dictation.

Once again, I activate those coordinates that quicken your own peace of body and mind, and encourage your healing capacities.

(*"Thank you."* 4:30 P.M.)

JUNE 22, 1984
3:07 P.M. FRIDAY

Now: I bid you another most fond good afternoon —

(*"Good afternoon, Seth."*)

— and we will continue dictation.

It is vital, then, that any therapist convinces the client that while the superbeing is a self-construction, and/or that the voices are hallucinations — this does not mean that the client is insane.

An effort should be made to help the client understand that <u>errors</u> of thought and belief are responsible for the condition — and that the removal of those erroneous beliefs can relieve the situation. The therapist should make it clear that he understands that the client is not <u>lying</u>, in ordinary terms, when he reports hearing voices from the devil.

According to the particular case in point, the therapist should then try to point out the errors of thought and belief involved, and also to explain their more or less habitual cast.

First, the ideas must be disentangled, and then the habitual behavior will begin to disintegrate. The therapist should also assure the client that on many subjects and topics of thought and conversation, the client operates quite well. The subject itself is so vast that, of course, an entire book could easily be devoted to it, so it is impossible to cover all the issues that may be involved with such cases here.

Some of the errors concern the misinterpretation of physical events. The individual — convinced he or she is being pursued by some secretive organization — again, may hear the sirens on a very real police car. The error is the assumption that the vehicle is pursuing the individual rather than some other party. The therapist can help the client learn to question his or her personal interpretation of such events.

All such cases can have their own peculiar complications. In the case of secondary personalities, the main operating portion who usually directs activity might be male, displaying all of the usual male characteristics. The secondary personality may seemingly be female, however, even speaking in a feminine-like voice. Or the opposite might be the case.

It is also possible for the individual to dress in male attire, while the secondary personality wears feminine clothes — or vice-versa.

(3:25.) What we are involved in mainly, however, are the characteristic periods of seeming amnesia, occurring usually involuntarily, often without any transition except perhaps for a headache.

In this category, I am not referring to individuals like Ruburt, who speak for another personality with a sense of ease and tranquillity, and whose resulting information is excellent knowledge — the obvious products of uncommon common sense that proves to be helpful to the individual and others.

Behind all of those instances we have been discussing, however, there is again the need for value fulfillment, that has been blocked largely by conflicting or even opposing beliefs.

(Very long pause at 3:31.) Regardless of how unbelievable it might seem to some readers, it is true that even the most destructive events are based upon misinterpretations of reality, opposing beliefs, and the inability to receive or express love. In fact, that kind of rage is the mark of a perfectionist caught in what seems to be the grasp of a world not only imperfect, but evil.

Take your break.

(3:34. Jane's vitals were taken. I did a couple of letters until she was ready to resume, then read the last line to her. Resume at 4:10.)

This brings us to another most dangerous belief — that the end justifies the means.

The greatest majority of destructive acts are committed in line with that belief. It leads to a disciplined overrigidity that gradually cuts down the range of human expression.

You should be able to see, in fact, that the problems we have been discussing begin by limiting the field of available choices, and thus curtailing the range of expression. The individual will try to express himself or herself to the best degree possible, and so each individual then begins a concentrated effort to seek out those avenues of expression still open. All of the constructive beliefs mentioned throughout this book should be applied to all of the instances in this chapter. The individual must feel safe and protected enough to seek its own development and aid in the fulfillment of others. End of dictation.

Once again I accelerate those coordinates that activate your own peace of body and mind, and increase your healing processes.

("Thank you." 4:18 P.M.)

JUNE 23, 1984
3:28 P.M. SATURDAY

(Yesterday after breakfast Jane had blood taken for tests, but we haven't heard anything about results yet. This noon I met Jeff Karder in the emergency room — just as I was thinking about him. He said he's worried about reports he's getting that Jane isn't as comfortable as she used to be. I said that such periods seemed to run in cycles, that I watch Jane and would always call someone if I thought anything else was amiss. Jane agreed with the cyclical description.)

Now I bid you another most fond good afternoon —

("Good afternoon, Seth.")

— and we will resume dictation.

One of the most rare and extraordinary developments that can occur in schizophrenic behavior is the construction of a seeming superbeing of remarkable power — one who is able to convince other people of his divinity.

Most such instances historically have involved males, who claim to have the powers of clairvoyance, prophecy, and omnipotence. Obviously, then, the affected individual was thought to be speaking for God when he gave orders or directives. We are dealing with "god-making," or "religionmaking" — whichever you prefer.

In almost all such instances, discipline is taught to believers through the inducement of fear. Put very loosely, the dogma says that you must love God or he will destroy you. The most unbelievable aspects of such dogmas should, it seems, make them very easy to see through. In many cases, however, the more preposterous the legends or dogmas, the more acceptable they become. In some strange fashion followers believe such stories to be true because they are not true. The inceptions of almost all religions have been involved one way or another with these schizophrenic episodes.

The person so involved must be extremely disturbed to begin with: up in arms against social, national, or religious issues, and therefore able to serve as a focus point for countless other individuals affected in the same manner.

(Long pause at 3:42.) <u>In a fashion</u>, Adolf Hitler fell into such a classification. Although he lacked that characteristic mark of speaking for a superbeing, this was because he frequently regarded <u>himself</u> as the superbeing. The trouble is that while such religions can also inspire people to acts of great sympathy, heroism and understanding, their existence rests upon drastic misreadings of the nature of reality.

If the major religions have been touched, then there have also been numberless smaller cults and sects throughout history into the present that bear that same stamp of great psychological power and energy, coupled with an inborn leaning toward self destruction and vengeance.

To varying degrees, other less striking individual cases can bear the same sense of magic and mystery.

There is certainly no need to romanticize schizophrenic behavior, for its romantic-like elements have long been coupled in the public mind in an unfortunate manner, seeming to place the madman and the genius in some kind of indefinable relationship. Such beliefs are apparent in statements such as: "Madness is the other end of sanity," or "All genius is touched with madness."

Beneath these ideas is the fear of the mind itself, the belief that its abilities are fine and dependable up to a point — but if it goes too far then it is in trouble.

What does it mean to go too far in that connotation? Usually it means that knowledge itself is somehow dangerous. Period.

In some cases, however, the constructed superbeing can deliver astute comments on national, social, or religious conditions.

Most such personages, however, begin to prophesy the end of the world, from which the chosen people — whoever they may be — will be saved. More than a few have rendered specific dates for this worldly foreclosure — dates which have come and gone. Many people still continue to follow the very same dogmas that seemed to have proven themselves wrong; the personage comes up with a newer excuse, or a newer date, and things go on as before.

Again, however, even in far simpler cases, the constructive personage will often make predictions that, incidentally, do not predict — and almost always give orders and directives that are to be followed without question.

There are many other deep psychological connections beneath schizophrenic behavior, but since this book is also devoted to other subjects, we will go on to other ways in which conflicting beliefs bring about mental or physical dilemmas.

End of dictation.

Once again, I bid you a fond early evening, and activate those coordinates that quicken your own peace of body and mind, and encourage the healing processes.

("Thank you." Once again, staff interrupted Jane twice while she was speaking for Seth. 4:25 P.M.)

CHAPTER 14

Nirvana, Right Is Might,
Onward Christian Soldiers, and the
Human Body as a Planet Worth Saving

JUNE 24, 1984
3:23 P.M. SUNDAY

(A *canker sore that began to erupt at supper time last evening really bothered me while I tried to sleep. I was up three times, and this morning it seemed the swelling and tenderness were worse than ever. To cut the story short, I'd used the pendulum last night, and it insisted that I'd developed the canker out of worry because I wasn't answering fan mail.*

(I used the pendulum again this morning, as soon as I was out of bed, and received the same answer. Last night it hadn't seemed to do any good. This time, though, almost as soon as I'd finished giving myself some gentle positive suggestions, I suddenly began to feel better. All at once I knew I'd be able to eat breakfast — maybe not in comfort, but at least eat. I felt the swelling begin to subside as though a balloon had been pricked.

(As I shaved, I felt the improvements continue — again, as if by magic. I said thanks to my subconscious. I'd felt so rough when I got up this morning that I'd considered seeking emergency medical aid — very rare for me. Through the day the improvements continued: supper was easier going than breakfast and lunch had been. And once again, I'd reinforced my faith in that simple tool, the pendulum — for me, at least.

(Jane, too, was doing better today. She'd had a sore gum for a couple of days, and that was better.)

Now I bid you another fond good afternoon.

(*"Good afternoon, Seth."*)

We will continue dictation, starting a new chapter, to be called: "Nirvana, Right is Might, Onward Christian Soldiers, and the Human Body as a Planet Worth Saving."

Few people are much concerned personally with the esoteric situations mentioned in our last chapter. Many people are involved, however, with various religious ideas and philosophies, whose effects are quite unfortunate in personal experience. The majority of individuals have bouts of poor health now and then, from which they recover — so that all in all a fairly comfortable medium is struck.

It is unfortunately often — but not <u>always</u> — true that individuals who carry strong religious feeling are often bothered more than usual by poor health and personal dilemmas. The fact is that religions have been the carriers of some of the best ideas that man has entertained — but it has also held most stubbornly to the most troublesome concepts that have plagued mankind.

You cannot divorce philosophy from life, for your thoughts and opinions give your life its meaning and impetus. There are some people who believe that life is meaningless, that it has no purpose, and that its multitudinous parts fell together through the workings of chance alone. Obviously I am speaking here of scientific dogma, but such dogma is far more religious than scientific, for it also expects to be believed without proof, on faith alone.

(*3:37.*) Such ideas are bound to color any of their followers' ideas about other subjects also: sexuality, economics, and certainly concepts of war and peace.

Again, each portion of nature is propelled by the inner vitality, energy, and life force within it. The physical body cannot flourish if the individual believes that it and its works are without meaning. Such philosophies do not give man a stake in nature, or in the universe.

All of life is seen as heading for extinction in any case. The entire concept of a soul, life after death, or even life from one generation to the next, becomes largely doubtful, to say the least. In such a philosophical world it would seem that man had no power at all.

(*3:43. Donna came in to take Jane's temp: 98.8. I didn't tell Jane, but a couple of times I'd actually fallen asleep for very brief periods while Seth spoke — something I'd never done before. The welcome feeling of release from tension and worry that I'd achieved through using the pendulum this morning was continuing. Indeed, I'd had trouble sticking to my work on* Dreams *this morning, even as I began to rebound with more energy and relaxation at the same time.*

(I read the last paragraph to Jane. Resume at 4:10)

As mentioned earlier, those concepts can have a hand in the development of would-be suicides, particularly of a young age, for they seem to effectively block a future.

The same ideas are so dead-ended, however, that they often trigger a different kind of response entirely, in which a scientist who has held to those beliefs most stubbornly, suddenly does a complete double-take. This can propel him or her into a rather severe schizophrenic reaction, in which the scientist now defends most fanatically the same ideas that he <u>rejected</u> most fanatically only a short time before.

With some variations, the same kind of "sudden conversion" can occur when a person who has berated religious concepts and beliefs suddenly does a double-take of a different kind, ending up as a twice-born Christian.

Both mechanisms suddenly line up the belief systems in one particular manner, knocking aside all doubts but accepting instead a strict obedience to the new belief system, and a new reorganization of life itself beneath that new cause.

End of dictation.

Once again, I quicken those coordinates that accelerate your own peace of mind and body, and so encourage the healing mechanisms.

("Thank you.")

(4:20 P.M. "I notice I didn't get any Darvoset yet," Jane said as soon as she was out of trance. Someone usually brings it around 4:00. A nurse did bring it within a few minutes.

(I'd left the house a little early this noon so that I'd have a bit of extra time to go up to room 522 at the hospital, to see if Joe Bumbalo was there — but he wasn't. I made the trip again after leaving Jane, and this time found him. We had a pleasant exchange for about half an hour. Joe lay in bed with his eyes closed the whole time, although he alertly followed our talk. He goes back on chemotherapy tomorrow. Margaret told me a couple of days ago that he'd gone back in the hospital because of uncontrolled blood sugar. This evening she told me the doctors were controlling the diabetes with insulin so Joe could accept the chemotherapy.

(When I pulled into the driveway at home, John Bumbalo came walking out of his garage with a large piece of lemon pie for me. Margaret and I had been kidding about her lemon pie at the hospital. She'd called John as I drove home.)

JUNE 26, 1984
3:31 P.M. TUESDAY

Now I bid you another most fond good afternoon —

("Good afternoon, Seth.")

— and we will continue dictation.

The phrase, "Might is right," can just as well be written the other way around.

For centuries it was taken for granted that God was on the side of the strongest, richest nation. Surely, it seemed, if a country was poor or downtrodden, it was because God had made it so.

Such ideas literally held people in chains, fostering slavery and other inhumane practices. The same unfortunately applies to the Eastern concept of nirvana, and to the Christian idea of heaven. Both have been used by those in power to hold down the masses of people, to justify shoddy and inadequate living conditions by promising future bliss in the world after death.

There are many differences between the ideas of nirvana and heaven, but each has been used not only to justify suffering, but also to teach people to seek pain. The idea has been that the more persecuted and maligned a person is, the greater will be the reward in a future existence.

I want to avoid concentration upon esoteric practices in this book, but they do sometimes impinge upon the subject matter at hand.

The ideas of penance, fasting to excess, the personal abuse of the body, such as self-flagellation — all of those practices are conducted in the belief that suffering is something to be sought in itself. In such a way pain becomes a sought-after goal, and pleasure becomes subverted into pain.

Quite ordinary people often believe, then, that suffering itself is a way toward personal development and spiritual knowledge. In matters of health, such beliefs can have most unfortunate results. They are often responsible for needless sacrifices of physical organs in imprudent operations.

Some individuals become anxious and worried if they think they are too happy — for to them it means that they are not paying sufficiently for their sins. They may be threatened by some undeniable danger, until finally in one way or another they seek out their own punishment once again — wondering all the time why they are so frequently besieged by poor health or disease.

This kind of syndrome can affect individuals, families, and to some extent entire nations. They mitigate directly against man's health, survival, and exuberance.

Constant fears about nuclear destruction, or other such catastrophes <u>can</u> also fall under this classification.

Take your break.

(4:04. Jane had heard the medicine cart in the hall, but a few minutes passed before a nurse came in with the Darvoset. Jane said she'd better close out the session.

(4:22.) End of dictation.

Once again, I accelerate those coordinates that activate your peace of body and mind, and encourage your own healing processes.

("Thank you."

(Peggy Gallagher visited briefly during the session, to tell me that a camera I wanted to buy was on sale at a certain store.

(I told Jane that I hoped Frank Longwell had gotten his young friend to mow the grass this afternoon, as he'd promised to do this morning, but nothing doing. As I drove up our road, I saw at once that the grass wasn't cut. The place looks terrible, although Frank said some of the wild flowers he planted out back are just beginning to show through the straw and grass mulch.

(Jane called tonight at 9:35, just as I was typing the session.)

JUNE 27, 1984
3:02 P.M. WEDNESDAY

(Jane doesn't appear to be doing too well — her body is up to something, I told her. Today her feet bothered her considerably. There is swelling on her right shoulder, and I also thought her cheeks looked swollen. I've seen such signs before, but do not recall what they meant, if anything. Today her temperature was 100 degrees — up again. She's had such swings in recent days, and ate little lunch and less supper, saying she had to take it very easy in order to keep the food down. No nurses have said anything to doctors, as far as I know.

(The day was quite cool, and intermittently cloudy. I thought it was going to rain, which meant that Frank wouldn't be doing the grass again. [And I was right about that.]

(I didn't think she'd want to have a session, or feel like it, but Jane said she did. When she began her voice was quite weak and distant at the beginning. Pauses as usual.)

I bid you another fond good afternoon.

("Good afternoon, Seth.")

We will resume dictation.

Large masses of people became so convinced of God's eventual vengeance and retribution that they began to plan for it.

Their lives became a way of avoiding pain instead of seeking out pleasure or satisfaction. This is true of individuals, but it also applies to many so-called survival groups, who congregate in one or another portion of the country, collecting supplies to carry them over the holocaust and to defend their families from those who might steal their provisions.

Most such people expect a period of chaotic time, in which all laws are broken down. Another version stresses the economic area, foreseeing the collapse of the economy, anarchy, and other conditions that pit one individual against the other.

These people believe, of course, that any given situation will worsen, and be carried to its most disastrous end. That attitude colors all of their other beliefs and actions. Some use religious dogma, and others rely upon scientific dogma to prove their cases, but in any case, they are presented with a world of deception and vengeance.

Good mental or physical health can hardly flourish under such conditions. There are instead most beneficial groups in this country and abroad, who actually, actively, <u>yet peacefully</u> join together to work for worldwide nuclear disarmament, and also to tackle such questions as nuclear waste. Their efforts are directed in other ways also, as they try to convince all areas of the world to share their wealth and foodstuffs equally.

These may be "highflying" goals, however they are positive in nature, aimed toward accomplishment and achievement, and they collect the energies of the people together in a way that stresses cooperation and understanding.

Again, the end does not justify the means — so no amount of war is ever going to produce a meaningful peace.

Such ideas affect every level of life, from the most microscopic onward. It is not that plants understand your ideas in usual terms — but that they do indeed pick up your intent, and in the arena of world survival, they have a stake.

I do not want to romanticize nonhuman life either, or to overestimate its resources, but nature also has its own ways — and in those ways it constantly works toward survival of life in general. Nature <u>may not bail you out</u>, but it will always be there, adding its own vitality and strength to the overall good and health of the planet.

Remember what I said earlier about the connections between disease and nondisease states. Communication flashes between viruses and microbes, and they can change in the wink of an eye. Once again, then, ideas <u>of the most optimistic nature</u> are the biologically pertinent ones.

Take your break.

(Resume at 3:52. Jane's voice was somewhat stronger, her pace a little faster.)

This is a good place to bring up again some extreme food practices, such as overfasting, and an <u>obsession</u> with so-called natural foods.

I am not talking about a natural and healthy interest in the purity of foodstuffs, but of a worrisome overconcern. This is often carried so far that no food seems perfectly satisfying, and the concentration becomes focused upon the <u>fear</u> of food, rather than upon its benefits.

Behind many such attitudes is the idea that the body itself is unworthy, and that starving it somehow cuts down on the appetites of the flesh. You usually end up with a flurry of different kinds of diets.

Some concentrate almost exclusively on protein, some on carbohydrates — particularly rice — but in any case the large natural range of available foods and nutrients are cut out.

This keeps the body in a state of constant turmoil. Some people are so convinced, in fact, that eating is wrong that they diet until they become ravenously hungry, then overeat and force themselves to vomit up the residue.

Other people, in a well-meaning attempt to watch their weight, skip their breakfasts entirely — a very poor procedure. It is far better to eat moderate amounts of food in all of the food ranges, and to consume smaller portions more often. I realize that your social mores also dictate your eating habits — but <u>four light meals</u> a day will overall serve you very well, and give the body a more steady, regulated nourishment.

These food ideas are important, since they are passed on from parents to children, and parents often use food as a way of rewarding a child's good behavior, thus starting the youngster out toward conditions of overweight.

End of dictation.

I bid you a fond early evening, and accelerate those forces that quicken your peace of body and mind, and release the healing processes.

(*"Thank you." End at 4:10 P.M.*)

JULY 4, 1984
4:04 P.M. WEDNESDAY

(*This morning I received a very upsetting phone call from Jeff Karder. He too is upset that Jane is obviously much more uncomfortable these days than she used to be — than two months ago, say. He doesn't want her to suffer. Jeff doesn't suggest antibiotics at this time, but told me that the ulcers on Jane's right knee and left hand won't heal themselves, and that the new swelling on the top of her right shoulder may turn into another such area. [It didn't.] Jane has a traveling infection, he believes, and he hopes it doesn't get into her bloodstream. I've suspected the same thing. Jeff said an operation would be needed on the knee to correct the condition.*

(*I had many questions after the call, of course. I felt sad for Jane and what was happening to both of us. I also felt angry at the role she's chosen, even while I thought I understood it, basically. When Jeff called I was reading the last portion of the first session in Jane's book,* The Individual and the Nature of Mass Events — *for April 18, 1977, in connection with a note I'm doing for* Dreams. *The passages are on death and suicide —* <u>natural</u> *death, no less, and how we continually interfere medically with people's chosen time of death. Hardly a coincidence, I realized.*

(*In interpreting those passages, I saw that Jane would have died, given her own choice, a couple of years ago, but her plan was interfered with by me and the hospital personnel. Although she obviously played a vital part in keep-*

ing herself alive, I believe that that action came after her own natural, chosen time of death had been subverted. She changed her mind, in other words. Otherwise, nothing would have kept her alive, no treatment of any sort.

(I was also angry that Jane hadn't allowed anything to come through in sessions about herself for some time. I think this means that her sinful self, or whatever, has once again clamped down. It doesn't want her to recover. The great question, then, is why those portions of the self would — and do — continue their terribly destructive ways, even to the point of <u>bringing about their own death</u> *— for if allowed to, I think, death would be the end result, the final step along their chosen path.*

(I've also thought for some time that there might be clues to Jane's seeming dilemmas in reincarnation — which Seth hasn't gone into at all. This is not permitted.

(I took Mass Events *to 330 with me. Jane was a bit better, yet still uncomfortable. She could keep some medications down, but was very careful about food. I'd forgotten to make her a promised corned-beef sandwich, and she'd been counting on that for supper. Georgia had told her Jeff had called me, and her version of the call was pessimistic indeed. Jane knew of Jeff's concerns.*

(Jeff suggested that we do nothing at the moment, while he monitors Jane's condition. Her temperature has varied, but has generally been okay. Yesterday afternoon it had been 100, but after supper it was down to 98.7. This morning it was a bit lower. I told her the swelling on her right shoulder looked a bit reduced. But her cheeks are swollen and somewhat blotchy, which Jeff had noticed this morning. Later in the afternoon the cheeks and shoulder both looked a bit better, and Jane acted better.

(Yesterday I'd told Jane that I knew her "body was up to something." But what? I said that I hoped it wasn't another case of her improving while getting worse — which I used to rant about in years past. We had a long talk. I said I wanted information on whether she wanted to live or die — or whether she was trying to die her own natural death, in line with that excellent information in Mass Events. *I wanted to know what her sinful self thought about what it was doing to her body, if it cared, if it even understood that it's protective actions threatened its own existence. Or was her death the ultimate goal of the sinful self? I said the situation must be a common one. I felt I was onto something here, but wasn't quite sure what — something close to the more basic human condition that is little understood.*

I told Jane it would be a joke if those portions of the self we're blaming for her condition, really are the truest, most simple and honest portions after all, and that their roles in bringing about her natural death were being subverted by our conscious-mind meddling and interference. Just where is the "truth"? I asked.

(The afternoon passed without Jane having a session. She'd cried several times as we talked — mourning most of all, I thought, that she would probably never get home again, see the house and grounds, and so on. I felt like crying myself, for I felt that she was right. She said she was too upset to have a session. I said I wanted stuff on her, not the book. She said she'd been having the longer sessions to get information she could use on herself — that each day she tried to put it to use. News to me. I said maybe she'd been trying too hard. By 4:25 she still hadn't had a session, and I didn't think she would.

(We also discussed Jane's fears that she'd done all she could in this life, and thus was ready to bow out of physical existence. I told her that if she wanted to leave I couldn't, and wouldn't try to hold her back, and that I'd never have her hooked up to survival equipment. I wouldn't want that done to me, either. And all the time we talked I couldn't help but just miss, just fail to understand exactly why she was doing what she was doing. Nor have I forgotten Seth's statement a few months ago that basically neither of us have done anything wrong.

(But so fearful and reluctant are we to face or to grasp ideas about death that run counter to what we've been taught, that we'll literally do almost anything to ourselves in order to prevent nature's plan from working in its own natural and creative way. How can we really go against what's been drummed into us since the day we were born?

(During our talk I'd cited a long list of things that in my view Jane has given up over the years, at the never-satisfied behest of portions of the personality that were now in complete control. It's all gone now except for her lying in bed, and she can't even do that in peace these days. She'd even given up all reading, even with the new glasses we so eagerly sought from Jim Baker. The supporting easel I'd made for her to use in reading, sits in the closet of 330. Jane used it just once. She said she doesn't use it or do any reading because of the longer sessions.

(After my nap I asked her why she didn't read more, to keep in touch with the world, and got quite a response from her. She got angry and shouted that she would read more if I wanted her to. I laughed — my first

*of the day, I said — and told her that she was only saying that because I
wanted her to read more — not because she'd suggested that she do so on her
own. Later, she did suggest I bring in some reading matter. I told her that*
Mass Events *was still a terrific book. "So why isn't it a household word?" I
asked. No answer.*

*(At the end of her outburst about reading, Jane ended up by saying some-
thing important — that her failure to read was <u>another example of her doing
something wrong</u> — "And that's what we're talking about, isn't it? All those
things I'm doing wrong?" Too true. When I said I wouldn't bug her any more
about reading, she said I talked like a martyr. So how can one win in such a
situation, when either way is rejected?*

*(There's no use going to all the work to present a detailed summary of the
complicated series of events that have transpired since June 28. Jane is still
very ill. I was surprised when she said she'd try to have a session today. At
times her voice was so weak I had to ask her to repeat phrases or words.*

("I'm going to skip the preliminaries," she said.)

The main issue involved, once again, is the trust of the body.

The condition itself is an unfortunate aspect of the hospital environment, but you leapt to the conclusion that the very worst was
involved. Ruburt did fall prey, <u>in your terms</u>, (underlined twice), to
a flu-like condition — but the additional fear added immeasurably,
prolonging the situation.

End of session.

("Thank you." 4:07 P.M.)

JULY 17, 1984
7:00 P.M. TUESDAY

Dictation: (Time, 7:00–7:10 P.M.)

*Outside of my house
there are sparrows
and a robin
outside of my door,
and maybe a crow
or a rabbit,
and it's nice to know
that they're there.*

The small woods are still
in the side yard,
and chipmunks and squirrels
are running free.
In the evening it's nice
to know it's all there.

The breeze blows
through the side trees and
the sweet smell of earth
comes through the
screen door, and there are
promises in the air
that remind me of
my girlhood
and the dreams that
drifted there.

JULY 18, 1984
4:00 P.M. WEDNESDAY

Dictation: (Time, 4:00–4:15 P.M. Revised July 19)

I'm looking forward to autumn,
which isn't so far away,
and I'd like to come alive
as fully in flesh as I ever have,
and let the quickness of autumn
bring all my life to newly rise in wisdom
and knowledge and time.
I don't want to die yet.
That's the purpose as clear as any I have.
I want to arouse and live with ease through my flesh
with some gallantry and love.

There are winds in the high Sierras —
wherever the hell they are —
but it's nice to know
that the universe sings
even in places I haven't been.

And there are high adventures that rise to circle the moon,
and shadows that leap
like wild asses
in worlds that whistle and curl.
For everywhere there is magic,
and it swirls through my molecules
with a secret life that dances
and splashes against
the rocky thoughts of my mind,
and there are new mornings happening
everywhere in all of my bodily parts.
Let me live while I wonder and wander
through my nature's multitudinous paths.

JULY 22, 1984
1:35 P.M. SUNDAY

Dictation: (Time, 1:35 P.M.)

The Cupboard said,
"I've got lots of cupcakes
and cookies, Mr. Bear.
I'd like to share them
with you — just you and me
alone. We'll have a little party
and maybe sing a little song."
The Bear said, "Whoops,
slow down, Mr. Cupboard.
While I'm sure your purposes
are good, I swear you can
be a mean cuss sometimes, for a
creature made up of
such lovely wood.
I know you've got a trick
here someplace, though I'm not
smart, so eat your cookies
alone, but God bless your
heart, dear heart."

Dictation: (Time, 2:15 P.M.)

I'd rather sit down
with a pussycat
out in the sun, where all
the secrets are free,
and dance on a path
smelling sweet buttercups
and chasing after
early fireflies
and cavort through tiny
mountain paths
where the air is
bright and free —
then take out a pair of
binoculars, and see
as far as I can see.
So here's to
pussycats and flowers,
and rainbows and lilac trees
too. So have a lovely
morning and smile at the
mountain air
because each day is
actually the prettiest
day you'll ever have.

Dictation: (Time, 2:27 P.M.)

The air has memories
of every place it's been,
so the coldest
air in the Arctic
remembers palm trees
and balmy winds,
and a breeze that blows
in Maine's deep woods
remembers southern
nights that glistened
years and years ago
around the coast of
southern France.

JULY 25, 1984
6:50 P.M. WEDNESDAY

Dictation: (Time, 6:50–7:00 P.M.)

The Queen of Frogs

The queen of frogs
adjusted her crown
and called for the finest
prince of the realm,
and while she waited she massaged
her beautiful manicured toes.
She said, "I'm sending you on a mission
as mysterious as can be,
for I want to collect
the loveliest nights and days
to decorate our kingdom walls.
We're going to have the most spectacular art gallery
that the world has ever known,
where we can contemplate
the shining nights and days,
and keep them for our own."

The prince blinked and said,
"Dear lovely queen, surely this you must not do,
for the world would weep itself
asleep, and soon die of a broken heart.
As it is, the beauties of nature belong to us all.
Nobody can steal them away,
for they exist by themselves
in the world of the mind
where no thieves can ever go."

JULY 27, 1984
2:17 P.M. FRIDAY

Dictation: (Time, 2:17–2:20 P.M.)

Suppose there was a puncture
way out in the air
in a place where nobody knew.
Well, I bet that somebody'd patch it up
from the other side
so that it lasted for a
hundred more years.

JULY 30, 1984
4:04 P.M. MONDAY

(After lunch today, I showed Jane the last two poems she's dictated at the hospital — those for July 25 and July 27. Then a little later she told me to turn down the TV and get out my pad. She dictated another.

There is a message
in a postbox
meant for me alone.
It may be in front
of some old barn,
hidden in Ohio,
or maybe it's in Timbuktu
or in some postbox
by the sea.
It's been there for centuries,
waiting just for me.
It may be far closer, though,
waiting for me where
my life and the message
sing the same lifesong.

(Jane said she didn't want to hear it when I asked her if she wanted me to read it back to her. I told her I liked it, but in retrospect I see that it's content is far more revealing than I'd first realized. I believe it literally deals with Jane's questioning over whether to live or die.

(Rather than go into more detail here, I'll move to the session, which Jane began quite a bit later. I was surprised that she said she'd have one: "I don't know whether I can do this, Bob, or how far I'll get, but I'm going to try . . . "

(I should add that after reading her the poetry and her new dictation, I read her the last three sessions for Seth's The Way Toward Health, *given on June 24, 26, and 27. Jane didn't ask for these, but left it up to me to pick out something to read.*

(Jane's Seth voice was average, her delivery good. I thought she carried off the little session very well.)

In any case, there are new lives growing and maturing within each individual, whatever his or her age or circumstances.

The idea of survival reaches far beyond this life experience, and each person has new physical and spiritual existences ever ready — for there is no such thing as extinction. Alive or dead in usual terms, you are always conscious and aware of yourselves, and you are always a part of universal ventures in which you have always been involved, whatever your states of consciousness.

You are supported, never abandoned, and always couched lovingly in the great yet intimate presence of All That Is, whose love forms your breath, your life, your death, as in which the unknown divinity is always blessed and ever known.

It is known and unknown, forming all stages of creativity, and you are held within it, graced to be a part of the divine framework of All That Is.

(End at 4:09 P.M.

("That can be the end of the book, you know. Or maybe I'll do a little more," Jane said. "Whatever happens, Bob, I'd like all of the material published someday, if it can be done. Not to put a burden on you. Maybe if you can't do it, you can get some help."

("What brought all of this on?" I asked, knowing quite well the answer.

("The whole thing," Jane said. "I don't know whether I'm going to live or die." She spoke quite matter-of-factly. "Whatever I'm going to do, I'm going to do."

("I know you've been thinking it over, whether you want to live or die," I said. "Ever since you stopped eating, around July 4. It's been obvious to me."

(Off and on through the afternoon I'd felt like crying, as I'd become more and more sure that Jane was indeed thinking things over. She had a smoke and we talked until about 4:40.

(Jane said she treasured every day we'd been together throughout our marriage. I did too — and in those 30 years I don't believe we'd been separated more than four or five days. I said I probably couldn't publish all of the material by myself. Also that I'd probably not marry again. Jane said I could take up with Sue — although I doubt if Sue would care to do that.

(I said I wished we'd never left Sayre, and she agreed. Maybe things would have been different. She said, "No autopsy." When I asked her if she wanted to be buried or cremated, she expressed no strong wish for either mode, but finally chose cremation — maybe because I said what would I do if I wanted to move out of town a few years after she'd been buried. She hadn't thought of that. She said as far as she knew her grandfather and grandmother and others were buried in Saratoga, though we aren't sure about her mother. Her father, Del, is buried somewhere in Florida, we guess — we don't know where.

(After I turned her I broke down crying when I tried to tell her how much I loved her. Jane cried too. I couldn't believe this was happening, even after all of the signs that have accumulated over the years. The import and impact of today's session made things quite clear.

(After I had her situated on her side, I sat back for my usual nap, but didn't actually sleep much. I felt terribly sad. Jane had talked about how much she loved nature, and how she wanted to see the house one more time, and the cats. I told her about the four deer — three bucks and a doe — that I'd seen out back this morning, nibbling away in the so-called wildflower garden. Some blood-red poppies are up now.

(Jane ate a little of several things for supper — about as she's been doing the last few days. This is actually an improvement for her, for since around July 4 she hasn't taken in any solid food with very few exceptions — and then only a crust, one might say. After watching her behavior as the month passed, I could see that she was indeed starving herself, and would die if she kept it up. She's lost a great deal of weight; her arms look skeletal — so do her legs to a lesser degree.

(After supper, I learned several things. Jane had been told by the nurses a few days ago that she could have morphine whenever she wanted it; it's

given by injection. She also said that yesterday she <u>resumed</u> taking her thyroid medication, which she'd stopped taking July 4 — the day of that last little session. She also revealed that she hasn't gone to hydro for three days, and will have to give in and go; she was trying to avoid more pain.

(I read the session to her at 6:55. "It's extremely well done," I said.

("Well, that's it," she said. "That's the end."

("Of the book, or the Seth material?"

("I don't know. We'll see. Maybe I'll start on something else and go right through it," she said. She almost laughed. "But right now I'm trying to get through each night and day."

(Her nights have been particularly rough, I learned. "If only I could get a little peace of mind, how wonderful it would be," she said.

(I asked her if she wanted to try some free association. I said I thought she'd broken that off because she was afraid it wouldn't work — although I'd thought it showed signs that it was working. I also thought she'd stopped free associating because it had collided with those deeply held beliefs that had led to her physical immobility. I told her that during the last month I'd given up hope, and that she must have, and that her condition was a perfect mirror of that loss for each of us. She seemed to agree.

(I'd like to add that while there's life there's hope, and that as Seth has said many times, one who doesn't want to die — as Jane said the other day she didn't — won't for any reason. But I told Jane that I couldn't ask her to do something she didn't want to do. I added that I wouldn't want to live under such conditions.

(And so there it is. Carla called for Jane at 9:15, as I was typing this material. She told me that Jane loved me, and that she was having "a better night." I asked Carla to give Jane my love. And the fact that my wife is having a better night may mean something, or not . . . I'd told her this afternoon that I'd been prepared to receive a call from the hospital at any time, telling me to get my ass down there because my wife was failing and the end was near. And Jane smiled and said that she'd been tempted many a time to have me called to come see her, especially late at night.

(I love you, Jane, and don't know whether to laugh or cry. I feel like the latter. I wish you the best, whether you leave or stay. Today's session says it all, I guess, for it means that better things lie ahead for you — and me — and if that's the case, what have we got to worry about?

(I will close on this note, though in all sincerity, I think those who are left behind have it far rougher than those who go . . .)

JULY 31, 1984
3:54 P.M. TUESDAY

(Jane ate a better lunch today — that is, not enough to keep a bird alive, but still an improvement over most of the month of July: A little soup, a little egg yolk, coffee, a little custard, chocolate milk, and so forth.

(After lunch I read her the session for yesterday, after she'd been unable to read it with either pair of her glasses. Her eyes behaved the same way yesterday. I ended up asking Jane if she wanted to try free association after we'd talked a while, but got no definite answer.

(She was so much in pain that I ended up giving her at least ten minutes of what I thought were good suggestions. Hypnosis may have entered in. The bout seemed to help her relax; her arms and hands became easier and looser. She seemed to lay in bed more easily, and referred to the experience several times through the afternoon. I'll try more such things. She loved the wild flowers I brought in from the house.

(Later I told Jane of a remark Frank Longwell had made the other day, after I'd explained to him that she'd been having a very rough time this month. "Well," Frank said, "she always does when she doesn't have the sessions." This got Jane thinking, I could see. Both of us have had the thought at times, but Frank's spontaneous remark hit the mark just right.

(I asked Jane if she thought the sessions served as a balance to those sinful-self, very restrictive ideas — that when she gave up on the sessions that other self was free to exert its power and beliefs. She didn't know, but I thought it a valid idea. I added that the whole bit put me on the spot, and always had, because I was never sure whether to insist that she have the sessions, or forget them. I'd always been cautious about asking her to keep holding them, for fear that they might come to dominate her life. It would be ironic indeed if it develops that the "truth" is more the other way around. It even appears to me right now, at least, that that more damaging avoidance of sessions has had a very negative impact.

("Get out your stuff," Jane said after I'd told her about Frank's remark and we had discussed it a little. She lay high up on the bed, her head back against her pillows. Her Seth voice was both strained and strong, I thought, although she had no trouble with the words. Her voice was different, though, and the rhythm was distinctly different than usual; she paused every few words.)

The sessions, like life itself, have been and are a gift, rising from the immense, never-ending creativity of existence.

Alone, they carry within themselves the splendor of unknown knowledge, and they arise from the deep founts of Ruburt's life, containing within themselves the neighborhood and world in which he grew, the power and vitality of the people he knew, the resourcefulness and energy that composed reality. Hidden within the sessions there is the splendid vitality of Father Trenton, his *(Jane's)* mother, his neighbors and teachers — but beyond that the sessions connect and unite the annals of existence as he has experienced them, so that in speaking with my voice, <u>and for me</u> *(quavering)*, he expresses the blessed vitality and acknowledgments of the universe, as even through the sessions the sweet universe acknowledges his own presence and being. And the two of you together also live within one life that expresses multitudinous voices, and sheds its own mercy, gladness, and joy, out into the world at large, enriching it, renewing the springtimes, and never truly ending.

Let us, then, continue.

(4:02 P.M. "That's it," Jane said. "I don't know what he meant by the "Let us continue," but that's the last sentence I got. I don't know — I couldn't tell whether it was a hello or a goodbye . . . "

(I read the session to her. "Well, I'd say it can be anything you want it to be."

(She nodded. "I feel so weird I don't know what to do."

("That may be a good sign — a sign of change. Let me know what you want to do."

(Jane said she felt "scared and panicky," and that, I knew, was a good sign. I told her we'd touched something that needed dragging out into the open. Before I could try anything like free association, however, Jane said she had more to give.

(4:10.) To one extent or another, Ruburt then speaks in the sessions for all peoples, for the united psyches that overflow with thoughts and feelings that are registered by the wind, giving voice to the private, intimate, yet connected lives of men and women throughout the centuries — so that many people, listening to or reading the sessions, hear their own inner voices also, and feel the contours of their own natures, and universal nature as well.

("That's all," she said at 4:14. I made notes and helped her have a cigarette until it was time to get ready to turn her at 4:30.

(I felt some small glimmers of hope about our progress this afternoon, and of course, hope it continues. Perhaps sessions will help Jane. I also mentioned several times that I'd like to have her return to the house. "But not to the bed there," I said, referring to the hospital bed we own. "I don't mean that at all. I mean I want to see you getting around somewhat, at least.")

AUGUST 1, 1984
3:13 P.M. WEDNESDAY

(Today Jane looked and acted somewhat better, following our talks and actions yesterday. I brought in the sessions for February 5 and 6, and read them to her after lunch. I selected them at random this morning, but picked just those I wanted, for their import is that Jane has no disease, as Seth has insisted all along. In other words, I told Jane, she doesn't have to surmount any physical debilitating disease that has bacteria or germs or microbes attached to it, and is labeled "incurable."

(The sessions also stressed her fears of being attacked by the world if she used her abilities. I'd had them too, but they are much minimized by now for me, and I want her to reach that belief plateau also. I know she can, I told her, and that it's vital for her if she wants to live. After all, hardly anything else could be worse in life than being attacked by her symptoms, so what's there to lose?

(The session for February 5 even stressed that the same energy that healed her right leg could also straighten it. I tried to go easy with what I said to her today, but ended up fearing I had overdone it in my eagerness to get things started. I thought Jane might get confused, being bombarded with so many ideas and suggestions from so many angles.

(She did agree to try for a session, however, even though I thought she didn't feel up to it. I'd mentioned her doing so, so as to help her use her creative abilities, since they are so much a part of her, whereas in times before I'd thought of asking her not to use those same abilities because I felt they were making her worse. I think that now I've learned — and hope to help teach Jane — that there's nothing for it but to use one's abilities full blast in every area — and that that resolve and action will conquer all and set her free — physically, creatively, and mentally.

(She lay back upon her bed and pillow, half crying at times, speaking with a choked voice often, and once again with a different rhythm — one broken by long pauses every few words, as yesterday.)

I bid you *(half crying)* a most fond and sympathetic afternoon.

("Thank you, Seth. The same to you."

(Long pause.) Ruburt is not going to die now, to the best of my knowledge.

He is still gathering up his resources, and became quite panic-stricken at the situation in general. He is still working toward recovery, though the fear and panic did slow down that recovery considerably — and by recovery I mean simply the return to conditions just before this recent hang-up.

(Delivery often strange, choked with emotion, long pauses.)

The thyroid medication will benefit, and I believe the food situation will slowly return to the period previously.

Let him take a break, and perhaps we can return briefly.

(3:21 Jane was again half crying. She felt panicky, which meant we were close to something. I asked her what it might be, but she didn't answer enough for me to pursue the subject.

("It'll take me a minute to get back to it."

("Okay." Word by careful word:

(3:27.) The session itself should reassure him enough to allow some of the panic to subside, so that he can begin to sense at least some return of composure. You have indeed been of invaluable support now.

(Jane lay so quietly, eyes closed, head tipping toward her left on her pillow, mouth open, that I thought she'd fallen asleep.)

Avoid what-is-wrong issues. Imperative.

(Long pause.) Instead, have him try to sense the rightness that still works within him. That rightness can then help dissolve or circumnavigate those other elements.

I bid you a hopeful good afternoon.

("Thank you."

(3:36 P.M. Jane asked me to read the session to her, and tell her what I thought of it. I said it was very good indeed — just what I'd expected and hoped for. It showed a resurgence of hope, that all was not lost. Jane wasn't so sure about the recovery, but I said I thought I'd seen signs of that the last few days, and now felt it would happen. Her appetite was slowly improving. Her arms and hands rest easier, and overall she seems a little more relaxed. I want to try more suggestion, like I'd done yesterday. I told Jane I realized it would be tougher for her to realize these things, but that I thought events would prove them out.

(I had her lay on her side while I checked TV, got supper ready, and so forth. I left at 7:15. Her vitals had been okay — 98.5, I believe. No prayer was said. Have a good night, sweetheart.)

AUGUST 2, 1984
3:21 P.M. THURSDAY

(Jane didn't call last night. She said that after I left her at 7:15 or so last night, following all the events of the day, she "passed out" and slept well for 2½ hours. She wasn't so comfortable later, though. She went to hydro this morning. Pain. Later in 330 she had to call for help because she couldn't work the nurses' call button, and one of the nurses hollered at her. Georgia then came to help.

(I was disappointed that Jane ate so little for lunch today. I had started feeling tired when I got to 330, so decided not to press any points. Maybe, I thought, we needed time to recover from the emotions of the last few days especially. I also felt that Jane's destiny was in her own hands, and that nothing anyone else was going to do would change that. So it is with each of us. Her recovery was up to her, then, although I still puzzled why she carried her situation to such extremes when she said she didn't want to die.

(Jane dictated this poem from 3:00–3:06.

> *Each woman, child and man*
> *is anonymous as*
> *we all are,*
> *yet each is secretly named*
> *as a royal brother and sister*
> *of nature's kingdom.*
> *We are saluted by the wind*
> *and acknowledged by stars*
> *as members of a family*
> *of eternal guise.*

(I read the poem to her at her request. Sometimes she doesn't want to hear them. She told me about a vivid dream she had last night, and I refer to an interpretation of the dream at the end of the session.

(Then I read her the Seth part of yesterday's session, but not my notes. Jane said she felt a little better today generally, and I thought she acted it. "I don't know if I'll have a session today or not," she said, "but keep your

paper and pen handy." And then she immediately began the session. Her words were loaded with emotion, more evenly delivered than yesterday's session had been, yet still the rhythm wasn't one of ease and speed.

(I was surprised that she had a session at all, figuring she might want to relax more today.)

I bid you a sympathetic, yet hopeful good afternoon.

("Good afternoon.")

Let Ruburt remind himself that his birth was not responsible for his mother's incapacity. He did not <u>rob her</u> of her own life by being born.

(In no time at all Jane's Seth voice had moved closer and closer to tears.)

He has no reason *(long pause)* to feel guilty, or to punish himself for his mother's situation. He did not <u>murder</u> her in any way by his birth. He is, therefore, no murderer or destroyer, or contemptible. He is not his mother's murderer, then, in any fashion, nor responsible for the breakup of his parents' marriage.

He has no such crime, or crimes, to repent of, or to punish himself for. He is not therefore an unnatural daughter of the earth.

Take a break.

(3:27. The tears were streaming down Jane's face as she came out of the session, and their flow increased as she cried more and more. She'd delivered her words in almost a grand sepulchral manner by the break. She sobbed, her face wet, her mouth contorted.

("Is that what this has been all about?" I asked, meaning the years of the symptoms. She didn't answer. I thought it was great that she was expressing deeply-felt emotion, just as I was surprised that she'd spontaneously — seemingly — chosen the subject matter for the session . . . This had to be good, I said.

("I always tried to buy her things to make up," Jane cried, her whole face twisted with tearful emotion. "I do not know whether she hated me or not. I guess she hated me."

("Well," I said several times, wherever she is now, I sure hope your mother understands what she did to you. I groped for words to express my anger, for watching my wife cry certainly aroused strong feelings within me. I felt like directing some very nasty barbs at Marie — especially when I remembered those old photos of Jane that I'd looked at a couple of days ago. How could a three-year-old child, standing in the snow on Middle Avenue in Saratoga Springs, be responsible for hurting anything — or anybody?

(I tried to reassure her several times. "You've never hurt anybody, sweet-heart — "

(Wouldn't you know it — at a time like this Carla came in to do Jane's vitals. As long as she was there, I asked Carla to get someone to clean out Jane's ears, for she'd been having difficulty hearing again lately.

(Carla hadn't been gone a minute when another nurse came in, and said she'd do Jane's ears a little later. I said fine.

(Jane wasn't crying by now, but her reddened eyes and face must have been revealing, though no one said anything. "You never hurt anyone," I said again. "I don't know what I'm trying to say." I held my tongue instead of cursing Marie, as I wanted to. "I'd better shut up, I guess, before I say more."

(3:47. Crying somewhat again, Jane resumed the session. I had to ask her to repeat some words. She lay back with her eyes closed most of the time.)

Tell Ruburt he is in no way responsible for killing his grandmother or the housekeeper.

There is, therefore, in those regards, no cause for self-punishment or penance *(crying)*, or turmoil. <u>He is therefore not damned in any manner</u> — neither by God or nature, and there is no reason for him to damn himself. He is therefore innocent, and pronounced so.

(3:50. A nurse's aide brought in Jane's vitamins. Then another one came in to say hello and talk about the rain we were getting in spurts. "If any more of those kids come in I'll scream," Jane said when they'd left. But they're all great people and a joy to see and depend upon, and obviously they like us.

(I read the session since break to Jane. "More," she said at 3:56. Her delivery was calmer now, more even.)

There is no reason either, to blame his mother, or to hold any grudge against her, for in no way did Marie understand the issues.

(Long pause, eyes closed.) Such attitudes and dire misinterpretations often occur as mistakes in reading life, as if you insert an extra vowel or syllable that does not belong, but change the interpretation of an entire passage. Let the mistake, then, be erased.

(Long pause at 4:01. "I guess that's it . . . "

(Not very long after the end of the session, Jane began making motions with both arms, raising them up from her body and rotating them. Her feet and toes also moved, and her head a little. The motions were reminiscent, on a smaller scale, of those she'd begun doing in October 1983, but eventually gave up on.

("What are you doing?" I asked. "Showing off?"

(Jane didn't answer. With her mouth closed tight she was making grunt-ing and keening sounds as she moved her body, over and over, expressing vocally the same efforts she was making physically. These motions too were a definite response to new freedom, and I reminded her that Seth had said earlier this year that once it's allowed to, the physical body will begin responding immediately. This was certainly a sign of that, I said, and some-thing I hadn't even thought of. The session and the motions certainly did signal new things.

(When I asked her, Jane said today's session and motions could be inter-preted as being related to her dream for last night. She'd dreamed that once certain things, events, were set into motion, they inevitably would continue in their motion until they came true — then the world would end. "Well," she said, "if I find out those things aren't true, then the world isn't going to end." I said this seemed like a symbolic statement, the dream, that old beliefs meant she had no hope of extricating herself from a foregone conclusion. But if those events between Jane and Marie <u>didn't</u> have to move on toward their inevitable end, as stated in the session today, then there was hope.

(This didn't mean that I didn't still feel bitterness toward Marie. Even if she didn't grasp the issues involved, as Seth said, did this give her the freedom to so abuse another? A large subject, I know, and one chosen by all involved, but still . . .

(After supper, Jane once again embarked upon a series of movements of her arms and hands especially. Other parts of her body were also respond-ing — it was as if once it understood that it were set free, it would try to move as best it could right away. Most heartening, Jane, and keep it up. Great things can happen!

(Carla called for Jane at 9:30, and told me that Jane was again doing those motions. My wife was already plunging in, then. Fine.)

AUGUST 3, 1984
2:59 P.M. FRIDAY

(Jane looked a bit more at ease when I got to 330. "Don't touch me," she said as she lay on her back watching the TV soap opera, The Young and the Restless, *as she did every noontime. "I just want to lay here and let the Darvoset take effect . . ."*

(She ate a rather skimpy lunch. At 2:59, as we talked, she began to speak about being scared and panicky again. Half crying and moaning in no time, arms and hands moving from where I'd propped them up. She did say her panicky feelings had to do with the session about her mother Marie yesterday, and a dream she'd had last night. Very good, I said, but she couldn't actually pin down the source or subject matter for her panic today. She continued half crying. "Read me — read me yesterday's session. I don't know what I'm doing," she cried, when I asked her if she was thinking about Marie.

(I read her the session at 2:48. Jane was moaning and crying. She didn't want to hear my notes for the session, or the poem she'd dictated yesterday. I thought it important that she hear the notes, but had no choice except to wait.

(Tearfully, moaning, at 2:58: "I'm going to try, Rob, to have a session. I'll do the best I can . . . I don't know if I can . . . All right, I'll try." Then, teary, with many pauses, eyes open most of the time:)

To live does not require any monumental effort.

He will not die, despite himself, so to speak. His living is the most natural thing in the world. He is, therefore, not abandoned. The mysterious, creative healing energies do sustain him. Forget the knees as much as possible, and the seeming impediments.

(Very long pause.) The body's motion already begins to assert itself. Let him find that motion. Above all, reassure him, and feel its presence. Again, the session should automatically help calm his mind and let the panic dissipate.

We will return.

("Okay for now," Jane said.

(3:03. She was still teary, her voice often choked with emotion. She took the Darvoset to help calm her down. It was raining heavily, just as it had done periodically yesterday afternoon. Reading today's session, so far, helped. Carla had said last night when she called that Jane was still doing the motions she'd begun yesterday. Now Jane told me a friend had visited earlier. When the motions had started up, Jane had asked her to leave, since she hadn't wanted to do the motions in front of someone else.

("Right now," Jane said, "the fear seems to be that despite myself I'm going to die."

("That's okay," I said. "It's just another fear. Just don't hide it. It'll go

away. But it shows how far things have gone — that it's time to back off from the point of death."

(Jane had a cigarette. I told her it was important that I read her my notes for yesterday's session, especially those pertaining to her mother. She finally agreed.

(3:14. I read the notes. Then I read the session for July 30 — at Jane's request — the first in this series regarding her death, the end of The Way Toward Health, *and so forth. I tried to put the situation in perspective: "You're trying to excise your fears of your mother, which in turn led to your being afraid of the world and your own fears of death, 'cause you carried your idea of protection from the world so far . . . "*

(3:30. "A little more session," Jane said. Her delivery was much calmer now.)

Remind Ruburt further *(pause)* that he did his best to help <u>your</u> mother, making efforts toward love and communication *(long pause)* that he felt you were not able to express toward your mother at times.

Remind him of his kindnesses to your apartment-house neighbor, Miss Callahan, to his many students, and of his love for you. Also remind him that <u>he did not deal with malice</u> toward his own mother. Do remind him affectionately and often that for many years he loved his mother deeply, and that his own existence made his grandfather experience a love that was a <u>light</u> in his later years.

These elements are all living and highly potent in the <u>affairs</u> of his life — so that <u>in no way</u> do his relationships with his mother *(pause)* become any isolated concentration, existing apart from the other affairs of life. Remind him that Ruburt loves nature, and always has. <u>Nature loves Ruburt</u>, and always has.

It may also be a good idea to read some portions of our late material over, substituting the name Jane rather than Ruburt. He is Jane to himself and to the universe and to you, and to his friends and his readers.

("Okay," Jane said at 3:40.

(We were talking at 3:45 when the phone rang. It was John Bumbalo. His father, Joe, had died at 2:00 P.M. John had just left the house, as Jane and I had left the rest home just before my mother died in November, 1973. Jane spoke to John, thanking him for looking after me. John told her I was "a wonderful man." I felt a surge of emotion, half unbelieving, when she told me. Jane began

to hum a song we both knew but couldn't place — perhaps an aria from an Italian or Spanish opera. She said she thought it was connected to Joe somehow.

(After a late supper I went over to see the Bumbalo family. Margaret and I hugged. She almost cried. I could tell they'd all been crying. Yet they had the Olympics on TV, and John offered me a scotch and soda. There was much laughing and joking too. Margaret asked me if I'd be an honorary pallbearer at Joe's funeral, and I said sure. She said I didn't have to do anything. The first thought that crossed my mind was that I didn't have a suit to wear — just my corduroys. I didn't mention this.

(I did no typing last night, but typed this session this morning after taking our cat, Billy, around the house on his morning jaunt. The phone rang at 10:25. It was Georgia. She put Jane on. "No big deal," my wife said, "but I had a crappy night. Would you come down earlier and maybe eat lunch with me?"

(Georgia said she'd order me a cold ham plate, and Jane and I made arrangements that I'd get there at noon — earlier wasn't necessary, she said. Jane wasn't going to hydro this morning, and Georgia was starting to bathe her in bed.

(This is the first time my wife has ever asked me to come at a different hour. I see it as a good thing, since I'd told her to do so, and that it may serve as excellent therapy and reinforcement of new beliefs.)

AUGUST 4, 1984
3:00 P.M. SATURDAY

(I got to 330 at 12:05, just as Jane was taking her Darvoset. She didn't feel very good, but seemed to improve a bit later. When the lunch tray came, along with the cold ham plate Georgia had ordered for me, I wasn't hungry. Jane also ate little, except for several cups of iced chocolate milk. I guess I got depressed when I saw that once again she just wasn't going to eat much.

(At 2:30 Jane began having panic attacks, just as she's been doing lately. Crying and moaning. She again could not tell me what their source was, although we were pretty sure the same things were involved — mostly her mother. I cleaned her close-up glasses for her and told her to put them on when she resisted. Then I told her to read yesterday's session as I held it for her. Something she wouldn't have done if I hadn't insisted. First she read the Seth material in the session, then the notes at my insistence.

("I guess I've let the fear get into everything," she said, tearfully.

(I too was upset and half angry. "You sure have," I said. "You've let it rule every bit of your life, every thought almost, and there sure isn't much left, is there?"

(Her panic didn't last nearly as long as it had yesterday, and I hoped her continued experience of it would lead to its dissipation. She repeated several times between sniffles that she'd try to have a session. "I'll do the best I can.")

Start again, slowly.

Tell Ruburt to tell himself that he can slowly but definitely make small adjustments in his thinking, feeling, belief — that even despite his panic he can feel those changes move around in his psyche.

Remind him that all his nature <u>does indeed</u> work to his benefit, and that signs of creative alterations and feeling begin to surface, like tiny shoots.

Again, he is not abandoned. He is in no way responsible for his mother's problems, and no matter how strong his fears, universal energy lifts him up regardless of all else. The session does automatically add its own sense of infinite devotedness by gathering together the healing abilities, which have their own soothing effect.

Sometimes it is not the words but the very sounds of the sessions which transfer calmness by directly affecting the body itself also.

The entire situation not only is temporary, but already has made its own turnabout, restoring the body and mind to an important degree.

(3:14. I read the session to Jane at her request. I hardly felt like it. I'd sensed anger again as the session progressed. I wondered what good it would do. Probably my own attitude and mood today, of course — yet the session could have been any one of a similar kind that Jane had given in the last ten years. And in all of those others she'd been in better shape to begin with — and still nothing had happened!

(I must have reached the point where I truly don't think she wants anything but what she's got — for after all, doesn't each of us create our own reality? And what's my part in all of this? Without doubt, my own frustrations and resentments were surfacing probably for my own safety.

(Jane seemed to feel and speak much better after the session. She went through another period of moving her arms and hands, and feet to a lesser extent, as I turned her at 4:30. I couldn't help but tell myself I'd seen the same thing many times before, without lasting results.

(Carla helped Jane call me at 9:05 P.M., just as I was finishing this session. She sounded fairly good. We exchanged words of love for each other.)

AUGUST 5, 1984
4:09 P.M. SUNDAY

(I was eating breakfast at 7:50 when I received a call from the hospital. The call scared me at that hour. The nurse said Jane wasn't good. They couldn't get her comfortable, she wasn't eating breakfast, and she wanted me to come down. Jan was to tell Jane at once if I'd see her. I left the breakfast, the cats, the house, turned off the lights, and drove down. I didn't think it was a life-or-death crisis, but the result of our conversations lately, and the sessions, the panic attacks, and so forth. It was raining heavily when I left the house.

(Jane was uncomfortable, up to her shoulders on two full chucks, propped and wedged so she couldn't move. I had two nurses hold her up while I got rid of the chucks. We got her positioned much more comfortably. Jane cried at times, but not excessively. She'd had Darvoset before I arrived. Actually, I felt her upset was another good sign.

(In fact, after a while I got my wife to resume eating breakfast. She did quite well, taking chocolate milk, coffee, a slice of toast and jelly, several bites of egg and bacon. My presence undoubtedly helped her resume eating.

(She had periodic bouts of panic as she ate, and we talked these out to some extent. I asked her to just not bury the feelings, and I don't think she did. Jane came up with several excellent insights. One of them is that she may have associated punishment with physical motion — this idea stemming from her days at the Catholic home, where the youngsters were made to kneel for long periods of time as punishment for various "wrongs." This came to Jane's consciousness as we watched a very creative skit on the TV program Sesame Street. I'd never heard her make this connection before.

(Another insight is that "the body has it's own rights." Seth has said this many times, as have I, but it evidently hadn't meant all that much to Jane before.

(At one time during breakfast when she became upset and panicky again, I repeated my use of suggestion/mild hypnosis as I had the other day. Again, results were good. Jane stared at me intently as I spoke each word.

(I told her about Joe Bumbalo's obituary notice that I'd found in

yesterday's paper, and that after I left 330 tonight I'd stop at the funeral home to see Joe and the family. Also, that I'd be going to the funeral tomorrow morning.

(One of the new nurses had her 20th birthday today. Staff had a party and lots of goodies to eat, so a nurse put together more food for Jane and me. Jane ate fairly well. She also felt instances of the panic, though, having to do with her mother and family events, and we talked those out.

(I hadn't realized that her grandfather, Joseph Burdo — "Little Daddy," as Jane had called him — had spent a couple of years in a hospital for TB when Jane had been around ten years old. I also understood as we talked that when Jane's grandfather had wanted to move out of the house on Middle Avenue, he had sold all the furniture and had the utilities turned off. Marie then succeeded in thwarting his plans and banned him from the house. To Jane this had seemed like <u>a second divorce in the family</u>*. This hurt the six-year old girl. Her parents had divorced when she was 3.*

(Jane cried as she told me things I hadn't heard before. I said she had to put the past in its place if ever she was to be free. She came up with a number of memories new to me — like going to the youth center on Saratoga Springs' lower Broadway on weekend evenings to dance and socialize, and so forth. She cited many things she'd enjoyed doing very much — running, skating, dancing, and just sheer walking for the fun of it. Even then she had loved nature.

(I was pleased. In view of all of those early enjoyable events she'd had, I suggested she try focusing on them in times of stress, instead of the negative ones we usually talk about. All in all, I think we learned a great deal, and that we had hope after all, in contrast to my mood yesterday.

(When I asked her if she wanted to have a session, she said in surprise that she had no idea for one, and was hardly ready or in the mood. I said she didn't have to. She was obviously getting restless and had been on her back long enough. But almost at once Jane began a session after all. She spoke slowly, eyes closed often, her voice still uneven and very emotional at times, even quavering.)

Once again, your help has been invaluable, rising also from a new sense of peace and power that is emerging in <u>your</u> psyche.

Those energies are coming to Ruburt's aid now. *(Long pause.)* The feelings of abandonment are being expressed. This is a therapeutic measure that will make way for healings, comfort and reassurance, by his putting together material in different fashions, rearranging experience, turning thoughts inside out.

(Very long pause at 4:20.) In many, even most upsetting experiences, there has been a resourceful power. Ruburt is now beginning to clear the way for expression again. More than the session words are important *(delivery very uneven)*, for underriding those, the healing energy is being translated in other ways.

He should remind himself to look for new signs, however small, of a new <u>ease</u>, for those signs will indeed now be making themselves known.

I bid you a most sympathetic and supportive afternoon.

("Good afternoon, Seth. Thank you very much."

(4:24 P.M. "I had to stop several times because of bladder spasms," Jane said, which helped account for her uneven delivery. She said that at the same time she'd felt panicky a couple of times, and she'd had a very catchy, well-known tune running through her head. "I don't know," she said. "I guess I was getting from Seth: 'Ruburt will make out okay in hydro,' because it's something I've been dreading."

(Jane didn't eat much for supper, which seemed okay. I was getting tired. I left at 7:15 and drove to the funeral home. I felt self-conscious about my blue jeans and shoes. I'd left the house so early and quickly I hadn't had time to plan for anything to wear more formally. I carried with me the jacket I usually wear when I nap at 330 — it looked a bit more presentable.

(But I soon discovered at the funeral home that it mattered not; people wore anything. I met John, Margaret, and others there, and signed a guest book. Joe lay in a deep crimson casket. I told John that he really did look peaceful, as at no other time in his life. It was the same feeling I'd had staring at my parents in their respective caskets. People laughed and joked. I told John I expected to attend the service tomorrow at the funeral home, that I was willing to be an honorary pallbearer, providing the times worked out. They all understood, since they knew I'd been at the hospital all day. I don't think I'd better consider being late to 330, after today's events. I told the Bumbalos I'd call if anything came up early in the day. John said they have enough food to feed me for a week, after it's all over. Life goes on, even in our reality.

(I expected a call from Carla and Jane as I typed this, but none has come through as I finish this session at 9:55 P.M. Sleep well, Jane.)

AUGUST 7, 1984
4:05 P.M. TUESDAY

(Here are the notes for activities of Monday, August 6:

(This morning I was dressed to go to Joe Bumbalo's funeral by 9:15. I didn't feel like hanging around the house until 9:45 — the service was at 10:00 — so I told Margaret Bumbalo I'd run down to the hospital to see Jane first, then walk over. Jane was better, surprised to see me, trying to decide whether to go to hydro [she didn't].

(I was one of six honorary pallbearers. We stood outside after the service, three in a row facing each other on the porch, while six others carried Joe's casket between us and down the steps to the hearse.

(I found the whole funeral experience quite interesting, though I understood little of what was going on. A priest gave a short talk at the funeral home, leading it off, maybe for shock value, by telling us that sooner or later every one of us would experience the same thing Joe Bumbalo had. The room was very impressive, with its beamed ceiling. I thought the timeless quality, of light and so forth, inside the large room where the casket lay was more than a little symbolic in itself, isolated as the room was from the apparent time of day, night, or season.

(I could see how each move of the burial process had been carefully evolved to help the bereaved family separate from the one who had died. After all, the process had been refined through the centuries.

(The priest in charge — there were three of them — said that Joe had planned much of the service himself, and that Joe had asked him: "Why are the good ones taken?" The priest enlarged the question to: "Why is anyone taken?"

(Booklets titled "The Catholic Burial Rite" were handed out as we entered the church, and I kept my copy. After trying to stuff it into jacket pockets during the service, I finally ended up carrying it out with me quite openly. Nobody challenged me, asking for its return. I wanted to show it to Jane.

(The booklet explains much — all of the multitude of sittings and standings and kneelings that we went through in the pews; the gifts carried to the altar by the Bumbalo grandchildren; the hymns we listened to; the selections from the Bible read by the various priests; the responses we gave to the appropriate passages recited by the head priest, who read from the Gospel of John and other Biblical passages.

(It was all part of the ritual, Jane said later as we went over the booklet together in 330. Only now she was surprised to see that it was printed all in English. In her day it had been printed in Latin on one page, with the English translation on the page opposite. The new way seemed very strange to her.

(The service wasn't as long as I'd thought it might be, though, and we were on our way to the cemetery shortly before noon, winding through the quiet tree-lined side streets. The day had turned hot and bright and humid — a beautiful day to be alive, actually, though I'd agreed with the priests when each of them said that Joe was in an even better place now.

(Perhaps 20–25 people were at graveside, compared to the much larger group at the church. The priests spoke briefly. They were perfectly sincere people, and I found it arresting to listen to them as they spoke of Jesus Christ, the afterlife, and so forth, with such utter sincerity and conviction. Their commitment was for life, I thought, and so was bound to be different than most other people's. I wondered how often they went through roughly the same procedures with the dead, and speculated about how their sincerity and love must have stood them in good stead at such often-repeated times. For each time, they had to ring true to those left behind, adding those necessary personal touches, and references and little stories, to match the personal history of the newly deceased.

(I didn't stay for the lowering of the casket. I don't know whether the immediate family did or not. John Bumbalo had made arrangements for someone to give me a ride back to the hospital, where my car was. Jane and I went over the booklet of burial rites after lunch. I felt peaceful and tired, and put off starting these notes for a long time.

(At the funeral home a friend had told me he didn't know how Jane and I stood it after all this time. I said you either rose to the occasion or you didn't. He agreed, and offered to help us in any way he could, which I told him I appreciated very much. I do.)

～

(August 7, 1984. Patty called me at noon and said Jane wanted me to come to 330 early if I could. I finished a sandwich and went down. She was doing fairly well by then, but had had a very rough morning. She'd gone to hydro, and hadn't fared too well: new people, students, had helped position

her, and hadn't done it right. Jane said she'd had a much better night than usual, though.

(I'd told her several times in recent days that I thought her right knee was draining considerably less as a rule, and that several other scabs on her body were showing signs of clearing up. The swelling on her left shoulder blade varies considerably in size from day to day.

(I was pretty quiet today, mostly because I felt tired and didn't know what else to do to try to get her to eat or be more open about physical motion. So I said nothing, feeling very frustrated. Jane ate little lunch, though she said she did better with breakfast. I decided to stop saying anything about either hydro or her eating, since it appeared to have no effect.

(I didn't expect her to have a session. When she did, her voice was quite uneven; she spoke with many pauses, at times in a peculiar pronunciation that I had trouble understanding. Eyes often closed.)

Do not take it for granted that the hydro situation has the worst connotations.

The knee material *(drainage)* is <u>drying up</u> from beneath *(long pause),* and that is also part of the therapeutic process. Motion <u>is</u> being redistributed, but faith in the process is again immensely important.

I will try to return *(long pause),* and portions of Ruburt's evening last night were considerably improved — that is, more peaceful.

(4:11. I read the session to Jane. Resume briefly, at 4:26:)

Again, the session itself will help promote the mind and body's sense of ease and comfort. I bid you then a supportive good evening.

("Thank you." 4:27 P.M. Jane ate very little for supper — then she threw it all up, so ended up without food since noon. I was frustrated and discouraged. She just will not eat. She called at 9:15 with Carla's help. She said something about she should eat something before the night passes. I don't know how she's going to manage that. I didn't ask.)

AUGUST 8, 1984
2:15 P.M. WEDNESDAY

(No session was held today, but I want to present a mix of poetry and notes.

(Jane ate little lunch. I didn't urge her to, or ask questions about hydro or anything else. She dictated the following poem from 2:15–2:28 P.M.)

High in the secret mountains
where the proclamations
of nature come,
I sense a new note full and free
as a whole new world in some
ancient sweet recipe.

The ingredients are
glittering and golden and bright
and filled with expectancy,
and that note swirls
curled inside nature's world
with the promise a salute,
a new book to emerge
up in the mountains
where the earth's
proclamations are made.

And there is a wind,
a rush and a power and the voice,
a voice that says nothing at all
yet forms new alphabets of life
that glitter and buzz and swarm
and shoot into fragments,
jigsaws of light, sweet bombs
of mystery that go shooting off
like seeds of flame,
with a fury and a power
and a secret
known to me alone.

(Then at 2:33–2:37 P.M.)

There are Mondays
stuck into corners
where children threw them
ages ago, so I gathered
them up and washed them out
and hung them up to dry.

The time winds quickly
dry them out
so they flap in the
new morning sun,
cosmic laundry.

(One of the first things I learned when I got to 330 today was that Jeff Karder had increased Jane's dosage of Darvoset to every two hours instead of three. Jane finally told me that she'd had a very rough morning, although during the night she'd mostly done rather well.

(Her talk veered around to the fact that once again she said she was thinking of dying — in her sleep, maybe — in order to get some peace of mind, and to give me some. The pain is really bothering her at times. She talked about how she'd loved life, and the great times we'd had before she got sick, and even after that for a long while. She also said she was surprised her life was ending at such an early age. She told me I'd have a great life after her death, and be free myself.

(She said all of this in that matter-of-fact voice she'd used the last time, that she'd told me similar things about her death, before Seth had said very recently that she <u>wasn't</u> going to die now, no matter what she thought or said. I kept that in mind. Yet here she was, treating the possibility of death quite seriously again.

(The swelling on her shoulder was up again, but I noticed there was no drainage at all from her knee, nor was there for the rest of the afternoon. Jane said she'd been picturing herself at the old apartments on Water Street [we'd ended up with two], and around town as she used to go — all as though she were taking the last grand tour. When she was finished with all of this she asked me what I thought. I said I didn't have anything to say. I no longer carry on like I used to, or get mad, and so forth. I could hardly make her do something she didn't want to do, but I didn't say that either. If she wanted to die that was it. The hell with it, I thought. I decided — again — that I was through worrying about whether she'd live or die, or whether she was starving herself to death, or whatever.

(Some interesting developments occurred as I prepared to rub her legs with Oil of Olay, as I always do before turning her on her side. When I pressed the main tendon/ligament under her left knee, I found it as taut and strong as steel — as usual. But the next second it suddenly gave way very flexibly. Beneath my hands it seemed to turn to rubber. Jane cried out *in surprise. Her leg began to quiver and the foot also moved. So did her head and shoulders as I massaged the leg for some while. Surprise: Seth had said her body had begun to turn itself around.*

(I found the same relative situation with the right leg. As I cautiously massaged it, it too began to move, including the foot, and the head and shoulders. Jane cried again, and kept on making a series of low moaning sounds, eyes closed, as I worked with the leg. I could tell she was both afraid of my touch, that it hurt, and that she hadn't expected the response in the leg or the motion.

(I told her I didn't want to overdo it, so I turned her on her side. After my nap, I turned her back. As I propped her left leg with the pillow, I discovered that it would still move, for the tendons were still soft. At the same time Jane was in pain — natural enough, I said — for according to conventional belief, muscles that hadn't been used were supposed to hurt. I also let loose with a few barbed comments, to the effect that she wasn't about to let the body do its thing, no matter what it wanted.

(She'd kept her body down for years, I said, and now when it moved she hurt and complained, even though presumably the motion was what she wanted. I confused her, I learned, for she couldn't tell the difference between my remarks about the body wanting freedom, and her grim desire to keep it down. I explained, and she seemed to get it straight. She was in a lot of pain, though, and I rang for the Darvoset again, since the staff was late with it.

(Jane was both surprised and pleased at the unexpected discovery of motion. I said we'd try it again tomorrow. In fact, after supper she began to hurt even more. I didn't know what to do except a few light touches of massage on the right upper leg. Even I was surprised to feel it move beneath my hand — that it could still do so after being held in that position for many months, following the fracture of the knee. Her abdomen still feels rock hard, though.

(I stayed over an extra half hour, trying to help her calm down, and seemed to eventually make some headway there. She asked me if I felt some hope, and I said yes — a strange question coming from someone who'd said earlier that they were strongly thinking of dying!

(I knew my own half-sarcastic remarks about her not letting the body go its own healing way obviously were in response to her earlier talk about dying. I don't think I overdid what I said — though of course anything like that bothers Jane, even when its true. Then most of all, I suppose — for I

express my feelings based upon my interpretation of what I see — I ended up thinking my remarks were the right way to go, for later she told me that I'd expressed some intuitive truths. Who knows — maybe something can be salvaged after all.

(Jane actually smiled as I was getting ready to leave after 7:30. "Maybe I'll get to go home after all?" she asked. "That's the idea," I said. I'd mentioned that thought a few days ago.)

AUGUST 9, 1984
3:58 P.M. THURSDAY

(Jane didn't call last night. I got there a few minutes early; she'd just been turned by Patty and was hurting a lot. However, she'd had a good night and morning, and had eaten some breakfast. I massaged under her left knee when she asked me to, almost at once, and was pleased to see the motion in her leg, and head and shoulders, return once again. She said she'd reassured herself through the night and morning that it was okay to move, that she trusted her body, and had had some movements.

(She'd had only a small amount of drainage from the knee. She didn't go to hydro this morning: "You've got to be kidding."

(At lunch time I told her I wanted her to have a session today if at all possible, by way of encouraging her new course. After a very light lunch, Darvoset, and so forth, I read her yesterday's session and poetry. She was all ready to try for a session, but I didn't push for it yet. I read her the short session for August 7, in which Seth had said that her physical improvements have already begun.

("I believe it can be said that they have," I told her. I said I hope they continue, that I want her home with me. Her left hand bothered her a lot, and I massaged it. Her arms and hands kept moving.

(3:15. Jane felt panicky again, and we talked. She wasn't sure of the cause. I thought her fear of motion was involved, as well as old family stuff, and she agreed. Half crying, she began more motions with her arms and hands. I rubbed her legs a bit and got more responses, but tried not to overdo it.

(Jane said she wanted to try for the session. Her voice was somewhat distressed, and with many pauses, but okay all in all. Eyes closed often.)

Events are as we stated them —

(Bea came in to see how we were doing; she said she was in charge tonight. I read the line back to Jane.)

— from the far country has come those proclamations.

(Long pause.) Ruburt is joyfully <u>understanding</u> the miracle of normal physical bodily motion. Again, the session itself does indeed physically rearrange, reorganize, so that the bodily and mental contents are filled with <u>soothing</u> healing messages and potions.

Ruburt will make it home alive, in a much better physical situation.

(Long pause.) I will perhaps briefly return.

("All right. Thank you."

(4:00 P.M. Jane said she still felt some panic, and was half crying. Lynn stopped by to tell us she'd bring Darvoset at 4:30 — half an hour late for some mysterious reason.

(I read the session to Jane. I called it excellent. The key, I said, was the reference to her understanding physical motion. I mentioned the joy Seth referred to, and Jane said she felt it, even as she cried while I helped her move her arms. I gave her eye drops and turned up the TV after she'd gone through various additional motions. I told her I wanted her home — that all of the rooms in the house were waiting for her.

(Jane's motions, in the legs especially, were quite startling as I started massaging them with Oil of Olay preparatory to turning her on her side. To my surprise I discovered that as I massaged those tendons underneath the knee, her foot began to move back and forth an inch — something she hasn't been able to do for months, at least, and proof that the left knee joint wasn't frozen. I congratulated her. It was also easier doing her arms and hands and other parts of her body after I turned her. And the turning itself went very easily indeed — she didn't cry at all, and seemed to be at some sort of peace. I told her she'd done well.

(In fact, she continued her motions without my asking her too. Supper didn't work out, though — after taking a half cup of soup she began to throw up, and lost it all. This upset me, yet Jane didn't feel bad about it, and I curbed my disappointment.

(I stayed with her until after 7:30. "You'd better get out of here," Jane said, meaning that the longer I stayed, the longer she'd keep up her motions. I was only concerned that she not overdo it, and have sore muscles later. I told her often how great it was to see her move, and that her motions only meant that her body was more than willing to cooperate if allowed to. I do

think she has either learned that by now, or is on the way. What counts is keeping it up, without trying too hard, and letting the body do its thing.

("If you keep on improving the way you did today," I said, "your progress will be spectacular." She agreed. And why not, I said. It was always possible. Miracles <u>are</u> nature unimpeded, as Seth has said. Anything will help, Jane, so let's see what happens.

(For now, at least, I'd settle for anything. Jane had said yesterday that she'd even be happy with a 30% improvement. Maybe she's on the way.

(9:25 P.M. Jane called, with Carla's help, just as I typed these lines. I told my wife once again that she'd done well today.)

AUGUST 11, 1984
4:09 P.M. SATURDAY

(Today I took Jane's acrylic painting she calls The Irises into 330. It's one of her best. She enjoyed seeing it. A couple of nurses were there when I unwrapped it. I told Jane that tomorrow I'd replace the oil portrait of mine that's been there on the bulletin board. In the meantime I shifted around other paintings I'd brought to 330 over the weeks, and took some things down from the wall. It looks nice.

(Jane was feeling very restless when I arrived, so I quickly turned her on her back. Still, she said she'd had a pretty good night for the most part, and a good morning. No hydro. She's kept in mind to remind herself of her trust in her body, and it's helped.

(She ate a much better lunch than usual, including a little solid food. After lunch I massaged both of her legs as I've been doing, and once again obtained good reactions. Arms and hands and head moved also.

(Jane asked that I read her some Seth material, so I picked the last nine sessions — starting with our new resolve and intent on July 30, after the long layoff since July 4. They're all short sessions, but now carry all of our hopes for the future, and so far have been paying off. We also talked of plans for the future.

(When Jane said she wanted to have a session, her voice was quite unsteady in trance, and I had to ask her to repeat a number of words.)

Now, again, Ruburt — Jane — will be able to go home again, in far better condition, able *(long pause)* finally to sit in a wheel-type chair.

The right leg <u>will</u> become much more mobile, so that the sitting is possible. There will be day-by-day —

(4:12. Unfortunately, a nurse interrupted us by bringing in Jane's dosage of Darvoset. She only stayed a few moments, but it was too long.)

I may or may not return — but he will sit on his back porch again.

("That's it," Jane finally said.

(4:14 P.M. Jane took the Darvoset — which she's getting every two hours or so. "Is there that possibility — getting better enough to sit on the back porch again?" she asked, half crying.

("Why not?" I said.

(She continued to make crying sounds, her face contorted. "Just the possibility of being able to go home and sit on my porch again . . . I want to believe it so, with all my heart and soul . . . "

("Okay," I said, "so let's work for that."

(I saw no drainage at all from her right knee, and I believe the swelling on her left shoulder had decreased considerably. She was quite uncomfortable at times through the afternoon, but all in all I think she was better, which means that our approach these days is helping considerably.)

AUGUST 13, 1984
3:45 P.M. MONDAY

(Jane didn't call last night. Rita and Patty were having trouble getting her comfortable on her back when I got to 330 today. I straightened her out, and she did much better. She didn't eat much lunch, though.

(Jane said she did motions at times during the night and this morning. I massaged her legs at 3:15, with good results once again. I see the feet and toes responding, and will concentrate more upon them tomorrow.

(After the massage, which lasted quite a while, she dictated this poem. Her feet were still moving. Eyes often closed, voice quiet, many pauses.

Way up beyond
the far hidden boulders
of the world
where all of nature's
proclamations rise
speeds a sweet swift message
in which dear secrets
are unrolled.

Seeds of motion,
sweet, glowing and mysterious
speak and move
the sockets with a
sudden unknown note
whose meaning is for
me alone.

Its source is higher
its message clear
though it speaks without words,
without the vowels
and syllables.

(At 4:26, after we'd been talking about various subjects like politics, which Jane enjoyed, she told me to turn down the TV. "I probably won't have more than a sentence or two.")

I merely want to reassure Ruburt of my presence, to let him know that I hereby assert again those statements I made concerning his sitting on the porch.

(Long pause.) Also, again, to tell him that regardless of the session's words, new nuances and motions are carried by the session itself.

I bid you a fond, reassuring good afternoon.

("Good afternoon."

(4:30 P.M. I'd had to ask Jane to repeat several words, so quiet was her dictation. The session Seth had referred to was that for last Saturday, August 11, when he'd first mentioned that Jane would be able again to sit on her back porch. He's referred to the same thing since then, also.

(It was time to turn my wife on her left side for half an hour, then take my nap. I massaged her legs and arms first, and once again received good responses. She did well, and is indeed responding to the new hope we're creating.)

AUGUST 16, 1984
4:37 P.M. THURSDAY

(From 3:47 to 3:57 Jane dictated this poem to me.

Behind the highest clouds
man has ever seen
there are mountains and
hidden coves from which all
true proclamations come.
Their sentences are silent
yet they contain a word that
releases and fills secret contracts
between the gods and man,
uttered long ago
uttered without a word or a whisper,
and speaking for me alone
with a magic note
and a secret message
and a sweet response
known to me alone.

(At 4:37 Jane said: "You might want to write this down. But the thought came to me that the not-eating might be the body's therapeutic fasting situation — it's own natural version of it."

("To what end?" I asked.

("The healing process."

(I didn't really understand her answer to my question, but she didn't seem up to me pressing the point, so I let it go. She still isn't eating enough to prevent weight loss. Ergo — if the not-eating persists, it will have extremely serious repercussions. She's already gone much too far with it.)

AUGUST 17, 1984
3:30 P.M. FRIDAY

(Georgia called at about 11:30 this morning. Jane asked me to come down to 330 early, so I did. I was working on Chapter 9 — just starting it — of Dreams. *Just as I was opening the garage door, I met a woman who had pulled into the driveway, who has a tumor and wanted to see Jane. She'd written us several times and I stopped answering after a while.*

(I talked to her for a few minutes, saying I had no choice but to leave. I heard her car radiator boiling, though it wasn't leaking. She followed me

down the hill and into the service station there, where I waved goodbye. I said I'd probably received her latest letter, but hadn't answered mail for some time.

(Jane wasn't nearly as much in poor shape as she'd been the other day when I was called down to 330 earlier in the morning. I massaged her left leg especially before lunch; it helped.

(After lunch I took down to billing a check I'd received yesterday from our insurance company. The rather small amount, $5,000, was a puzzle. I didn't know what it was for. Neither did the people in billing.

(Strange, I said to Jane when finally I got back to 330. Maybe the whole insurance mess will be reopened in more confusion. I should have known that the calm of the last few months was deceptive. Our bill has run up again to around $55,000 — and here insurance hasn't been sending me any checks. My idea that the hospital might be billing them quarterly or something like that must have been wishful thinking. I'm going to forget the whole business if at all possible.

(Once again Jane ate very little for lunch, although Georgia had said she did okay for breakfast. She's still starving, essentially. Jane and Georgia talked and smoked while I was down to billing. Jane said she'd have a session later, then changed her mind as I got ready to do mail. Her voice was very shaky, not very distinct, rather high-pitched and with little inflection. Eyes open and closed.)

I bid you a most sympathetic and therapeutic afternoon.

Ruburt should not be afraid, or ashamed, of the panicky feelings. They should also <u>be</u> expressed, and again, they then clear the road for new energy.

The additional motion you have seen arises naturally as the seasons do, and will bring a growing sense of ease.

Now signs of composure will be noticeable. You have again been of most valuable aid. Read the session back to him. We may or may not return, but my presence, attention, and energy are with him.

(All right," Jane said.

(3:36 P.M. The "ashamed" bit was new to me. "That's probably why I had the session," Jane said. She said she'd felt ashamed of the panic at times, and agreed with me that if the shame was used to possibly suppress the panic, it — the panic — would last longer.

(I'll have to admit I was surprised when my wife said she felt shame at the panic. I hadn't thought there was anything left for her to hide from me —

but upon reflection I saw that her behavior was quite typical, quite secretive. Maybe I should have figured something like that was going on — but on the other hand, how can I be responsible, except possibly in a minor way?

(It's events like this that make me despair, for once again I see Jane going along in the same old way, and wonder what, if anything, has been learned out of all of this. How can one say much has been learned, I wondered, if my wife is at death's door, and is currently starving herself? Each challenge we have to meet and surmount is at a lower level, and simply to break it or surmount it leaves one only back at the next level from which the fall took place. There's never a surge up a few rungs on the ladder, from which we can look back in triumph.

(As I massaged Jane's left leg, she made so much noise — moaning — that Georgia came in. I explained the benefits, and showed her what I was doing. Georgia understood. After the session I massaged all of Jane's limbs — and once again achieved excellent results. Jane had more motions in her legs and feet especially. And in spite of those good results, once again I wondered: What did you have to do to even get back to the perch from which you'd recently fallen?)

AUGUST 23, 1984
2:46 P.M. THURSDAY

(These notes are for August 22:

(We did one thing, surprisingly, that made us both feel very good. Jane was telling me that an aide who took care of her this morning, and who is living apart from her husband and has three kids, looked at a second-hand washing machine this noon but couldn't afford the $130 cost. "Tell her we'll pay for it," I said, or words to that effect. Maybe I said, "We can get it for her." It would save her going to the laundromat to do the wash, though it made no provision for the drying part of the chore. Jane at once enthusiastically agreed. As though on signal, the aide came in to empty Jane's Foley, and we explained our idea to her. Predictably, she said no at first, but we talked her into it.

("No one's ever done anything like that for me," she said. We explained, not in great detail, that others have helped us. It was decided I'd give her the cash tomorrow, rather than have her or the store send me the bill. She couldn't believe it. She kissed each of us. We asked her not to tell anyone,

though I expect she'll tell Georgia, her closest friend in the hospital. She thanked us again before she left work.

(I haven't seen Jane so enthusiastic about doing anything for a long time. She positively bubbled with pleasure, and I knew at once that we'd made the right decision. This could have very beneficial therapeutic effects on my wife, I realized. Helping another in this fashion was a breakthrough for us. I'd often wondered what else I — or anyone else — could do to help Jane, and here a possible solution lay right before us all the time . . .)

~

(August 23. This morning the ringing telephone got me out of bed at 5:45 A.M. It couldn't be anyone except someone at the hospital, I thought as I ran out of the bedroom. It was Shawn, the night nurse. I talked to Jane: "I'm not dying or anything, but could you come down now? I'm so uncomfortable . . . "

(I fed the cats and shaved, and arrived at 330 before 7:00 A.M. Jane was very sore. I got two night-shift aides to help me get the chuck out from under her, and we gradually got her more comfortable. She didn't look so hot, with her face all screwed up in pain. Darvoset helped calm her down. I saw that the swollen bubble of fluid on her left shoulder blade was way up — this was causing much of her discomfort. She didn't know whether to stay on her side or go on her back at first, but the shifting of her position helped, actually. Mary, the head nurse, came in and I said the bubble should be drained to relieve the pressure. She agreed: "They'll stick a needle in it." She made a note on a chart and left, very pleasant — but no action was taken during the day. No doctor showed up.

(At breakfast Jane said that later today she wanted to have a short session if at all possible. She seemed to feel better as the day progressed. I'd taken the notebook with Chapter 9 of Dreams *to the hospital with me. I was working on it when she told me to shut the door and get out the notebook for sessions.*

(Jane's voice was halting, almost high-pitched, with a sort of unusual sing-song delivery. Her eyes were half closed most of the time.)

A most fond good afternoon.

("Good afternoon, Seth.")

The giving away of the money in order to help with someone else's current need was, in it's own way, a stroke of genius, regardless of its seeming simplicity and childishness.

Because of Ruburt's mixture of symbolic and literal natures, the gesture gave him an excellent, definite sense of self-approval <u>in a way</u> that he has not experienced in some time. Highly valuable, this is responsible for the beginning consumption of solid food.

Your own behavior was impeccably correct in agreeing, and also in your very early morning visit.

I cannot stress these points too strongly. I also strongly suggest that small amounts be thusly given to people whose needs are known to you or Ruburt. The results can be turning points toward action and motion. I recommend that such activity begin at once. Of course, the books have helped people in greater ways, but we want quick inoculations, so to speak, of this specific type of self-approval.

The body is showing even more signs of activity, and this kind of behavior mentioned will beautifully reinforce new ease of motion.

Your own acquiescence to the money recommendations is also highly pertinent.

I may or may not return — but again, the session itself will encourage more composure and faith. I may indeed <u>possibly</u> return, but I want you two to discuss the session.

(*"Thank you."*

(*3:00 P.M. Jane's feet had begun moving in concert as the session progressed. I read the session to her. We didn't get to discuss it much because Frank Longwell visited. I told him the red maple he'd help plant in the back yard had evidently died but he said it may not really be dead.*

(*I had good results from massaging Jane's limbs and helping them to move. This noon she sampled several different foods, to my surprise, some things dietary had sent up on her tray for me, at the request of Georgia. I've seen a little improvement in her eating the last few days, but today is the best so far.*)

AUGUST 30, 1984
2:50 P.M. THURSDAY

(*Yesterday when I got to 330 at 12:45 Jane lay on her side. She looked very poor — gaunt from eating far too little — like an aged fetus, I thought, in her drawn-up position.*

(*"I may have chosen death," she said weakly.*

*("You have," I said frankly. "It won't be long now. I don't see you chang-
ing your ways now. It's too late."*

*("I don't want to hear about it," she said. "Turn up the TV." Her
favorite soap opera was on.*

*(That little exchange pretty much sums up our attitudes these days,
and Jane's worsening physical condition. She ate some lunch yesterday, but
little supper. Today she ate less lunch. I reminded her that I had to go to the
dentist at 4:15. This at once compressed her ideas of the time in which to do
anything, although I didn't feel any pressure. She asked me about the time
quite often.*

*(After a meager lunch she said that last night she got a flash, like an
"ear pop," that she wasn't going to die at this time. It was very brief but very
clear. I'd known she had something to tell me after lunch, but hadn't expected
this. I had absolutely no reaction to the news at all — and at once remembered my total lack of reaction when our lawyer had told me that the insurance business was settled. I was evidently so numb from repeated doses of fear
and concern and negativity and Jane's worsening situation daily, that I
couldn't react. I didn't believe or disbelieve it. I was afraid to hope, perhaps.*

*(Anyhow, Jane seemed to feel a bit better about it, so I went along when
she even talked about a session this afternoon. I had her help me fill out the
menu, for I'd decided it was useless for me to continue putting items on it
that she never touched.*

*(Then she said her legs clamored for action exercises, so I massaged her
left leg particularly. Her legs and feet moved pretty well.*

*(Jane could still hurry things up when she wanted to — hence the early
session because I was leaving later. I must be more negative than I thought
after all this time, for I didn't believe her when she said she wasn't going to
die now. For it certainly does seem that her life is almost over. When she says
these days that she's going to die, I agree with her.*

*(Her Seth voice wasn't strong at all, and I had trouble understanding
some of the half-quavering words. Eyes half closed most of the time.)*

We will dismiss preliminaries.

Ruburt's feeling is true: he is not ready to die yet — he will not
die yet. There is a difference between feeling a certain way, and knowing the feeling is true — that is, it is true you feel, perhaps, that A is
B, but you can be completely wrong in your interpretation. Because
you feel that, say, A and B are one, <u>this does not make them so</u>.

Of course, many of the difficulties are caused by the environment, and the sooner he can return home the better, regardless of how presumptive this may seem.

He must regain that determination to return, <u>and so should you</u> make every effort to do the same; your <u>feelings</u> that the affair is hopeless do not mean that the affair <u>is</u> hopeless — and this must be as clearly understood as possible.

Moving the imagination in that direction is highly important. It is indeed possible for you two to do this — that vital move of creative, imaginative motion.

Again, the session alone will indeed help, and restore some tranquillity.

Take a moment. I will hopefully then return.

(2:59. "Oh God," Jane said, using an expression that's become one of her favorites. "Give me a puff. As soon as I said I'd do it — the session — I got scared. It shows how you've got to get those feelings out. I wish I could yell and scream, but I can't . . . " I read her the session. "Oh, my arms," she said. I'd felt them, and she was holding them as rigid as bent metal rods.

(3:06. "I guess I will do a little more. It's very hard, oh God . . . ")

Again, it is vital that Ruburt express those feelings of panic, thereby releasing them outward. That release also relieves the muscles and rearranges structures, like putting crystal together in a new form.

The session itself will again help relieve . . .*

(3:08. "Oh, Bob, that's all," she said, half crying. "I wish I could scream out." I'd told her to do just that more than once.

(We talked a little. Jane seemed more concerned about when I'd leave for the dentist than anything else. So restricted has her world become.

(When she finally asked me what I thought of the session, I had trouble expressing any hope, versus those negative feelings I've been aware of for so long now. I did say things like, "This morning while working on Chapter 9 for Dreams *I had to reread some sessions from back in 1981 — and they're perfect. They go into exact detail as to what was wrong, and they fit today like a glove. Only look where we are now — a lot worse off." What had happened to the four years?*

(I did finally express some anger as the time approached for me to leave. I accused Jane of not caring about the emotional storms I was going through. This came about when I tried to make her arms comfortable, and found her

holding herself as rigid as could be — after all she's supposed to know and have learned. It got to me. I felt blown away by such behavior.

("But I do care," Jane protested. "I care a lot. I've even thought of dying to let you go free."

("Believe me," I said, "I've had the thought. I'd be lying if I said I hadn't . . . "

(I should add that I didn't mean I wished she'd die so that I'd be free. I want her to live — with me, at home, working and singing. I thought of this in the dentist's chair. I forgot to tell her when I got back at supper time, but will tomorrow. Jane called just as I was typing this session.)

*[Note on Sept. 9, 1984, four days after Jane's death — Seth's last words, trying to help to the last.]

EPILOGUE

S o there you have it: the last book. The end of the Seth material —
or is it? Now that my emotions have calmed down somewhat after
proofreading *The Way Toward Health,* I can deal with that question at
least a little bit.

During her last days in the hospital Jane simply stopped eating,
and I knew that her transition to another reality was near. I was
with her when she died in her sleep at that early-morning hour in
September 1984. As always, Seth had done his part, and more, as the
record in *The Way Toward Health* shows. Yet he too acquiesced to
Jane's death when she made her decision to go. There were no
protests on his part, no recriminations about his voice "being stilled
forever," for example. Nor did I feel any sort of rebellion — only a
state of numb acceptance.

Although I told myself that I knew Jane still lived, I wasn't used to
being in the presence of physical death. I made two ball-point pen
drawings of my wife while she lay on her side with her beautiful eyes
still open; they were blue flecked with hazel, and were as clear and
peaceful as those of a child. I had the vague idea that I'd use the
drawings as references for portraits that I would paint of her. They
would be unique, I thought. (I have yet to paint those particular
images, but still plan to do so.)

Jane had been a devoted Catholic in her youth. Since she had died in a Catholic hospital, I called for a priest to speak at her bedside. I tried, but could not cry as he spoke: "Loving and merciful God, we entrust our sister to you. You loved her greatly in this life . . . " The priest promised to send me a copy of his eulogy.

In the days that followed I attended to the cremation Jane had decided upon long ago, took care of legal matters, paid bills, spoke briefly with a few friends. Our gravesite is not in Elmira. Later, when I could be alone, my tears began to come. I cried each day for more than a year. Yet the day after my wife's death I'd gone back to work, finishing Volume 2 of *Dreams, "Evolution," and Value Fulfillment.* What else was I to do?

And as Jane survives, so does her work. Although one can say that her life is over in this reality, her lifework isn't. Many have written that her books are new each time they read them — that they're constantly finding new material in them. This happens with me, too. It also happens with the audio tapes from Jane's ESP class, as she speaks for Seth, or as herself in exchanges with students, or as she speaks and sings in her trance language, Sumari. What wonderful signs of survival all of these things are!

Yet there can be even more to come out of the great bulk of Jane's work. The 15 three-ring binders containing her poems, all neatly typed, for example; her essays and journals; other blocks of unpublished Seth material, one of which I mentioned in the Introduction; an unfinished autobiography that perhaps I could put into publishable shape; likewise, passages from an unfinished fourth *Oversoul Seven* novel, in which Jane dealt with Seven's childhood; a book of her paintings, with commentary; several early novels that I still believe merit publishing. Enough there to do for the rest of my life, certainly, and perhaps for others to carry on after I join my wife.

Over the years Jane's and my work led to our receiving many thousands of letters, not only from this country but from abroad, too. I still gratefully receive letters almost every day, and still struggle to answer each one in some fashion. Without the responses of others, Jane and I often said, where would we be? Except for a few missives that may have escaped us in the very beginning, I've saved them all.

When Jane published *The Seth Material* in 1970, we were quite unprepared for the impact her work would have. Boxes and boxes of letters are now at Yale University Library, where their privacy is protected. I have many more to send now. I love every letter we've ever received, even the ones that are not so nice. In my opinion, friendships with those we've never met physically are rare things to know and experience. Often those friends gave of themselves in ways we couldn't equal. They still do.

Also, copies of all of the Seth sessions — regular, private, and for ESP class — are in the collection of our papers at Yale. Much other material is there also: I've spent several years assembling it. Practically all of this is open to the public, free of charge, with but a few restrictions as to how much can be copied for personal use. Sometimes my permission is required.

I'm proud to have helped Jane and Seth make their contributions in our complex and very creative system of things in this reality. I thank them — just as I thank each and every one of you, dear readers, for your past, present, and future contributions. Each one of us is part of the great mystery of All That Is, then, which we explore together, yet each in our own way.

As Seth said in the session for July 31, 1984, in *The Way Toward Health,* "The sessions, like life itself, have been and are a gift, rising from the immense, never-ending creativity of existence."

I like ending this epilogue on such a note.

Robert F. Butts
Elmira, New York
September 1997

INDEX

New Seth Books, Online Seth Courses
Seth Conferences & Workshops

"THE EARLY SESSIONS" – BY JANE ROBERTS

"The Early Sessions" are the first 510 sessions dictated by Seth during the first six years of his relationship with Jane Roberts and her husband, Robert F. Butts. Published in nine volumes, these new Seth books offer fresh insights from Seth on a vast array of topics.

"THE PERSONAL SESSIONS" – BY JANE ROBERTS

"The Personal Sessions," originally referred to as "the deleted sessions," are Seth-dictated sessions that Jane Roberts and Robert F. Butts considered to be of a highly personal nature, and therefore kept separate from the main body of the Seth material.

THE SETH AUDIO COLLECTION

These audios consist of rare recordings of Seth speaking through Jane Roberts during her classes in Elmira, New York in the 1970s, and recorded by her student, Rick Stack. This collection represents the best of Seth's comments gleaned from over 120 class sessions.

ONLINE SETH COURSES

This in-home learning experience offers an intensive immersion into some of the most important concepts presented in the Seth material. (Includes live online interactive webinars with instructor Rick Stack.)

SETH CONFERENCES & WORKSHOPS

These gatherings offer a unique opportunity to meet people of like mind, increase your understanding of both inner and outer reality, and enhance your ability to create your ideal life.

For further information, contact New Awareness Network, Inc.
(516) 869-9108 between 9:00 A.M. – 5:00 P.M. ET
sumari@sethcenter.com, or visit our web sites:
www.sethcenter.com
www.sethlearningcenter.org
www.sethconference.org

ALSO FROM AMBER-ALLEN PUBLISHING

Seth Speaks by Jane Roberts. In this essential guide to conscious living, Seth clearly and powerfully articulates the concept that we create our own reality according to our beliefs.

The Nature of Personal Reality by Jane Roberts. Seth explains how the conscious mind directs unconscious activity, and has at its command all the powers of the inner self.

The Nature of the Psyche by Jane Roberts. Seth reveals a startling new concept of self, answering questions about many aspects of the psyche, including love, dreams, sexuality, and death.

The Individual and the Nature of Mass Events by Jane Roberts. Extending the idea that we create our own reality, Seth explores the connection between personal beliefs and world events.

The Magical Approach by Jane Roberts. Seth discusses how we can live our lives spontaneously, creatively, and according to our own natural rhythms.

The "Unknown" Reality, Volumes One and Two by Jane Roberts. Exploring the interdependence of multiple selves, Seth explains how understanding unknown dimensions can change the world as we know it.

Dreams, "Evolution," and Value Fulfillment, Volumes One and Two by Jane Roberts. These books answer crucial questions about the entire significance of Seth's system of thought, as he takes us on an odyssey to identify the origins of our universe and our species.

The Oversoul Seven Trilogy by Jane Roberts. The adventures of Oversoul Seven are an intriguing fantasy, a mind-altering exploration of our being, and a vibrant celebration of life.

The Seven Spiritual Laws of Success by Deepak Chopra. In this abridged "One Hour of Wisdom" edition of his classic best-selling book, Chopra gathers the most powerful pearls of wisdom, and offers a life-altering perspective on the attainment of success.

ALSO FROM AMBER-ALLEN PUBLISHING

The Four Agreements by don Miguel Ruiz with Janet Mills. Based on ancient Toltec wisdom, The Four Agreements offer a powerful code of conduct that can rapidly transform our lives to a new experience of freedom, true happiness, and love.

The Four Agreements Companion Book by don Miguel Ruiz with Janet Mills. This companion book offers additional insights, practice ideas, questions and answers about applying The Four Agreements, and true stories from people who have already changed their lives.

The Mastery of Love by don Miguel Ruiz. Using insightful stories to bring his message to life, Ruiz shows us how to heal our emotional wounds, recover the freedom and joy that are our birthright, and restore the spirit of playfulness that is vital to loving relationships.

The Circle of Fire by don Miguel Ruiz with Janet Mills. In this beautiful collection of essays and prayers, Ruiz inspires us to enter into a new and loving relationship with ourselves, with our fellow humans, and with all of creation.

The Voice of Knowledge by don Miguel Ruiz with Janet Mills. In this life-altering book, Ruiz reminds us of a profound and simple truth: the only way to end our emotional suffering and restore our joy in living is to stop believing in lies — mainly about ourselves.

The Fifth Agreement by don Miguel Ruiz and don Jose Ruiz with Janet Mills. Ruiz joins his son to encourage us to see the truth, to recover our authenticity, and to change the message we deliver to ourselves and to everyone around us.

For information about other bestselling titles from
Amber-Allen Publishing, please visit us online.
www.amberallen.com